Story Central

Teacher Edition 6

macmillan education

Dave Tucker

Macmillan Education
4 Crinan Street
London N1 9XW
A division of Macmillan Publishers Limited

Companies and representatives throughout the world

ISBN 978-0-230-45244-2
Pack ISBN 978-0-230-45245-9

First published 2015

Teacher Edition credits:
Designed by Red Phoenix Design
Page make-up by Mike Brain Graphic Design Limited
Illustrated by Steven Wood (Advocate Art)
Cover design by Wild Apple Design Ltd

Student Book credits:
Text © Viv Lambert ELT Limited and Mo Choy Design Ltd 2015
Design and illustration © Macmillan Publishers Limited 2015
The authors have asserted their rights to be identified as the authors of this work in accordance with the Copyright, Designs and Patents Act 1988.

Designed by Wild Apple Design Ltd
Illustrated by Ilias Arahovitis (Beehive Illustration) pp8, 9, 45; Monica Auriemma (Sylvie Poggio Artist Agency) pp30–31, 32; Andre Bock (Beehive Illustration) pp60–61, 62; Stephanie Dominguez pp90–91, 92; Pablo Gallego (Beehive Illustration) pp39, 47, 77, 97; Gary Hanna pp70–71, 72; Kevin Hopgood pp38, 40–41, 42; Alvaro Iglesias (Advocate Art) pp37, 57; Mike Love (Bright Illustration) pp10–11, 12; Andre Ricci Martinez (Organisart) pp20–21, 22; Patricia Moffat pp50–51, 52; Dan Netherton p24; Ismael Pinteno (Advocate Art) pp80–81, 82; Laszlo Veres (Beehive Illustration) pp14, 15, 29, 34, 49, 55, 94; Steven Wood (Advocate Art) pp4–104 (border design and main character artwork), 4–5, 6–7, 10, 13, 20, 23, 30, 33, 40, 43, 50, 53, 60, 63, 70, 73, 80, 83, 90, 93.
Cover design by Wild Apple Design Ltd
Cover artwork by Steven Wood (Advocate Art)
Cover photographs by Paul Bricknell
Picture research by Victoria Gaunt

The authors and publishers would like to thank the following for permission to reproduce their photographs:
Alamy/uniors Bildarchiv GmbH p44(3), Alamy/imageBROKER p54(2), Alamy/Justin Eckersall p89(tr), Alamy/Elena Elisseeva p18(tr), Alamy/Eureka p44(2), Alamy/Eye-Stock p35(sweater), Alamy/epa European pressphoto agency b.v. p49, Alamy/Tim Gainey p95(r), Alamy/Blend Images p58, Alamy/Geoffrey Kidd p17(tr), Alamy/ACE STOCK LIMITED p75(r), Alamy/Paul Maguire p44 (Background), Alamy/Wavebreak Media ltd p67(m), Alamy/OJO Images Ltd p85(t), Alamy/Andrew Payne p35(trash), Alamy/PhotoAlto p88(bl), Alamy/Eduardo Pucheta Photo p64(tc), Alamy/James Schwabel p28(tm), Alamy/tbkmedia.de p64(b), Alamy/Juice Images p67(l), Alamy/CJWinch Animal World Photography p75(l), Alamy/Horizons WWP p28(bl); **Corbis**/Tobias Hase/dpa p95(l), Corbis/Stefan Huwiler/imagebroker p44(4), Corbis/Blue Jean Images p17(br), Corbis/Victoria Bonn-Meuser/dpa p25, Corbis/Splash News p35(car), Corbis/Mark Moffett/Minden Pictures p9(r), Corbis/Tui De Roy/Minden Pictures p48(br), Corbis/Hill Street Studios/Blend Images p64(t), Corbis/Sandro Vannini p9(m), Corbis/Robert Harding World Imagery p9(l); **Getty Images** p28(tl), Getty Images/AFP p48(tm), Getty Images/Paul Biris p65(r), Getty Images/Monkey Business Images p85(c), Getty Images/Cavan Images p89(bl), Getty Images/DAJ p18(bl), Getty Images/Robert Daly p79(boy), Getty Images/Danita Delimont p65(l), Getty Images/George Doyle p59(r),Getty Images/Compassionate Eye p74(t), Getty Images/Blend Images/JGI/Jamie Grill p67(r), Getty Images/Justin Horrocks p88(br), Getty Images/Fabrice LEROUGE p85(b), Getty Images/James Merrell p19(b), Getty Images/meshaphoto p74(b), Getty Images/Daniel Milchev p69, Getty Images/MIXA p27(tl), Getty Images/Buero Monaco p88(bm), Getty Images/David Muir p27(tr), Getty Images/Charlotte Nation p27(b), Getty Images/DEA/G. DAGLI ORTI p17(tm), Getty Images/Alan Pappe p89(br), Getty Images/Ray Pfortner p28(tr), Getty Images/Cultura/Floresco Productions p19(t), Getty Images/Helen H. Richardson p48(tr), Getty Images/The Asahi Shimbun p55(m, r), Getty Images/Stanislav Solntsev p79(girl), Getty Images/Image Source p79(DJ), Getty Images/Hill Street Studios p64(bc), Getty Images/sturti pp68(c), 88(tr), Getty Images/Lauri Wiberg p15; **Glow Images**/Werner Forman Archive p17(bm); **Image 100** p44(1); **Lebrecht Music & Arts**/culture-images p54(4); **Photoshot**/Bilderlounge p18(bm), Photoshot/Fotofeeling p25, **Rex**/c.W. Disney/Everett p54(1), Rex/NEWS PICTURES p55(l); **Science Photo Library**/Jim Edds p48(tl); **Stockbyte**/PunchStock/Getty Images p56(c); **Superstock**/Biosphoto p35(turtle), Superstock/Stock Connection p94(background), Superstock/age footstock p54(3), Superstock/Nice Monkey p24(background), Superstock/Sasty Photo p17(tl); **Thinkstock** pp28(bm), 37, Thinkstock/ajt p34, Thinkstock/azgek p18(br), Thinkstock/BananaStock p68(t), Thinkstock/KatarzynaBialasiewicz p18(tmr), Thinkstock/JeremyKeithBrown p44(5), Thinkstock/Jani Bryson p59(l), Thinkstock/gnagel p64(background), Thinkstock/g0rZh p48(bl),Thinkstock/hammett79 p75(m), Thinkstock/lculig p18(tml), Thinkstock/SvitlanaMartyn p18(tl), Thinkstock/mihalec p35(bottle), Thinkstock/szefei p74(tc), Thinkstock/trekandshoot p28(br), Thinkstock/ucagavagna p84, Thinkstock/YanLev p88(tl), Thinkstock/InteractiveZoom p17(bl).
Commissioned photographs by MMStudios pp16, 26, 36, 46, 56, 66, 76, 86, 96.
Prop artwork by Carla Drury

Reader credits:
Text, design and illustration © Macmillan Publishers Limited 2015
Written by Viv Lambert ELT Limited and Mo Choy Design Limited 2015
The authors have asserted their rights to be identified as the authors of this work in accordance with the Copyright, Designs and Patents Act 1988.

Page design and art editing by Wild Apple Design Ltd
Storyboard layouts by Carrie Webb (Red Phoenix Design)
The Tomb of the Ancient Dog illustrated by Mike Love (Bright Agency); Icarus illustrated by André Martinez Ricci (Organisart); The Frog Hunt illustrated by Monica Auriemma (Sylvie Poggio Artist Agency); Master Mind Returns illustrated by Kevin Hopgood; The Legend of the Lost Island illustrated by Patricia Moffat; Just Dance! illustrated by Andrew Bock (Beehive Illustration); An Unusual Friendship illustrated by Gary Hanna; The Stolen Painting illustrated by Ismael Pinteno (Advocate Art); A Fairy Tale Life illustrated by Stephanie Dominguez.
Cover design by Wild Apple Design Ltd
Cover artwork; front cover, Patricia Moffat, Kevin Hopgood, and André Martinez Ricci (Organisart); back cover, Monica Auriemma (Sylvie Poggio Artist Agency) and Stephanie Dominguez.

Activity Book credits:
Text, design and illustration © Macmillan Publishers Limited 2015
Written by Viv Lambert ELT Limited, Mo Choy Design Ltd, and Suzanne Gaynor
Additional material written by Tracy Traynor
The authors have asserted their rights to be identified as the authors of this work in accordance with the Copyright, Designs and Patents Act 1988.

Designed by Liz Adcock
Page make-up by Carrie Webb (Red Phoenix Design)
Illustrated by Monica Auriemma (Sylvie Poggio Artist Agency) pp24–25; Steve Colgan (Beehive Illustration) pp12, 15, 19, 23, 28, 31, 36, 43, 52, 60, 70; Russ Daff (Beehive Illustration) pp78, 79, 81, 83, 84, 85, 87, 88, 89, 90, 91, 93, 95, 101; Stephanie Dominguez pp72–73; Nick Harris (Beehive Illustration) pp10, 11, 20, 27, 35, 39, 42, 44, 55, 66, 67; Kevin Hopgood p33; Andrés Martínez Ricci (The Organisation) pp16–17; Bethan Matthews (Sylvie Poggio Artist Agency) pp14, 22, 23, 46, 54, 62, 71; Patricia Moffat pp40–41; Andrew Painter pp4, 13, 21, 29, 37, 45, 53, 61, 69, 77; Ismael Pinteno (Advocate Art) pp64–65; Laszlo Veres (Beehive Illustration) pp6, 30, 38; Steven Wood (Advocate Art) pp3–77.
Cover design by Wild Apple Design Ltd
Cover illustration by Steven Wood (Advocate Art)

Printed and bound in Thailand

2019 2018 2017 2016 2015
10 9 8 7 6 5 4 3 2 1

Contents

Student Book Contents

Competencies

me	act	think	learn	communicate
Activities that encourage children to accept responsibility and reflect on the consequences of lifestyle choices.	Activities that develop societal understanding and identification of children's own circumstances in a wider context.	Activities that develop critical thinking skills to reflect upon, manipulate, process, and interpret information.	Activities that foster learner autonomy, and allow children to demonstrate and put into practice learning strategies.	Activities that promote interpersonal and collaborative skills, develop teamwork, and allow children to express opinions and ideas.

Philosophy and Methodology

Philosophy

1 Language is power.

Story Central empowers children to communicate effectively and develop their knowledge of the world around them through stories. The course enables children to become critical and active readers, writers, and storytellers through its strong focus on literacy development.

2 An empowered teacher empowers students and changes lives.

Story Central provides teachers with all the support they need to deliver effective and inspiring lessons. Children will respond to the meaningful texts and activities, ensuring that both teachers and children feel a real sense of achievement. Children will develop the skills they need to participate fully in their lives both inside and outside the classroom.

3 The child is not a blank slate.

Children bring their culture, beliefs and a rich inner world to the classroom. Our materials respect this and recognize that this is key to engaging and interesting children in learning English.

4 Nurturing critical and creative thinking will help children become well-rounded and innovative adults.

Story Central actively encourages creative, divergent, and playful thinking, and consistently supports the acquisition of academic knowledge.

Methodology

Literacy

Reading and writing skills are developed throughout the course. Each chapter is based around a story. An extract is introduced in Student Book Lesson 3, allowing opportunities to develop reading skills and encouraging children to think creatively as they analyze the language in a meaningful context, and predict story developments. The full story is given in the beautifully illustrated Reader. Use of the Reader is fully integrated and the story links together the chapter theme and target language, providing language-rich input and enabling holistic learning. Activities engage children's interest and imagination as they are encouraged to read for pleasure. After children have read the story, their writing skills are developed through personal responses and creative writing. A love of literature is further fostered by the Oral Storytelling Videos.

Critical Literacy

Story Central takes children beyond understanding texts. The material and activities helps them analyze and respond, as they develop the skills of questioning and interpreting the information they encounter. Opportunities are given for discussion of the story's meaning and how the values expressed relate to their lives and the world around them. Children are supported in expressing their opinions through presentations, role play, and extended writing. These essential skills will empower them to use language effectively later in life.

Critical and Creative Thinking

Critical and creative thinking are actively encouraged. Children are given every opportunity to figure things out for themselves and share their ideas. Vocabulary is presented in context, requiring them to use textual and visual clues to process and deduce meaning. Prediction, reflection, and drawing conclusions all play an important part in developing an imaginative and reflective response.

A Cool Place to Hang Out With Friends!

Story Central is a cool club where kids hang out with their friends and read great books. They also share ideas and stories, plan events, do homework, and drink milkshakes! In *Story Central* you can explore, discover, learn, research, and interact. It's the sort of place where kids really want to be!

Children will love getting to know the fun characters who hang out in Story Central. They appear in Lesson 3 and Lesson 5 in every chapter.

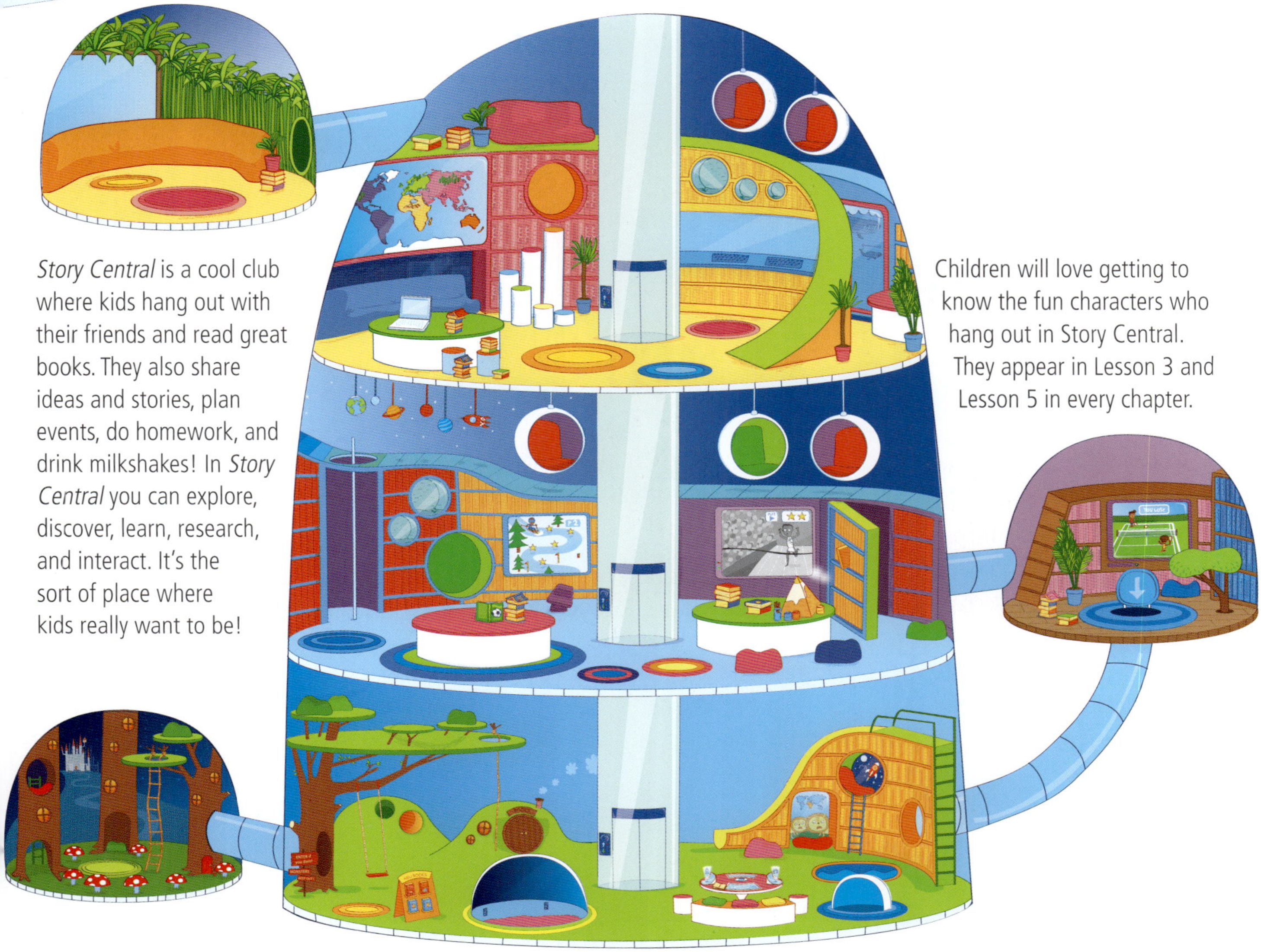

Level 6 Characters

Scarlett is an art student who runs *Story Central* with her twin brother, Rufus. She enjoys painting, poetry, and other creative activities.

Rufus studies IT. He shows everyone how to use the technology at *Story Central*—and fixes things when they break!

Hamish is Scarlett and Rufus's clever dog. He thinks a lot …

Yasmin is 14 years old. She is fascinated by science and nature and loves finding out about them at *Story Central*.

Angelo is 14 too. He loves literature, acting, and singing—and he has his own film blog!

Component Overview

For the Student

Student Book

Consists of 9 thematic chapters, featuring a story extract, literacy development, competency coverage, CLIL content, and project work. Focuses on developing critical thinking, creativity, communication, and collaboration.

Reader

Consists of 9 stories of different genres and styles. Focuses on promoting critical literacy and reading skills through developing a love of reading.

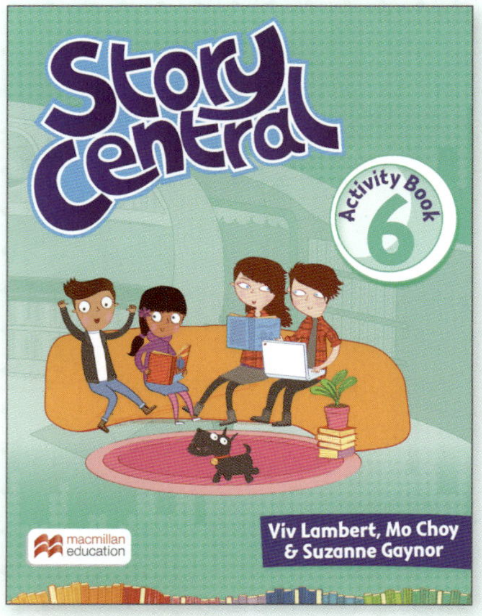

Activity Book

Consists of follow-on lessons for every Student Book lesson. Focuses on consolidating key language and skills, and developing creative use of language in writing.

Student's App

Consists of enjoyable and motivating games for children to play outside the classroom, with rewards and challenges to encourage repeat use. Focuses on practicing key vocabulary.

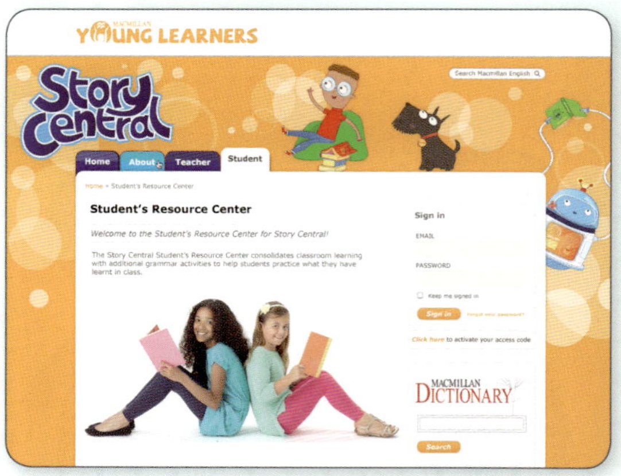

Student's Resource Center

Consists of downloadable supplementary materials including further grammar practice and videos that children can watch over and over. Focuses on consolidating and extending language learning.

For the Teacher

Teacher Edition

Consists of teaching notes for each lesson of the Student Book, Reader, and Activity Book, and suggestions on when and how to use digital components. Focuses on providing clear and concise support for lesson planning and teaching.

Class Audio CDs

Contain all key texts, stories, songs, and dialogues.

Oral Storytelling Videos feature additional stories with mesmerizing narration set in *Story Central*. These are related to Chapters 1, 3, 5, 7, and 9.

Music Videos will get children singing! They can follow the lyrics on screen for the songs from Chapters 2, 6, 8, and 9.

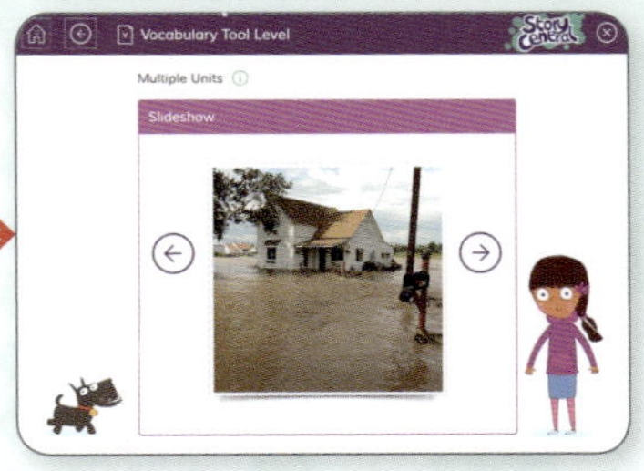

The **Vocabulary Tool** presents all of the target vocab from Lessons 1 and 6 with a clear audio model which will help children remember the words.

Presentation Kit

Consists of a downloadable digital version of the Student Book, Reader, and Activity Book, to be used in class, with integrated audio, video, interactive activities, answer keys, and teaching tips. Focuses on promoting "heads-up" and interactive learning.

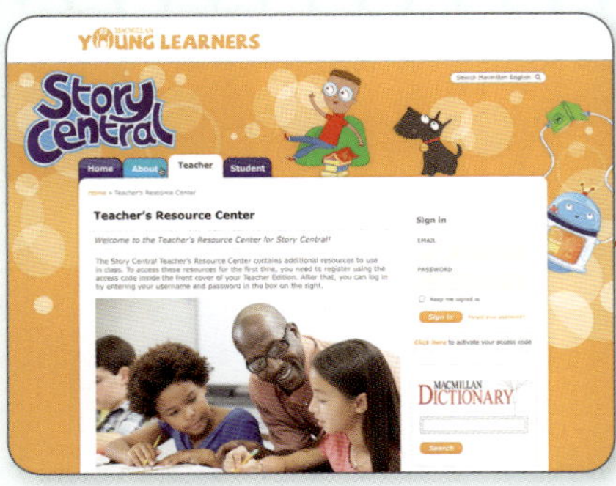

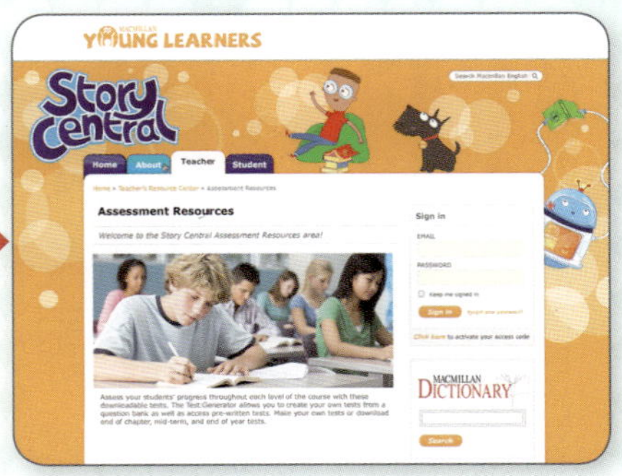

Teacher's Resource Center

Consists of additional resources and ideas to extend lessons and learning, and give further practice of key language. Focuses on giving teachers flexibility and the means to deliver dynamic and varied lessons.

Test Generator

Pre-written tests for each chapter, mid-year, and end-of-year are available to download from the Teacher's Resource Center. In addition, the Test Generator allows teachers to customize and create new tests from a bank of activities.

Teaching with Story Central

Lesson 1 Vocabulary

High-impact openers introduce the chapter theme to create interest and engage children.

Fun activities **consolidate new language** and provide opportunities for extra practice.

Vocabulary is introduced through visual and audio clues to develop **critical thinking skills**, encouraging children to deduce meaning.

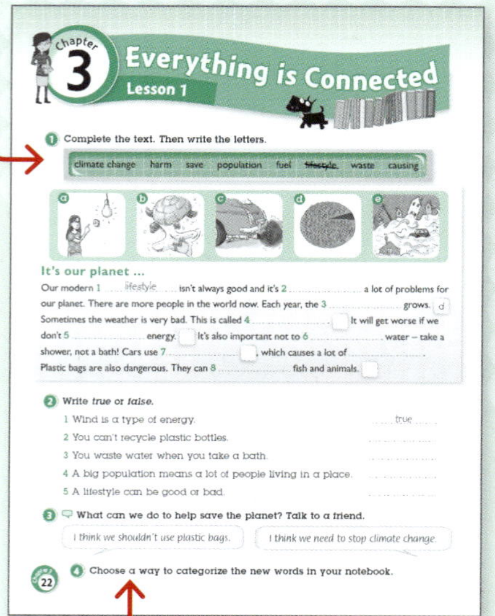

Children use the **clues** to deduce meaning of the vocabulary.

Categorization activities **empower children** by giving them **choices** about how they learn.

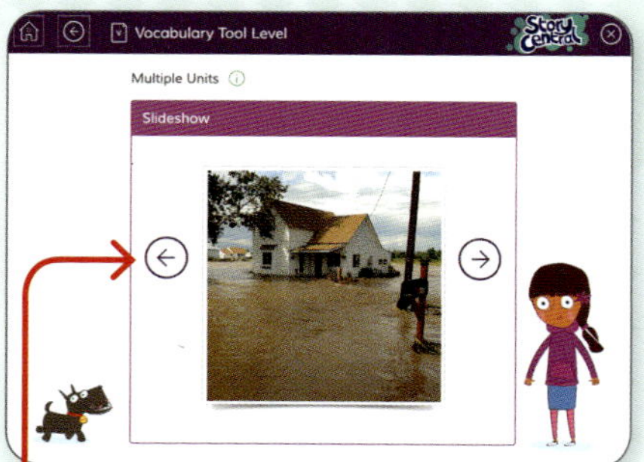

The **Vocabulary Tool** provides clear audio models of the new words to reinforce learning (available in the Presentation Kit).

Lesson 2 Grammar

Grammar is presented clearly and accessibly, recycling Lesson 1 vocabulary.

Further grammar practice in the Activity Book consolidates language.

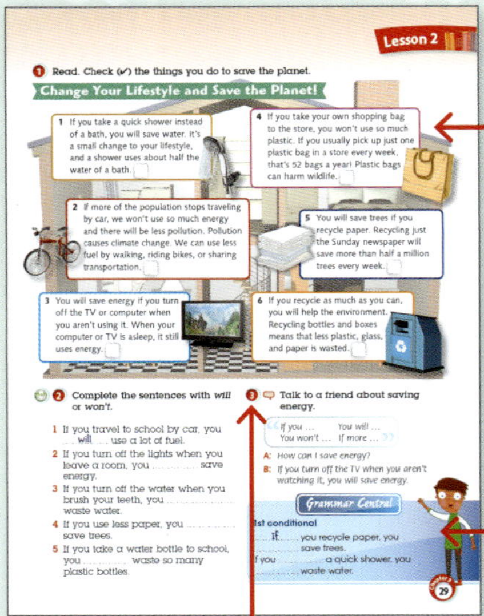

Grammar Central encourages children to complete the grammar structures themselves and provides a useful reference for activities.

Grammar Reference sections in the Student Book (pp. 98–103) and Activity Book (pp. 96–104) provide further practice and support.

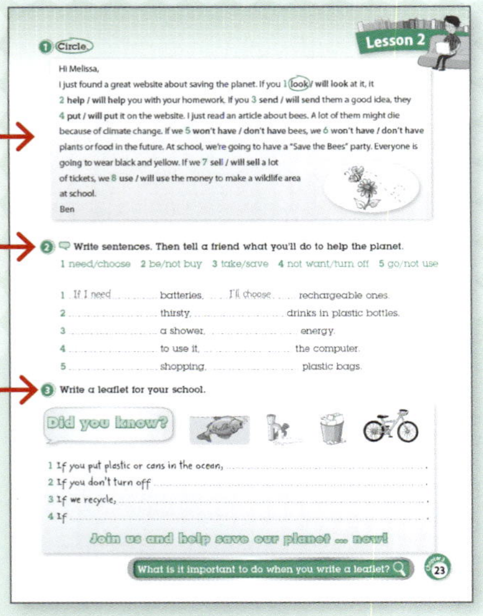

Speaking activities give children the opportunity to use the new grammar in a meaningful context.

Writing activities provide well-supported and progressive development of writing skills.

Supplementary **grammar worksheets** can be downloaded from the Teacher's Resource Center to further consolidate learning in class or as homework.

Engaging **grammar activities** are available on the Student's Resource Center for additional home study and practice.

Lesson 3 Reading: Story Extract

A **functional dialogue** featuring the *Story Central* characters introduces and gives practice in useful everyday language.

Children predict what the story is about before reading, to develop **visual literacy**.

Comprehension questions about the story extract check understanding.

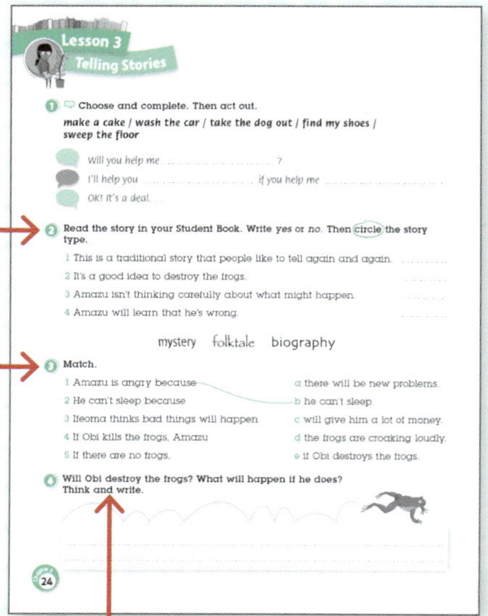

The **story extract** (beginning, middle, or end) engages children but leaves plenty to the imagination.

Comprehension and prediction questions develop reading skills and strategies.

A **prediction activity** asks children to use their **imagination** to figure out what will happen in the story.

Reader

Children read the whole story in their Reader.

A wide variety of story genres and narrative styles gives a **rich literary experience**.

Beautiful illustrations motivate children to **read for pleasure** and develop **a lifelong love of reading**.

Extensive language input allows **holistic language learning**, with the focus on overall understanding.

Lesson 4 Reading Comprehension and Critical Literacy

After reading the story in the Reader, children answer comprehension questions which help develop **reading strategies**.

The **Writing Tools** feature helps children identify and apply techniques to improve their writing.

Graphic organizer activities develop **study skills**.

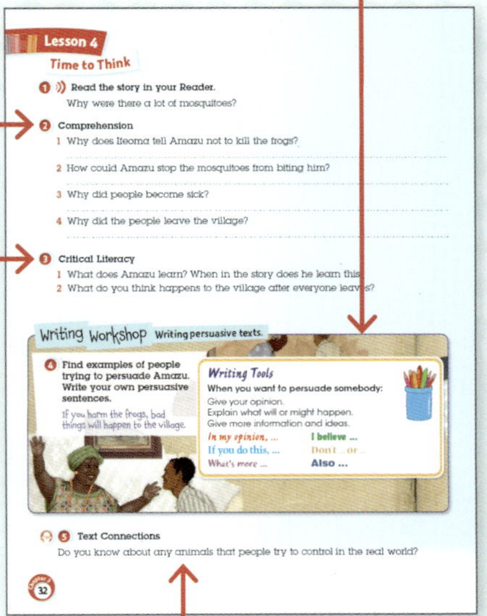
Lesson 4
Time to Think
1 Read the story in your Reader.
Why were there a lot of mosquitoes?
2 Comprehension
1 Why does Ifeoma tell Amazu not to kill the frogs?
2 How could Amazu stop the mosquitoes from biting him?
3 Why did people become sick?
4 Why did the people leave the village?
3 Critical Literacy
1 What does Amazu learn? When in the story does he learn this?
2 What do you think happens to the village after everyone leaves?
Writing Workshop Writing persuasive texts.
4 Find examples of people trying to persuade Amazu. Write your own persuasive sentences.
If you harm the frogs, bad things will happen to the village.
Writing Tools
When you want to persuade somebody:
Give your opinion.
Explain what will or might happen.
Give more information and ideas.
In my opinion, ... I believe ...
If you do this, ... Don't ... or ...
What's more ... Also ...
5 Text Connections
Do you know about any animals that people try to control in the real world?
32

Children practice the Student Book **Writing Tools** techniques.

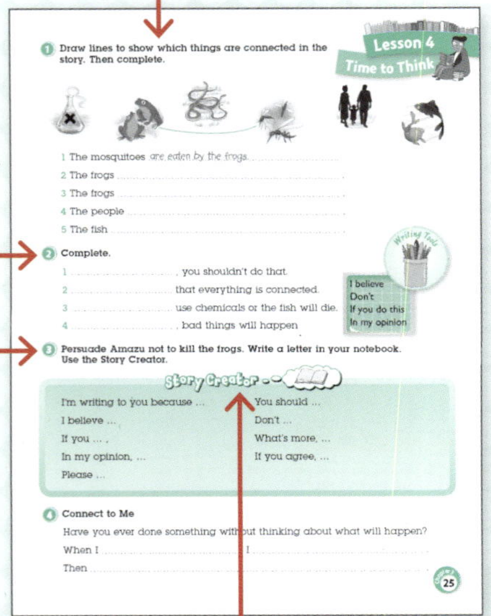
Lesson 4
Time to Think
1 Draw lines to show which things are connected in the story. Then complete.
1 The mosquitoes are eaten by the frogs.
2 The frogs
3 The frogs
4 The people
5 The fish
2 Complete.
1 ..., you shouldn't do that.
2 ... that everything is connected.
3 ... use chemicals or the fish will die.
4 ... bad things will happen.
I believe
Don't
If you do this
In my opinion
3 Persuade Amazu not to kill the frogs. Write a letter in your notebook. Use the Story Creator.
Story Creator
I'm writing to you because ... You should ...
I believe ... Don't ...
If you ..., What's more, ...
In my opinion, ... If you agree, ...
Please ...
4 Connect to Me
Have you ever done something without thinking about what will happen?
When I ... I ...
Then ...
25

Critical literacy activities encourage children to analyze the text, reflecting on the main issues, and getting inspiration for their own writing.

Personalization questions prompt children to make links between the story and other texts / their own lives, providing opportunities for discussion and self-expression.

Supported **writing activities** give children the opportunity to respond imaginatively to the story.

Story Creator supports children in producing their own stories.

In the **Oral Storytelling Videos** professional storytellers act out and bring to life a different story on a related theme for Chapters 1, 3, 5, 7, and 9 (available in the Presentation Kit).

Teaching notes and worksheets for the Oral Storytelling Videos provide activities ideas to support comprehension and enhance enjoyment (downloadable from the Teacher's Resource Center). A **Literacy Handbook** gives support and ideas for developing literacy skills with young learners.

Lesson 5 Grammar and Reading

In the Book Club the *Story Central* characters present new **grammar** in a lively, meaningful context which recycles the vocabulary from the chapter.

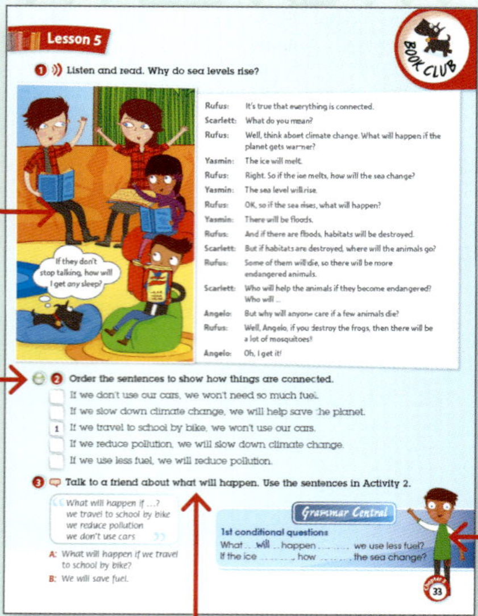
Lesson 5

BOOK CLUB

1 Listen and read. Why do sea levels rise?

Rufus: It's true that everything is connected.
Scarlett: What do you mean?
Rufus: Well, think about climate change. What will happen if the planet gets warmer?
Yasmin: The ice will melt.
Rufus: Right. So if the ice melts, how will the sea change?
Yasmin: The sea level will rise.
Rufus: OK, so if the sea rises, what will happen?
Yasmin: There will be floods.
Rufus: And if there are floods, habitats will be destroyed.
Scarlett: But if habitats are destroyed, where will the animals go?
Rufus: Some of them will die, so there will be more endangered animals.
Scarlett: Who will help the animals if they become endangered? Who will ...
Angelo: But why will anyone care if a few animals die?
Rufus: Well, Angelo, if you destroy the frogs, then there will be a lot of mosquitoes!
Angelo: Oh, I get it!

2 Order the sentences to show how things are connected.
- [ ] If we don't use our cars, we won't need so much fuel.
- [ ] If we slow down climate change, we will help save the planet.
- 1 If we travel to school by bike, we won't use our cars.
- [ ] If we reduce pollution, we will slow down climate change.
- [ ] If we use less fuel, we will reduce pollution.

3 Talk to a friend about what will happen. Use the sentences in Activity 2.

What will happen if ...?
we travel to school by bike
we reduce pollution
we don't use cars

A: What will happen if we travel to school by bike?
B: We will save fuel.

Grammar Central
1st conditional questions
What ... will ... happen .... we use less fuel?
If the ice .... , how .... the sea change?

33

Grammar Central encourages children to complete the grammar structures themselves and provides a useful reference.

Grammar Reference sections in the Student Book (pp. 98–103) and Activity Book (pp. 96–104) provide further practice and support.

Children are given the opportunity for controlled **written practice** of the new structures.

Speaking activities give children the opportunity to use the new grammar in a meaningful context.

Grammar practice activities give staggered support.

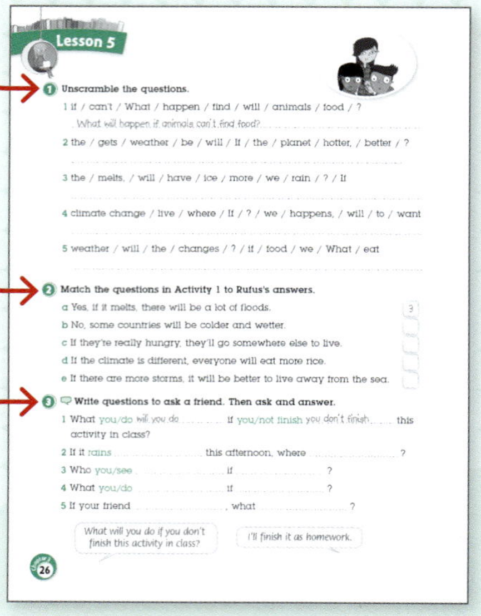
Lesson 5

1 Unscramble the questions.
1 if / can't / What / happen / find / will / animals / food / ?
What will happen if animals can't find food?
2 the / gets / weather / be / will / If / the / planet / hotter, / better / ?
3 the / melts, / will / have / ice / more / we / rain / ? / If
4 climate change / live / where / If / ? / we / happens, / will / to / want
5 weather / will / the / changes / ? / if / food / we / What / eat

2 Match the questions in Activity 1 to Rufus's answers.
a Yes, if it melts, there will be a lot of floods. 3
b No, some countries will be colder and wetter.
c If they're really hungry, they'll go somewhere else to live.
d If the climate is different, everyone will eat more rice.
e If there are more storms, it will be better to live away from the sea.

3 Write questions to ask a friend. Then ask and answer.
1 What you/do will you do .... if you/not finish you don't finish .... this activity in class?
2 If it rains .... this afternoon, where .... ?
3 Who you/see .... if .... ?
4 What you/do .... if .... ?
5 If your friend .... , what .... ?

What will you do if you don't finish this activity in class?
I'll finish it as homework.

26

A **guided writing** activity consolidates grammar and progressively develops writing skills.

Supplementary **grammar worksheets** can be downloaded from the Teacher's Resource Center to further consolidate learning in class or as homework.

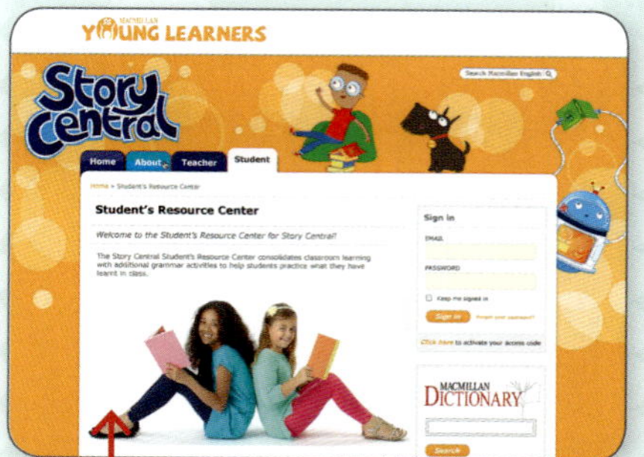

Engaging **grammar activities** are available on the Student's Resource Center for additional home study and practice.

Lesson 6 Vocabulary, Listening or Song, and Spelling

A variety of interesting **listening activities** and catchy **songs** present new vocabulary in a fun, memorable, and motivating context.

Vocabulary is introduced through textual and visual clues to develop **critical thinking skills** (deduction of meaning).

Word work activities consolidate vocabulary and help develop strategies for memorizing vocabulary.

Lesson 6

1 Listen and circle on the map. Where were the toys found?

2 Listen again and order the sentences.

- [ ] Strong **currents** took them to the USA, Alaska, Japan, Australia, and South America.
- [ ] The **cargo ship** left the **port** in Hong Kong.
- [ ] The boxes **broke down** and the plastic ducks floated far across the ocean.
- [ ] Twelve enormous **containers** fell into the ocean.
- 1 A **factory** in Hong Kong made thousands of plastic toys.
- [ ] They will take years to break down and will leave **chemicals** in the ocean.
- [ ] There was a **storm** in the ocean.

3 Talk to a friend and retell the story. Use the words in the text.

A: *What happened?*
B: *The toys left the port in Hong Kong in a cargo ship.*

Spelling Central

Circle the words with a *k* sound. Write the words in the chart. Can you add more *k* sound words?

c	k	ck	ch
container			

34

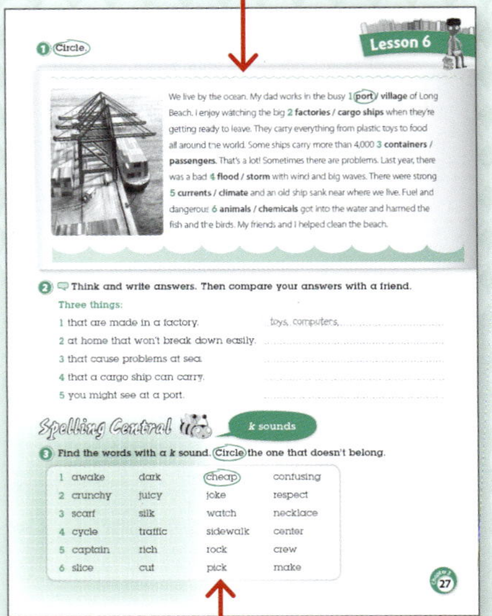

Lesson 6

1 Circle.

We live by the ocean. My dad works in the busy 1 **port / village** of Long Beach. I enjoy watching the big 2 **factories / cargo ships** when they're getting ready to leave. They carry everything from plastic toys to food all around the world. Some ships carry more than 4,000 3 **containers / passengers.** That's a lot! Sometimes there are problems. Last year, there was a bad 4 **flood / storm** with wind and big waves. There were strong 5 **currents / climate** and an old ship sank near where we live. Fuel and dangerous 6 **animals / chemicals** got into the water and harmed the fish and the birds. My friends and I helped clean the beach.

2 Think and write answers. Then compare your answers with a friend.

Three things:

1 that are made in a factory. toys, computers,
2 at home that won't break down easily.
3 that cause problems at sea.
4 that a cargo ship can carry.
5 you might see at a port.

Spelling Central — *k* sounds

3 Find the words with a *k* sound. Circle the one that doesn't belong.

1	awake	dark	cheap	confusing
2	crunchy	juicy	joke	respect
3	scarf	silk	watch	necklace
4	cycle	traffic	sidewalk	center
5	captain	rich	rock	crew
6	slice	cut	pick	make

27

Speaking activities give practice in a meaningful context to develop fluency.

Spelling tips are covered and practiced in **Spelling Central**.

Children identify and practice the spellings from the Student Book **Spelling Central** feature.

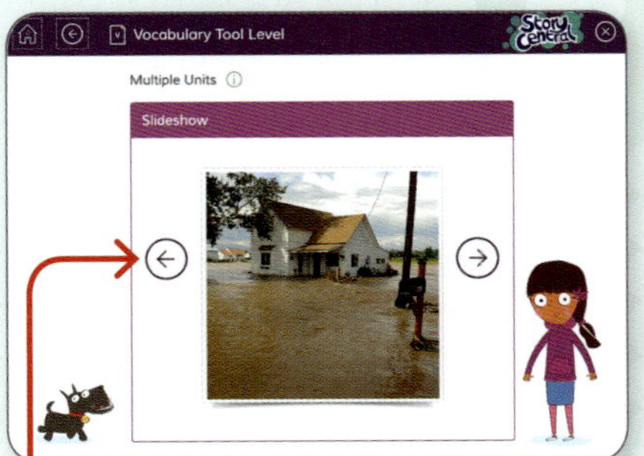

Music Videos for Chapters 2, 6, 8, and 9 encourage children to sing along to the music, consolidating the learning of the target vocabulary (available in the Presentation Kit).

The **Vocabulary Tool** provides clear audio models of the new words to reinforce learning (available in the Presentation Kit).

The lively clan of The Inks on the **Student's App** provide children with motivating and challenging games to practice the chapter vocabulary from Lesson 1 and Lesson 6 outside the classroom.

Lesson 7 CLIL

The **CLIL** focus gives the opportunity to find out about other curricular areas (such as science, math, social science) through English.

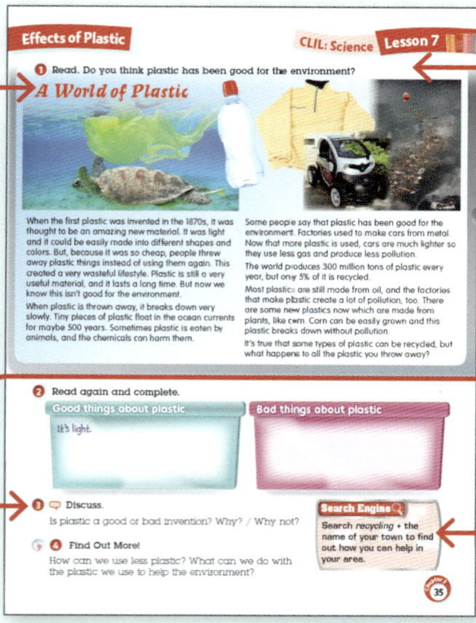

Additional **Audio** is available in the Presentation Kit.

Children are encouraged to express their own opinions in a class discussion.

Search Engine gives tips to help children search for information online, developing their information literacy.

Children use their **Find Out More!** research to make an Info Card and complete a mini-project extending the CLIL topic.

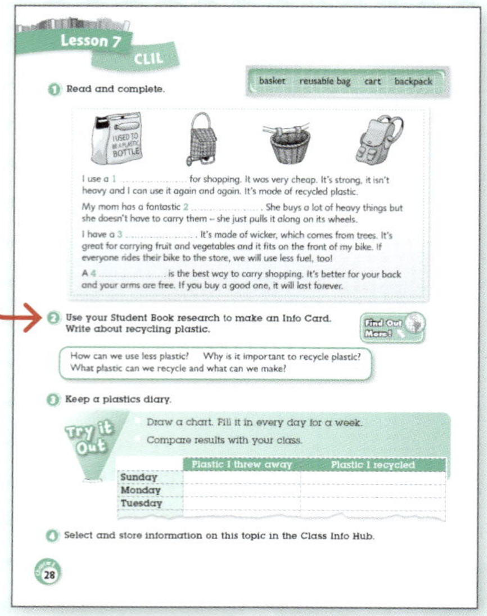

Lesson 8 Project

Children do a **writing project** that relates to the chapter theme.

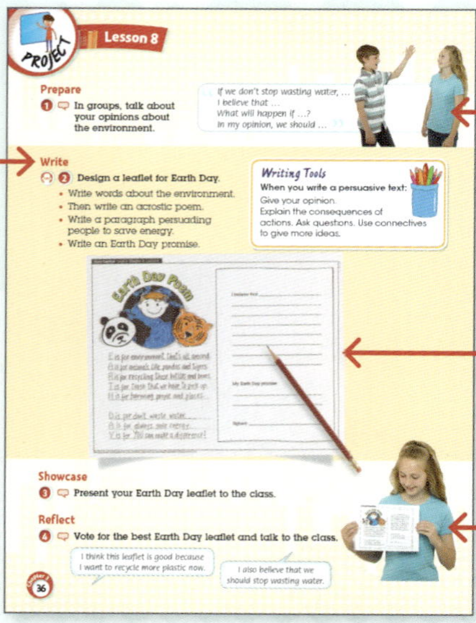

A **group discussion** helps children prepare.

A clear **structure** is given to support writing.

The children then **present** their project to the class.

An ongoing **quiz** for children to complete in pairs reviews language, gives speaking practice, and rounds off the chapter.

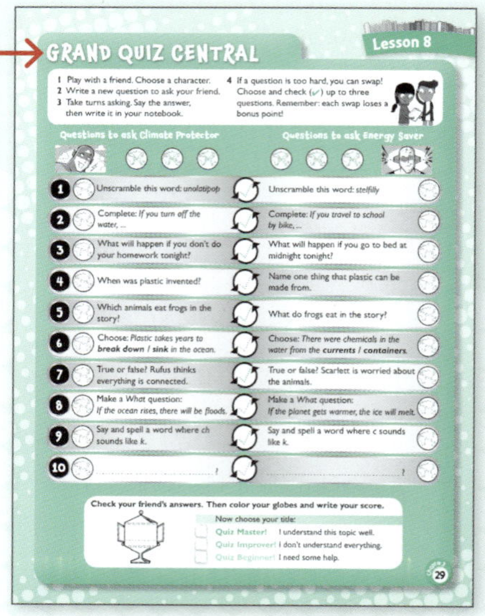

Each CLIL lesson has an optional **graphic organizer** template to help children organize their findings (downloadable from the Teacher's Resource Center).

Where necessary, printable **Writing templates** are supplied for Lesson 8 (downloadable from the Teacher's Resource Center).

Review

The Review lesson provides **further practice and consolidation** of language from the chapter.

Children reflect on their own progress and color in Hamish's bones to record their progress (**self-evaluation**).

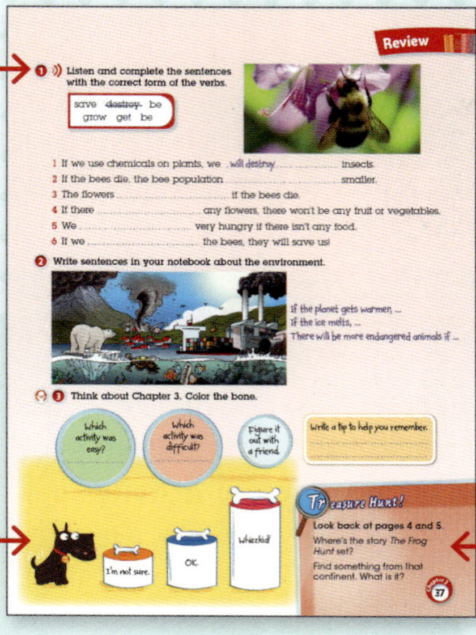
Review

1 Listen and complete the sentences with the correct form of the verbs.

save ~~destroy~~ be
grow get be

1 If we use chemicals on plants, we ...will destroy... insects.
2 If the bees die, the bee population .... smaller.
3 The flowers .... if the bees die.
4 If there .... any flowers, there won't be any fruit or vegetables.
5 We .... very hungry if there isn't any food.
6 If we .... the bees, they will save us!

2 Write sentences in your notebook about the environment.

If the planet gets warmer, ...
If the ice melts, ...
There will be more endangered animals if ...

3 Think about Chapter 3. Color the bone.

Which activity was easy?
Which activity was difficult?
Figure it out with a friend.
Write a tip to help you remember.

I'm not sure.
OK.
Whizzkid!

Treasure Hunt!
Look back at pages 4 and 5.
Where's the story *The Frog Hunt* set?
Find something from that continent. What is it?

37

A fun **Treasure Hunt!** activity takes children back to the Welcome section (pp. 4–5) to find an item from the chapter.

CEYLT (**Cambridge YLE**)-style activities practicing the language from each chapter are in the Activity Book pp. 78–95. These help prepare for the Reading and Writing, and Listening papers of the Cambridge English Flyers Exam.

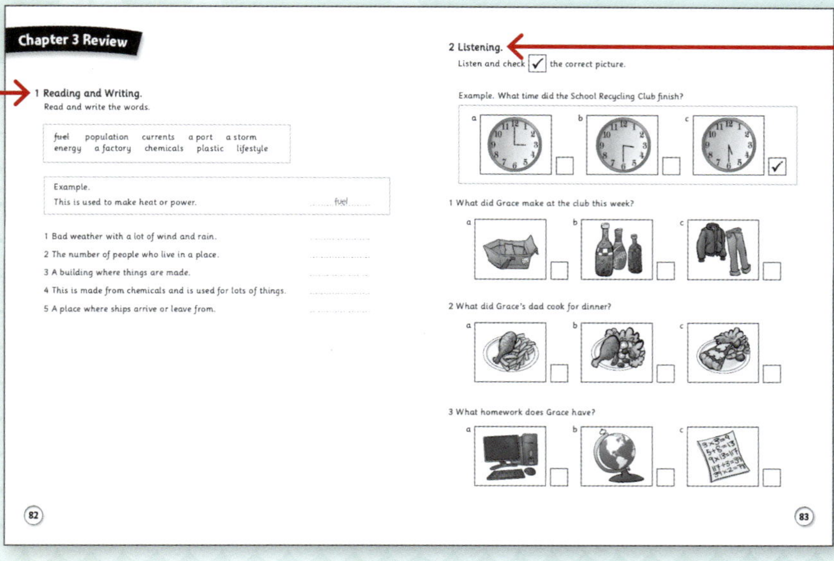
Chapter 3 Review

1 Reading and Writing.
Read and write the words.

fuel population currents a port a storm
energy a factory chemicals plastic lifestyle

Example.
This is used to make heat or power. ....fuel........

1 Bad weather with a lot of wind and rain. ....
2 The number of people who live in a place. ....
3 A building where things are made. ....
4 This is made from chemicals and is used for lots of things. ....
5 A place where ships arrive or leave from. ....

2 Listening.
Listen and check ✓ the correct picture.

Example. What time did the School Recycling Club finish?

1 What did Grace make at the club this week?

2 What did Grace's dad cook for dinner?

3 What homework does Grace have?

82

83

Class audio for the listening activities is at the end of Class CD2.

The Teacher's Resource Center provides a wealth of assessment support including pre-written chapter, mid-year, and end-of-year tests, plus a **Test Generator** to create customized class tests. **CEYLT** (**Cambridge YLE**)-style speaking prompts and tips are also available.

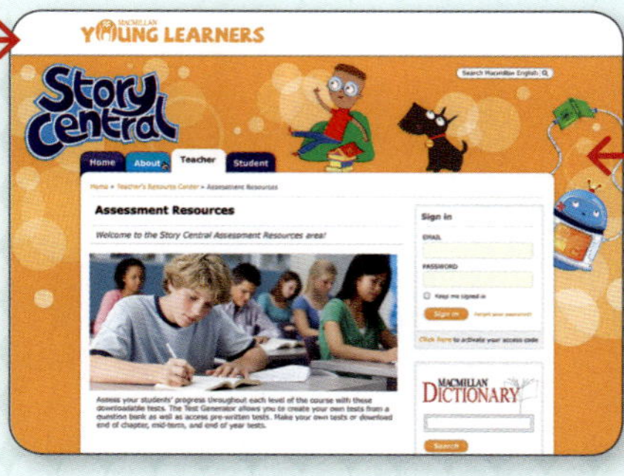

Festival worksheets and teaching notes to be used during the year bring the world outside into the classroom and help to foster an understanding of different cultures.

Teacher Edition Overview

Chapter Overview

An **Overview** at the start of every chapter provides a quick reference point to show what is covered.
The **Competency Focus** shows where competencies are developed throughout the chapter.
The **Digital Overview** shows the variety of digital resources available for the chapter.

Student Book and Activity Book Lessons

Each lesson opens with the lesson objectives, key language, and any materials required.

A **Warmer** activity introduces children to the lesson topic, activating prior knowledge, and getting the children energized!

Reduced pages for the **Student Book** and the **Activity Book** give easy reference to the components being used.

A **Cooler** activity allows children to review language learned in a fun context.

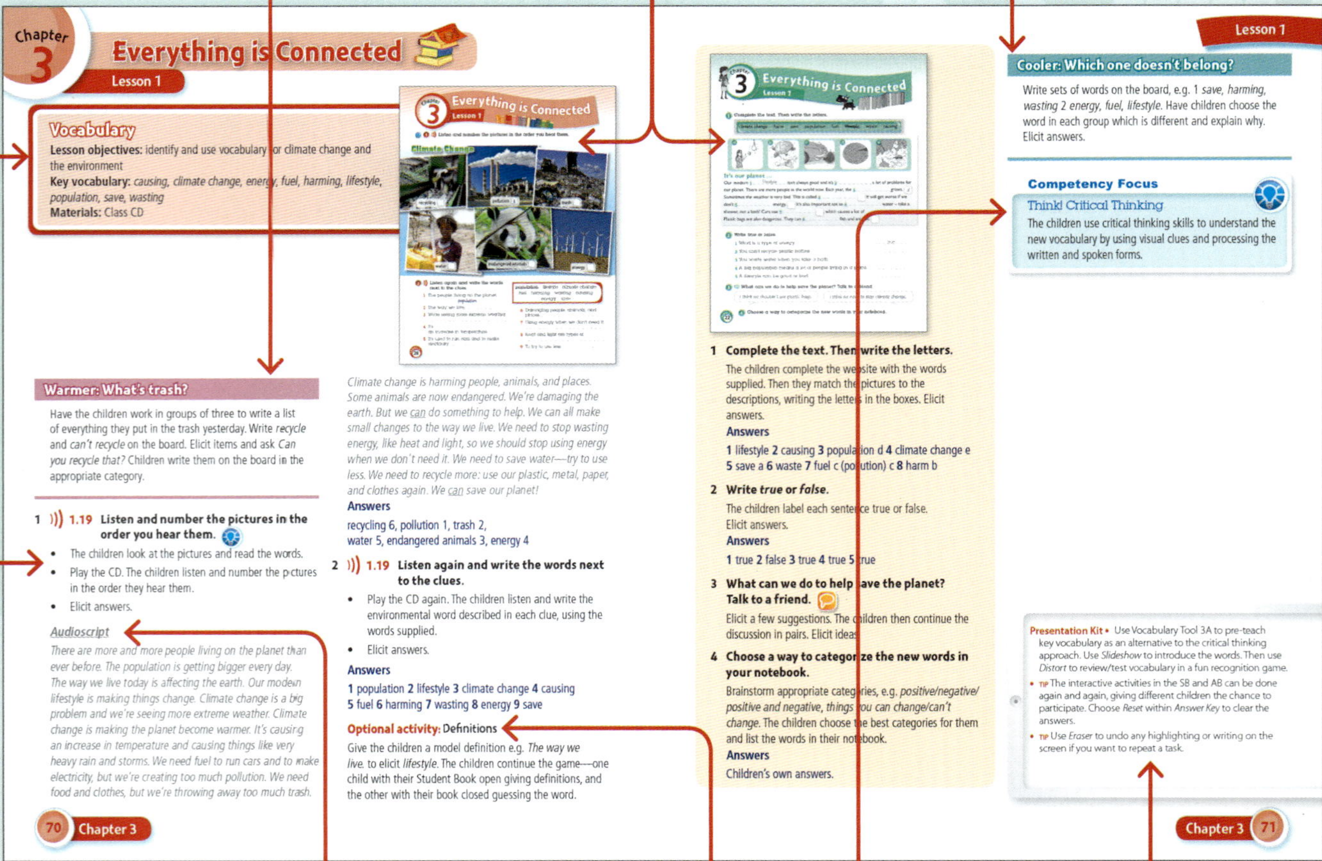
Chapter 3 Everything is Connected
Lesson 1

Vocabulary
Lesson objectives: identify and use vocabulary for climate change and the environment
Key vocabulary: *causing, climate change, energy, fuel, harming, lifestyle, population, save, wasting*
Materials: Class CD

Warmer: What's trash?
Have the children work in groups of three to write a list of everything they put in the trash yesterday. Write *recycle* and *can't recycle* on the board. Elicit items and ask *Can you recycle that?* Children write them on the board in the appropriate category.

1 1.19 **Listen and number the pictures in the order you hear them.**
- The children look at the pictures and read the words.
- Play the CD. The children listen and number the pictures in the order they hear them.
- Elicit answers.

Audioscript
There are more and more people living on the planet than ever before. The population is getting bigger every day. The way we live today is affecting the earth. Our modern lifestyle is making things change. Climate change is a big problem and we're seeing more extreme weather. Climate change is making the planet become warmer. It's causing an increase in temperature and causing things like very heavy rain and storms. We need fuel to run cars and to make electricity, but we're creating too much pollution. We need food and clothes, but we're throwing away too much trash.

Climate change is harming people, animals, and places. Some animals are now endangered. We're damaging the earth. But we can do something to help. We can all make small changes to the way we live. We need to stop wasting energy, like heat and light, so we should stop using energy when we don't need it. We need to save water—try to use less. We need to recycle more: use our plastic, metal, paper, and clothes again. We can save our planet!

Answers
recycling 6, pollution 1, trash 2, water 5, endangered animals 3, energy 4

2 1.19 **Listen again and write the words next to the clues.**
- Play the CD again. The children listen and write the environmental word described in each clue, using the words supplied.
- Elicit answers.

Answers
1 population 2 lifestyle 3 climate change 4 causing 5 fuel 6 harming 7 wasting 8 energy 9 save

Optional activity: Definitions
Give the children a model definition e.g. *The way we live,* to elicit *lifestyle*. The children continue the game—one child with their Student Book open giving definitions, and the other with their book closed guessing the word.

70 Chapter 3

1 **Complete the text. Then write the letters.**
The children complete the website with the words supplied. Then they match the pictures to the descriptions, writing the letters in the boxes. Elicit answers.
Answers
1 lifestyle 2 causing 3 population d 4 climate change e 5 save a 6 waste 7 fuel c (pollution) c 8 harm b

2 **Write *true* or *false*.**
The children label each sentence true or false. Elicit answers.
Answers
1 true 2 false 3 true 4 true 5 true

3 **What can we do to help save the planet? Talk to a friend.**
Elicit a few suggestions. The children then continue the discussion in pairs. Elicit ideas.

4 **Choose a way to categorize the new words in your notebook.**
Brainstorm appropriate categories, e.g. *positive/negative/ positive and negative, things you can change/can't change*. The children choose the best categories for them and list the words in their notebook.
Answers
Children's own answers.

Lesson 1

Cooler: Which one doesn't belong?
Write sets of words on the board, e.g. 1 *save, harming, wasting* 2 *energy, fuel, lifestyle.* Have children choose the word in each group which is different and explain why. Elicit answers.

Competency Focus
Think! Critical Thinking
The children use critical thinking skills to understand the new vocabulary by using visual clues and processing the written and spoken forms.

Presentation Kit • Use Vocabulary Tool 3A to pre-teach key vocabulary as an alternative to the critical thinking approach. Use *Slideshow* to introduce the words. Then use *Distort* to review/test vocabulary in a fun recognition game.
- TIP The interactive activities in the SB and AB can be done again and again, giving different children the chance to participate. Choose *Reset* within *Answer Key* to clear the answers.
- TIP Use *Eraser* to undo any highlighting or writing on the screen if you want to repeat a task.

Chapter 3 71

Teacher's notes are carefully structured to give clear guidance at a glance.

Audioscripts are provided (unless they appear in the Student Book or Reader). Audioscripts for the Activity Book Chapter Reviews are available on pp. 223–4.

The **Competency Focus** shows how competencies are developed in the lesson.

Teaching notes suggest how and when to use the **digital components**.

Optional activities allow you to extend lessons and offer opportunities for further practice and personalization.

Reader

The **Reader** lesson contains a range of additional activities that you can use as you please. You can get children to read the Reader story at home or in class.

Reading Strategy helps you develop children's literacy, with further explanation and activities in the **Literacy Handbook** on the Teacher's Resource Center.

Story Time helps you get the most out of the Reader, helping you become a more effective storyteller in the classroom.

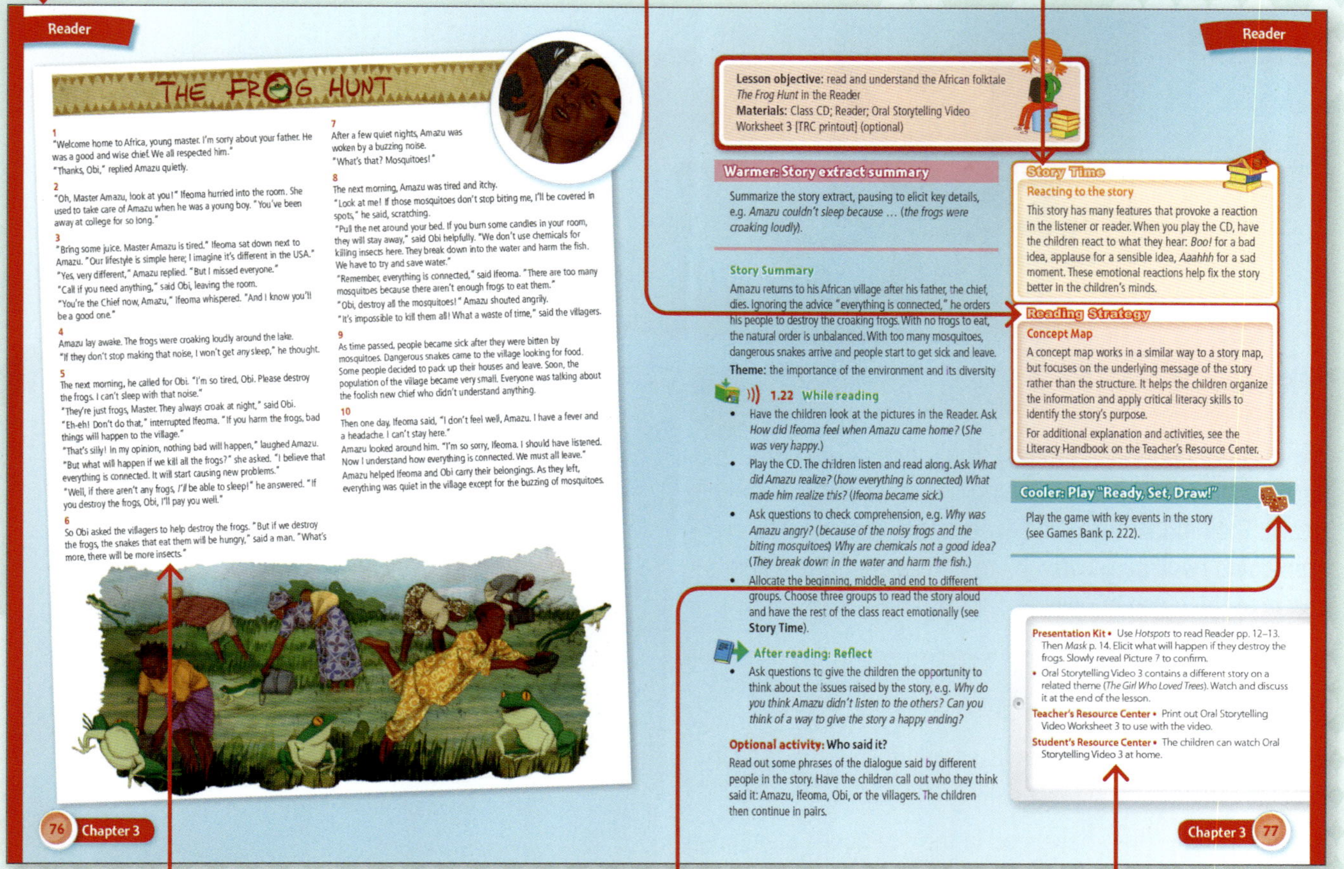

Reader

THE FROG HUNT

1
"Welcome home to Africa, young master. I'm sorry about your father. He was a good and wise chief. We all respected him."
"Thanks, Obi," replied Amazu quietly.

2
"Oh, Master Amazu, look at you!" Ifeoma hurried into the room. She used to take care of Amazu when he was a young boy. "You've been away at college for so long."

3
"Bring some juice. Master Amazu is tired." Ifeoma sat down next to Amazu. "Our lifestyle is simple here; I imagine it's different in the USA."
"Yes, very different," Amazu replied. "But I missed everyone."
"Call if you need anything," said Obi, leaving the room.
"You're the Chief now, Amazu," Ifeoma whispered. "And I know you'll be a good one."

4
Amazu lay awake. The frogs were croaking loudly around the lake.
"If they don't stop making that noise, I won't get *any* sleep," he thought.

5
The next morning, he called for Obi. "I'm so tired, Obi. Please destroy the frogs. I can't sleep with that noise."
"They're just frogs, Master. They always croak at night," said Obi.
"Eh-eh! Don't do that," interrupted Ifeoma. "If you harm the frogs, bad things will happen to the village."
"That's silly! In my opinion, nothing bad will happen," laughed Amazu.
"But what will happen if we kill all the frogs?" she asked. "I believe that everything is connected. It will start causing new problems."
"Well, if there aren't any frogs, *I'll* be able to sleep!" he answered. "If you destroy the frogs, Obi, I'll pay you well."

6
So Obi asked the villagers to help destroy the frogs. "But if we destroy the frogs, the snakes that eat them will be hungry," said a man. "What's more, there will be more insects."

7
After a few quiet nights, Amazu was woken by a buzzing noise.
"What's that? Mosquitoes!"

8
The next morning, Amazu was tired and itchy.
"Look at me! If those mosquitoes don't stop biting me, I'll be covered in spots," he said, scratching.
"Pull the net around your bed. If you burn some candles in your room, they will stay away," said Obi helpfully. "We don't use chemicals for killing insects here. They break down into the water and harm the fish. We have to try and save water."
"Remember, everything is connected," said Ifeoma. "There are too many mosquitoes because there aren't enough frogs to eat them."
"Obi, destroy all the mosquitoes!" Amazu shouted angrily.
"It's impossible to kill them all! What a waste of time," said the villagers.

9
As time passed, people became sick after they were bitten by mosquitoes. Dangerous snakes came to the village looking for food. Some people decided to pack up their houses and leave. Soon, the population of the village became very small. Everyone was talking about the foolish new chief who didn't understand anything.

10
Then one day, Ifeoma said, "I don't feel well, Amazu. I have a fever and a headache. I can't stay here."
Amazu looked around him. "I'm so sorry, Ifeoma. I should have listened. Now I understand how everything is connected. We must all leave."
Amazu helped Ifeoma and Obi carry their belongings. As they left, everything was quiet in the village except for the buzzing of mosquitoes.

76 Chapter 3

Reader

Lesson objective: read and understand the African folktale *The Frog Hunt* in the Reader
Materials: Class CD; Reader; Oral Storytelling Video Worksheet 3 [TRC printout] (optional)

Warmer: Story extract summary

Summarize the story extract, pausing to elicit key details, e.g. *Amazu couldn't sleep because … (the frogs were croaking loudly).*

Story Summary

Amazu returns to his African village after his father, the chief, dies. Ignoring the advice "everything is connected," he orders his people to destroy the croaking frogs. With no frogs to eat, the natural order is unbalanced. With too many mosquitoes, dangerous snakes arrive and people start to get sick and leave.
Theme: the importance of the environment and its diversity

1.22 While reading

- Have the children look at the pictures in the Reader. Ask *How did Ifeoma feel when Amazu came home? (She was very happy.)*
- Play the CD. The children listen and read along. Ask *What did Amazu realize? (how everything is connected) What made him realize this? (Ifeoma became sick.)*
- Ask questions to check comprehension, e.g. *Why was Amazu angry? (because of the noisy frogs and the biting mosquitoes) Why are chemicals not a good idea? (They break down in the water and harm the fish.)*
- Allocate the beginning, middle, and end to different groups. Choose three groups to read the story aloud and have the rest of the class react emotionally (see **Story Time**).

After reading: Reflect

- Ask questions to give the children the opportunity to think about the issues raised by the story, e.g. *Why do you think Amazu didn't listen to the others? Can you think of a way to give the story a happy ending?*

Optional activity: Who said it?

Read out some phrases of the dialogue said by different people in the story. Have the children call out who they think said it: Amazu, Ifeoma, Obi, or the villagers. The children then continue in pairs.

Story Time

Reacting to the story

This story has many features that provoke a reaction in the listener or reader. When you play the CD, have the children react to what they hear: *Boo!* for a bad idea, applause for a sensible idea, *Aaahhh* for a sad moment. These emotional reactions help fix the story better in the children's minds.

Reading Strategy

Concept Map

A concept map works in a similar way to a story map, but focuses on the underlying message of the story rather than the structure. It helps the children organize the information and apply critical literacy skills to identify the story's purpose.

For additional explanation and activities, see the Literacy Handbook on the Teacher's Resource Center.

Cooler: Play "Ready, Set, Draw!"

Play the game with key events in the story (see Games Bank p. 222).

Presentation Kit • Use *Hotspots* to read Reader pp. 12–13. Then *Mask* p. 14. Elicit what will happen if they destroy the frogs. Slowly reveal Picture 7 to confirm.
• Oral Storytelling Video 3 contains a different story on a related theme (*The Girl Who Loved Trees*). Watch and discuss it at the end of the lesson.
Teacher's Resource Center • Print out Oral Storytelling Video Worksheet 3 to use with the video.
Student's Resource Center • The children can watch Oral Storytelling Video 3 at home.

Chapter 3 77

The full text of the Reader story is provided, giving easy reference to the component being used.

The **Games Bank** (p. 222) gives details of popular and easy-to-use games that can be played in different lessons to engage, stimulate and motivate children.

Teaching notes suggest how and when to use the **digital components**.

Story Central

Lesson objectives: introduce *Story Central* 6; sing the course song
Materials: Class CD

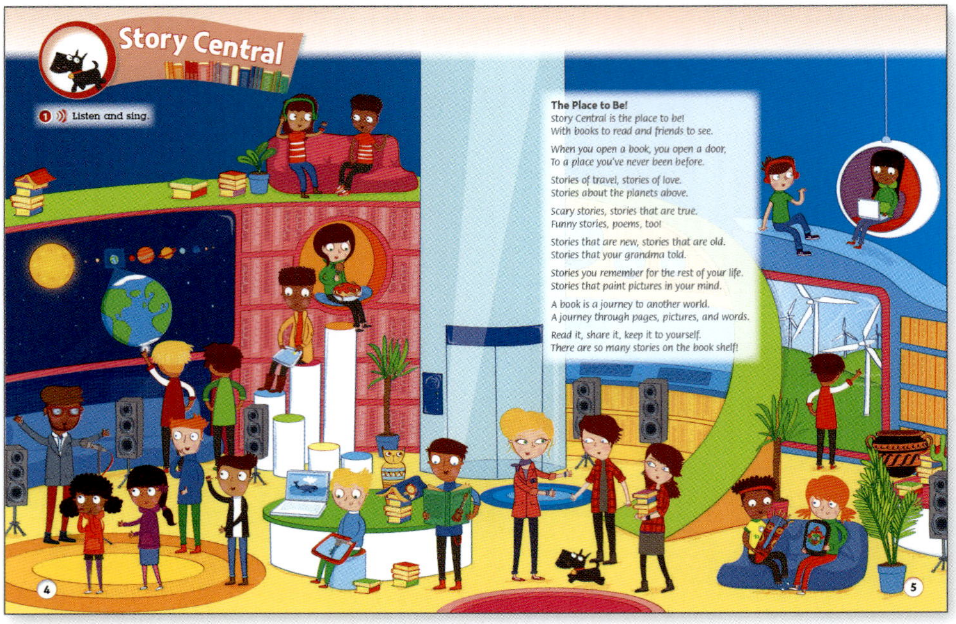

Warmer: Play "I Spy"

The children open their Student Book to pp. 4–5. Write *I spy with my little eye something beginning with …* on the board. Then model the game, using *I spy with my little eye something beginning with "p"* to elicit *planet*. The children continue the game in pairs.

1 1.2 Listen and sing.

- Play the CD. The children listen and follow the song in their book.
- Elicit stories they have read in the categories mentioned in the song.
- Play the CD again for the children to sing along.
- Divide the class into two groups. Play the CD again and have the two groups sing alternate lines. (This gives them more time to prepare for their next line.)

Optional activity: Play "Ready, Set, Draw!"

Play the game with key vocabulary from this lesson (see Games Bank p. 222).

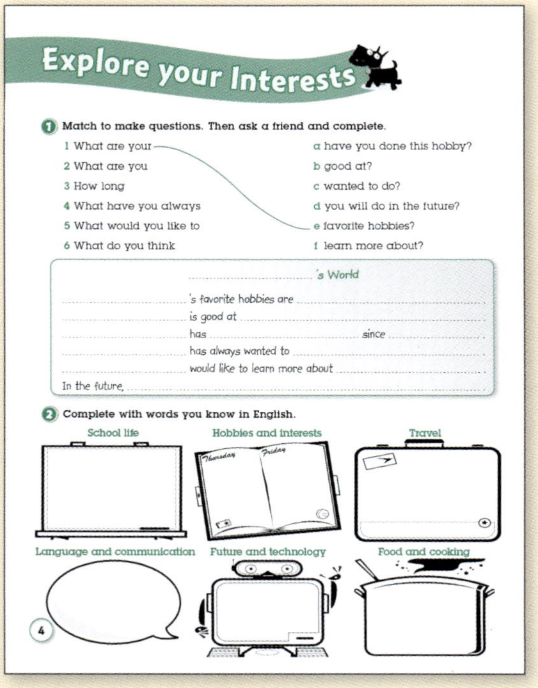

Explore your Interests

1 Match to make questions. Then ask a friend and complete.

1 What are your — a have you done this hobby?
2 What are you — b good at?
3 How long — c wanted to do?
4 What have you always — d you will do in the future?
5 What would you like to — e favorite hobbies?
6 What do you think — f learn more about?

……'s World
……'s favorite hobbies are ……
…… is good at ……
…… has …… since ……
…… has always wanted to ……
…… would like to learn more about ……
In the future, ……

2 Complete with words you know in English.

4

1 Match to make questions. Then ask a friend and complete.

The children match the openings and endings to make questions. Elicit responses. They then take turns asking and answering the questions in pairs, and complete the profile with their friend's information. Ask children to read out their texts.

Answers

1 e **2** b **3** a **4** c **5** f **6** d

2 Complete with words you know in English.

Elicit an example for each category. The children write as many words as they can for each category. Elicit answers, asking children to write them on the board.

Answers

Children's own answers.

Cooler: Sing and mime

1.2

Agree on a mime for each story type. Play the CD again for the children to sing along and mime.

Presentation Kit • All SB and AB pages can be shown on the board. For "heads-up" teaching activities, have the children close their book so you have their full attention.

- The Navigation Pane (horizontal bar, bottom of screen) helps you navigate and gives access to *Audio*, *Answer Key*, etc. The Tool Bar (side) contains tools to use on the screen, e.g. *Hotspots*, *Pointer*.
- Use *Spotlight* on the people on SB pp. 4–5. Elicit what they are doing, e.g. *He's pointing*.

Explore Your Interests

Lesson objectives: talk about interests and hobbies; preview some of the course themes
Key language: *What are you interested in? I'm good at … I've always wanted to … I'd like to learn more about … In the future, I think I will …*
Materials: Class CD; alphabet pages (Warmer)

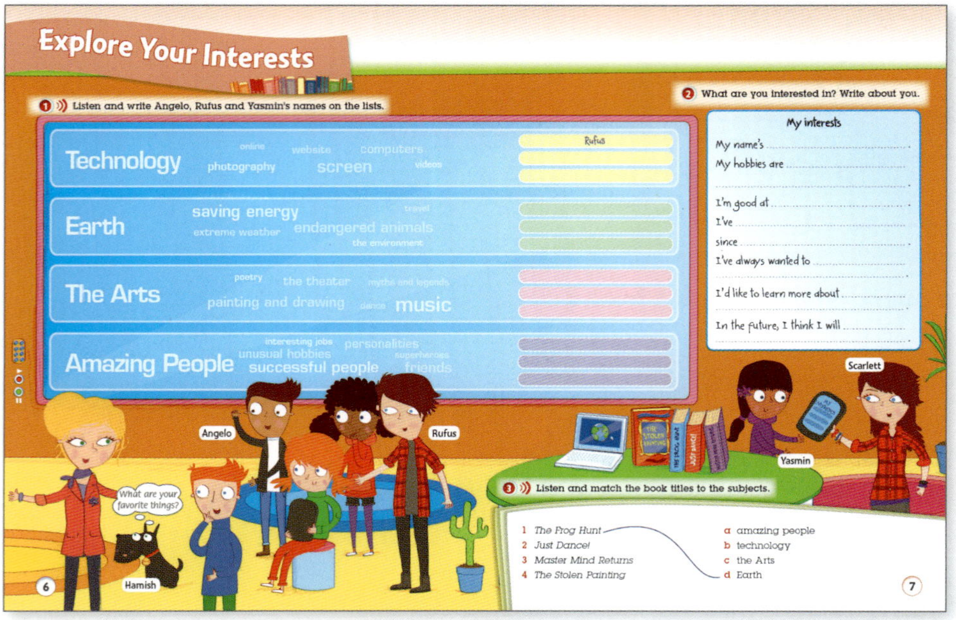

Warmer: Play "Hobbies A–Z"

Prepare an answer page for each team (the title *Hobbies* + the alphabet written vertically). Put the class into teams. Give them two minutes to write a hobby for as many letters of the alphabet as possible. Ask the team with the most words to read their list, then ask other teams to say any other words. A correct answer wins a point. The team with the most points wins.

1 1.3 Listen and write Angelo, Rufus, and Yasmin's names on the lists.

- Play the CD. The children listen and write *Angelo*, *Rufus*, or *Yasmin* in the correct place.
- Elicit answers.

<u>*Audioscript*</u>

Ava: *Welcome to the Story Central Open Day. My name's Ava, and I started Story Central five years ago. It was a small place. There was only one floor, but now we have this fantastic building with three floors. I used to work alone, but now there is a whole team of people working in the Story Central office.*
I believe that everyone can learn something when they play and have fun. I also believe that everyone can succeed when they follow their dreams and do the things they enjoy most. I always loved books and reading, and imagining fantasy worlds. That's why I started Story Central. So today is about just that! Having fun, finding out what interests you, and learning something new.
So, let's get started. Just choose the talks and classes you want to go to and put your name on the list. There's more information about them on the screens, or ask Rufus or Scarlett.
Wow! This place is fantastic. What are you guys interested in? Rufus, I know you like computers—we've talked about that already.
Rufus: *Yes, I'm really interested in the future and technology. I think life will be very different in the future. I also want to learn more about the environment.*
Ava: *You're Angelo, aren't you?*

Angelo: *That's right. I'm going to go to the presentation on theater. I've always liked singing and dancing and I'd like to work in the theater. Yasmin loves geography and science. I'm going to put her name next to the Earth. She loves superheroes, too.*

Answers

Technology: Rufus *Earth:* Rufus, Yasmin
The Arts: Angelo *Amazing People:* Yasmin

2 What are you interested in? Write about you.

- Ask *What do you like to do? What are you good at?* Elicit responses.
- The children complete the form with their own details.

3 1.4 Listen and match the book titles to the subjects.

- Play the CD. The children match each title to the subject.
- Elicit answers.

Audioscript

Scarlett: *Hi, everyone. I've chosen some books to go with our Open Day's categories. So, if you want some stories to read afterward, come and take a look. We'll be talking about the stories in Book Club, too, through the semester—so let me know if you want to join. Yasmin, can you help me sort these books into categories, please?*
Yasmin: *Sure. Oh! What are they about?*
Scarlett: *Um,* Master Mind Returns, *that's a fantastic superhero story. He can do amazing things.*
The Stolen Painting *isn't really about art—it's a smart story that's told using email and cell phone messages.*
Just Dance! *That's about a boy who goes to theater school to learn to dance.*
The Frog Hunt *is an interesting story about what happens when wildlife is destroyed.*

Answers

1 d **2** c **3** a **4** b

Optional activity: Alliterative profile

The children work in pairs. Give each pair a different letter to use in writing a profile, e.g. *G: My name's Gregory. My hobbies are gardening and golf. I'm good at geography. I'd like to learn more about giraffes. In the future, I think I will be a geologist!*

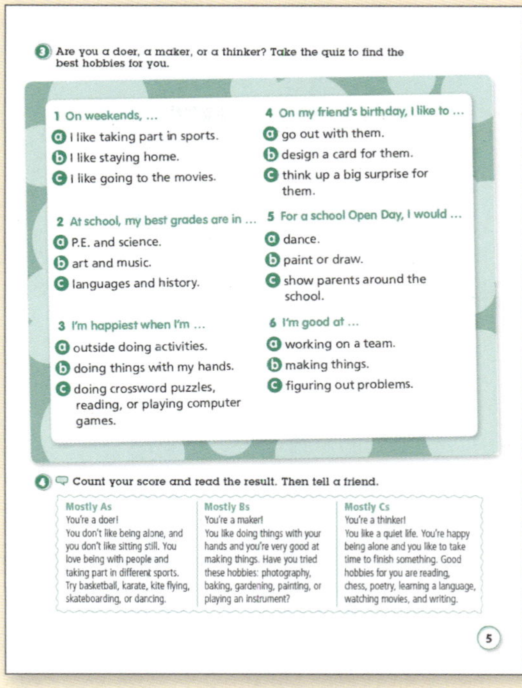

3 Are you a doer, a maker, or a thinker? Take the quiz to find the best hobbies for you.

1 On weekends, …
a I like taking part in sports.
b I like staying home.
c I like going to the movies.

2 At school, my best grades are in …
a P.E. and science.
b art and music.
c languages and history.

3 I'm happiest when I'm …
a outside doing activities.
b doing things with my hands.
c doing crossword puzzles, reading, or playing computer games.

4 On my friend's birthday, I like to …
a go out with them.
b design a card for them.
c think up a big surprise for them.

5 For a school Open Day, I would …
a dance.
b paint or draw.
c show parents around the school.

6 I'm good at …
a working on a team.
b making things.
c figuring out problems.

4 Count your score and read the result. Then tell a friend.

Mostly As	Mostly Bs	Mostly Cs
You're a doer! You don't like being alone, and you don't like sitting still. You love being with people and taking part in different sports. Try basketball, karate, kite flying, skateboarding, or dancing.	You're a maker! You like doing things with your hands and you're very good at making things. Have you tried these hobbies: photography, baking, gardening, painting, or playing an instrument?	You're a thinker! You like a quiet life. You're happy being alone and you like to take time to finish something. Good hobbies for you are reading, chess, poetry, learning a language, watching movies, and writing.

5

3 Are you a doer, a maker, or a thinker? Take the quiz to find the best hobbies for you.

The children circle the correct answers for them.

4 Count your score and read the result. Then tell a friend.

The children figure out which letter they circled most and read the corresponding text to find out the best hobbies for them. They discuss the result in pairs.

Cooler: Play "Tic-Tac-Toe"

Play the game with questions related to interests and hobbies (see Games Bank p. 222).

Presentation Kit • Choose *Hotspots* to see what you can do on each page. The buttons in the Navigation Pane show which activities are interactive—here, SB Activities 1 and 3.

- In groups, encourage the children to imagine a famous person and think up details about them using the SB Activity 2 prompts. Choose a group to use *Pen* to write in a detail each. The class guesses who they are describing. Use *Eraser* to clear and repeat with a different group.

Chapter 1 Mysteries and Monsters Overview

The children will:

- use critical thinking skills to identify archeology vocabulary.
- talk about possible and certain things using *must*, *might*, and *can't*.
- read and understand a story about a mysterious dog.
- describe mysterious creatures.
- find out about the Bermuda Triangle.
- write the opening of a mystery story.

Key Vocabulary

Archeology: archeologist, bracelets, guard, mask, mummy, statues, throne, tomb
Mysterious creatures: beast, blood, disappeared, exist, imaginary, prove, unexplained, unusual

Key Grammar

must be / might be

- It must be a chair.
- They might be earrings or they might be bracelets.

can't be / must be / might be

- I don't believe it. It can't be true.
- It walks on two legs. It might be a man.
- It must be true. There's a picture of it.

Reading Skills

Story: *The Tomb of the Ancient Dog*
Genre: modern mystery story

Literacy Development

- use reading skills to understand and predict content
- relate story theme to personal experience
- use sense verbs to set the scene

Functional Language

- I went to bed at midnight last night.
- You must be tired.
- Yes, I am.

Spelling

Words with prefix *un*– or *dis*–

CLIL: History—Mystery of the Bermuda Triangle

The children find out what happens in the Bermuda Triangle.

Competency Focus

The children will:

use critical thinking skills to deduce the meaning of new vocabulary. (Lesson 1)	activate new vocabulary and apply new grammar knowledge. (Lesson 2)	work in pairs to act out a dialogue. (Lesson 3)	relate the story and story theme to their personal experience. (Lesson 4)	develop an understanding of a mystery by carrying out research. (Lesson 7)
predict the content of a story. (Lesson 3)	apply new grammar rules in a familiar context. (Lesson 5)	work in pairs to talk about different creatures. (Lesson 6)	invent and write their own mystery story opening. (Lesson 8)	
			evaluate their own progress in the chapter. (Review)	

Digital Overview

Presentation Kit

Projectable Student Book, Activity Book, and Reader pages

- Vocabulary Tool 1A: Archeology
- Vocabulary Tool 1B: Mysterious creatures
- Oral Storytelling Video 1: *The Golden Duck*
- Interactive versions of selected SB and AB activities
- Integrated *Audio* and *Answer Key* for all activities

Teacher's Resource Center

Resources for planning, lesson delivery, and homework

- Class Planner Chapter 1
- Worksheets to print out (including notes and answers):
  - Grammar Worksheet 1A: *must be / might be*
  - Grammar Worksheet 1B: *can't be / must be / might be*
  - Oral Storytelling Video Worksheet 1: *The Golden Duck*
  - CLIL Graphic Organizer 1
  - Writing Template 1
  - Test Chapter 1
- Test Generator
- Literacy Handbook

Student's Resource Center

Resources for consolidation and practice at home

- Interactive Grammar 1A: *must be / might be*
- Interactive Grammar 1B: *can't be / must be / might be*
- Vocabulary Tool 1A: Archeology
- Vocabulary Tool 1B: Mysterious creatures
- Oral Storytelling Video 1: *The Golden Duck*

Student's App

Vocabulary games: Archeology and mysterious creatures

Watch the Oral Storytelling Video

Mysteries and Monsters

Lesson 1

Vocabulary

Lesson objective: identify and use vocabulary associated with Egypt and archeology

Key vocabulary: *archeologist, bracelets, guard, mask, mummy, statues, throne, tomb*

Materials: Class CD

Chapter 1 Mysteries and Monsters
Lesson 1

1 Listen and complete the facts.

2 Listen again and write the words next to the clues.

~~tomb~~ statues guard bracelets mummy mask throne archeologist

1 The room with the mummy. tomb
2 He looked for things from the past.
3 To keep the tomb safe and protect it.
4 There are .... of animals, made of gold.
5 The chair that King Tutankhamun sat on.
6 There are boxes of jewelry; earrings and
7 His body is still inside.
8 On its face it's wearing a

8

Warmer: Play "Ready, Set, Draw!"

Play the game with *pyramid, camel, desert, river, museum, pharaoh*, etc. (see Games Bank p. 222).

1 1.5 Listen and complete the facts.

- Throughout the Student Book and Activity Book, an example is generally given at the beginning of an activity. You can use this to talk through how the activity is done or encourage the children to use as a guide to help promote more independent learning.
- Play the CD. The children listen and complete the facts. Elicit answers. Whenever you elicit answers, remember to check with the class to see if they agree.

Audioscript

Boy: *Look at this tour. It looks amazing. You can actually go inside the room—it's Tutankhamun's tomb. Howard Carter discovered it in 1922.*
Girl: *Who's Howard Carter?*
Boy: *He traveled around the world and looked for things from the past. He was an archeologist. Wow, look, you can go down the steps. There are two statues of the King. The statues guard the tomb. They stand outside the tomb and keep it safe—they protect it.*
Girl: *Why? What's in the tomb?*
Boy: *There's a lot of treasure. There are more statues, of animals made of gold, and you can see the throne—the chair that King Tutankhamun sat on. There are boxes of jewelry: earrings and bracelets.*
Girl: *Can you see Tutankhamun's mummy? His body is still inside.*
Boy: *Yes, you can. The mummy is lying down, and you can see its famous gold mask.*
Girl: *Wow! Was he really rich?*
Boy: *Yes, he was. He was a pharaoh and the King of Egypt at the age of nine.*
Girl: *How did he die?*
Boy: *No one knows. It's a mystery … but he was very young.*
Girl: *How old was he when he died?*
Boy: *He was only 19.*

Answers

1922, 9, 19

2 1.5 Listen again and write the words next to the clues.

- Play the CD again. The children listen and write the object/person described in each clue, using the words supplied.
- Elicit answers.

Answers

1 tomb **2** archeologist **3** guard **4** statues **5** throne
6 bracelets **7** mummy **8** mask

Optional activity: True or false?

Say *Archeologists protect the tomb and keep it safe. True or false?* Elicit *False—The statues protect the tomb.* The children work in pairs, taking turns making up a true or false sentence using information on the page, and responding appropriately.

Chapter 1

Mysteries and Monsters

Lesson 1

1 Complete the words.

1 b.racelets....... 2 t.......... 3 m.......... 4 a.......... 5 m.......... 6 s..........

2 Complete the rules for the game.

~~tomb~~ statues guards bracelets mummy mask archeologist

Can you find the treasure in the 1 ....tomb.... ? You're an 2 .... You have to get past the two gold 3 .... – they're the 4 .... of the tomb – and find your way to Tutankhamun. But hurry! You have to take the 5 .... from the face of the 6 .... before the thieves get there! On the way, you can collect 7 .... to wear on your arm. These give you extra powers. Oh, and watch out for snakes! Good luck!

3 Make questions with words from Activities 1 and 2. Ask and answer.

How does a mummy make you feel?

It makes me feel scared!

4 Choose a way to categorize the new words in your notebook.

Chapter 1 6

1 Complete the words.

The children complete the labels for the items pictured. Elicit answers.

Answers

1 bracelets **2** throne **3** mask **4** archeologist **5** mummy **6** statues

2 Complete the rules for the game.

Say *There are two guards. They guard the tomb.* Point out that *guard* is both a noun and a verb. The children complete the text using the words supplied. Elicit answers.

Answers

1 tomb **2** archeologist **3** statues **4** guards **5** mask **6** mummy **7** bracelets

3 Make questions with words from Activities 1 and 2. Ask and answer.

The children make questions to ask and answer in pairs. Have pairs ask and answer for the class.

4 Choose a way to categorize the new words in your notebook.

Brainstorm appropriate categories, e.g. *people/things and places, small objects/big objects, useful/decorative/useful and decorative.* The children choose the best categories for them and list the words in their notebook. Remind them that organizing vocabulary makes it easier to memorize.

Answers

Children's own answers.

Cooler: Next word

Say sentences from the Activity 1 audioscript. Pause before key words and have the children write the next word. Elicit answers.

Competency Focus

Think! Critical Thinking

The children use critical thinking skills to understand the new vocabulary by using visual clues and processing the written and spoken forms.

Presentation Kit • All SB and AB pages can be shown on the board. Use them for "heads-up" teaching and reference throughout the lesson.

- TIP All audio is accessible within the SB/AB pages: look for *Audio* in the Navigation Pane.
- Use Vocabulary Tool 1A to pre-teach key vocabulary. Use *Slideshow* to introduce the words, one after the other. Select once to show the item and word, and choose *Audio* to hear it. Then use *Flash* to review/test vocabulary by choosing items in random order and quick succession.

Grammar

Lesson objective: talk about things which are certain or possible
Key grammar: *must be, might be*
Secondary language: *corridor, steps, thieves, treasure*
Materials: pictures of mystery objects (optional); Grammar Worksheet 1A [TRC printout] (optional)

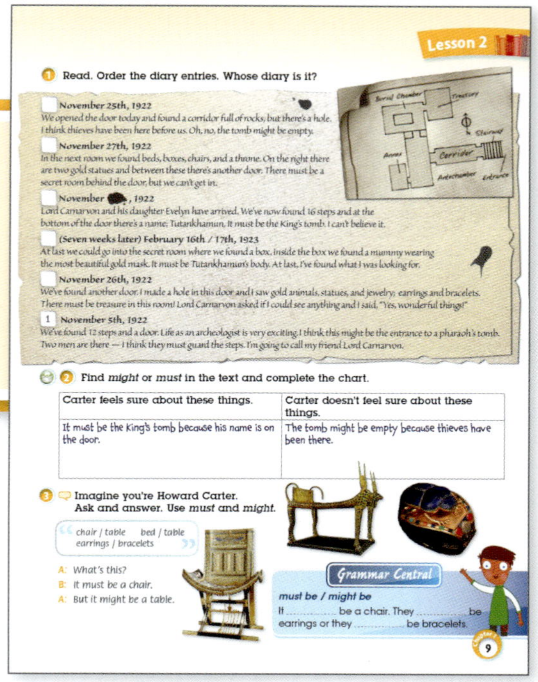

Lesson 2

1 Read. Order the diary entries. Whose diary is it?

November 25th, 1922
We opened the door today and found a corridor full of rocks, but there's a hole. I think thieves have been here before us. Oh, no, the tomb might be empty.

November 27th, 1922
In the next room we found beds, boxes, chairs, and a throne. On the right there are two gold statues and between these there's another door. There must be a secret room behind the door, but we can't get in.

November , 1922
Lord Carnarvon and his daughter Evelyn have arrived. We've now found 16 steps and at the bottom of the door there's a name: Tutankhamun. It must be the King's tomb. I can't believe it.

(Seven weeks later) February 16th / 17th, 1923
At last we could go into the secret room where we found a box. Inside the box we found a mummy wearing the most beautiful gold mask. It must be Tutankhamun's body. At last, I've found what I was looking for.

November 26th, 1922
We've found another door. I made a hole in this door and I saw gold animals, statues, and jewelry; earrings and bracelets. There must be treasure in this room! Lord Carnarvon asked if I could see anything and I said, "Yes, wonderful things!"

1 **November 5th, 1922**
We've found 12 steps and a door. Life as an archeologist is very exciting. I think this might be the entrance to a pharaoh's tomb. Two men are there — I think they must guard the steps. I'm going to call my friend Lord Carnarvon.

2 Find *might* or *must* in the text and complete the chart.

Carter feels sure about these things.	Carter doesn't feel sure about these things.
It must be the King's tomb because his name is on the door.	The tomb might be empty because thieves have been there.

3 Imagine you're Howard Carter. Ask and answer. Use *must* and *might*.

chair / table bed / table
earrings / bracelets

A: What's this?
B: It must be a chair.
A: But it might be a table.

Grammar Central
must be / might be
It .... be a chair. They .... be earrings or they .... be bracelets.

9

Warmer: Scrambled sentences

Review key vocabulary (*tomb, statues, guard, bracelets, mummy, mask, throne, archeologist*). Then write scrambled versions of the words on the board. Have the children unscramble the words in pairs. Ask children to write the answers on the board.

1 Read. Order the diary entries. Whose diary is it?

- Have the children look at the text. Ask *What is this?* (*a diary*) *Why did the person write it?* (*to record things that happened*)
- They then read the diary. Ask *Whose diary is it?* (*Howard Carter's*) Ask *How did you know?* (*It talks about discovering Tutankhamun's tomb so it must be his.*)

Answers

3, 5, 2, 6, 4, 1

2 Find *might* or *must* in the text and complete the chart.

- Write *might* and *must* on the board. Elicit which is used when you are sure (*must*) and not sure (*might*).
- The children complete the chart in pairs, using *might / must* and giving an appropriate reason each time.
- Elicit answers.

Answers

Carter feels sure about these things: It must be the king's tomb because his name is on the door. The two men must guard the steps because they are at the entrance. There must be treasure in the room because he saw gold animals, statues, and jewelry. There must be a secret room because there is a door with two gold statues. It must be Tutankhamun's body because it's in his tomb and it's wearing the most beautiful gold mask.

Carter doesn't feel sure about these things: The tomb might be empty because thieves have been there. This might be the entrance to a pharaoh's tomb because there's a big door and there are two statues.

Grammar Central

must be / might be

Have the children complete the grammar examples. Elicit answers. Elicit the rules for using *must be* (*when we're sure*) and *might be* (*when we're not sure*). They write further examples in their notebook. See also the Grammar Reference sections in the Student Book (p. 98) and Activity Book (p. 96) for further explanation and practice.

Grammar Central Answers: must, might, might

3 Imagine you're Howard Carter. Ask and answer. Use *must* and *might*.

- Choose two children to read the example dialogue.
- Divide the class into pairs to practice the dialogue using *must* and *might*. Have pairs perform for the class.

Optional activity: Mystery objects

Show the children a selection of pictures of strange objects, and say that you are not sure what they are. Have them discuss in pairs what they might/must be. Elicit ideas.

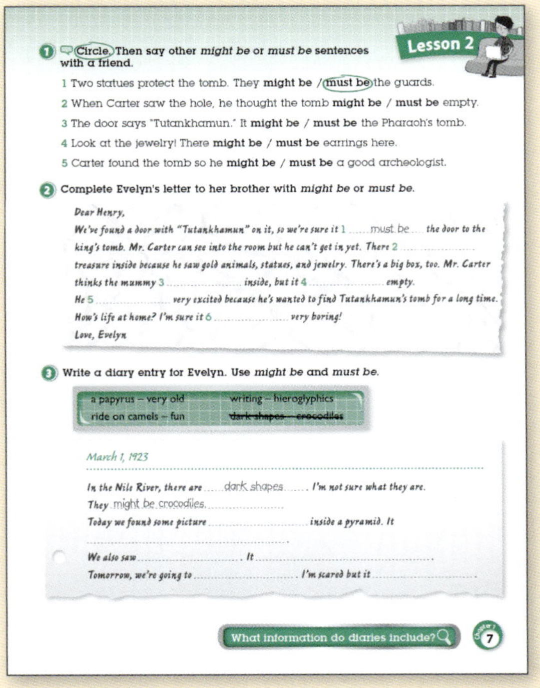

Lesson 2

1 Circle. Then say other *might be* or *must be* sentences with a friend.

1 Two statues protect the tomb. They **might be** / **must be** the guards.
2 When Carter saw the hole, he thought the tomb **might be** / **must be** empty.
3 The door says "Tutankhamun." It **might be** / **must be** the Pharaoh's tomb.
4 Look at the jewelry! There **might be** / **must be** earrings here.
5 Carter found the tomb so he **might be** / **must be** a good archeologist.

2 Complete Evelyn's letter to her brother with *might be* or *must be*.

Dear Henry,
We've found a door with "Tutankhamun" on it, so we're sure it 1 ...must be... the door to the king's tomb. Mr. Carter can see into the room but he can't get in yet. There 2 .... treasure inside because he saw gold animals, statues, and jewelry. There's a big box, too. Mr. Carter thinks the mummy 3 .... inside, but it 4 .... empty.
He 5 .... very excited because he's wanted to find Tutankhamun's tomb for a long time.
How's life at home? I'm sure it 6 .... very boring!
Love, Evelyn

3 Write a diary entry for Evelyn. Use *might be* and *must be*.

a papyrus – very old | writing – hieroglyphics
ride on camels – fun | ~~dark shapes – crocodiles~~

March 1, 1923
In the Nile River, there are ...dark shapes.... I'm not sure what they are.
They ...might be crocodiles.........
Today we found some picture .... inside a pyramid. It ....
We also saw .... It ....
Tomorrow, we're going to .... I'm scared but it ....

What information do diaries include?

7

Cooler: Action time

Ask the class to stand. Agree actions for *must be* (e.g. both hands on your head) and *might be* (a shrug). Say sentences featuring *must be* and *might be* in random order. The children respond by doing the correct mime. As they become more confident, you can speed up the prompts to make it more fun. Have children take over your role as prompt and say the *must be/might* be sentences.

1 Circle. Then say other *might be* or *must be* sentences with a friend.

The children complete the sentences by circling *might be* or *must be*. Then they work in pairs, taking turns making up sentences with *might be* and *must be*. Elicit answers, then call on pairs to say their sentences for the class.

Answers

1 must be **2** might be **3** must be **4** might be **5** must be

2 Complete Evelyn's letter to her brother with *might be* or *must be.*

Have the children look at the text and say which letter looks different from usual. (*d*) Explain that this is not a conventional *d* but it is sometimes used in handwriting. The children complete the text using *might be* or *must be*. Elicit answers.

Answers

1 must be **2** must be **3** might be **4** might be **5** must be **6** must be

3 Write a diary entry for Evelyn. Use *might be* and *must be.*

The children write a diary entry for Evelyn using the prompts supplied. Then they compare with a friend. Elicit responses. Ask *What information do diaries include?* (*activities, thoughts, feelings*)

Answers

dark shapes, might be crocodiles
writing, must be hieroglyphics
papyrus, must be very old
ride on camels, might be fun

Competency Focus

Learn

The children integrate previously acquired vocabulary into new grammar and structure and adapt the language to show an understanding of the topic.

Presentation Kit • Ask children to use *Highlighter* to show the information they used each time to order the paragraphs in SB Activity 1.

• Children use *Pen* to circle answers in AB Activity 1 and write answers in AB Activity 2. Have the class confirm or adjust the answers before using *Answer Key*.

Teacher's Resource Center • Print out Grammar Worksheet 1A for extra practice after SB Activity 2.

Student's Resource Center • Alert the children to the online Interactive Grammar 1A practice for ongoing consolidation and review.

Reading: Story Extract

Lesson objectives: predict people's feelings; use the title and pictures to predict story content; read the extract from the modern mystery story *The Tomb of the Ancient Dog* (middle)
Functional language: *I went to bed at ... You must be ... Yes, I am.*
Secondary language: *howl, beast, footprints*
Materials: Class CD; a bag and various objects (Warmer)

Warmer: Mystery bag

Use a bag with a selection of objects not usually seen in the classroom, e.g. a piece of fruit, a bank card, a cell phone, etc. Invite children to feel inside the bag and say what they think or are sure they have found, using *It might be* ... or *It must be* ... as appropriate. Then they check if they were correct. The children can continue playing this game in pairs with the contents of their schoolbags.

Functional language

1 1.6 Listen and read.

- Play the CD. The children listen and read along. Ask *How does Rufus feel?* (*tired*) *Does Scarlett feel sorry for him?*
- Play the CD again, pausing for them to repeat.
- Divide the class into pairs to practice the dialogue.

2 Imagine different situations. Talk to a friend about how you think they're feeling.

- Choose two children to read the example dialogue. Elicit other examples using the prompts supplied.
- The children practice in pairs. Have pairs act out a dialogue for the class.

Before reading

3 Look at the story. How do you think the characters feel?

- Have the children study the story title and pictures to figure out how the characters feel. Elicit ideas.

4 1.7 Read the story extract and answer.

- Play the CD. The children listen and read along. Have them answer question 1. Elicit the answer.
- Play the CD again so they can write their ideas for questions 2 and 3. Encourage them to use the reading skills they have practiced in earlier levels (e.g. using the title, pictures, and context) to infer meaning and make predictions.

- Elicit answers, but do not confirm predictions: explain that they will have to read the story to find out.

Answers

1 No, he doesn't. He thinks it might be a dog or it might be the wind. **2** Children's own answers. **3** Because he wants to solve the mystery.

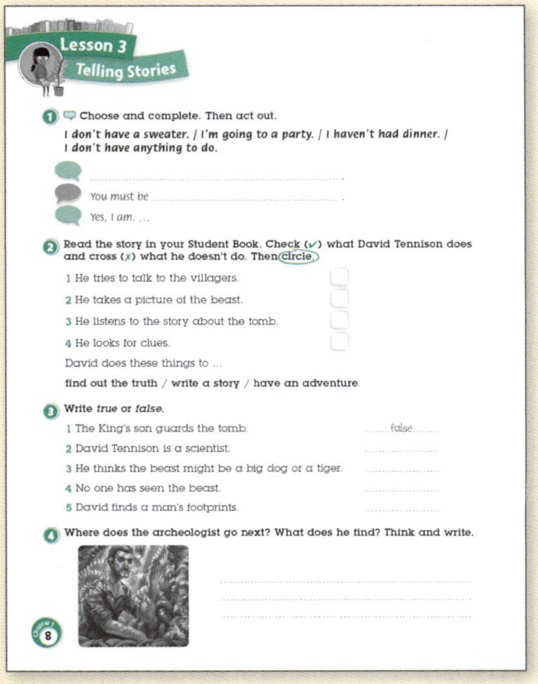

Lesson 3
Telling Stories

1 Choose and complete. Then act out.

I don't have a sweater. / I'm going to a party. / I haven't had dinner. / I don't have anything to do.

....

You must be ....

Yes, I am. ...

2 Read the story in your Student Book. Check (✓) what David Tennison does and cross (✗) what he doesn't do. Then circle.

1 He tries to talk to the villagers.

2 He takes a picture of the beast.

3 He listens to the story about the tomb.

4 He looks for clues.

David does these things to ...

find out the truth / write a story / have an adventure.

3 Write *true* or *false*.

1 The King's son guards the tomb. ......*false*......

2 David Tennison is a scientist. ....

3 He thinks the beast might be a big dog or a tiger. ....

4 No one has seen the beast. ....

5 David finds a man's footprints. ....

4 Where does the archeologist go next? What does he find? Think and write.

8

1 Choose and complete. Then act out.

The children choose one of the sentences supplied and complete the dialogue. They then act it out in pairs. Encourage the children to use what they know to adapt and extend the dialogue. Have pairs act out their dialogue for the class.

2 Read the story in your Student Book. Check (✓) what David Tennison does and cross (✗) what he doesn't do. Then circle.

The children read the Student Book story extract again. They check/cross what David Tennison does/doesn't do. They then think about why he does these things, circling the correct option. Elicit answers.

Answers

1 ✓ **2** ✗ **3** ✓ **4** ✓

Circled: find out the truth

3 Write *true* or *false*.

The children write true or false for each sentence about the story extract. Elicit answers.

Answers

1 false **2** false **3** true **4** false **5** false

4 Where does the archeologist go next? What does he find? Think and write.

Elicit suggestions on where David Tennison goes next. The children write their own ideas, then compare with a friend. Elicit ideas.

Answers

Children's own answers.

Cooler: Mime the story extract

1.7

Play the CD again and have the children mime all the actions in the dialogue.

Competency Focus

Collaborate and Communicate

The children work together to practice, perform, and adapt the new functional language.

Think! Critical Thinking

The children use critical thinking skills to identify how the characters feel.

Presentation Kit • Have the children use *Spotlight* to identify the details in the story which help them answer SB Activity 3, e.g. words like *terrifying*, *scared*; the characters' facial expressions; the mysterious colors and shadows used in the pictures.

- TIP Choose the double arrows at the top of the Tool Bar to reveal the function of each button.
- TIP Within *Hotspots*, use the arrows to navigate through the activities in a lesson.

THE TOMB OF THE ANCIENT DOG

1
It was a warm evening. The insects were chirping in the grass and the air smelled of jasmine flowers. In the distance, a creature was howling in the moonlight.

2
Man: A ... an enormous beast. Horrible, yellow eyes. It's coming … help me! Aaargh!

3
Two days later …
Mr. O: You aren't from here. Are you looking for the beast?
David: I'm here to solve a mystery. A man is in the hospital after visiting the tomb.
Mr. O: People say a creature is the guard of the tomb. Are you a policeman?
David: No, I'm an archeologist. My name's David Tennison.

4
Mr. O: The story is true. Stay away from the tomb at night. A king lived here many years ago. Dogs guarded his home. There was a battle and he died.

5
His only son and the dogs escaped. But one dog stayed and guarded the king's body and his treasure—statues, thrones, jewelry; everything was gold. Thieves came to steal the treasure, but no one left alive.

6
Mr. O: The king's son built this tomb. That faithful dog still guards the tomb now. On stormy nights, people hear its terrifying howl. It has scared men to death.

7
David: It's an unusual story, but it can't be true. I believe in science. I'm sure we'll solve this mystery. It might be a dog or it might be the wind.

8
Mr. O: You should talk to people in the village!
David: I've tried. They're too scared to talk about it.

9
Villager 1: I've seen an enormous black beast drinking by the lake.
Villager 2: It disappeared behind the tomb.

10
Later …
David: These footprints might be from a big dog, or a tiger.
And this must be from the man's shirt.

11
David: This doesn't prove anything. I need to go into the tomb.

13
David: It's just a statue.

14
David: What?

16
David: Aargh!

17
David: There isn't a beast—it's a trap!

18
David: Of course! In ancient times, they made traps to stop thieves from stealing things from inside tombs.

19
David: There must be treasure inside. But that doesn't explain the footprints. Hm … Where's Mr. Ong?

20
David: Good, he's home.

21
David: Woooah! Down boy!

22
Mr. O: Who's there?
David: You're up late. You must be tired.

23
Mr. O: Oh, David, it's you. I never go to bed early.
David: I didn't know you had a dog.
Mr. O: Um, I keep it as a guard dog.

24
Later …
David: So, you see, there isn't a mysterious beast. It's a trap to stop thieves from stealing the treasure.

25
David: Are you hiding something, Mr. Ong?
Mr. O: Yes, I am. You've solved the mystery. Now I can tell my story.

26
Mr. O: No one knows that the king was my great-great-great-great-grandfather. He lost everything in battle, except the treasure in the tomb. This secret has been with our family for many years. The story of the beast has kept it safe.

27
David: So you let the dog out at night, and everyone believes the creature is real.
Mr. O: That's right. Please don't tell anyone. My father told me to take care of the tomb, but I'm getting old.

28
David: Your secret is safe. But I have a better idea. Let's turn the tomb into a museum. The treasure will be safe, and the villagers will be able to learn the real story about your family.

29
Nine months later …
David: You can stop worrying about the tomb now.
Mr. O: You've made me happy.
Visitor: That's beautiful! I didn't know the history of the village before.

Lesson objective: read and understand the modern mystery story *The Tomb of the Ancient Dog* in the Reader
Materials: Class CD; Reader; Oral Storytelling Video Worksheet 1 [TRC printout] (optional); *yes/no* signs (Warmer)

Warmer: Yes or no?

Stick papers with *yes* and *no* on opposite sides of the classroom. The children point to *yes* if the word appeared in the story and *no* if it did not. Call out words, e.g. (yes) *a dog, a mystery, a tomb*; (no) *a wolf, Tutankhamun, a vet*. For *yes* words, elicit a sentence using the word.

Story Summary

David Tennison, an archeologist, decides to investigate a mysterious creature which has been scaring people close to an ancient tomb. He discovers that an old man, Mr. Ong, has pretended that his dog is a dangerous beast in order to guard his family's tomb and treasure.

Theme: the importance of preserving the past

1.8 While reading

- Have the children look at the pictures in the Reader. Ask *Who are the main characters in the story?*
- Play the CD. The children listen and read along. Ask *What does David Tennison discover? (that Mr. Ong is using his dog to guard the tomb)*
- Ask questions to check comprehension, e.g. *Why does David think there must be treasure? (There's a trap.) Why is there a trap? (to stop thieves)*
- Have the class read the story aloud. Encourage them to move around the classroom as they do so (see **Story Time**), with children taking turns being Mr. Ong, David, and the villagers.

After reading: Reflect

- Ask questions to give the children the opportunity to think about the issues raised by the story, e.g. *How did the people feel at the end of the story? What would you do in Mr. Ong's situation? Why do you think people believed the story of the dog?*

Optional activity: Who said it?

Read out a line of dialogue from the story to elicit who said it. Then have the children continue the activity in pairs.

Story Time

Moving storytelling

Use a story's locations to make storytelling more dramatic. Move around the classroom as you read, taking the children with you—it increases their feeling of being involved in the story. Encourage them to move around when they role-play any scenes from the story.

Reading Strategy

Anticipation Guide

Anticipating what will happen helps the children engage with the story and the characters by using their own knowledge to predict the plot. It also prepares them to analyze the story and answer "while reading" or "after reading" comprehension questions.

For additional explanation and activities, see the Literacy Handbook on the Teacher's Resource Center.

Cooler: One long sentence

Elicit ten key words the children think cover the whole story and write them on the board. They work in pairs to summarize the story using at least eight of these words in one sentence. Remind them to use words like *and, but, because, so*, etc., to join pieces of information. Elicit sentences.

Presentation Kit • Display the Reader story. Use *Spotlight* to review the story extract. Elicit story predictions before the children read the rest of it.

• Oral Storytelling Video 1 contains a different story on a related theme (*The Golden Duck*). Watch and discuss it at the end of the lesson.

Teacher's Resource Center • Print out Oral Storytelling Video Worksheet 1 to help you get the most out of the video.

Student's Resource Center • The children can watch Oral Storytelling Video 1 at home.

Reading Comprehension and Critical Literacy

Lesson objectives: understand and evaluate the story; relate story theme to personal experience; focus on the use of sense verbs to set the scene and create mystery

Materials: Class CD; Reader; Oral Storytelling Video Worksheet 1 [TRC printout] (optional)

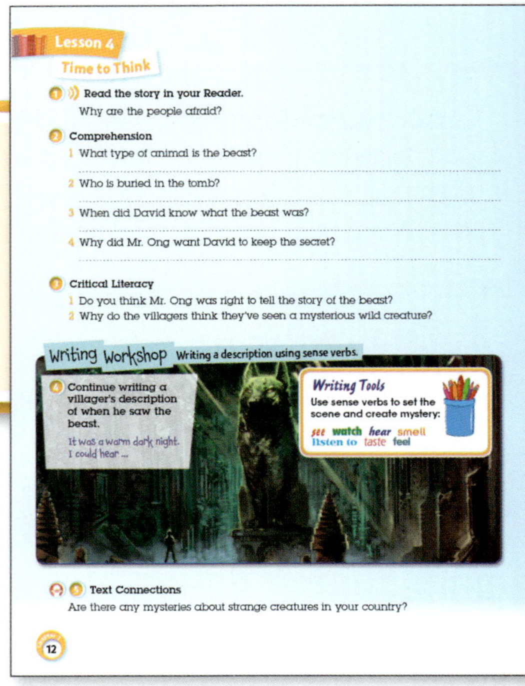
Lesson 4

Time to Think

1 Read the story in your Reader.
Why are the people afraid?

2 Comprehension
1 What type of animal is the beast?
2 Who is buried in the tomb?
3 When did David know what the beast was?
4 Why did Mr. Ong want David to keep the secret?

3 Critical Literacy
1 Do you think Mr. Ong was right to tell the story of the beast?
2 Why do the villagers think they've seen a mysterious wild creature?

Writing Workshop Writing a description using sense verbs.

4 Continue writing a villager's description of when he saw the beast.
It was a warm dark night. I could hear ...

Writing Tools
Use sense verbs to set the scene and create mystery:
see watch hear smell listen to taste feel

5 Text Connections
Are there any mysteries about strange creatures in your country?

12

Note: Please ensure that your class has read the Reader story before you do this lesson.

Warmer: Play "Bingo"

Write on the board in random order: *insects, beast, mystery, policeman, throne, howl, wind, scared, thieves, grandfather, museum, history*. Have the children draw a 3 x 2 Bingo grid, then choose and write the six words they think will be the first to occur in the story. The children cross them off as you say them. When all six are crossed off, they call out *Bingo!*

1 1.8 Read the story in your Reader.

- Have the children read the story. (Alternatively, play the CD and have them read along.)
- Elicit whether the children were correct in their predictions in Lesson 3 Activity 4. Ask *Why are the people afraid? (because they have seen and heard a mysterious beast at night)*

2 Comprehension

- The children write answers to the first three questions. Elicit answers.
- Discuss question 4. Ask the children to justify their answers.

Answers

1 It's a dog. **2** A king/Mr. Ong's great-great-great-great-grandfather. **3** When he visited Mr. Ong and saw his dog. **4** Because he wanted to keep the tomb safe.

3 Critical Literacy

- The children discuss the answers in pairs.
- Elicit ideas and have a class discussion. Encourage children to give reasons for their opinions. Empathizing with the characters and imagining themselves in their situations helps children engage creatively with the story.
- In class discussions like this, it is important that the children respect everyone's right to be heard. If they interrupt each other a lot, you could introduce a "walkie-talkie" rule: only one person at a time speaks. You could even use a prop, like a ruler, to represent the walkie-talkie, with the children passing it around. Phase this out in the course of the year so that the children learn the correct way to behave without the prompt.

Answers

1 Children's own answers. **2** They heard a creature howling/saw the dog statue.

Writing Workshop

Writing a description using sense verbs

4 Continue writing a villager's description of when he saw the beast.

Have a child read the example. Elicit other ideas, using sense verbs from the **Writing Tools** box. The children write their description in their notebook, then compare with a friend. Elicit responses.

Answers

Children's own answers.

5 Text Connections

- Ask *Are there any mysteries about strange creatures in this country?* Elicit ideas and discuss as a class.

Optional activity: Visualization

Have the children close their eyes. Say *Imagine you are in Mr. Ong's house with David, the archeologist. Look around. What can you see? What furniture is there? What can you hear/smell/feel?* The children open their eyes and tell a friend what they imagined.

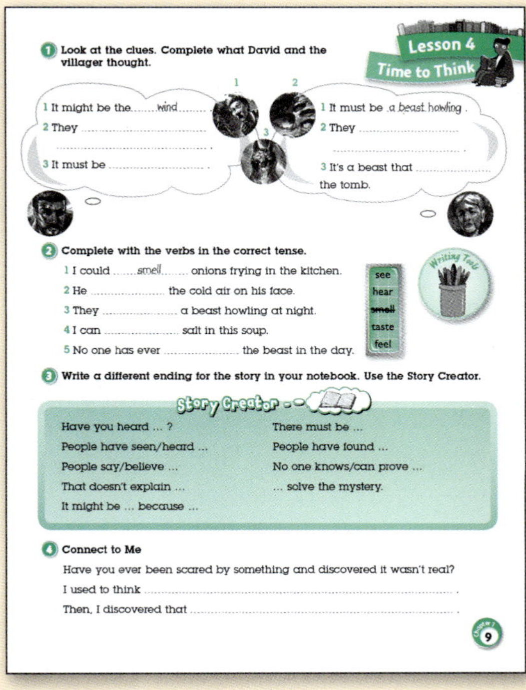

Lesson 4
Time to Think

1 Look at the clues. Complete what David and the villager thought.

1 It might be the ....wind.......
2 They ....
3 It must be ....

1 It must be .a beast howling .
2 They ....
3 It's a beast that .... the tomb.

2 Complete with the verbs in the correct tense.

1 I could ....smell....... onions frying in the kitchen.
2 He .... the cold air on his face.
3 They .... a beast howling at night.
4 I can .... salt in this soup.
5 No one has ever .... the beast in the day.

see / hear / ~~smell~~ / taste / feel

Writing Tools

3 Write a different ending for the story in your notebook. Use the Story Creator.

Story Creator

Have you heard ... ?	There must be ...
People have seen/heard ...	People have found ...
People say/believe ...	No one knows/can prove ...
That doesn't explain ...	... solve the mystery.
It might be ... because ...	

4 Connect to Me

Have you ever been scared by something and discovered it wasn't real?
I used to think ....
Then, I discovered that ....

Chapter 1 9

1 Look at the clues. Complete what David and the villager thought.

The children look at the pictures and complete the sentences using *might* and *must*. Elicit responses.

Answers (suggested)

David: **1** wind **2** might be from a dog or a tiger **3** a trap
Villager: **1** a beast howling **2** must be the beast's footprints **3** guards

2 Complete with the verbs in the correct tense.

The children complete the sentences using the verbs supplied in the correct tense. Elicit answers.

Answers

1 smell **2** felt **3** heard **4** taste **5** seen

3 Write a different ending for the story in your notebook. Use the Story Creator.

Use the **Story Creator** prompts to elicit ideas. The children write a different ending for the story in their notebook, then compare with a friend. Have children read out their texts for the class.

4 Connect to Me

Elicit examples of things that have scared the children but which were not real. (e.g. *strange shapes in the dark that looked like monsters*) The children write their own response, then compare with a friend. Elicit responses.

Cooler: Crazy sentences

Refer to the sentences in Activity 2 of the Activity Book. Have a child read out the beginning of sentence 1 (*I could smell*), then part of sentence 3 (*a beast howling*), and part of sentence 4 (*in this soup*). Write the crazy sentence on the board: *I could smell a beast howling in this soup!* The children work in pairs to make new crazy sentences. Elicit sentences.

Competency Focus

Me: Critical Literacy

The children use critical literacy skills to reflect on the story and how the characters acted, and think of similar stories from their own country.

Presentation Kit • Have children use *Pen* to write answers for SB Activity 2. If the class disagrees, use *Eraser* to clear for another child to write. Confirm answers using *Answer Key*. Choose to show the answers all at once or one by one.

- If you haven't already, watch Oral Storytelling Video 1, which contains a different story on a related theme.

Teacher's Resource Center • If you haven't already, print out Oral Storytelling Video Worksheet 1 for support activities on the new story.

Grammar and Reading

Lesson objective: talk about possible things and things we are certain are true/not true

Key grammar: *can't be, must be, might be*

Secondary language: *reminds me of, costume, joke*

Materials: Class CD; Grammar Worksheet 1B [TRC printout] (optional); animal pictures from Internet (optional)

Lesson 5

BOOK CLUB

1 Listen and read. Who believes that Bigfoot is real?

Angelo: The story reminds me of Bigfoot. Do you know about the mystery of Bigfoot?
Yasmin: Yes, I do. It's a creature that walks on two legs. People say it lives in the forests in North America, but it can't be true.
Angelo: It must be true because people have taken pictures of it.
Yasmin: Hm. Bigfoot can't be real. No one has ever found a dead Bigfoot. It must be a man in a costume. It's a joke.
Angelo: It can't be a man in a costume. Men's feet aren't 60 cm. long.
Yasmin: No, but a man might wear boots that are 60 cm. long.
Angelo: True, but I've seen a video of Bigfoot on the Internet. That can't be a joke.
Yasmin: Yes, it can. I've seen a video of a dog talking. Dogs can't talk so that must be a joke!

2 Complete with *must*, *might*, or *can't*.

1 It ....must........ be real. I've seen pictures.
2 Bigfoot .... be real. Nobody has found a dead one.
3 It walks on two legs. It .... be a man in a costume.
4 Dogs can't talk. It .... be a joke.
5 The story .... be true. I don't believe it.

3 Talk to a friend about Bigfoot. Give reasons.

It might be real. It must be a joke. The story can't be true. It can't be a man.

A: *What do you think about Bigfoot?*
B: *It might be real because people have taken pictures of it.*

Grammar Central

can't be / must be / might be

I don't believe it. It .... be true.
It walks on two legs. It .... be a man.
It .... be true. There's a picture of it.

13

Warmer: Missing vowels

Write on the board a sentence from the story featuring *must be* or *might be*, e.g. *And this must be from the man's shirt.*, omitting the vowels. Ask the children to write the correct sentence in their notebook. Elicit answers. Ask children to write in the missing vowels on the board. Repeat with other sentences from the story.

1 1.9 Listen and read. Who believes that Bigfoot is real?

- Play the CD. The children listen and read along. Ask *What do you think Bigfoot is?* and elicit suggestions.
- Play the CD again and ask *Who believes that Bigfoot is real?* (*Angelo*)
- Elicit answers.

Grammar Central

can't be / must be / might be

Have the children complete the grammar examples. Elicit answers. Elicit when we use *might* (*when we're not sure*), *must be* (*when we're sure something is true*), and *can't be* (*when we're sure something isn't true*). They write further examples in their notebook. See also the Grammar Reference sections in the Student Book (p. 98) and Activity Book (p. 96) for further explanation and practice.

Grammar Central Answers: can't, might, must

AB Answers Activity 2: 1 It can't be true … **2** It might be true … **3** It can't be true … **4** It must be true … + Children's own reasons

2 Complete with *must, might,* or *can't.*

- Draw the children's attention to the example. Elicit why the answer is *must*. (*because Angelo is sure it is true*)
- Have the children complete the activity.
- Elicit answers.

Answers

1 must **2** can't **3** might **4** must **5** can't

3 Talk to a friend about Bigfoot. Give reasons.

- Ask two children to read out the example dialogue. Then have the children talk about it in pairs, using the prompts supplied.
- Elicit opinions, and have a class discussion.

Optional activity: What's the animal?

Download a selection of animal pictures from the Internet. Increase the image size until it is just a blurred patch of color in the middle of the animal. Then reduce the size of the image little by little and ask the children to guess what animal it is and why, e.g. *It might be a lion—it's the right color./It can't be a tiger—it's not orange and black.*, etc. When they finally see enough of the animal to be sure, they identify it using *It must be …*

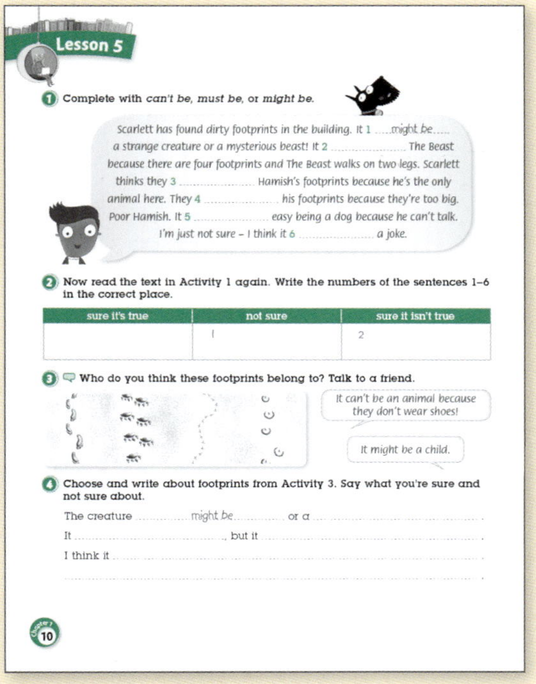

Lesson 5

1 Complete with *can't be, must be,* or *might be.*

Scarlett has found dirty footprints in the building. It 1 ....might be..... a strange creature or a mysterious beast! It 2 .... The Beast because there are four footprints and The Beast walks on two legs. Scarlett thinks they 3 .... Hamish's footprints because he's the only animal here. They 4 .... his footprints because they're too big. Poor Hamish. It 5 .... easy being a dog because he can't talk. I'm just not sure – I think it 6 .... a joke.

2 Now read the text in Activity 1 again. Write the numbers of the sentences 1–6 in the correct place.

sure it's true	not sure	sure it isn't true
	1	2

3 Who do you think these footprints belong to? Talk to a friend.

4 Choose and write about footprints from Activity 3. Say what you're sure and not sure about.

The creature ....might be.... or a ....

It .... , but it ....

I think it ....

Chapter 1 10

1 Complete with *can't be, must be, or might be.*

The children complete the text by writing *can't be*, *must be*, or *might be*. Elicit answers.

Answers

1 might be **2** can't be **3** must be **4** can't be **5** can't be **6** might be

2 Now read the text in Activity 1 again. Write the numbers of the sentences 1–6 in the correct place.

The children read the Activity 1 sentences with numbered blanks. They decide if the person is sure the sentence is true, is not sure if it's true, or is sure it isn't true, writing the number in the correct column. Elicit answers.

Answers

sure it's true: 3
not sure: 1, 6
sure it isn't true: 2, 4, 5

3 Who do you think these footprints belong to? Talk to a friend.

The children discuss in pairs who made each set of footprints. Elicit ideas.

4 Choose and write about footprints from Activity 3. Say what you're sure and not sure about.

The children choose a set of footprints. They speculate about what made the footprints, writing sentences using *can't be*, *might be*, and *must be*. Then they compare with a friend. Elicit answers.

Answers

Children's own answers.

Cooler: Can't/might/must be true

Create three sections on the board, each with a heading: *CAN'T, MIGHT, MUST*. Say *I drive a big car*. The children decide whether this statement can't, might, or must be true and stand by the corresponding section. Elicit opinions using *It can't be … / It might be … / It must be …*, then confirm the answer. Repeat with other sentences.

Competency Focus

Learn

The children demonstrate their understanding of the new language by reading the dialogue and completing the activity.

- TIP The interactive activities in the SB and AB can be repeated, giving different children the chance to participate. Choose *Reset* within *Answer Key* to clear the answers.
- Use *Hotspots* to enlarge Grammar Central. Display the corresponding SB Grammar Reference page as a pop-up.

Teacher's Resource Center • For extra grammar practice, print out Grammar Worksheet 1B.

Student's Resource Center • The children can use Interactive Grammar 1B at home.

Vocabulary, Listening, and Spelling

Lesson objectives: talk about mysterious creatures; practice spelling words with the prefix *un–* or *dis–*
Key vocabulary: *beast, blood, disappeared, exist, imaginary, prove, unexplained, unusual*
Secondary language: *scales, spines*
Materials: Class CD

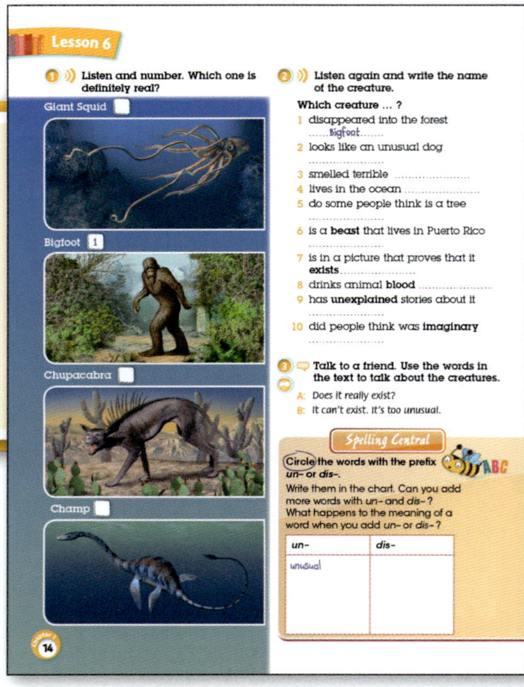

Warmer: Pre-teach vocabulary

Pre-teach the vocabulary by giving definitions or sentences showing the words in context, e.g. *When something is there and then it is not, you say it has disappeared.* Repeat the definitions/sentences, stopping before the key vocabulary word to elicit it from the class.

1 1.10 Listen and number. Which one is definitely real?

- Have the children look at the pictures. Play the CD twice. The children listen and number the pictures, then decide which one is definitely real.
- Elicit answers.

Audioscript

Boy 1: *I saw this creature last year in the forest in North America. It was three meters tall, with dark brown hair. It was walking on two legs like us, and it smelled terrible. It disappeared into the forest but I found enormous footprints—they were 60 cm. long. There are a lot of unexplained stories about it.*
Girl 1: *Champ is a monster that lives at the bottom of Lake Champlain in Vermont in the United States. It can't be a fish or a snake. It's too big. It's about 60 meters long. It looks like a dinosaur with a long tail and a long neck. A picture of the monster proves that it exists. Some people say it might be a tree, but many disagree.*
Boy 2: *Chupacabra is a beast that lives in Puerto Rico, Mexico, and the United States. It looks like an unusual dog, but it has scales and sharp spines on its back. It has sharp teeth and it drinks the blood of other animals. A chupacabra killed sheep on my grandpa's farm.*
Girl 2: *The Giant Squid is a real sea monster! These creatures live at the bottom of the ocean and can grow up to 13 meters long. Its eye can be as big as a human head! For many years, people thought these creatures were imaginary, but now we know the Giant Squid really does exist.*

Answers

Giant Squid 4, Bigfoot 1, Chupacabra 3, Champ 2
The Giant Squid is real.

2 1.10 Listen again and write the name of the creature.

- Play the CD again. The children listen and write the name of the creature described in each clue.
- Elicit answers.

Answers

1 Bigfoot **2** Chupacabra **3** Bigfoot **4** Giant Squid **5** Champ **6** Chupacabra **7** Champ **8** Chupacabra **9** Bigfoot **10** Giant Squid

3 Talk to a friend. Use the words in the text to talk about the creatures.

- Choose two children to read the example dialogue. Elicit other examples using words from the text.
- The children practice in pairs. Have pairs act out a dialogue for the class.

Spelling Central

Words with the prefix *un–* or *dis–*

Have the children find words starting *un–* or *dis–* on the page and complete the chart. They then add other words in each category. (e.g. *unhappy, unkind; disagree, dislike*) Ask *How do un– and dis– change words?* (*They give it the opposite meaning.*)

Answers

un: unusual, unexplained
dis: disappeared

Optional activity: True or false?

Divide the class into pairs. The children take turns making a true/false sentence about the mystery creatures in Activity 1 and responding *true* or *false*, as appropriate.

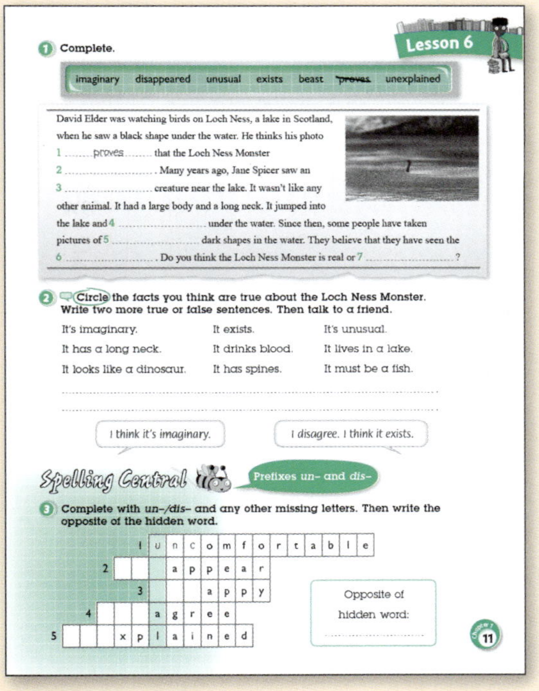

Lesson 6

1 Complete.

imaginary disappeared unusual exists beast ~~proves~~ unexplained

David Elder was watching birds on Loch Ness, a lake in Scotland, when he saw a black shape under the water. He thinks his photo 1 ......proves...... that the Loch Ness Monster 2 .... Many years ago, Jane Spicer saw an 3 .... creature near the lake. It wasn't like any other animal. It had a large body and a long neck. It jumped into the lake and 4 .... under the water. Since then, some people have taken pictures of 5 .... dark shapes in the water. They believe that they have seen the 6 .... Do you think the Loch Ness Monster is real or 7 .... ?

2 Circle the facts you think are true about the Loch Ness Monster. Write two more true or false sentences. Then talk to a friend.

It's imaginary. It exists. It's unusual.
It has a long neck. It drinks blood. It lives in a lake.
It looks like a dinosaur. It has spines. It must be a fish.

I think it's imaginary.
I disagree. I think it exists.

Spelling Central — Prefixes un– and dis–

3 Complete with un–/dis– and any other missing letters. Then write the opposite of the hidden word.

1 u n c o m f o r t a b l e
2 _ _ _ a p p e a r
3 _ _ _ a p p y
4 _ _ _ a g r e e
5 _ _ _ x p l a i n e d

Opposite of hidden word: ....

11

1 Complete.

The children complete the text with the words supplied. Elicit answers.

Answers

1 proves **2** exists **3** unusual **4** disappeared **5** unexplained **6** beast **7** imaginary

2 Circle the facts you think are true about the Loch Ness Monster. Write two more true or false sentences. Then talk to a friend.

The children circle the sentences they think are true. Then they write two more true or false sentences. They discuss these with a friend.

Answers

Children's own answers.

3 Complete with *un–/dis–* and any other missing letters. Then write the opposite of the hidden word.

To practice the **Spelling Central** feature, the children complete the words using the prefixes *un–* or *dis–* and any other missing letters. They identify the hidden word on the shaded boxes, then write its opposite.

Answers

uncomfortable, **dis**appear, **unh**appy, **dis**agree, **une**xplained
Opposite of hidden word: unusual

Cooler: Spelling Bee

Use **Spelling Central** words. For each prompt (e.g. *appear*), the children spell out the opposite (e.g. *disappear*).

Competency Focus

Collaborate and Communicate

The children develop their communication skills by talking to friends, incorporating the new language learned.

Presentation Kit • Use Vocabulary Tool 1B to pre-teach key vocabulary. Use *Slideshow* to introduce the words. Select once to show the item and the word, and choose *Audio* to hear it. Then use *Picture Dictionary* to review/test vocabulary by playing the cards game.

- On the SB page, choose *Audio* on the Navigation Pane to see the lyrics highlighted as the audio plays.
- Children use *Highlighter* to identify the words which illustrate the SB spelling feature (here, words with the prefix *un–* or *dis–*).

CLIL: History—Mystery of the Bermuda Triangle

Lesson objective: find out about what happens in the Bermuda Triangle
Materials: map showing Central America/the Bermuda Triangle (Warmer); CLIL Graphic Organizer 1 [TRC printout] (optional)

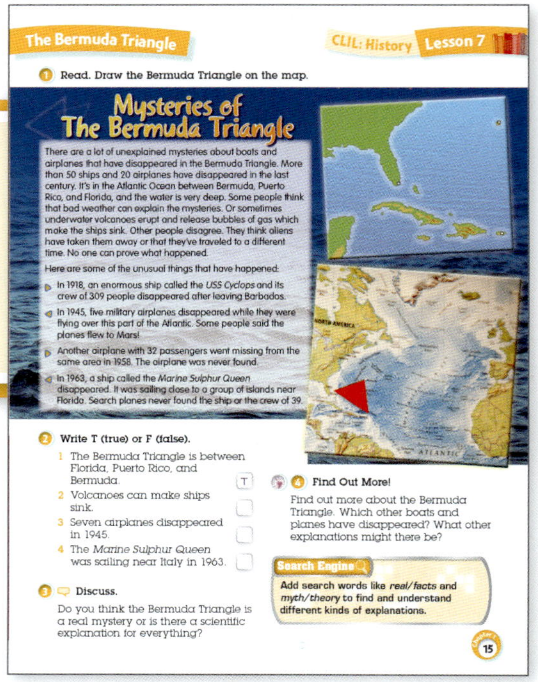
The Bermuda Triangle

CLIL: History Lesson 7

1 Read. Draw the Bermuda Triangle on the map.

Mysteries of The Bermuda Triangle

There are a lot of unexplained mysteries about boats and airplanes that have disappeared in the Bermuda Triangle. More than 50 ships and 20 airplanes have disappeared in the last century. It's in the Atlantic Ocean between Bermuda, Puerto Rico, and Florida, and the water is very deep. Some people think that bad weather can explain the mysteries. Or sometimes underwater volcanoes erupt and release bubbles of gas which make the ships sink. Other people disagree. They think aliens have taken them away or that they've traveled to a different time. No one can prove what happened.

Here are some of the unusual things that have happened:

- In 1918, an enormous ship called the *USS Cyclops* and its crew of 309 people disappeared after leaving Barbados.
- In 1945, five military airplanes disappeared while they were flying over this part of the Atlantic. Some people said the planes flew to Mars!
- Another airplane with 32 passengers went missing from the same area in 1958. The airplane was never found.
- In 1963, a ship called the *Marine Sulphur Queen* disappeared. It was sailing close to a group of islands near Florida. Search planes never found the ship or the crew of 39.

2 Write T (true) or F (false).

1 The Bermuda Triangle is between Florida, Puerto Rico, and Bermuda. T
2 Volcanoes can make ships sink.
3 Seven airplanes disappeared in 1945.
4 The *Marine Sulphur Queen* was sailing near Italy in 1963.

3 Discuss.

Do you think the Bermuda Triangle is a real mystery or is there a scientific explanation for everything?

4 Find Out More!

Find out more about the Bermuda Triangle. Which other boats and planes have disappeared? What other explanations might there be?

Search Engine

Add search words like *real/facts* and *myth/theory* to find and understand different kinds of explanations.

Chapter 1 15

Warmer: Name the countries

Show an unlabeled map of Central America and the surrounding area. The children work in pairs to see how many of the countries they can name on the map. Set ten countries as a target. Elicit answers and write the correct names on the board.

1 Read. Draw the Bermuda Triangle on the map.

- Have the children look at the map and find any of the countries they named.
- The children read the article quickly and then draw the Bermuda Triangle on the map. They compare their triangles in small groups.

Answer

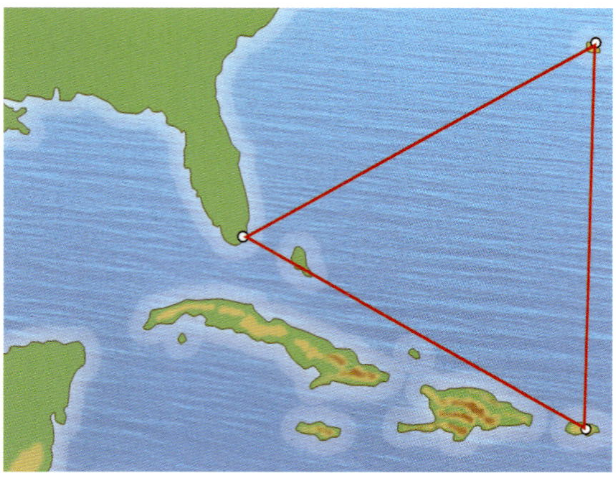

2 Write T (true) or F (false).

- The children read the text again and decide true or false for the other sentences. Elicit answers, including the correct version of the false sentences.
- Have children make up other true/false sentences about the text to ask the class.

Answers

1 T **2** T **3** F **4** F

3 Discuss.

- Have a child read out the discussion question.
- Put children into small groups to talk about their ideas.
- Share ideas in a class discussion.

4 Find Out More!

- The children research the Bermuda Triangle to find out about other lost craft and possible explanations. The **Search Engine** feature gives support on where to look. The children will need to complete this research before doing the follow-up activity in the Activity Book. (It could be set as homework.)

Optional activity: Remember the numbers

The children read the text again, paying particular attention to the numbers. Have them close their books. Write the numbers *50, 20, 1918, 309, 5, 32, 1963* on the board. The children talk to a friend to try and remember the significance of the numbers. Elicit answers.

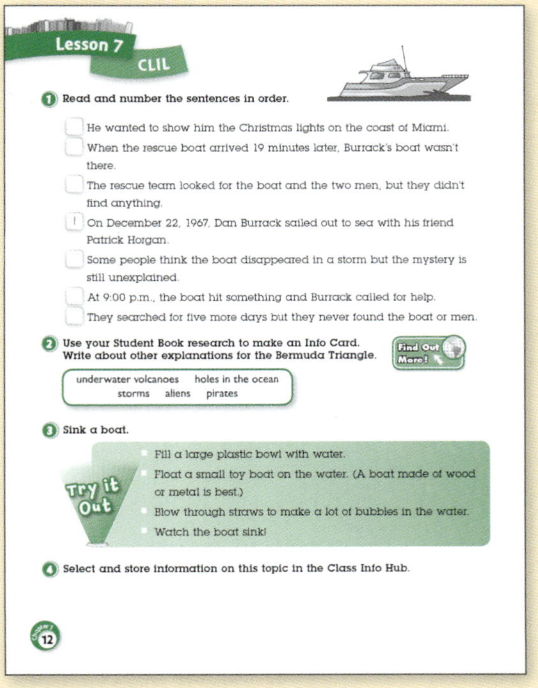
Lesson 7 CLIL

1 Read and number the sentences in order.

- [ ] He wanted to show him the Christmas lights on the coast of Miami.
- [ ] When the rescue boat arrived 19 minutes later, Burrack's boat wasn't there.
- [ ] The rescue team looked for the boat and the two men, but they didn't find anything.
- [1] On December 22, 1967, Dan Burrack sailed out to sea with his friend Patrick Horgan.
- [ ] Some people think the boat disappeared in a storm but the mystery is still unexplained.
- [ ] At 9:00 p.m., the boat hit something and Burrack called for help.
- [ ] They searched for five more days but they never found the boat or men.

2 Use your Student Book research to make an Info Card. Write about other explanations for the Bermuda Triangle. Find Out More!

underwater volcanoes holes in the ocean storms aliens pirates

3 Sink a boat.

Try it Out
- Fill a large plastic bowl with water.
- Float a small toy boat on the water. (A boat made of wood or metal is best.)
- Blow through straws to make a lot of bubbles in the water.
- Watch the boat sink!

4 Select and store information on this topic in the Class Info Hub.

12

1 Read and number the sentences in order.

The children number the sentences in order to make a logical paragraph. Elicit answers.

Answers

2, 4, 5, 1, 7, 3, 6

2 Use your Student Book research to make an Info Card. Write about other explanations for the Bermuda Triangle.

Divide the class into groups. Have the children pool the information they learned from their research in the Student Book and the Activity Book. The children write about and illustrate their ideas individually. Have the groups present their Info Cards to the class.

3 Sink a boat.

In their groups, the children follow the **Try It Out** instructions to sink a boat. Ask groups to demonstrate for the class.

4 Select and store information on this topic in the Class Info Hub.

Create an Info Hub to file the five best Info Cards and the best example of any larger project work in each topic. This will motivate the children to work creatively and also help them develop critical assessment skills. You can use the Info Hub as a resource for fast finishers or as an extension activity at the end of a lesson. Archive photos of the Activity 3 experiment and the five best Info Cards (by class vote) in a folder called **Chapter 1 The Bermuda Triangle**.

Cooler: Play "Disappearing Text"

Play the game with text from the lesson (see Games Bank p. 222).

Competency Focus

Act

The children carry out research to find out about the Bermuda Triangle. This helps them expand their learning and relate it to their world, both inside and outside the classroom.

Presentation Kit • Display the SB page on the board to do Activity 1 for an alternative "heads-up" introduction to the topic. This helps the children engage. Use *Pointer* to help them follow the text as you or children read it aloud.

• TIP Research and store links to pictures about the Bermuda Triangle in *Notepad* to help the children with Activity 4 Find Out More!

Teacher's Resource Center • Print out CLIL Graphic Organizer 1 for the children to use in collating their Find Out More! research.

Writing Project

Lesson objectives: review language from Chapter 1; write a mystery story opening and present it to the class
Materials: Writing Template 1 [TRC printout] (optional)

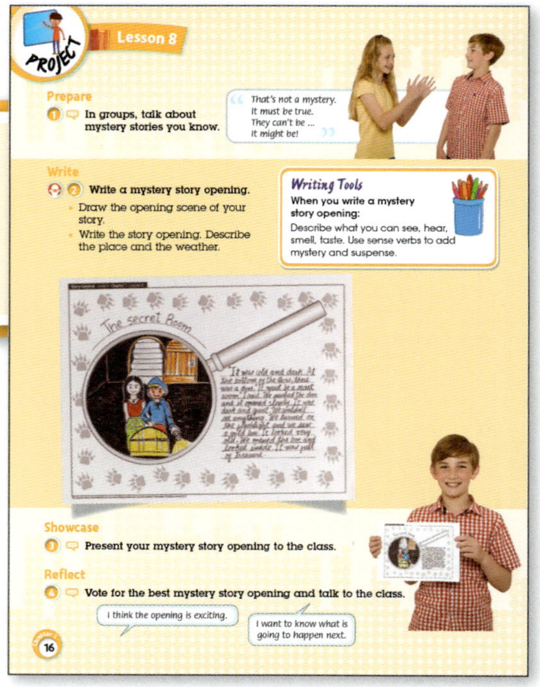
PROJECT Lesson 8

Prepare
1 In groups, talk about mystery stories you know.

That's not a mystery.
It must be true.
They can't be ...
It might be!

Write
2 Write a mystery story opening.
- Draw the opening scene of your story.
- Write the story opening. Describe the place and the weather.

Writing Tools
When you write a mystery story opening:
Describe what you can see, hear, smell, taste. Use sense verbs to add mystery and suspense.

Showcase
3 Present your mystery story opening to the class.

Reflect
4 Vote for the best mystery story opening and talk to the class.

I think the opening is exciting.
I want to know what is going to happen next.

16

Warmer: Play "Back to the Board"

Play the game with key vocabulary: *disappeared, unusual, exist, beast, prove, blood, unexplained, imaginary* (see Games Bank p. 222).

Prepare

1 In groups, talk about mystery stories you know.

- Elicit from the class any famous mystery stories they know and write some key words on the board.
- Have the children talk about the mystery stories in small groups of three or four.
- Ask groups to share one of the stories they have discussed with the class.

Write

2 Write a mystery story opening.

- Have a child read the example. Ask the children to read the **Writing Tools** box and find examples in the text. (e.g. *cold, dark, quiet, smell, feel*, etc.)
- The children write a story opening using the example as a model. Encourage them to include details of place and weather and remind them to use sense verbs.
- Monitor and help where necessary.

Showcase

3 Present your mystery story opening to the class.

- Choose children to read their mystery story openings to the class. Ask the class to listen and count the sense verbs.

Reflect

4 Vote for the best mystery story opening and talk to the class.

- Have the children comment on which mystery story was the best and why. Have a class vote to identify their favorite.

Optional activity: Invent a school mystery

Have the children work in pairs to write a mystery story about their school using sense verbs and interesting adjectives. They can also illustrate the story. Have the children display their stories for the class to read. Elicit ideas on which mystery story would make a good movie!

Competency Focus

Me

The children invent and write their own mystery story opening, exploring their imagination and creativity.

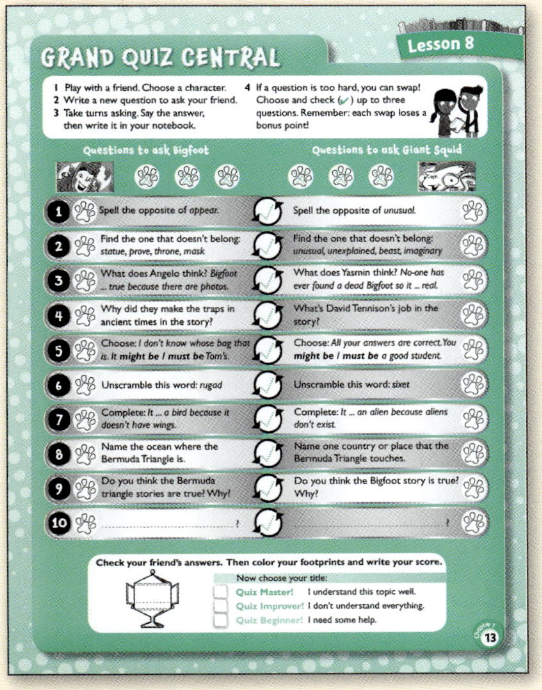
GRAND QUIZ CENTRAL

Lesson 8

1 Play with a friend. Choose a character.
2 Write a new question to ask your friend.
3 Take turns asking. Say the answer, then write it in your notebook.
4 If a question is too hard, you can swap! Choose and check (✓) up to three questions. Remember: each swap loses a bonus point!

	Questions to ask Bigfoot	Questions to ask Giant Squid
1	Spell the opposite of *appear.*	Spell the opposite of *unusual.*
2	Find the one that doesn't belong: *statue, prove, throne, mask*	Find the one that doesn't belong: *unusual, unexplained, beast, imaginary*
3	What does Angelo think? *Bigfoot ... true because there are photos.*	What does Yasmin think? *No-one has ever found a dead Bigfoot so it ... real.*
4	Why did they make the traps in ancient times in the story?	What's David Tennison's job in the story?
5	Choose: *I don't know whose bag that is. It* **might be / must be** *Tom's.*	Choose: *All your answers are correct. You* **might be / must be** *a good student.*
6	Unscramble this word: *rugad*	Unscramble this word: sixet
7	Complete: *It ... a bird because it doesn't have wings.*	Complete: *It ... an alien because aliens don't exist.*
8	Name the ocean where the Bermuda Triangle is.	Name one country or place that the Bermuda Triangle touches.
9	Do you think the Bermuda triangle stories are true? Why?	Do you think the Bigfoot story is true? Why?
10	...............................?	...............................?

Check your friend's answers. Then color your footprints and write your score.

Now choose your title:

- Quiz Master! I understand this topic well.
- Quiz Improver! I don't understand everything.
- Quiz Beginner! I need some help.

Chapter 1 13

Grand Quiz Central

Explain the game. The children play in pairs. They choose a character and answer questions from that character's section. They take turns asking questions. They give answers orally and in writing in their notebook. They can choose up to three questions to swap if their own question is too difficult. (They will get a bonus point for each of the three they do <u>not</u> swap.) They write question 10 using language from the chapter. They color in a symbol for each correct answer. They tally and write their score (adding in any swap symbols they did not use), then evaluate and check their Quiz title.

Answers

1 disappear / usual **2** prove / beast **3** must be / can't be **4** to stop thieves stealing from tombs / an archeologist **5** might be / must be **6** guard / exist **7** can't be / can't be **8** the Atlantic Ocean / Bermuda or Puerto Rico or Florida **9–10** Children's own answers.

Cooler: Play "The Chain Game"

Play the game with mystery story sentences, e.g. *I could see a light. I heard a noise.*, etc. (see Games Bank p. 222).

Presentation Kit • Have children use *Highlighter* to identify examples in the model text of sense verbs, saying each time which sense the verb refers to.

- TIP Choose *Help* at any time to access FAQs on using the materials.
- TIP Position the Navigation Pane on the left or right of the screen, depending on where you want to stand at the board. Choose *Swap sides* to change.

Teacher's Resource Center • Print out Writing Template 1 to use for the SB writing activity.

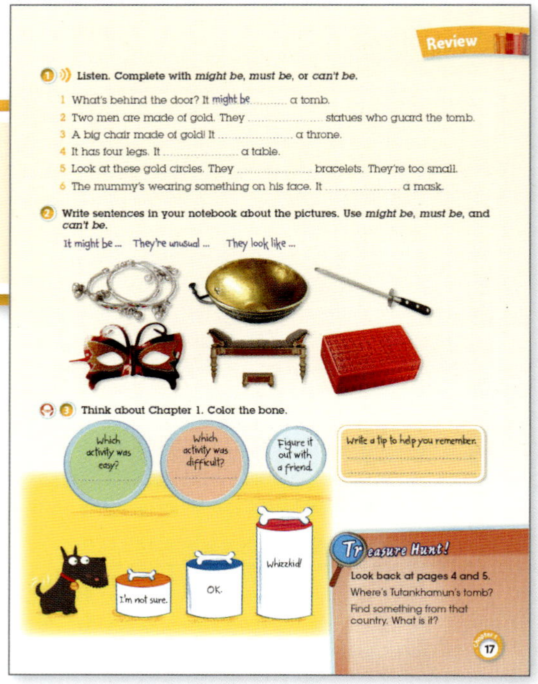

Review

1 Listen. Complete with *might be*, *must be*, or *can't be*.

1 What's behind the door? It might be .... a tomb.
2 Two men are made of gold. They .... statues who guard the tomb.
3 A big chair made of gold! It .... a throne.
4 It has four legs. It .... a table.
5 Look at these gold circles. They .... bracelets. They're too small.
6 The mummy's wearing something on his face. It .... a mask.

2 Write sentences in your notebook about the pictures. Use *might be*, *must be*, and *can't be*.

It might be ... They're unusual ... They look like ...

3 Think about Chapter 1. Color the bone.

Which activity was easy?
Which activity was difficult?
Figure it out with a friend.
Write a tip to help you remember.
I'm not sure.
OK.
Whizzkid!

Treasure Hunt!
Look back at pages 4 and 5.
Where's Tutankhamun's tomb?
Find something from that country. What is it?

Chapter 1
17

Language Review

Lesson objective: review language from Chapter 1
Materials: Class CD

Warmer: Play "Collocations"

Play the game with collocations from the chapter, e.g. *solve/the mystery, it might/be true, I don't/believe it, it smells/terrible, unexplained/mysteries, Bermuda/Triangle*, etc. (see Games Bank p. 222).

1 1.11 Listen. Complete with *might be*, *must be*, or *can't be*.

- Play the CD twice. The children listen and complete the sentences. Elicit answers.

Audioscript

Lord C: *Can you see anything?*
Howard C: *Yes, wonderful things.*
Lord C: *What's behind the door? Is it a tomb?*
Howard C: *I don't know. It might be a tomb. Let's open it.*
Evelyn: *Look at these two men made of gold.*
Howard C: *They're statues. They guard the tomb.*
Evelyn: *Look at this beautiful gold chair. It's very big. It must be a throne!*
Lord C: *And what's this? It has four legs. Is it a bed or a table?*
Howard C: *I don't know. It's very unusual.*
Evelyn: *Look at these—are they bracelets?*
Howard C: *They're very small gold circles. They're too small. They must be earrings. Wow! Look in this box. It's a mummy! It must be Tutankhamun's body!*
Lord C: *Look at his face! What a beautiful mask!*

Answers

1 might be **2** must be **3** must be **4** might be **5** can't be **6** must be

2 Write sentences in your notebook about the pictures. Use *might be*, *must be*, and *can't be*.

- Elicit some suggestions for the first picture. Introduce an idea that the children will disagree with to elicit a sentence with *can't be*, e.g. *It might be something you can eat.*
- The children write sentences in their notebook, then compare in pairs.
- Elicit sentences.

Answers

Children's own answers.

3 Think about Chapter 1. Color the bone.

- Have the children look back at Chapter 1 and color the bone to evaluate their progress (self-evaluation).
- Discuss ideas for making a memorable example sentence, e.g. practicing pronunciation, drawing pictures, or inventing actions to help remember, etc. The children choose and write a tip in their Student Book.

Treasure Hunt

Ask *Where's Tutankhamun's tomb?* (*Egypt*) Have the children look at pp. 4–5 to find something from Egypt. (*cat mummy*)

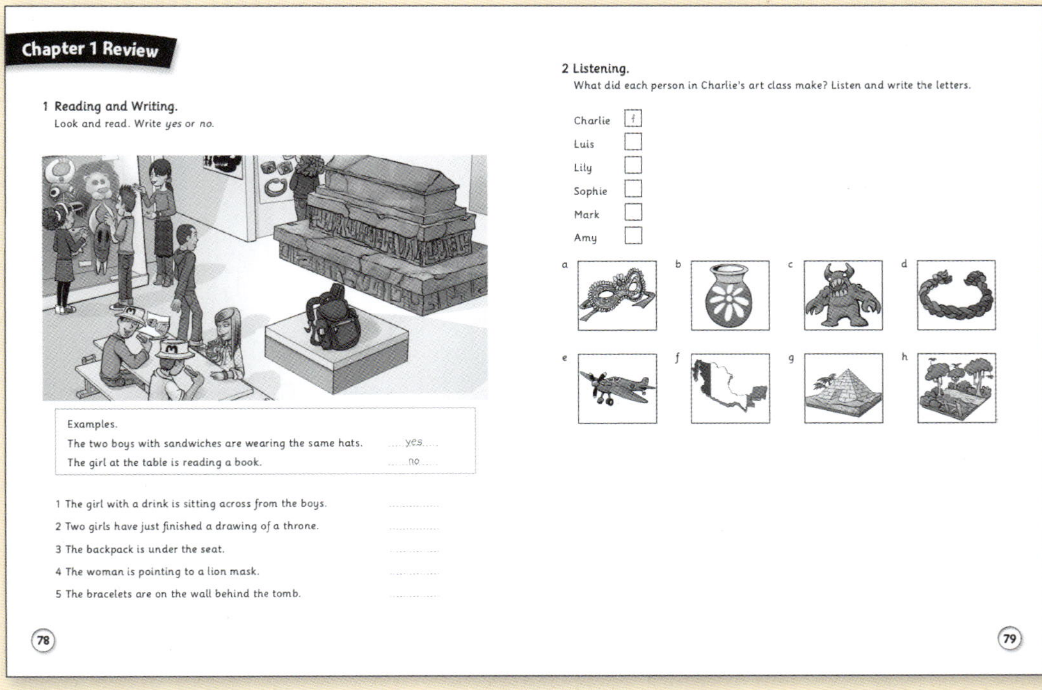

Chapter 1 Review

1 Reading and Writing.
Look and read. Write *yes* or *no*.

Examples.
The two boys with sandwiches are wearing the same hats. ....yes....
The girl at the table is reading a book. ....no....

1 The girl with a drink is sitting across from the boys. ....
2 Two girls have just finished a drawing of a throne. ....
3 The backpack is under the seat. ....
4 The woman is pointing to a lion mask. ....
5 The bracelets are on the wall behind the tomb. ....

78

2 Listening.
What did each person in Charlie's art class make? Listen and write the letters.

Charlie f
Luis
Lily
Sophie
Mark
Amy

a b c d
e f g h

79

1 Reading and Writing. Look and read. Write *yes* or *no*.

The children use the picture to respond *yes* or *no* to each sentence. Check answers.

Answers

1 yes **2** no **3** no **4** yes **5** yes

2 2.31 Listening. What did each person in Charlie's art class make? Listen and write the letters.

Play the CD twice. The children write the letter of the correct object for each person. Check answers.

Answers (Audioscript on p. 223)

Luis c, Lily g, Sophie a, Mark h, Amy d

Competency Focus

Me: Self-evaluation

The children reflect on the chapter, express their personal opinions about their own progress, and look for ways to improve. This encourages them to evaluate and make decisions about what they need to revisit and how they can learn better.

Cooler: Play "Sentence Builders"

Play the game with sentences featuring words from **Spelling Central** (see Games Bank p. 222).

Teacher's Resource Center • Print out Test Chapter 1 to use at the end of this lesson. The Test Generator also allows you to create customized tests.

- TIP Use the drop-down Menu at the top left of the screen to access the AB Review pages.
- For the CEYLT (Cambridge YLE) exam preparation activities on the AB page, choose *Audio* to access the recordings.

Student's App • Encourage the children to play the games on their smartphone/tablet as a fun way to review the chapter vocabulary.

Chapter 2

Get Crafty
Overview

The children will:

- use critical thinking skills to identify craft verbs and activities.
- talk about hobbies using verb + *–ing* or *to* + verb.
- read and understand a Greek myth.
- talk about wishes using *wish* + simple past.
- describe themselves using personality adjectives.
- find out about yarn bombing (a type of street art).
- write a wish poem.

Key Vocabulary

Craft activities and verbs: decide, enjoy, models, offer, pottery, practice, sewing, suggest
Personality adjectives: artistic, creative, imaginative, logical, patient, practical, sociable, sporty

Key Grammar

verb + *–ing*, *to* + verb

- How did you learn to make candles?
- I practiced making them with my friend.

wish + simple past

- I wish I were good at dancing.
- She wishes she could be on TV.
- He wishes he didn't have to go to school.

Reading Skills

Story: *Icarus*
Genre: Greek myth

Literacy Development

- use reading skills to understand and predict content
- relate story theme to personal experience
- use *so that* to give a reason and *or* to give the result of an action

Functional Language

- Please stop singing!
- But I enjoy singing.
- Well, I don't enjoy listening!

Spelling

Adjectives ending in *–ive* or *–al*

CLIL: Art—Cool creations

The children find out about yarn bombing, a type of street art.

Competency Focus

The children will:

use critical thinking skills to deduce the meaning of new vocabulary. (Lesson 1) predict the content of a story. (Lesson 3)	activate new vocabulary and apply new grammar knowledge. (Lesson 2) apply new grammar rules in a familiar context. (Lesson 5)	work in pairs to act out a dialogue. (Lesson 3) work in pairs to describe themselves. (Lesson 6)	relate the story and story theme to their personal experience. (Lesson 4) invent and write a wish poem. (Lesson 8) evaluate their own progress in the chapter. (Review)	develop an understanding of art by carrying out research. (Lesson 7)

Digital Overview

Presentation Kit

Projectable Student Book, Activity Book, and Reader pages

- Vocabulary Tool 2A: Craft activities and verbs
- Vocabulary Tool 2B: Personality adjectives
- Music Video 2: *What Are You Like?*
- Interactive versions of selected SB and AB activities
- Integrated *Audio* and *Answer Key* for all activities

Teacher's Resource Center

Resources for planning, lesson delivery, and homework

- Class Planner Chapter 2
- Worksheets to print out (including notes and answers):
  - Grammar Worksheet 2A: verb + *–ing* / to + verb
  - Grammar Worksheet 2B: *wish* + simple past
  - CLIL Graphic Organizer 2
  - Writing Template 2
  - Festival Worksheet: Halloween
  - Test Chapter 2
- Test Generator
- Literacy Handbook

Student's Resource Center

Resources for consolidation and practice at home

- Interactive Grammar 2A: verb + *–ing* / to + verb
- Interactive Grammar 2B: *wish* + simple past
- Vocabulary Tool 2A: Craft activities and verbs
- Vocabulary Tool 2B: Personality adjectives
- Music Video 2: *Whct Are You Like?*

Student's App

Vocabulary games: Craft activities/verbs and personality adjectives

Watch the Music Video

Chapter 2

Get Crafty

Lesson 1

Vocabulary

Lesson objectives: identify and use vocabulary for craft activities
Key vocabulary: *decide, enjoy, models, offer, pottery, practice, sewing, suggest*
Materials: Class CD; alphabet pages (Warmer)

Chapter 2 Get Crafty Lesson 1

1 Listen and check (✔) the activities they talk about.

painting ☐ sewing ☐ jewelry making ☐ cookie decorating ☐
paper model making ☐ pottery painting ✔ birthday card making ☐

2 Listen again and write the missing words.

enjoy suggest practice ~~decide~~ pottery models offer sewing

1 I don't know. I can't ....decide....
2 Can you help? What do you ....?
3 You .... art and you've always painted.
4 Why don't you paint some ....? A pot or a plate?
5 You just need to .... and bake more cookies!
6 You can make a pencil case in the .... workshop.
7 You can make paper .... of airplanes or birds.
8 I can .... the cookies to all my friends.

Chapter 2 18

Warmer: Play "At home A–Z"

Prepare an answer page for each team (the title *Things to do at home* + the alphabet written vertically). Put the class into teams. Give them two minutes to write a hobby for as many letters of the alphabet as possible. Ask the team with the most words to read their list, then ask other teams to say any other words. A correct answer wins a point. The team with the most points wins.

1 1.12 Listen and check (✔) the activities they talk about.

- Ask the children to look at the pictures of the different craft activities and read the words.
- Play the CD twice. The children listen and check the activities they hear.
- Elicit answers. Whenever you elicit answers, remember to check with the class to see if they agree.

Audioscript

Dad: *Amy, you're going to be one year older next week! What do you want to do for your birthday?*
Amy: *Hm, I think I want to go to Cool and Creative with some friends.*
Dad: *OK, that's a good idea. What do you want to do there?*
Amy: *I don't know. I can't decide. There are so many activities. Can you help? What do you suggest?*
Dad: *You enjoy art and you've always painted. Why don't you paint some pottery? A pot or a plate?*
Amy: *Hm. I really enjoy painting, but I don't want to paint pots and plates.*
Dad: *What about decorating cookies?*
Amy: *I'm not very good at baking.*
Dad: *Yes, you are—you can bake. You just need to practice and bake more cookies!*
Amy: *What do you think they make in the sewing workshop?*
Dad: *I think you can make a pencil case or a case for your cell phone. Or, look! You can make paper models of airplanes or birds. They look amazing.*
Amy: *Hm. Sounds difficult. I think I'll decorate cookies. Then I can offer the cookies to all of my friends.*
Dad: *Great idea. They'll love that.*

Answers

✔ *next to:* painting, sewing, cookie decorating, paper model making, pottery painting

2 1.12 Listen again and write the missing words.

- Play the CD again. The children listen and complete the sentences, using the words supplied.
- Elicit answers.

Answers

1 decide **2** suggest **3** enjoy **4** pottery **5** practice **6** sewing **7** models **8** offer

Optional activity: Suggest activities

Say *I want to do some activities too, but I can't decide! Does anyone have any ideas?* Elicit suggestions using *Why don't you …? / You can make …* phrases. Reject some ideas with a reason and accept others. The children continue the activity in pairs.

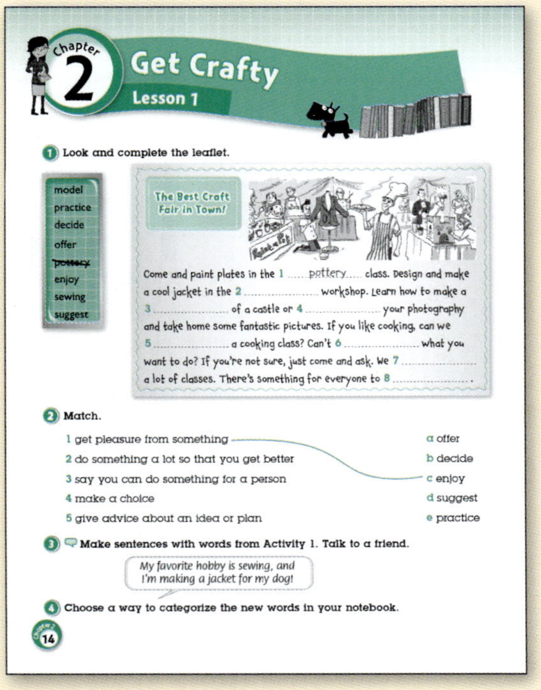

Chapter 2 **Get Crafty**
Lesson 1

1 **Look and complete the leaflet.**

model
practice
decide
offer
~~pottery~~
enjoy
sewing
suggest

The Best Craft Fair in Town!

Come and paint plates in the 1 ...pottery... class. Design and make a cool jacket in the 2 .... workshop. Learn how to make a 3 .... of a castle or 4 .... your photography and take home some fantastic pictures. If you like cooking, can we 5 .... a cooking class? Can't 6 .... what you want to do? If you're not sure, just come and ask. We 7 .... a lot of classes. There's something for everyone to 8 ....

2 **Match.**

1 get pleasure from something — a offer
2 do something a lot so that you get better — b decide
3 say you can do something for a person — c enjoy
4 make a choice — d suggest
5 give advice about an idea or plan — e practice

3 **Make sentences with words from Activity 1. Talk to a friend.**

My favorite hobby is sewing, and I'm making a jacket for my dog!

4 **Choose a way to categorize the new words in your notebook.**

Chapter 2 14

1 Look and complete the leaflet.

The children complete the text using the words supplied. Elicit answers.

Answers

1 pottery **2** sewing **3** model **4** practice **5** suggest
6 decide **7** offer **8** enjoy

2 Match.

The children match the definitions and words. Elicit answers.

Answers

1 c **2** e **3** a **4** b **5** d

3 Make sentences with words from Activity 1. Talk to a friend.

Elicit a few sentences using words from Activity 1. The children then talk in pairs, taking turns making up sentences using the words.

4 Choose a way to categorize the new words in your notebook.

Brainstorm appropriate categories, e.g. *verbs/nouns*, *alphabetical order*. The children choose the best categories for them and list the words in their notebook.

Answers

Children's own answers.

Cooler: Mime time

Mime one of the activities in Student Book Activity 1 for the class and have them guess what you are doing. The children continue the activity in pairs.

Competency Focus

Think! Critical Thinking

The children use critical thinking skills to understand the new vocabulary by using visual clues and processing the written and spoken forms.

- **Presentation Kit** • Use Vocabulary Tool 2A to pre-teach key vocabulary. Use *Slideshow* to introduce the words. Then use *Spotlight* to review/test vocabulary, focusing on the pictures one by one in the images dictionary.
- Play "Kim's Game" with the new vocabulary. Display the SB page. Use *Stopwatch* to give the class one minute to memorize the words, then one minute to recall them. Repeat several times.
- TIP Most audioscripts appear on the SB page. If not, choose the arrow on the *Audio* pop-up to show them.

Grammar

Lesson objective: talk about different activities using verb + *–ing* or *to* + verb

Key grammar: verb + *–ing*, *to* + verb

Secondary language: *keeping bees, melting the wax, beekeeping suit*

Materials: Grammar Worksheet 2A [TRC printout] (optional)

Lesson 2

1 Read. When did Charlie start making candles?

Hello again, Akiko,

You asked me about my hobbies. Well, I have an unusual hobby. I keep bees! About three years ago, I heard about keeping bees in the city and decided to try it. My aunt, who lives in the countryside, keeps bees and she offered to help me.

At first I was a little nervous, but then I stopped feeling scared and learned to be gentle and calm around the bees. The first time we collected honey, I was so excited I wanted to taste it before it went into the jars!

After about two years, my aunt suggested making candles with the wax from the bees. I started going to a class after school and learned to make candles. I practiced melting the wax and making different shapes and models.

I really enjoy keeping bees. I'm sending you a picture of me in my beekeeping suit and another one of me and my sister making candles.

Tell me about your hobbies in your next email.

Love, Charlie

2 Find these verbs in the text and complete the chart.

~~decide~~ learn suggest practice ~~stop~~ want offer start enjoy learn

verb + verb + *–ing*	verb + *to* + verb
stopped feeling	decided to try

3 Talk to a friend about your hobbies.

When did you start …?
Who suggested …?
Why did you decide …?
How often do you practice … ?

A: When did you start playing the guitar?
B: I started playing it about two years ago.

Grammar Central

Verb + *-ing* / *to* + verb

How did you learn .... candles?
I practiced .... them with my friend.

19

Warmer: Play "Back to the Board"

Play the game with vocabulary from Lesson 1, e.g. *decide, enjoy, practice, suggest, pottery, models, offer, sewing* (see Games Bank p. 222).

1 Read. When did Charlie start making candles?

- Have the children look at the pictures. Ask *What is happening? What can you see?*
- Give the children two minutes to read the text, then ask *When did Charlie start making candles?* (*about one year ago*) *What kind of text is this? A letter/phone call/email?* (*an email—last sentence says "in your next email"*)

2 Find these verbs in the text and complete the chart.

- Elicit why *stop* and *decide* are in different columns. (stop *followed by verb + –*ing; decide *followed by* to + *verb*)
- The children complete the chart, finding each verb in the text and writing the whole phrase in the correct column.
- Elicit answers.

Answers

*verb + verb + –*ing*:* stopped feeling, suggested making, started going, practiced melting/making, enjoy keeping
verb + to *+ verb:* decided to try, offered to help, learned to be, wanted to taste, learned to make

Grammar Central

verb + *–ing* / *to* + verb

Have the children complete the grammar examples. Elicit answers. Elicit examples of when we use verb + *–ing* and *to* + verb. Explain that they will need to learn and remember these! Have them write further examples in their notebook. See also the Grammar Reference sections in the Student Book (p. 98) and Activity Book (p. 97) for further explanation and practice.

Grammar Central Answers: to make, making

3 Talk to a friend about your hobbies.

- Tell the children one of your hobbies. Have children use the question prompts to ask you about it.
- The children work in pairs, asking and answering about their hobbies.

Optional activity: Guess the craft

Divide the class into pairs. The children take turns secretly choosing a craft, and asking questions using *this* to identify it, e.g. *When did you start doing this? Why did you decide to do this?* Before they start, elicit possible questions from the children, e.g. *How often do you practice doing this? Why do you enjoy doing this?*, etc.

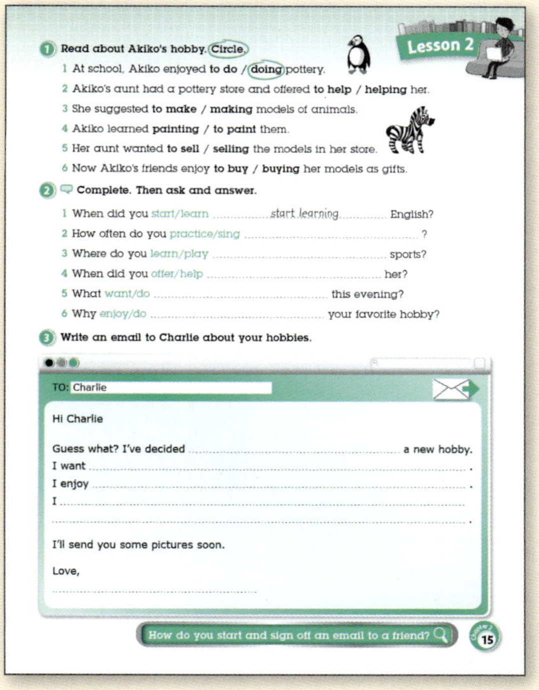

Lesson 2

1 Read about Akiko's hobby. Circle.

1 At school, Akiko enjoyed **to do** / **doing** pottery.
2 Akiko's aunt had a pottery store and offered **to help** / **helping** her.
3 She suggested **to make** / **making** models of animals.
4 Akiko learned **painting** / **to paint** them.
5 Her aunt wanted **to sell** / **selling** the models in her store.
6 Now Akiko's friends enjoy **to buy** / **buying** her models as gifts.

2 Complete. Then ask and answer.

1 When did you start/learn ....start learning.......... English?
2 How often do you practice/sing .... ?
3 Where do you learn/play .... sports?
4 When did you offer/help .... her?
5 What want/do .... this evening?
6 Why enjoy/do .... your favorite hobby?

3 Write an email to Charlie about your hobbies.

TO: Charlie

Hi Charlie

Guess what? I've decided .... a new hobby.
I want ....
I enjoy ....
I ....
....

I'll send you some pictures soon.

Love,
....

How do you start and sign off an email to a friend?

Chapter 2 15

1 Read about Akiko's hobby. Circle.

The children complete the sentences by circling the correct option for each one. Elicit answers.

Answers

1 doing **2** to help **3** making **4** to paint **5** to sell **6** buying

2 Complete. Then ask and answer.

The children complete the sentences using the prompts to make the correct verb form (verb + verb + *–ing* or verb + *to* + verb). Elicit answers, asking children to write them on the board.

Answers

1 start learning **2** practice singing **3** learn to play
4 offer to help **5** do you want to do **6** do you enjoy doing

3 Write an email to Charlie about your hobbies.

The children write an email about their hobbies. They then compare with a friend. Ask children to read extracts from their emails. Ask *How do you start and sign off an email to a friend?* (*Hi, Hello, Dear + first name / Love, Love from, See you soon + first name*)

Answers

Children's own answers.

Cooler: Play "Ready, Set, Draw!"

Play the game with phrases from Lessons 1 and 2 (see Games Bank p. 222).

Competency Focus

Learn

The children integrate previously acquired vocabulary into new grammar and structure and adapt the language to show an understanding of the topic.

Presentation Kit • Use *Hotspots* to enlarge the SB Grammar Central box. Use *Highlighter* to focus on key grammar structures.

• TIP Use *Eraser* to undo any highlighting or writing on the screen if you want to repeat a task.

Teacher's Resource Center • For extra grammar practice, print out Grammar Worksheet 2A.

Student's Resource Center • The children can use Interactive Grammar 2A at home.

Reading: Story Extract

Lesson objectives: make and reinforce firm requests; use the title and pictures to predict story content; read the extract from the Greek myth *Icarus* (middle)
Functional language: *Please stop …! But I enjoy … Well, I don't enjoy …!*
Secondary language: *tied the strings, flapped*
Materials: Class CD

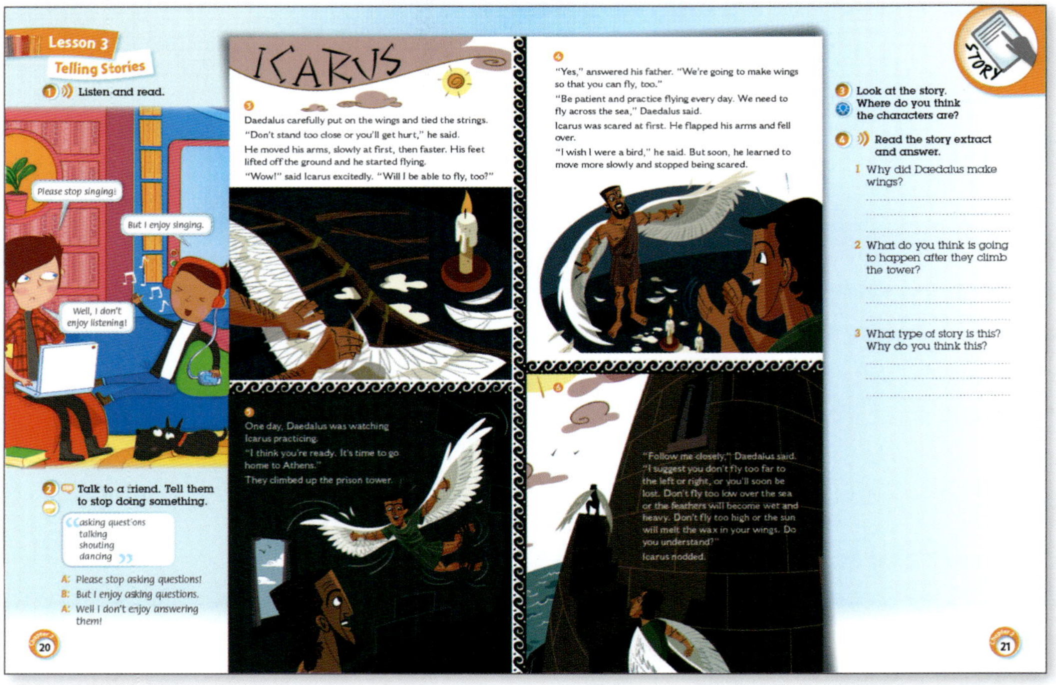
Lesson 3
Telling Stories
1 Listen and read.

2 Talk to a friend. Tell them to stop doing something.
asking questions
talking
shouting
dancing
A: Please stop asking questions!
B: But I enjoy asking questions.
A: Well I don't enjoy answering them!
20

ICARUS

3
Daedalus carefully put on the wings and tied the strings.
"Don't stand too close or you'll get hurt," he said.
He moved his arms, slowly at first, then faster. His feet lifted off the ground and he started flying.
"Wow!" said Icarus excitedly. "Will I be able to fly, too?"

4
"Yes," answered his father. "We're going to make wings so that you can fly, too."
"Be patient and practice flying every day. We need to fly across the sea," Daedalus said.
Icarus was scared at first. He flapped his arms and fell over.
"I wish I were a bird," he said. But soon, he learned to move more slowly and stopped being scared.

5
One day, Daedalus was watching Icarus practicing.
"I think you're ready. It's time to go home to Athens."
They climbed up the prison tower.

6
"Follow me closely," Daedalus said. "I suggest you don't fly too far to the left or right, or you'll soon be lost. Don't fly too low over the sea or the feathers will become wet and heavy. Don't fly too high or the sun will melt the wax in your wings. Do you understand?"
Icarus nodded.

STORY
3 Look at the story. Where do you think the characters are?
4 Read the story extract and answer.
1 Why did Daedalus make wings?
2 What do you think is going to happen after they climb the tower?
3 What type of story is this? Why do you think this?
21

Warmer: Play "Sentence Builders"

Play the game with key sentences from the text on p. 19 of the Student Book, e.g. *I practiced melting the wax and making different shapes and models.* (see Games Bank p. 222).

Functional language

1 1.13 Listen and read.

- Play the CD. The children listen and read along. Ask *Is Rufus happy?* (no) *Why not?* (*Angelo is being noisy.*) *Is he polite?* (*Yes, but he gives his true opinion.*)
- Play the CD again, pausing for the children to repeat.
- Divide the class into pairs to practice the dialogue.

2 Talk to a friend. Tell them to stop doing something.

- Choose two children to read the example dialogue. Elicit other examples of this situation in school or at home using the prompts supplied.
- The children practice in pairs. Have pairs perform a dialogue for the class.

Before reading

3 Look at the story. Where do you think the characters are?

- Have the children study the story title and pictures to figure out where the characters are. Ask *Is this in the past, present, or future? Is it in this country? How do you know?*

4 1.14 Read the story extract and answer.

- Play the CD. The children listen and read along. Have them answer question 1. Elicit the answer.

- Play the CD again so they can write their ideas for questions 2 and 3. Encourage them to use reading skills (e.g. using the title, pictures, and context) to infer meaning and make predictions.
- Elicit answers, but do not confirm predictions: explain that they will have to read the story to find out.

Answers

1 Because he wanted to fly/to go home to Athens.
2 Children's own answers. **3** A myth/Greek myth/Children's own answers.

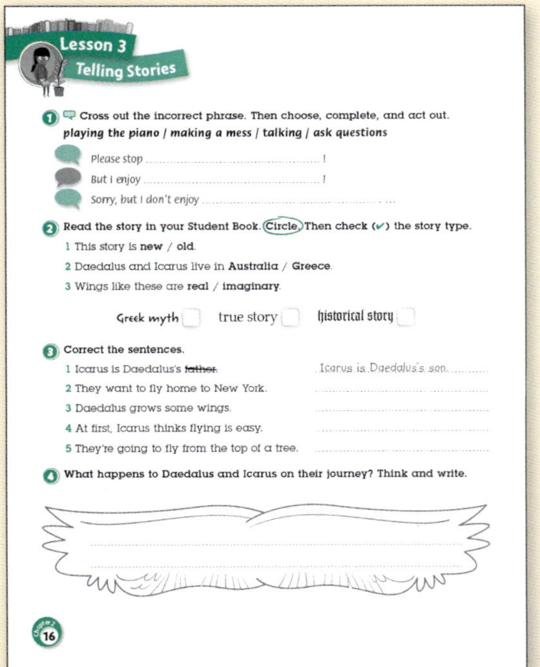

Lesson 3
Telling Stories

1 Cross out the incorrect phrase. Then choose, complete, and act out.
playing the piano / making a mess / talking / ask questions

Please stop .... !
But I enjoy .... !
Sorry, but I don't enjoy ....

2 Read the story in your Student Book. Circle. Then check (✓) the story type.
1 This story is **new** / **old**.
2 Daedalus and Icarus live in **Australia** / **Greece**.
3 Wings like these are **real** / **imaginary**.

Greek myth ☐ true story ☐ historical story ☐

3 Correct the sentences.
1 Icarus is Daedalus's ~~father~~. Icarus is Daedalus's son.
2 They want to fly home to New York. ....
3 Daedalus grows some wings. ....
4 At first, Icarus thinks flying is easy. ....
5 They're going to fly from the top of a tree. ....

4 What happens to Daedalus and Icarus on their journey? Think and write.

16

1 Cross out the incorrect phrase. Then choose, complete, and act out.

The children identify which phrase is incorrect. (*ask questions*) They then choose one of the others and act out the dialogue in pairs. Encourage them to use what they know to adapt and extend the dialogue. Have pairs act out their dialogue for the class.

2 Read the story in your Student Book. Circle. Then check (✓) the story type.

The children read the Student Book story extract again, then complete the sentences by circling the correct option. Then they check the correct story genre. Elicit answers.

Answers

1 old **2** Greece **3** imaginary
✔ *by:* Greek myth

3 Correct the sentences.

The children score through the incorrect detail and write each sentence correctly. Elicit answers.

Answers

1 Icarus is Daedalus's son. **2** They want to fly home to Athens. **3** Daedalus makes some wings. **4** At first, Icarus thinks flying is hard. **5** They're going to fly from the top of the tower.

4 What happens to Daedalus and Icarus on their journey? Think and write.

Elicit suggestions. The children write their own ideas, then compare with a friend. Elicit ideas.

Answers

Children's own answers.

Cooler: Play "Change the Text"

Play the game with a summary of the story extract (see Games Bank p. 222).

Competency Focus

Collaborate and Communicate

The children work together to practice, perform, and adapt the new functional language learned.

Think

The children use critical thinking skills to identify the setting of the story by looking at the text and story artwork.

Presentation Kit • In AB Activity 2, have children use *Pen* to circle answers. If the class thinks an answer is wrong, use *Eraser* to clear so another child can have a turn.
- For the interactive activity (AB Activity 3), choose *Reset* within *Answer Key* to clear the answers to give different children the chance to participate.
- TIP Choose *Audio* on the SB page to access recordings for listening activities.
- TIP Switch easily between the SB/AB using the Navigation Pane.

ICARUS

1
Daedalus looked out through the prison window. The sky was blue and he could hear the sea around the island.

"I wish we could go home," he said sadly. But men were guarding the tower.

2
Just then, a feather floated in through the window. Daedalus looked at the feather, then at his son Icarus. Then he started emptying the feathers from his pillow.

"What are you doing?" asked Icarus.

"I've decided to make some wings so that we can escape," replied Daedalus.

3
He collected sticks and string and, using the wax from candles, began sticking the feathers together. Icarus wanted to offer help but Daedalus was a skilled and creative craftsman, and soon a beautiful pair of wings lay in front of them.

Daedalus carefully put on the wings and tied the strings. "Don't stand too close or you'll get hurt," he said. He moved his arms, slowly at first, then faster. His feet lifted off the ground and he started flying.

"Wow!" said Icarus excitedly. "Will I be able to fly, too?"

4
"Yes," answered his father. "We're going to make wings so that you can fly, too."

"Be patient and practice flying every day. We need to fly across the sea," Daedalus said.

Icarus was scared at first. He flapped his arms and fell over.

"I wish I were a bird," he said. But soon he learned to move more slowly and stopped being scared.

5
One day, Daedalus was watching Icarus practicing.

"I think you're ready. It's time to go home to Athens."

They climbed up the prison tower.

6
"Follow me closely," Daedalus said. "I suggest you don't fly too far to the left or right, or you'll soon be lost. Don't fly too low over the sea or the feathers will become wet and heavy. Don't fly too high or the sun will melt the wax in your wings. Do you understand?"

Icarus nodded.

7
At the top of the tower, Daedalus took a deep breath and jumped. As he fell, the air lifted him up and he started to fly. Icarus followed.

8
Soon, they were flying over the sea like two big white birds. Icarus was excited. He enjoyed flying. It was easy! There were ships below him. He saw birds in the sky and wanted to fly as high as them. The birds flew higher, turning left and right. Icarus followed them, laughing, and forgetting everything Daedalus had said.

9
"Don't fly too high!" shouted Daedalus, "Or your wings will break." But Icarus was too far away to hear. It was getting hotter the higher he went. The wax began melting and the feathers started falling from his wings. The wings started bending. Icarus flapped faster, but it was too late. The wings broke, and Icarus fell a long, long way down into the sea.

11
Daedalus looked at the feathers floating on the water, and cried.

Lesson objective: read and understand the Greek myth *Icarus* in the Reader
Materials: Class CD; Reader

Warmer: Who did it?

Recap the story extract by describing an action from the story and have the children say if Daedalus, Icarus, or both of them did it, e.g. *He fell over.* (*Icarus*)

Story Summary

Daedalus makes wings from feathers so he and his son, Icarus, can escape from prison. Daedalus warns Icarus not to be over-confident when he flies. Icarus does not listen. He flies too close to the sun, his wings melt, and he falls into the sea.

Theme: the importance of listening to your parents

1.15 While reading

- Have the children look at the pictures in the Reader. Ask *Are they able to fly?* (*yes*)
- Play the CD. The children listen and read along. Ask *Did Icarus fly to Athens?* (*no*) *How did Daedalus feel at the end of the story?* (*very sad*) *Why?* (*because Icarus died*)
- Ask questions to check comprehension, e.g. *Why couldn't they leave the tower?* (*they were in prison and there were guards outside*) *Did Icarus understand the advice Daedalus gave him?* (*Yes, but he enjoyed flying too much and forgot his advice.*)
- Elicit reflections on how the children have felt when doing something for the first time (see **Story Time**). Then have the class read the story aloud, with children taking turns being Daedalus and Icarus.

After reading: Reflect

- Ask questions to give the children the opportunity to think about the issues raised by the story, e.g. *Why do you think Icarus flew so close to the sun? Do you know people who do dangerous things nowadays—dangerous sports or other activities?*

Optional activity: Role-play

The children imagine that Daedalus rescues Icarus. Elicit suggestions of what Daedalus and Icarus might say. Have them role-play the dialogue between father and son in pairs. Have pairs perform their dialogue for the class.

Story Time

Role-playing

Stories like this, featuring dialogue with clearly expressed objectives, are good for role-playing. Support the children's understanding of the situation by encouraging them to relate it to their own experiences (e.g. learning to swim, ride a bike, etc.).

Reading Strategy

Summarizing

Summarizing helps the children focus on the most important points in a text and identify any underlying message. It activates critical reading skills and improves memory. At this level, it needs to be practiced more explicitly and frequently, to enable the children to implement it in all their subjects.

For additional explanation and activities, see the Literacy Handbook on the Teacher's Resource Center.

Cooler: Tell the story

Have the children re-tell the story of Icarus around the class, with each child saying one word. You start with the first word *Daedalus* … and indicate the next child to continue.

Presentation Kit • Have the children recall their predictions for what is going to happen after Daedalus and Icarus climb the tower. Use *Mask* to cover Reader p. 10. Ask *What is going to happen?* Slowly uncover Picture 7. The children raise their hand to answer as soon as they know.

• Use *Spotlight* to focus on Pictures 8 and 9. Elicit what is happening. Ask *How does Icarus feel? How does his father feel? What will happen now?* Elicit ideas, then show Picture 10 to confirm.

Reading Comprehension and Critical Literacy

Lesson objectives: understand and evaluate the story; relate story theme to personal experience; focus on *so that* to give a reason and *or* to give the result of an action

Materials: Class CD; Reader

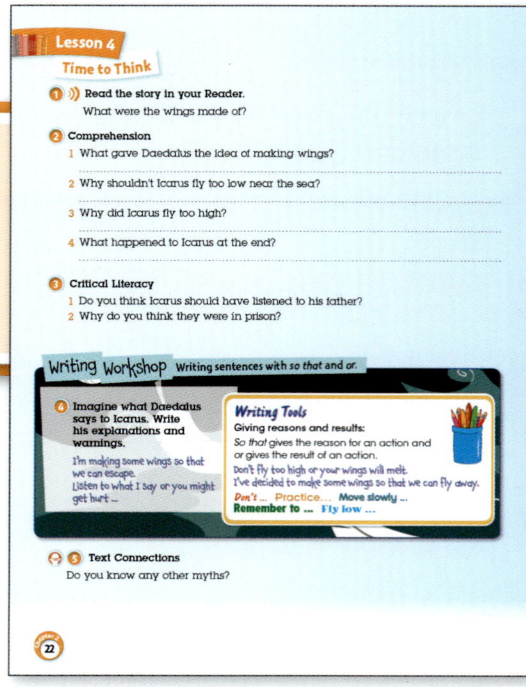
Lesson 4
Time to Think
1 Read the story in your Reader.
What were the wings made of?
2 Comprehension
1 What gave Daedalus the idea of making wings?
2 Why shouldn't Icarus fly too low near the sea?
3 Why did Icarus fly too high?
4 What happened to Icarus at the end?
3 Critical Literacy
1 Do you think Icarus should have listened to his father?
2 Why do you think they were in prison?
Writing Workshop Writing sentences with *so that* and *or*.
4 Imagine what Daedalus says to Icarus. Write his explanations and warnings.
I'm making some wings so that we can escape.
Listen to what I say or you might get hurt ...
Writing Tools
Giving reasons and results:
So that gives the reason for an action and *or* gives the result of an action.
Don't fly too high or your wings will melt.
I've decided to make some wings so that we can fly away.
Don't ... Practice ... Move slowly ...
Remember to ... Fly low ...
5 Text Connections
Do you know any other myths?
22

Note: Please ensure that your class has read the Reader story before you do this lesson.

Warmer: Play "Collocations"

Play the game with phrases from the story, e.g. *guard/the tower, put on/the wings, collect/sticks, don't fly/too high, practice/flying, wanted to/fly high, started/melting, fell/down* (see Games Bank p. 222).

1 1.15 Read the story in your Reader.

- Have the children read the story. (Alternatively, play the CD and have them read along.)
- Elicit whether the children were correct in their predictions in Lesson 3 Activity 4. Ask *What were the wings made of?* (*sticks, string, wax, feathers*)

2 Comprehension

- The children write answers to the first three questions. Elicit answers.
- Discuss question 4. Ask the children to justify their answers.

Answers

1 A feather floated through the window. **2** Because the feathers will become wet and heavy. **3** He wanted to fly as high as the birds. **4** He fell into the sea/drowned/died.

3 Critical Literacy

- Have the children discuss the answers to the questions with a friend.
- Elicit ideas and have a class discussion. Encourage children to give reasons for their opinions. Analyzing the characters' behavior and attitudes in this way develops critical literacy.

Answers

Children's own answers.

Writing Workshop

Writing sentences with *so that* and *or*

4 Imagine what Daedalus says to Icarus. Write his explanations and warnings.

Have a child read the example. Elicit other examples of *so that* and *or*, using phrases from the **Writing Tools** box. The children write their explanations and warnings in their notebook, then compare with a friend. Elicit responses.

Answers

Children's own answers.

5 Text Connections

- Ask *Do you know any other myths?* Elicit ideas and discuss as a class.

Optional activity: A different ending

Ask the children to imagine a different ending to the story. Elicit ideas as a class, then put the children into pairs to write their ideas. Elicit responses.

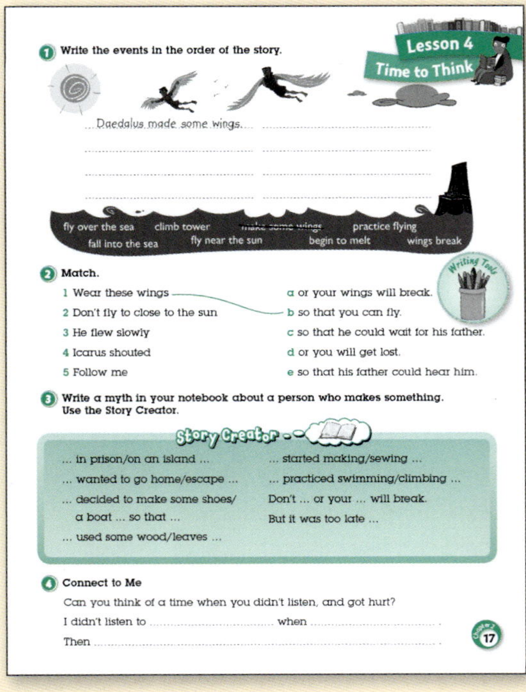
Lesson 4
Time to Think

1 Write the events in the order of the story.

...Daedalus made some wings....

fly over the sea · climb tower · ~~make some wings~~ · practice flying · fall into the sea · fly near the sun · begin to melt · wings break

2 Match.

1 Wear these wings — a or your wings will break.
2 Don't fly to close to the sun — b so that you can fly.
3 He flew slowly — c so that he could wait for his father.
4 Icarus shouted — d or you will get lost.
5 Follow me — e so that his father could hear him.

3 Write a myth in your notebook about a person who makes something. Use the Story Creator.

Story Creator

... in prison/on an island ...
... wanted to go home/escape ...
... decided to make some shoes/ a boat ... so that ...
... used some wood/leaves ...
... started making/sewing ...
... practiced swimming/climbing ...
Don't ... or your ... will break.
But it was too late ...

4 Connect to Me
Can you think of a time when you didn't listen, and got hurt?
I didn't listen to .... when ....
Then ....

17

1 Write the events in the order of the story.

The children use the prompts supplied to write the events of the story in the order they happened, using short sentences. Elicit answers.

Answers

1 Daedalus made some wings. **2** They practiced flying. **3** They climbed the tower. **4** They flew over the sea. **5** Icarus flew near the sun. **6** The wings began to melt. **7** The wings broke. **8** Icarus fell into the sea.

2 Match.

The children match the sentence halves. Elicit answers.

Answers

1 b **2** a **3** c **4** e **5** d

3 Write a myth in your notebook about a person who makes something. Use the Story Creator.

Use the **Story Creator** prompts to elicit ideas. The children write a myth in their notebook about a person who makes something, then compare with a friend. Have children read out their texts for the class.

4 Connect to Me

Elicit examples of a time when not listening meant someone got hurt. (e.g. *running in a busy place*) The children write their own response, then compare with a friend. Elicit responses.

Cooler: Myths and morals

Write morals from the story on the board, e.g. *always listen to your parents*, *be careful in the sun*, etc. Elicit further morals that children noticed in this story and other stories. Take a class vote on the most important moral in today's world.

Competency Focus

Me: Critical Literacy

The children use critical literacy skills to reflect on the story and the characters and think of other similar stories.

Presentation Kit • TIP You can use *Hotspots* to show one enlarged picture of the Reader at a time for a guided retelling of the story.

- TIP Use the arrows in the Navigation Pane to go to previous or later lessons, or between *Hotspots*.
- Have children use *Pen* to write answers for AB Activity 1. Elicit agreement from the class each time. Use *Eraser* to clear and let another child answer if the sentence is wrong or in the wrong place. Use *Answer Key* to confirm.

Grammar and Reading

Lesson objective: talk about wishes using *wish* + simple past
Key grammar: *wish* + simple past
Secondary language: *drown, happy ending*
Materials: Class CD; Grammar Worksheet 2B [TRC printout] (optional)

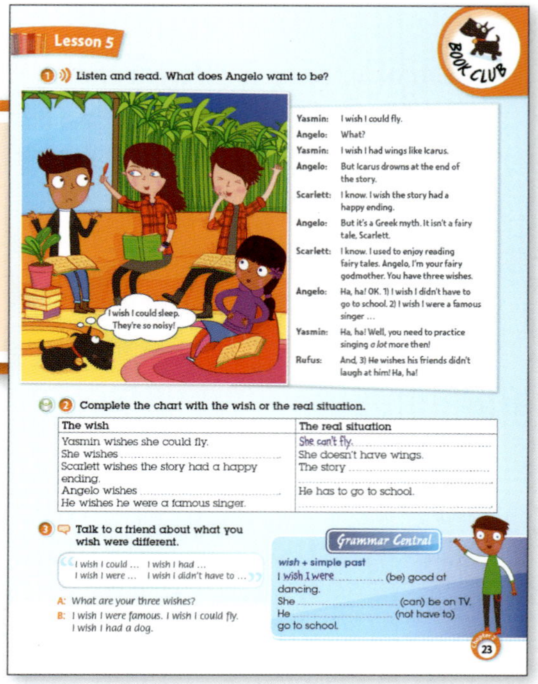
Lesson 5

BOOK CLUB

1 Listen and read. What does Angelo want to be?

Yasmin: I wish I could fly.
Angelo: What?
Yasmin: I wish I had wings like Icarus.
Angelo: But Icarus drowns at the end of the story.
Scarlett: I know. I wish the story had a happy ending.
Angelo: But it's a Greek myth. It isn't a fairy tale, Scarlett.
Scarlett: I know. I used to enjoy reading fairy tales. Angelo, I'm your fairy godmother. You have three wishes.
Angelo: Ha, ha! OK. 1) I wish I didn't have to go to school. 2) I wish I were a famous singer …
Yasmin: Ha, ha! Well, you need to practice singing *a lot* more then!
Rufus: And, 3) He wishes his friends didn't laugh at him! Ha, ha!

2 Complete the chart with the wish or the real situation.

The wish	The real situation
Yasmin wishes she could fly.	She can't fly.
She wishes ………	She doesn't have wings.
Scarlett wishes the story had a happy ending.	The story ………
Angelo wishes ………	He has to go to school.
He wishes he were a famous singer.	………

3 Talk to a friend about what you wish were different.

I wish I could … I wish I had …
I wish I were … I wish I didn't have to …

A: *What are your three wishes?*
B: *I wish I were famous. I wish I could fly. I wish I had a dog.*

Grammar Central
wish + simple past
I wish I were ……… (be) good at dancing.
She ……… (can) be on TV.
He ……… (not have to) go to school.

23

Warmer: Spot the mistakes

Retell the story of Icarus, but with key facts changed, e.g. *Daedalus and Icarus were on vacation. Daedalus got the idea to make some wings when he saw a plane. He made the wings from plastic and paper. He fell into the swimming pool.* When the children hear something incorrect, they say *Stop!* and tell you what it should be.

1 1.16 Listen and read. What does Angelo want to be?

- Play the CD. The children listen and read along. Ask *Who does Scarlett pretend to be?* (*Angelo's fairy godmother*)
- Play the CD again and ask *What does Angelo want to be?* (*a famous singer*) Elicit answers.

2 Complete the chart with the wish or the real situation.

- Ask two children to read out the first wish and the example real situation.
- Have the children complete the chart, referring to the dialogue in Activity 1.
- Elicit answers.

Answers

The wish / The real situation:
Yasmin wishes she could fly. / She can't fly.
She wishes she had wings. / She doesn't have wings.
Scarlett wishes the story had a happy ending. / It has a sad ending. *or* It doesn't have a happy ending.
Angelo wishes he didn't have to go to school. / He has to go to school.
He wishes he were a famous singer. / He isn't a famous singer.

Grammar Central

wish + simple past

Have the children complete the grammar examples. Elicit answers. Then elicit when we use *wish* + simple past. (*to talk about things which are not probable, or very difficult to have or do*) The children write more examples in their notebook. See also the Grammar Reference sections in the Student Book (p. 98) and Activity Book (p. 97) for further explanation and practice.

Grammar Central Answers: wish I were, wishes she could, wishes he didn't have to

3 Talk to a friend about what you wish were different.

- Choose two children to read the example dialogue.
- Divide the class into pairs to practice the dialogue using the prompts supplied and their own wishes. Have pairs perform for the class.

Optional activity: Difficult situations

Elicit some difficult situations (*bullying, in trouble with parents, having an argument with a friend, forgetting books, not doing homework*). Have the children imagine what someone might say in these situations and write examples using *I wish* … in their notebook. Have the children compare sentences in pairs. Elicit responses.

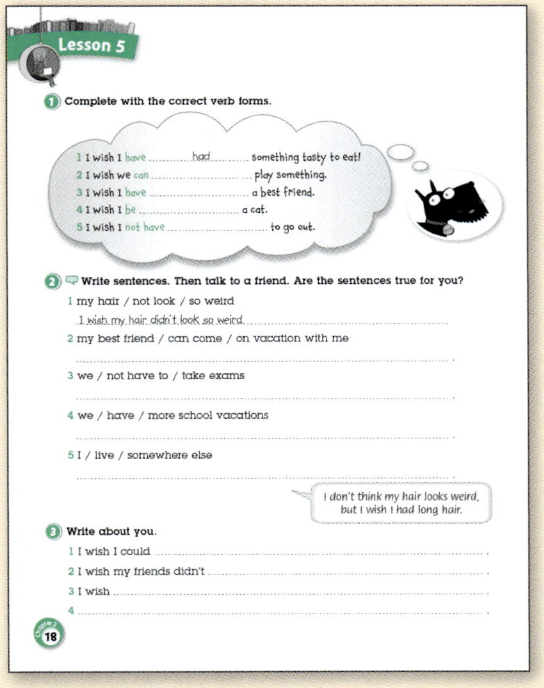

Lesson 5

1 Complete with the correct verb forms.

1 I wish I have .... had .... something tasty to eat!
2 I wish we can .... play something.
3 I wish I have .... a best friend.
4 I wish I be .... a cat.
5 I wish I not have .... to go out.

2 Write sentences. Then talk to a friend. Are the sentences true for you?

1 my hair / not look / so weird
I wish my hair didn't look so weird.
2 my best friend / can come / on vacation with me
....
3 we / not have to / take exams
....
4 we / have / more school vacations
....
5 I / live / somewhere else
....

I don't think my hair looks weird, but I wish I had long hair.

3 Write about you.

1 I wish I could ....
2 I wish my friends didn't ....
3 I wish ....
4 ....

Chapter 2 18

1 Complete with the correct verb forms.

The children complete the *I wish* sentences by writing the correct form of the verb prompts. Elicit answers.

Answers

1 had **2** could **3** had **4** were **5** didn't have

2 Write sentences. Then talk to a friend. Are the sentences true for you?

The children use the prompts to write sentences. Then they discuss the sentences with a friend, saying whether they are true or not.

Answers

1 I wish my hair didn't look so weird. **2** I wish my best friend could come on vacation with me. **3** I wish we didn't have to take exams. **4** I wish we had more school vacations. **5** I wish I lived somewhere else.

3 Write about you.

Elicit a possible answer for each sentence. The children complete the sentences with their own ideas, then they compare with a friend. Elicit responses.

Answers

Children's own answers.

Cooler: Play "Tic-Tac-Toe"

Play the game with *wish* + simple past sentences, e.g. *wish/have/purple hair*, *wish/swim fast*, etc. (see Games Bank p. 222).

Competency Focus

Learn

The children demonstrate their understanding of the new language by reading the dialogue and completing the activity.

Presentation Kit • Use *Mask* to hide key words/phrases in SB Activity 1, e.g. *I wish I ~~had~~ wings like Icarus*. Elicit the complete sentence.

• Have children use *Pen* to write AB Activity 3 answers. The class raises their hand if they have the same response. Use *Eraser* to clear and have children with different answers use *Pen* to write their responses.

Teacher's Resource Center • For extra grammar practice, print out Grammar Worksheet 2B.

Student's Resource Center • The children can use Interactive Grammar 2B at home.

Vocabulary, Song, and Spelling

Lesson objectives: identify and use personality adjectives; practice spelling adjectives that end with *–ive* or *–al*
Key vocabulary: *artistic, creative, imaginative, logical, patient, practical, sociable, sporty*
Secondary language: *get things done, a fantasy land*
Materials: Class CD

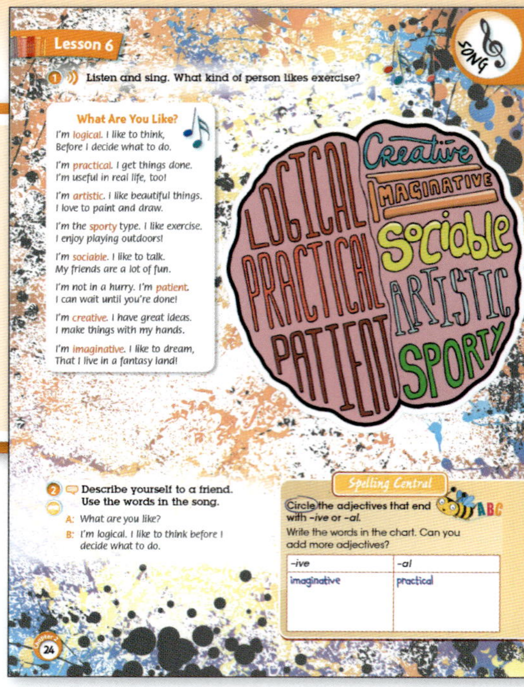

Warmer: Pre-teach vocabulary

Pre-teach the vocabulary using mimes. Call out the words for the class to do the correct mime. Then make sentences for the class to complete, e.g. *A person who is good at painting pictures is …* (*artistic*). *A person who is good at soccer and tennis is …* (*sporty*)., etc.

1 🔊 **1.17 Listen and sing. What kind of person likes exercise?**

- Play the CD. The children listen and think about the different types of people mentioned. Ask *What kind of person likes exercise?* (*a sporty person*)
- Play the CD again for the children to sing along.

2 Describe yourself to a friend. Use the words in the song.

- Read the example with the class. Tell them that they do not have to tell the truth! In pairs, they describe themselves using words from the song. After each statement they ask each other if it is true or false.

Spelling Central

Adjectives that end with *–ive* or *–al*

Read out the *–ive* and *–al* adjectives in the song, pausing to elicit the ending, e.g. *imaginat—ive! logic—al!* Have the children find *–ive* and *–al* words on the page and complete the chart. They then add other words in each category. (e.g. *positive, negative*; *magical, historical, musical*)

Answers

–ive: imaginative, creative
–al: practical, logical

Optional activity: **Family qualities**

Ask the children if other people in their family have the qualities mentioned in the song. Elicit examples and have each child write and illustrate a short text about two members of their family. These pictures and texts can be used to make a wall display.

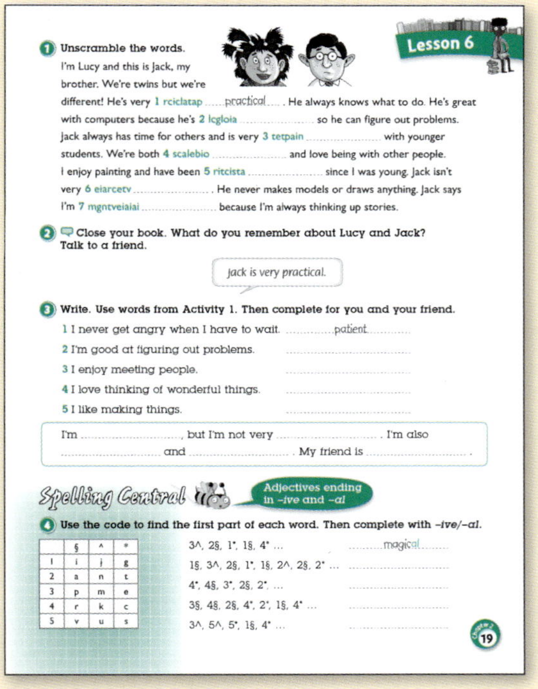

Lesson 6

1 Unscramble the words.

I'm Lucy and this is Jack, my brother. We're twins but we're different! He's very 1 rciclatap ......practical..... He always knows what to do. He's great with computers because he's 2 lcgloia .... so he can figure out problems. Jack always has time for others and is very 3 tetpain .... with younger students. We're both 4 scalebio .... and love being with other people. I enjoy painting and have been 5 ritcista .... since I was young. Jack isn't very 6 eiarcetv .... He never makes models or draws anything. Jack says I'm 7 mgntveiaiai .... because I'm always thinking up stories.

2 Close your book. What do you remember about Lucy and Jack? Talk to a friend.

Jack is very practical.

3 Write. Use words from Activity 1. Then complete for you and your friend.

1 I never get angry when I have to wait. ....patient............
2 I'm good at figuring out problems. ....
3 I enjoy meeting people. ....
4 I love thinking of wonderful things. ....
5 I like making things. ....

I'm ...., but I'm not very .... I'm also .... and .... My friend is ....

Spelling Central — Adjectives ending in *–ive* and *–al*

4 Use the code to find the first part of each word. Then complete with *–ive*/*–al*.

	§	^	*
1	i	j	g
2	a	n	t
3	p	m	e
4	r	k	c
5	v	u	s

3^, 2§, 1*, 1§, 4* ... .magical........
1§, 3^, 2§, 1*, 1§, 2^, 2§, 2* ... .
4*, 4§, 3*, 2§, 2* ... .
3§, 4§, 2§, 4*, 2*, 1§, 4* ... .
3^, 5^, 5*, 1§, 4* ... .

Chapter 2 19

1 Unscramble the words.

The children complete the text by unscrambling the word prompts. Elicit answers. Check difficult spellings, e.g. *patient, sociable, imaginative.*

Answers

1 practical **2** logical **3** patient **4** sociable **5** artistic **6** creative **7** imaginative

2 Close your book. What do you remember about Lucy and Jack? Talk to a friend.

The children close their Activity Book and recall in pairs what they can remember about Lucy and Jack.

3 Write. Use words from Activity 1. Then complete for you and your friend.

The children write the adjective for each definition. Elicit answers. The children then complete the summary, describing themselves and a friend.

Answers

1 patient **2** logical **3** sociable **4** imaginative **5** creative

4 Use the code to find the first part of each word. Then complete with *-ive*/*-al*.

To practice the **Spelling Central** feature, the children use the chart to decode the word beginnings. They then complete the words with *–ive* or *–al*. Elicit answers.

Answers

1 magical **2** imaginative **3** creative **4** practical **5** musical

Cooler: Sing the song

1.17

Divide the class into two groups. Explain to the children that one group will sing the first part of each line, and the other group will sing the "definition." Play the CD and have them sing along, then swap the roles of the groups.

Competency Focus

Collaborate and Communicate

The children work together to share their ideas on the topic, incorporating the new vocabulary.

Presentation Kit • Use Vocabulary Tool 2B to pre-teach key vocabulary. Use *Slideshow* to introduce the words. Then use *Find the Pairs* to review/test vocabulary in a matching game.

- After SB Activity 2, choose Music Video 2 and encourage the children to sing along, using the graphic lyrics on screen. Associating movements with words makes them more memorable. Pause *Video* for the children to continue singing.

Student's Resource Center • Encourage the children to share Music Video 2 at home with their family.

CLIL: Art—Cool creations

Lesson objective: find out about yarn bombing (a type of street art)
Materials: ten pictures of different styles of art (Warmer); colored yarn; CLIL Graphic Organizer 2 [TRC printout] (optional)

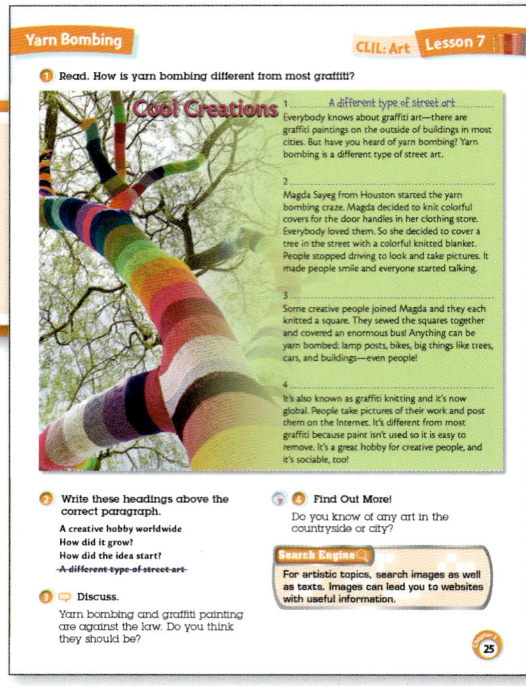
Yarn Bombing

CLIL: Art Lesson 7

1 Read. How is yarn bombing different from most graffiti?

Cool Creations

1 A different type of street art

Everybody knows about graffiti art—there are graffiti paintings on the outside of buildings in most cities. But have you heard of yarn bombing? Yarn bombing is a different type of street art.

2

Magda Sayeg from Houston started the yarn bombing craze. Magda decided to knit colorful covers for the door handles in her clothing store. Everybody loved them. So she decided to cover a tree in the street with a colorful knitted blanket. People stopped driving to look and take pictures. It made people smile and everyone started talking.

3

Some creative people joined Magda and they each knitted a square. They sewed the squares together and covered an enormous bus! Anything can be yarn bombed: lamp posts, bikes, big things like trees, cars, and buildings—even people!

4

It's also known as graffiti knitting and it's now global. People take pictures of their work and post them on the Internet. It's different from most graffiti because paint isn't used so it is easy to remove. It's a great hobby for creative people, and it's sociable, too!

2 Write these headings above the correct paragraph.

A creative hobby worldwide
How did it grow?
How did the idea start?
~~A different type of street art~~

3 Discuss.

Yarn bombing and graffiti painting are against the law. Do you think they should be?

4 Find Out More!

Do you know of any art in the countryside or city?

Search Engine

For artistic topics, search images as well as texts. Images can lead you to websites with useful information.

25

Warmer: My favorite art

Show the children ten different works of art (include famous paintings, modern art, graffiti art, sculpture, art using recycled objects, art using people, etc.). Have the children talk in groups and agree on their three favorite pieces. Have children tell the class why they agreed on their choices.

1 Read. How is yarn bombing different from most graffiti?

- Have the children look at the picture. Ask *What can you see? Where is it?* (*Houston*) *What has happened* (*A tree has been covered in colorful yarn.*)
- Have the children read the text. Ask *How is yarn bombing different from most graffiti?* (*because paint isn't used so it's easy to remove*)

2 Write these headings above the correct paragraph.

- The children decide which heading belongs to each paragraph.
- Elicit answers, including a reason each time.

Answers

1 A different type of street art **2** How did the idea start? **3** How did it grow? **4** A creative hobby worldwide

3 Discuss.

- Have a child read out the discussion question.
- Have the children talk about their ideas in pairs, then share ideas as a class.

4 Find Out More!

- The children research other art forms in the countryside or city. The **Search Engine** feature gives support on where to look. The children will need to complete this research before doing the follow-up activity in the Activity Book. (It could be set as homework.)

Optional activity: Yarn bomb our town!

Have the children work in pairs to decide on a landmark in their town that they think would be good for yarn bombing. Divide the class into groups to discuss their idea, then prepare a presentation and illustration for it. The groups present their ideas to the class.

Lesson 7 CLIL

1 Read and sort into two paragraphs by drawing arrows.

Graffiti — Sand art

1 It's a type of street art.
2 It's usually done on beaches.
3 It's found on walls in cities.
4 The artists usually use colorful paints.
5 The artists make models.
6 Sand and water are used.
7 Popular shapes are animals, people, and castles.
8 Artists write words and paint pictures.
9 Artists have to be very patient.
10 Artists usually work very quickly.
11 It lasts a long time and is difficult to remove.
12 It disappears when it rains.

2 Use your Student Book research to make an Info Card. Write about different types of art and graffiti.

Find Out More!

sand stones chalk flowers ice in the city in the countryside

3 Yarn bomb your classroom.

Try it Out

- Choose an object to yarn bomb, e.g. a pen or pencil.
- Carefully wrap brightly colored yarn around it.

4 Select and store information on this topic in the Class Info Hub.

20

1 Read and sort into two paragraphs by drawing arrows.

The children decide for each sentence whether it describes graffiti or sand art, drawing a line from the sentence to the appropriate picture. Elicit answers.

Answers

Graffiti: 1, 3, 4, 8, 10, 11
Sand art: 2, 5, 6, 7, 9, 12

2 Use your Student Book research to make an Info Card. Write about different types of art and graffiti.

Divide the class into groups. Have the children pool the information they learned from their research in the Student Book and the Activity Book. The children write about and illustrate their ideas individually. Have the groups present their Info Cards to the class.

3 Yarn bomb your classroom.

In their groups, the children follow the **Try It Out** instructions to yarn bomb an object in their classroom. Then they show the class what they have yarn bombed.

4 Select and store information on this topic in the Class Info Hub.

Have the children vote for the five most interesting Info Cards. Archive these in your Class Hub (see p. 41) in a folder called **Chapter 2 Art and Graffiti**.

Cooler: Play "Disappearing Text"

Play the game with the last paragraph of the Student Book Activity 1 text (see Games Bank p. 222).

Competency Focus

Act

The children carry out research to find out about art in the countryside or city. This helps them expand their learning and relate it to their world, both inside and outside the classroom.

Presentation Kit • Use *Notepad* to store links to the different works of art for the Warmer.

- As support for less confident children, you could elicit findings orally before the children do AB Activity 2. Use *Highlighter* on the word bank options (sand, stones, etc.), one at a time, to elicit information and ideas from the class about different types of art and graffiti.

Teacher's Resource Center • Print out CLIL Graphic Organizer 2 for the children to use in collating their Find Out More! research.

Writing Project

Lesson objectives: review language from Chapter 2; write a wish poem and present it to the class
Materials: Writing Template 2 [TRC printout] (optional)

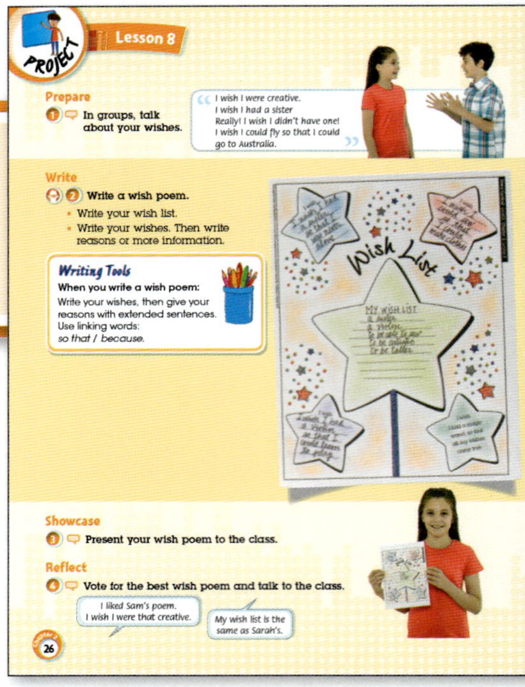

Warmer: If you wish you were ...

Say *Stand up if you wish you were rich*. The children stand up or stay seated, as appropriate. Repeat with other wishes, e.g. *if you wish you were a soccer player/astronaut, if you wish you lived in another country*, etc. Each time, give the children a different action to do, e.g. *raise your hand, stand on one foot, pretend to be a dog*, etc.

Prepare

1 In groups, talk about your wishes.

- Divide the class into groups of four. Tell the children they have two minutes to say as many wishes as they can about themselves, but they cannot repeat a wish.
- Then ask *What was the best wish in your group?* Give the groups a minute to decide. Elicit ideas.

Write

2 Write a wish poem.

- Have the children read the example list and the wishes that make up the poem.
- Read the **Writing Tools** box together. Have the children think of one wish and tell a friend, using linking words to give their reasons.
- The children write their own wish list, then use this to write wishes for a wish poem. Give support as necessary.
- They compare poems with a friend.

Showcase

3 Present your wish poem to the class.

- Choose children to read their poem to the class. Ask the class to listen and say which ones have similar wishes.

Reflect

4 Vote for the best wish poem and talk to the class.

- Have the children comment on which poem was the best and why. Have a class vote to identify their favorite.

Optional activity: I wish ...

Tell the class they are going to imagine they are someone else and think up wishes for that person. Elicit ideas—they can be friends, family, famous people, or fictional characters. Divide the class into pairs. Each pair chooses a person and writes four wishes for them. Elicit responses.

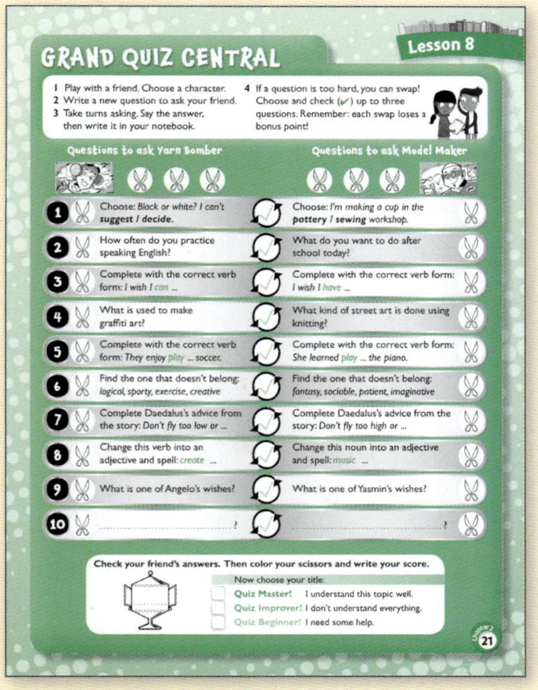

GRAND QUIZ CENTRAL

Lesson 8

1 Play with a friend. Choose a character.
2 Write a new question to ask your friend.
3 Take turns asking. Say the answer, then write it in your notebook.
4 If a question is too hard, you can swap! Choose and check (✔) up to three questions. Remember: each swap loses a bonus point!

	Questions to ask Yarn Bomber	Questions to ask Model Maker
1	Choose: *Black or white? I can't* **suggest / decide.**	Choose: *I'm making a cup in the* **pottery / sewing** *workshop.*
2	How often do you practice speaking English?	What do you want to do after school today?
3	Complete with the correct verb form: *I wish I can …*	Complete with the correct verb form: *I wish I have …*
4	What is used to make graffiti art?	What kind of street art is done using knitting?
5	Complete with the correct verb form: *They enjoy play … soccer.*	Complete with the correct verb form: *She learned play … the piano.*
6	Find the one that doesn't belong: *logical, sporty, exercise, creative*	Find the one that doesn't belong: *fantasy, sociable, patient, imaginative*
7	Complete Daedalus's advice from the story: *Don't fly too low or …*	Complete Daedalus's advice from the story: *Don't fly too high or …*
8	Change this verb into an adjective and spell: *create* …	Change this noun into an adjective and spell: *music* …
9	What is one of Angelo's wishes?	What is one of Yasmin's wishes?
10	……………………………?	……………………………?

Check your friend's answers. Then color your scissors and write your score.

Now choose your title:
- Quiz Master! I understand this topic well.
- Quiz Improver! I don't understand everything.
- Quiz Beginner! I need some help.

Chapter 2 21

Grand Quiz Central

See p. 43 for details of how to take the quiz.

Answers

1 decide / pottery **2** Children's own answers. **3** I wish I could + verb / I wish I had + noun **4** paint / yarn bombing **5** playing / to play **6** exercise / fantasy **7** your wings will become heavy and wet. / your wings will melt. **8** creative / musical **9** He wishes he didn't have to go to school/were a famous singer/his friends didn't laugh at him. / She wishes she could fly/the story had a happy ending/she had wings. **10** Children's own answers.

Cooler: Play "The Chain Game"

Play the game starting with the phrase *I wish* … (see Games Bank p. 222).

Competency Focus

Me

The children write their own wish poems. They develop an understanding about realistic goals for the future.

Presentation Kit • Use *Stopwatch* to give the children two minutes to study the SB Prepare box and come up with as many different wishes as they can. Elicit two different ideas from each group.

Teacher's Resource Center • Print out Writing Template 2 to use for the SB writing activity.

Student's Resource Center • Encourage the children to share Vocabulary Tools 1A–2B at home to reinforce vocabulary learning.

Language Review

Lesson objective: review language from Chapter 2
Materials: Class CD

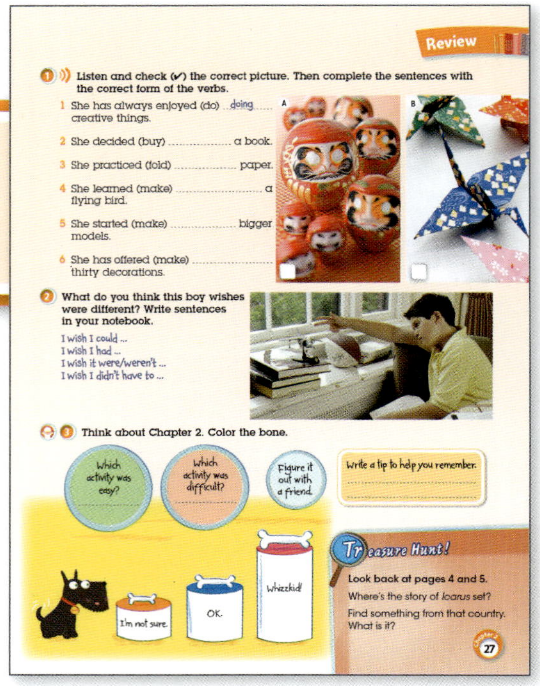
Review

1 Listen and check (✔) the correct picture. Then complete the sentences with the correct form of the verbs.

1 She has always enjoyed (do) doing ... creative things.
2 She decided (buy) ... a book.
3 She practiced (fold) ... paper.
4 She learned (make) ... a flying bird.
5 She started (make) ... bigger models.
6 She has offered (make) ... thirty decorations.

2 What do you think this boy wishes were different? Write sentences in your notebook.

I wish I could ...
I wish I had ...
I wish it were/weren't ...
I wish I didn't have to ...

3 Think about Chapter 2. Color the bone.

Which activity was easy?
Which activity was difficult?
Figure it out with a friend.
Write a tip to help you remember.
I'm not sure.
OK.
Whizzkid!

Treasure Hunt!
Look back at pages 4 and 5.
Where's the story of Icarus set?
Find something from that country. What is it?

27

Warmer: Play "Collocations"

Play the game using collocations from the chapter, e.g. *feeling/scared, climb/the tower, fly/too high*, etc. (see Games Bank p. 222).

1 1.18 Listen and check (✔) the correct picture. Then complete the sentences with the correct form of the verbs.

- Have the children look at the pictures. Ask *What can you see?*
- Play the CD and have the children listen and check the correct picture.
- Play the CD again for the children to check their answers.
- Elicit answers.

Audioscript

I'm really artistic and I've always enjoyed doing creative things and making models, so I decided to buy a book about origami. Origami is the Japanese art of folding paper to make models. The pictures were difficult to understand at first but I was very patient. I practiced folding the paper and making simple shapes. After a week, I learned to make a flying bird. Then, I started making bigger and more difficult models of flowers, to use for decorations. It's not very sociable but I really enjoy sitting quietly and being creative sometimes. I've offered to make thirty decorations for my sister's party. I just wish I could make them more quickly!

Answers

✔ *by:* Picture B
1 doing **2** to buy **3** folding **4** to make **5** making / to make **6** to make

2 What do you think this boy wishes were different? Write sentences in your notebook.

- Elicit from the class one sentence about the boy and his wishes. Write it on the board. Remind the children of the past verb after *wish*.
- The children write sentences in their notebook and compare their sentences in pairs.

Answers

Children's own answers.

3 Think about Chapter 2. Color the bone.

- Have the children look back at Chapter 2 and color the bone to evaluate their progress (self-evaluation).
- Discuss ideas for improving your grammar, e.g. check work carefully, look for mistakes, ask a friend to check. The children choose and write a tip in their Student Book.

Treasure Hunt

Ask *Where is the story* Icarus *set?* (*Greece*) Have the children look at pp. 4–5 to find something from Greece. (*a large pot with handles*)

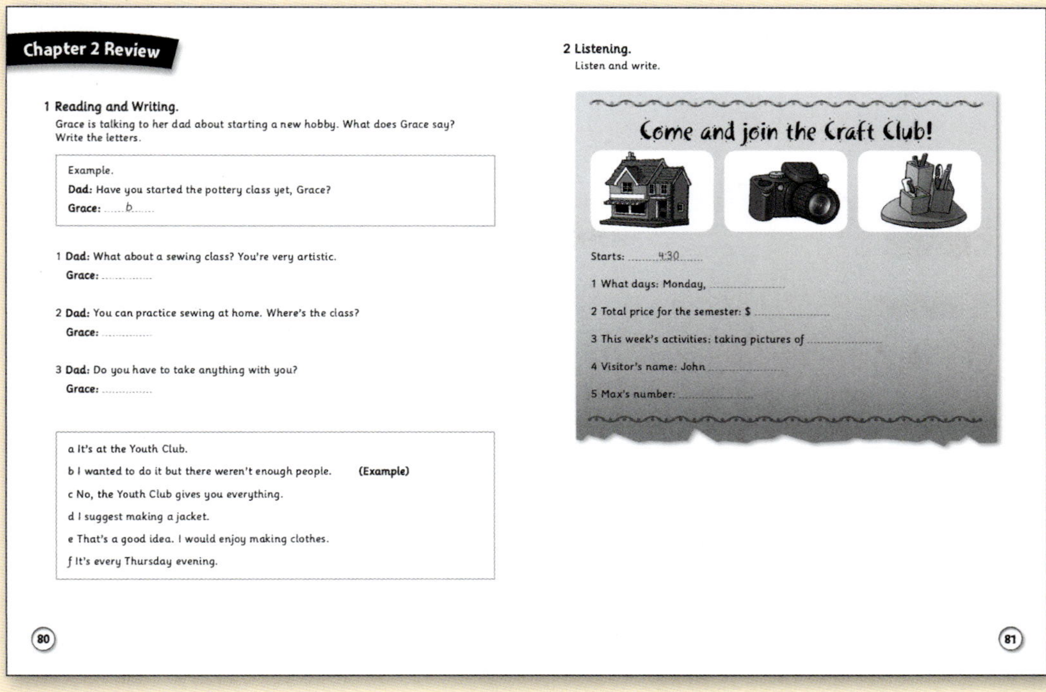

Chapter 2 Review

1 Reading and Writing.
Grace is talking to her dad about starting a new hobby. What does Grace say? Write the letters.

Example.
Dad: Have you started the pottery class yet, Grace?
Grace: ...... b ......

1 **Dad:** What about a sewing class? You're very artistic.
Grace: ....

2 **Dad:** You can practice sewing at home. Where's the class?
Grace: ....

3 **Dad:** Do you have to take anything with you?
Grace: ....

a It's at the Youth Club.
b I wanted to do it but there weren't enough people. **(Example)**
c No, the Youth Club gives you everything.
d I suggest making a jacket.
e That's a good idea. I would enjoy making clothes.
f It's every Thursday evening.

80

2 Listening.
Listen and write.

Come and join the Craft Club!

Starts: .... 4:30 ....
1 What days: Monday, ...
2 Total price for the semester: $ ....
3 This week's activities: taking pictures of ....
4 Visitor's name: John ....
5 Max's number: ....

81

1 Reading and Writing. Grace is talking to her dad about starting a new hobby. What does Grace say? Write the letters.

The children read the questions and write the letter for the appropriate response each time. Check answers.

Answers

1 e **2** a **3** c

2 2.32 Listening. Listen and write.

The children read the notice. Play the CD twice. They listen and write a single-word answer for each prompt. Check answers.

Answers (Audioscript on p. 223)

1 Thursday **2** 14 **3** wildlife **4** BAILEY **5** 786 394 7742

Competency Focus

Me: Self-evaluation

The children reflect on the chapter, express their personal opinions about their own progress, and look for ways to improve. This encourages them to evaluate and make decisions about what they need to revisit and how they can learn better.

Cooler: Class quiz

Ask the children some questions about things they learned in Chapter 2, e.g. *Where did yarn bombing begin?* (*Houston*) *Why did Icarus fly too high?* (*He wanted to fly as high as the birds.*) Then divide the class into pairs and have them write five more questions about the stories, facts, or pictures in the chapter. Elicit questions and answers.

Presentation Kit • Display the SB page. Choose *Image* in the Navigation Pane to give feedback on Treasure Hunt. Elicit where *Icarus* is set and ask children to use *Pen* to find and circle something from that country.

Teacher's Resource Center • Print out Test Chapter 2 to use at the end of this lesson. The Test Generator also allows you to create customized tests.

• Print out Festival Worksheet: Halloween to expand the children's knowledge of celebrations throughout the world.

Chapter 3

Everything is Connected

Overview

The children will:

- use critical thinking skills to identify climate change vocabulary.
- talk about lifestyle and the environment using the 1st conditional.
- read and understand an African folktale.
- ask and answer questions using the 1st conditional.
- describe transportation processes.
- find out about the effects of plastic on the environment.
- write an Earth Day leaflet.

Key Vocabulary

Climate change: causing, climate change, energy, fuel, harming, lifestyle, population, save, wasting
Ocean transportation: broke down, cargo ship, chemicals, containers, currents, factory, port, storm

Key Grammar

1st conditional

- If you recycle paper, you will save trees.
- If you take a shower, you won't waste water.

1st conditional questions

- What will happen if we use less fuel?
- If the ice melts, how will the sea change?

Reading Skills

Story: *The Frog Hunt*
Genre: African folktale

Literacy Development

- use reading skills to understand and predict content
- relate story theme to personal experience
- use persuasive language

Functional Language

- Will you help me do my math homework?
- I'll help you with your math if you help me with my art.
- OK! It's a deal!

Spelling

Words with a *k* sound (*c*, *k*, *ck*, *ch*)

CLIL: Science—Effects of plastic

The children find out about the effects of plastic on the environment.

Competency Focus

The children will:

use critical thinking skills to deduce the meaning of new vocabulary. (Lesson 1)	activate new vocabulary and apply new grammar knowledge. (Lesson 2)	work in pairs to act out a dialogue. (Lesson 3)	relate the story and story theme to their personal experience. (Lesson 4)	develop an understanding of resources by carrying out research. (Lesson 7)
predict the content of a story. (Lesson 3)	apply new grammar rules in a familiar context. (Lesson 5)	work in pairs to retell the story. (Lesson 6)	invent and write their own Earth Day leaflet. (Lesson 8)	
			evaluate their own progress in the chapter. (Review)	

Digital Overview

Presentation Kit

Projectable Student Book, Activity Book, and Reader pages

- Vocabulary Tool 3A: Climate change and the environment
- Vocabulary Tool 3B: Ocean transportation
- Oral Storytelling Video 3: *The Girl Who Loved Trees*
- Interactive versions of selected SB and AB activities
- Integrated *Audio* and *Answer Key* for all activities

Teacher's Resource Center

Resources for planning, lesson delivery, and homework

- Class Planner Chapter 3
- Worksheets to print out (including notes and answers):
  - Grammar Worksheet 3A: 1st conditional
  - Grammar Worksheet 3B: 1st conditional questions
  - Oral Storytelling Video Worksheet 3: *The Girl Who Loved Trees*
  - CLIL Graphic Organizer 3
  - Writing Template 3
  - Festival Worksheet: New Year's Eve
  - Test Chapter 3
- Test Generator
- Speaking Assessment: CEYLT
- Literacy Handbook

Student's Resource Center

Resources for consolidation and practice at home

- Interactive Grammar 3A: 1st conditional
- Interactive Grammar 3B: 1st conditional questions
- Vocabulary Tool 3A: Climate change and the environment
- Vocabulary Tool 3B: Ocean transportation
- Oral Storytelling Video 3: *The Girl Who Loved Trees*

Student's App

Vocabulary games: Climate change/the environment and ocean transportation

Watch the Oral Storytelling Video

Everything is Connected

Lesson 1

Vocabulary

Lesson objectives: identify and use vocabulary for climate change and the environment

Key vocabulary: *causing, climate change, energy, fuel, harming, lifestyle, population, save, wasting*

Materials: Class CD

Chapter 3 Everything is Connected Lesson 1

1 Listen and number the pictures in the order you hear them.

Climate Change

recycling

pollution 1

trash

water

endangered animals

energy

2 Listen again and write the words next to the clues.

~~population~~ lifestyle climate change fuel harming wasting causing energy save

1 The people living on the planet. ..population..
2 The way we live. ....
3 We're seeing more extreme weather. ....
4 It's .... an increase in temperature.
5 It's used to run cars and to make electricity. ....
6 Damaging people, animals, and places. ....
7 Using energy when we don't need it. ....
8 Heat and light are types of ....
9 To try to use less. ....

Chapter 3 28

Warmer: What's trash?

Have the children work in groups of three to write a list of everything they put in the trash yesterday. Write *recycle* and *can't recycle* on the board. Elicit items and ask *Can you recycle that?* Children write them on the board in the appropriate category.

1 1.19 Listen and number the pictures in the order you hear them.

- The children look at the pictures and read the words.
- Play the CD. The children listen and number the pictures in the order they hear them.
- Elicit answers.

Audioscript

There are more and more people living on the planet than ever before. The population is getting bigger every day. The way we live today is affecting the earth. Our modern lifestyle is making things change. Climate change is a big problem and we're seeing more extreme weather. Climate change is making the planet become warmer. It's causing an increase in temperature and causing things like very heavy rain and storms. We need fuel to run cars and to make electricity, but we're creating too much pollution. We need food and clothes, but we're throwing away too much trash. Climate change is harming people, animals, and places. Some animals are now endangered. We're damaging the earth. But we can do something to help. We can all make small changes to the way we live. We need to stop wasting energy, like heat and light, so we should stop using energy when we don't need it. We need to save water—try to use less. We need to recycle more: use our plastic, metal, paper, and clothes again. We can save our planet!

Answers

recycling 6, pollution 1, trash 2, water 5, endangered animals 3, energy 4

2 1.19 Listen again and write the words next to the clues.

- Play the CD again. The children listen and write the environmental word described in each clue, using the words supplied.
- Elicit answers.

Answers

1 population **2** lifestyle **3** climate change **4** causing **5** fuel **6** harming **7** wasting **8** energy **9** save

Optional activity: Definitions

Give the children a model definition e.g. *The way we live.* to elicit *lifestyle*. The children continue the game—one child with their Student Book open giving definitions, and the other with their book closed guessing the word.

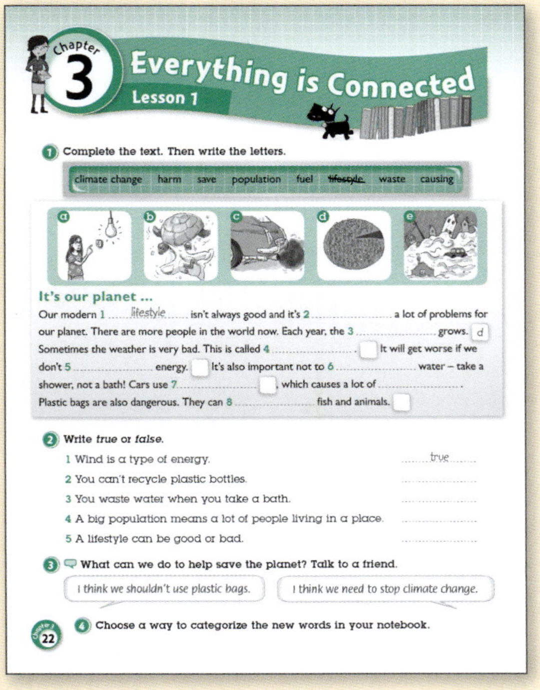

Chapter 3 Everything is Connected
Lesson 1

1 Complete the text. Then write the letters.

climate change harm save population fuel ~~lifestyle~~ waste causing

a b c d e

It's our planet ...

Our modern 1 ......lifestyle...... isn't always good and it's 2 .... a lot of problems for our planet. There are more people in the world now. Each year, the 3 .... grows. [d] Sometimes the weather is very bad. This is called 4 .... [ ] It will get worse if we don't 5 .... energy. [ ] It's also important not to 6 .... water – take a shower, not a bath! Cars use 7 .... [ ], which causes a lot of .... Plastic bags are also dangerous. They can 8 .... fish and animals. [ ]

2 Write *true* or *false*.

1 Wind is a type of energy. ......true......
2 You can't recycle plastic bottles. ....
3 You waste water when you take a bath. ....
4 A big population means a lot of people living in a place. ....
5 A lifestyle can be good or bad. ....

3 What can we do to help save the planet? Talk to a friend.

I think we shouldn't use plastic bags.
I think we need to stop climate change.

4 Choose a way to categorize the new words in your notebook.

Chapter 3 22

1 Complete the text. Then write the letters.

The children complete the website with the words supplied. Then they match the pictures to the descriptions, writing the letters in the boxes. Elicit answers.

Answers

1 lifestyle **2** causing **3** population d **4** climate change e **5** save a **6** waste **7** fuel (pollution) c **8** harm b

2 Write *true* or *false*.

The children label each sentence true or false. Elicit answers.

Answers

1 true **2** false **3** true **4** true **5** true

3 What can we do to help save the planet? Talk to a friend.

Elicit a few suggestions. The children then continue the discussion in pairs. Elicit ideas.

4 Choose a way to categorize the new words in your notebook.

Brainstorm appropriate categories, e.g. *positive/negative/positive and negative, things you can change/can't change*. The children choose the best categories for them and list the words in their notebook.

Answers

Children's own answers.

Cooler: Which one doesn't belong?

Write sets of words on the board, e.g. 1 *save, harming, wasting* 2 *energy, fuel, lifestyle*. Have children choose the word in each group which is different and explain why. Elicit answers.

Competency Focus

Think! Critical Thinking

The children use critical thinking skills to understand the new vocabulary by using visual clues and processing the written and spoken forms.

Presentation Kit • Use Vocabulary Tool 3A to pre-teach key vocabulary as an alternative to the critical thinking approach. Use *Slideshow* to introduce the words. Then use *Distort* to review/test vocabulary in a fun recognition game.

- TIP The interactive activities in the SB and AB can be done again and again, giving different children the chance to participate. Choose *Reset* within *Answer Key* to clear the answers.
- TIP Use *Eraser* to undo any highlighting or writing on the screen if you want to repeat a task.

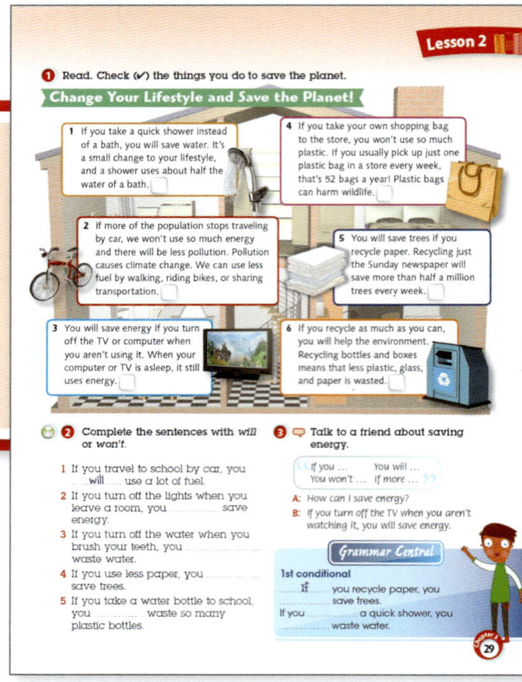
Lesson 2

1 Read. Check (✓) the things you do to save the planet.

Change Your Lifestyle and Save the Planet!

1 If you take a quick shower instead of a bath, you will save water. It's a small change to your lifestyle, and a shower uses about half the water of a bath. ☐

2 If more of the population stops traveling by car, we won't use so much energy and there will be less pollution. Pollution causes climate change. We can use less fuel by walking, riding bikes, or sharing transportation. ☐

3 You will save energy if you turn off the TV or computer when you aren't using it. When your computer or TV is asleep, it still uses energy. ☐

4 If you take your own shopping bag to the store, you won't use so much plastic. If you usually pick up just one plastic bag in a store every week, that's 52 bags a year! Plastic bags can harm wildlife. ☐

5 You will save trees if you recycle paper. Recycling just the Sunday newspaper will save more than half a million trees every week. ☐

6 If you recycle as much as you can, you will help the environment. Recycling bottles and boxes means that less plastic, glass, and paper is wasted. ☐

2 Complete the sentences with *will* or *won't*.

1 If you travel to school by car, you ..will.. use a lot of fuel.
2 If you turn off the lights when you leave a room, you .... save energy.
3 If you turn off the water when you brush your teeth, you .... waste water.
4 If you use less paper, you .... save trees.
5 If you take a water bottle to school, you .... waste so many plastic bottles.

3 Talk to a friend about saving energy.

If you ... You will ... You won't ... If more ...

A: *How can I save energy?*
B: *If you turn off the TV when you aren't watching it, you will save energy.*

Grammar Central

1st conditional
..If.. you recycle paper, you .... save trees.
If you .... a quick shower, you .... waste water.

Chapter 3 29

Grammar

Lesson objective: talk about lifestyle and the environment using the 1st conditional

Key grammar: 1st conditional

Secondary language: *instead of, harm, wildlife*

Materials: Grammar Worksheet 3A [TRC printout] (optional); pieces of paper with sentence words (Cooler)

Warmer: Scrambled words

Write scrambled versions of the key vocabulary items from Lesson 1 on the board. As soon as a child has an answer, invite them to come to the board and write the word next to the scrambled version.

1 Read. Check (✓) the things you do to save the planet.

- Have the children look quickly at the text and the pictures. Ask *Where do you think this text comes from?* (*a magazine/website*)
- Have the children read the first paragraph of the text. Ask *Do you usually take a shower or a bath?* If they answer *shower*, point out they can check the box.
- Have the children continue. Then ask for a show of hands for each paragraph by those children who checked the box. Ask the children to keep a count to identify which is the most popular item.

Answers

Children's own answers.

2 Complete the sentences with *will* or *won't*.

- Ask the children to identify which part of the text gives the information to complete the example sentence. (*paragraph 2*) Point out that the sentence wording is not exactly the same in the text, so they need to read and understand to complete the sentence.
- Have the children complete the sentences individually and then compare with a friend.
- Elicit answers.

Answers

1 will **2** will **3** won't **4** will **5** won't

Grammar Central

1st conditional

Have the children complete the grammar examples. Elicit answers. Then elicit the rules for using the 1st conditional. (If + *present tense verb to introduce the situation, followed by a verb in the future* (will/won't) *to state the result of these actions.*) The children write more examples in their notebook. See also the Grammar Reference sections in the Student Book (p. 99) and Activity Book (p. 98) for further explanation and practice.

Grammar Central Answers: If, will, take, won't

AB Answers Activity 1: 1 will get/'ll get **2** If, won't be **3** goes **4** If, will tell/'ll tell **5** If, won't waste **6** wants

3 Talk to a friend about saving energy.

- Choose two children to read the example dialogue.
- Divide the class into pairs. The children practice dialogues using the prompts supplied.
- Have pairs perform a dialogue for the class.

Optional activity: 1st conditional sentences

Make 1st conditional sentences around the class. Start off with *If I take a shower not a bath, …* The first child completes the sentence, e.g. *… I will save water*. Continue, with children taking turns starting and completing a sentence.

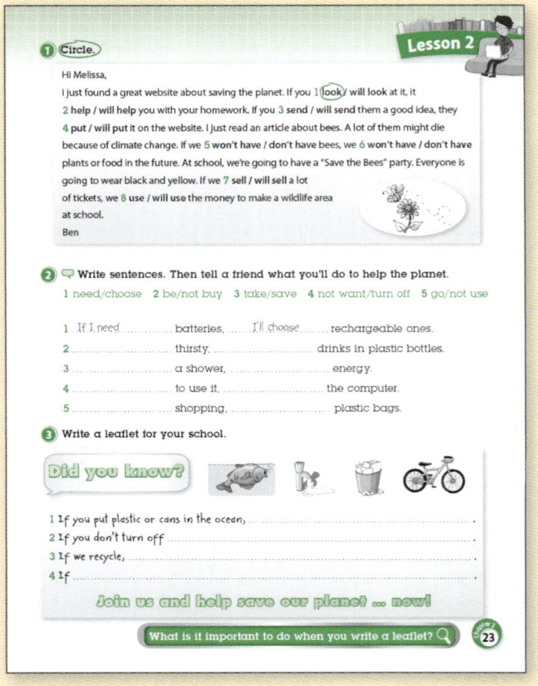

Lesson 2

1 Circle.

Hi Melissa,

I just found a great website about saving the planet. If you 1 look / will look at it, it 2 help / will help you with your homework. If you 3 send / will send them a good idea, they 4 put / will put it on the website. I just read an article about bees. A lot of them might die because of climate change. If we 5 won't have / don't have bees, we 6 won't have / don't have plants or food in the future. At school, we're going to have a "Save the Bees" party. Everyone is going to wear black and yellow. If we 7 sell / will sell a lot of tickets, we 8 use / will use the money to make a wildlife area at school.

Ben

2 Write sentences. Then tell a friend what you'll do to help the planet.

1 need/choose 2 be/not buy 3 take/save 4 not want/turn off 5 go/not use

1 If I need ………… batteries, …I'll choose… rechargeable ones.
2 ………… thirsty, ………… drinks in plastic bottles.
3 ………… a shower, ………… energy.
4 ………… to use it, ………… the computer.
5 ………… shopping, ………… plastic bags.

3 Write a leaflet for your school.

Did you know?

1 If you put plastic or cans in the ocean, …………
2 If you don't turn off …………
3 If we recycle, …………
4 If …………

Join us and help save our planet … now!

What is it important to do when you write a leaflet?

Chapter 3 23

1 Circle.

The children complete the text by circling the correct option from the two given each time. Elicit answers.

Answers

1 look **2** will help **3** send **4** will put **5** don't have **6** won't have **7** sell **8** will use

2 Write sentences. Then tell a friend what you'll do to help the planet.

The children complete the sentences using the words supplied. They then discuss with a friend what they will do to help the planet.

Answers

1 If I need, I'll choose **2** If I'm, I won't buy **3** If I take, I'll save **4** If I don't want, I'll turn off **5** If I go, I won't use

3 Write a leaflet for your school.

The children complete the leaflet using the picture prompts supplied. Then they compare with a friend. Elicit answers. Ask *What is it important to do when you write a leaflet?* (*make sure the text is simple but informative and interesting, the facts are correct, and that it looks attractive*)

Answers

Children's own answers.

Cooler: Scrambled sentences

Write each word of the following sentence on a separate piece of paper (big enough to be read by the class): *If you recycle as much as you can, you will help the environment.* Choose 13 children and give each child a piece of paper in random order. Have the children stand and face the class. The class then put the children in the correct order to make the correct sentence. Repeat with other sentences and different children.

Competency Focus

Learn

The children integrate previously acquired vocabulary into new grammar and structure and adapt the language to show an understanding of the topic.

Presentation Kit • Use *Notepad* for the Warmer activity, asking different children to write the word correctly each time.

• TIP You can move the *Answer Key* pop-up window around the screen to have the activity and the answers side by side. Hold the cursor over the colored band at the top of the window.

Teacher's Resource Center • For extra grammar practice, print out Grammar Worksheet 3A.

Student's Resource Center • The children can use Interactive Grammar 3A at home.

Reading: Story Extract

Lesson objectives: ask for help and agree on a deal; use the title and pictures to predict story content; read the extract from the African folktale *The Frog Hunt* (middle)
Functional language: *Will you help me … ? I'll help you with … if you help me with … OK! It's a deal!*
Secondary language: *croaking, destroy, connected*
Materials: Class CD; pieces of paper with half-sentences (Warmer)

Warmer: Make sentences

Stick half-sentences on the board in random order, each one on a piece of paper, e.g. *If we play a game … / If we study a lot … / … we'll learn a lot. / … we'll have some fun.*, etc. Have the children work in pairs to see how many different complete sentences they can make orally in one minute. Elicit suggestions.

Functional language

1 1.20 Listen and read.

- Play the CD. The children listen and read along. Ask *What do Angelo and Yasmin need help with?* (*math, art*)
- Play the CD again, pausing for them to repeat.
- Divide the class into pairs to practice the dialogue.

2 Talk to a friend. Take turns asking for help and making a deal.

- Choose two children to read the example dialogue. Elicit other examples using the prompts supplied.
- The children practice in pairs.
- Have pairs perform a dialogue for the class.

Before reading

3 Look at the story. What do you think the problem is?

- Have the children study the story title and pictures to figure out what the problem is. Elicit ideas.

4 1.21 Read the story extract and answer.

- Play the CD. The children listen and read along. Have them answer question 1. Elicit the answer.
- Play the CD again so they can write their ideas for questions 2 and 3. Encourage them to use reading skills (e.g. using the title, pictures, and context) to infer meaning and make predictions.

- Elicit answers, but do not confirm predictions: explain that they will have to read the story to find out.

Answers

1 Because they are noisy and he can't sleep. **2** Children's own answers. **3** Yes (it's a traditional tale). / Children's own answers.

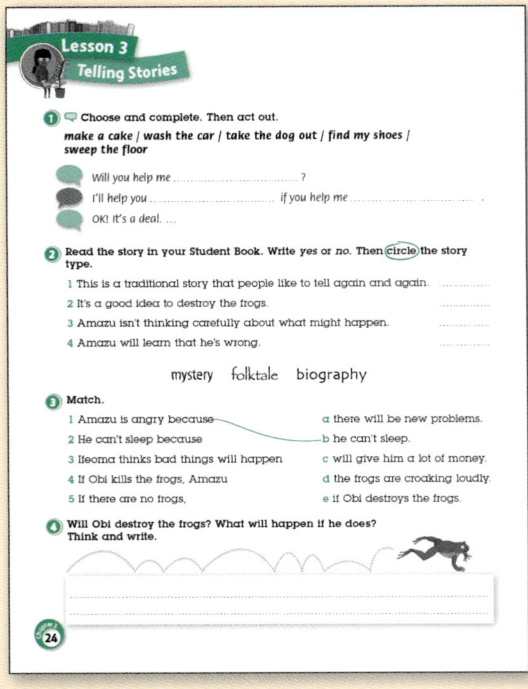

Lesson 3
Telling Stories

1 Choose and complete. Then act out.

make a cake / wash the car / take the dog out / find my shoes / sweep the floor

Will you help me ......?
I'll help you ...... if you help me ......
OK! It's a deal. ...

2 Read the story in your Student Book. Write *yes* or *no*. Then circle the story type.

1 This is a traditional story that people like to tell again and again. ......
2 It's a good idea to destroy the frogs. ......
3 Amazu isn't thinking carefully about what might happen. ......
4 Amazu will learn that he's wrong. ......

mystery folktale biography

3 Match.

1 Amazu is angry because — a there will be new problems.
2 He can't sleep because — b he can't sleep.
3 Ifeoma thinks bad things will happen — c will give him a lot of money.
4 If Obi kills the frogs, Amazu — d the frogs are croaking loudly.
5 If there are no frogs, — e if Obi destroys the frogs.

4 Will Obi destroy the frogs? What will happen if he does? Think and write.

Chapter 3 24

1 Choose and complete. Then act out.

The children choose one of the sentences supplied and complete the dialogue. They then act it out in pairs. Encourage the children to use what they know to adapt and extend the dialogue. Have pairs act out their dialogue for the class.

2 Read the story in your Student Book. Write *yes* or *no*. Then circle the story type.

The children read the Student Book story extract again, then write *yes* or *no* for each sentence. Then they circle the correct story type. Elicit answers.

Answers

1 yes **2** no **3** yes **4** yes
Circled: folktale

3 Match.

The children match the sentence halves. Elicit answers.

Answers

1 b **2** d **3** e **4** c **5** a

4 Will Obi destroy the frogs? What will happen if he does? Think and write.

Elicit suggestions on whether Obi will destroy the frogs and what will happen if he does. The children write their own ideas, then compare with a friend. Elicit ideas.

Answers

Children's own answers.

Cooler: Stand up!

1.21

Play the story extract again. Divide the class into three groups. Have the children listen to and follow the story in their books. Instruct one group to stand up and sit down every time they hear the word *frogs*, one group to do the same for *if*, and the other group to do the same for *will*. This encourages children to pay close attention to the story and its syntax, and also have some fun!

Competency Focus

Collaborate and Communicate

The children work together to practice, perform, and adapt the new functional language learned.

Think

The children use critical thinking skills to identify the context of the story by looking at the text and story artwork.

Presentation Kit • Do not be afraid to turn off the screen! Children benefit from variety and sometimes you will want to work just with books or without prompts. Work the Presentation Kit materials into your teaching in the way that suits you best.

- TIP *Hotspots* shows which activities are interactive—here, AB Activity 3.
- Have the children close their books. Then, use *Mask* to slowly reveal the SB story extract. Encourage the children to use the pictures to figure out the context of the story.

THE FROG HUNT

1
"Welcome home to Africa, young master. I'm sorry about your father. He was a good and wise chief. We all respected him."

"Thanks, Obi," replied Amazu quietly.

2
"Oh, Master Amazu, look at you!" Ifeoma hurried into the room. She used to take care of Amazu when he was a young boy. "You've been away at college for so long."

3
"Bring some juice. Master Amazu is tired." Ifeoma sat down next to Amazu. "Our lifestyle is simple here; I imagine it's different in the USA."

"Yes, very different," Amazu replied. "But I missed everyone."

"Call if you need anything," said Obi, leaving the room.

"You're the Chief now, Amazu," Ifeoma whispered. "And I know you'll be a good one."

4
Amazu lay awake. The frogs were croaking loudly around the lake.

"If they don't stop making that noise, I won't get *any* sleep," he thought.

5
The next morning, he called for Obi. "I'm so tired, Obi. Please destroy the frogs. I can't sleep with that noise."

"They're just frogs, Master. They always croak at night," said Obi.

"Eh-eh! Don't do that," interrupted Ifeoma. "If you harm the frogs, bad things will happen to the village."

"That's silly! In my opinion, nothing bad will happen," laughed Amazu.

"But what will happen if we kill all the frogs?" she asked. "I believe that everything is connected. It will start causing new problems."

"Well, if there aren't any frogs, *I'll* be able to sleep!" he answered. "If you destroy the frogs, Obi, I'll pay you well."

6
So Obi asked the villagers to help destroy the frogs. "But if we destroy the frogs, the snakes that eat them will be hungry," said a man. "What's more, there will be more insects."

7
After a few quiet nights, Amazu was woken by a buzzing noise.

"What's that? Mosquitoes!"

8
The next morning, Amazu was tired and itchy.

"Look at me! If those mosquitoes don't stop biting me, I'll be covered in spots," he said, scratching.

"Pull the net around your bed. If you burn some candles in your room, they will stay away," said Obi helpfully. "We don't use chemicals for killing insects here. They break down into the water and harm the fish. We have to try and save water."

"Remember, everything is connected," said Ifeoma. "There are too many mosquitoes because there aren't enough frogs to eat them."

"Obi, destroy all the mosquitoes!" Amazu shouted angrily.

"It's impossible to kill them all! What a waste of time," said the villagers.

9
As time passed, people became sick after they were bitten by mosquitoes. Dangerous snakes came to the village looking for food. Some people decided to pack up their houses and leave. Soon, the population of the village became very small. Everyone was talking about the foolish new chief who didn't understand anything.

10
Then one day, Ifeoma said, "I don't feel well, Amazu. I have a fever and a headache. I can't stay here."

Amazu looked around him. "I'm so sorry, Ifeoma. I should have listened. Now I understand how everything is connected. We must all leave."

Amazu helped Ifeoma and Obi carry their belongings. As they left, everything was quiet in the village except for the buzzing of mosquitoes.

Lesson objective: read and understand the African folktale *The Frog Hunt* in the Reader
Materials: Class CD; Reader; Oral Storytelling Video Worksheet 3 [TRC printout] (optional)

Warmer: Story extract summary

Summarize the story extract, pausing to elicit key details, e.g. *Amazu couldn't sleep because …* (*the frogs were croaking loudly*).

Story Summary

Amazu returns to his African village after his father, the chief, dies. Ignoring the advice "everything is connected," he orders his people to destroy the croaking frogs. With no frogs to eat, the natural order is unbalanced. With too many mosquitoes, dangerous snakes arrive and people start to get sick and leave.

Theme: the importance of the environment and its diversity

1.22 While reading

- Have the children look at the pictures in the Reader. Ask *How did Ifeoma feel when Amazu came home?* (*She was very happy.*)
- Play the CD. The children listen and read along. Ask *What did Amazu realize?* (*how everything is connected*) *What made him realize this?* (*Ifeoma became sick.*)
- Ask questions to check comprehension, e.g. *Why was Amazu angry?* (*because of the noisy frogs and the biting mosquitoes*) *Why are chemicals not a good idea?* (*They break down in the water and harm the fish.*)
- Allocate the beginning, middle, and end to different groups. Choose three groups to read the story aloud and have the rest of the class react emotionally (see **Story Time**).

After reading: Reflect

- Ask questions to give the children the opportunity to think about the issues raised by the story, e.g. *Why do you think Amazu didn't listen to the others? Can you think of a way to give the story a happy ending?*

Optional activity: Who said it?

Read out some phrases of the dialogue said by different people in the story. Have the children call out who they think said it: Amazu, Ifeoma, Obi, or the villagers. The children then continue in pairs.

Story Time

Reacting to the story

This story has many features that provoke a reaction in the listener or reader. When you play the CD, have the children react to what they hear: *Boo!* for a bad idea, applause for a sensible idea, *Aaahhh* for a sad moment. These emotional reactions help fix the story better in the children's minds.

Reading Strategy

Concept Map

A concept map works in a similar way to a story map, but focuses on the underlying message of the story rather than the structure. It helps the children organize the information and apply critical literacy skills to identify the story's purpose.

For additional explanation and activities, see the Literacy Handbook on the Teacher's Resource Center.

Cooler: Play "Ready, Set, Draw!"

Play the game with key events in the story (see Games Bank p. 222).

Presentation Kit • Use *Hotspots* to read Reader pp. 12–13. Then *Mask* p. 14. Elicit what will happen if they destroy the frogs. Slowly reveal Picture 7 to confirm.

- Oral Storytelling Video 3 contains a different story on a related theme (*The Girl Who Loved Trees*). Watch and discuss it at the end of the lesson.

Teacher's Resource Center • Print out Oral Storytelling Video Worksheet 3 to use with the video.

Student's Resource Center • The children can watch Oral Storytelling Video 3 at home.

Reading Comprehension and Critical Literacy

Lesson objectives: understand and evaluate the story; relate story theme to personal experience; focus on phrases used to persuade people
Materials: Class CD; Reader; Oral Storytelling Video Worksheet 3 [TRC printout] (optional)

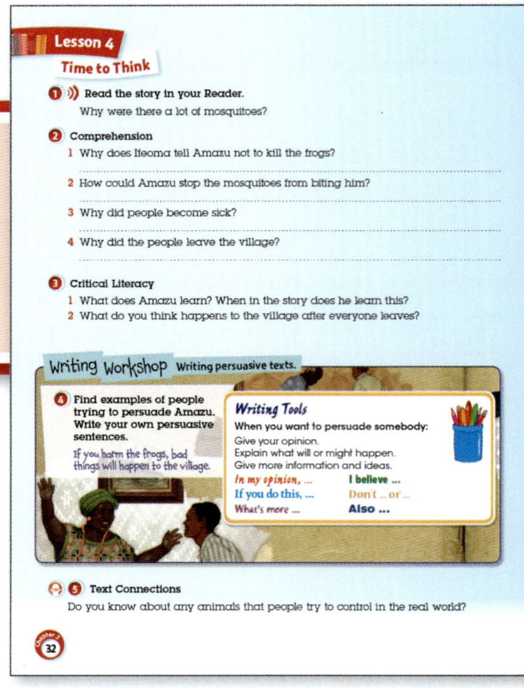
Lesson 4
Time to Think

1 Read the story in your Reader.
Why were there a lot of mosquitoes?

2 Comprehension
1 Why does Ifeoma tell Amazu not to kill the frogs?
2 How could Amazu stop the mosquitoes from biting him?
3 Why did people become sick?
4 Why did the people leave the village?

3 Critical Literacy
1 What does Amazu learn? When in the story does he learn this?
2 What do you think happens to the village after everyone leaves?

Writing Workshop Writing persuasive texts.

4 Find examples of people trying to persuade Amazu. Write your own persuasive sentences.
If you harm the frogs, bad things will happen to the village.

Writing Tools
When you want to persuade somebody:
Give your opinion.
Explain what will or might happen.
Give more information and ideas.
In my opinion, ... I believe ...
If you do this, ... Don't ... or ...
What's more ... Also ...

5 Text Connections
Do you know about any animals that people try to control in the real world?

32

Note: Please ensure that your class has read the Reader story before you do this lesson.

Warmer: True or False?

Make statements to elicit true or false, e.g. *Amazu really likes the sound of the frogs croaking.* (*false*) Elicit correct versions of the false statements, e.g. *Amazu doesn't like the sound of the frogs because it keeps him awake.* Invite children to make up their own statements.

1 1.22 Read the story in your Reader.

- Have the children read the story. (Alternatively, play the CD and have them read along.)
- Elicit whether the children were correct in their predictions in Lesson 3 Activity 4. Ask *Why were there a lot of mosquitoes?* (*because frogs eat mosquitoes and there weren't enough frogs to eat them*)

2 Comprehension

- The children write answers to the first three questions. Elicit answers.
- Discuss question 4. Ask the children to justify their answers.

Answers

1 Because bad things will happen. / Because it will start causing new problems. **2** He could pull the net around his bed and burn candles in his room. **3** Because they were bitten by mosquitoes. / Because the mosquitoes bit them. **4** Because they wanted to get away from the mosquitoes.

3 Critical Literacy

- The children discuss answers with a friend. Elicit ideas and have a class discussion. Encourage children to consider the reasoning behind the characters' actions and if they agree with their behavior. Tackling broader issues like this helps children engage constructively with the story.

Answers

1 He learns that everything is connected. He learns it at the end of the story when they leave the village.
2 Children's own answers.

Writing Workshop

Writing persuasive texts

4 Find examples of people trying to persuade Amazu. Write your own persuasive sentences.

Have a child read the example. Have them find examples in the story. Elicit other sentences, using phrases from the **Writing Tools** box. The children write persuasive sentences in their notebook, then compare with a friend. Elicit responses.

Answers

If you harm the frogs, bad things will happen to the village. If we kill the frogs, it will start causing new problems. If we destroy the frogs, the snakes that eat them will be hungry/there will be more insects. Children's own answers.

5 Text Connections

- Ask *What animals do people try to control in the real world?* Elicit ideas and discuss as a class.

Optional activity: Persuade your parents

Ask the children to think of something they would really like to do, but their parents do not allow (e.g. staying up late). Have the children write sentences persuading their parents using the guidelines in the **Writing Tools** box. Elicit answers.

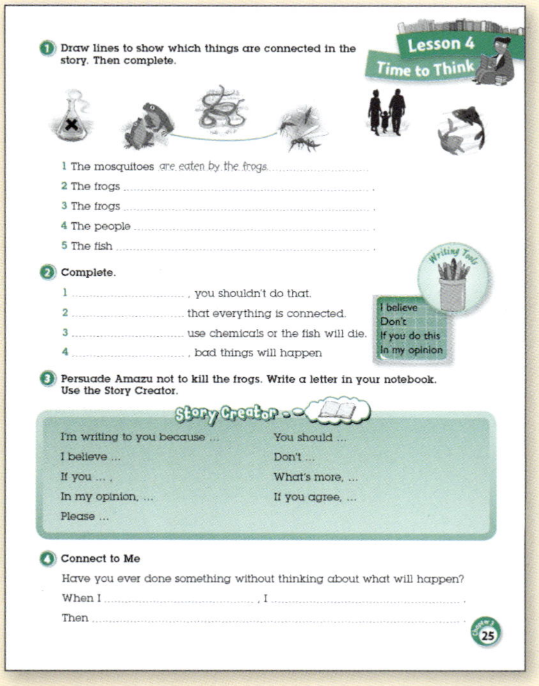

Lesson 4
Time to Think

1 Draw lines to show which things are connected in the story. Then complete.

1 The mosquitoes *are eaten by the frogs*
2 The frogs ....
3 The frogs ....
4 The people ....
5 The fish ....

2 Complete.

1 ...., you shouldn't do that.
2 .... that everything is connected.
3 .... use chemicals or the fish will die.
4 ...., bad things will happen

Writing Tools
I believe
Don't
If you do this
In my opinion

3 Persuade Amazu not to kill the frogs. Write a letter in your notebook. Use the Story Creator.

Story Creator

I'm writing to you because ...	You should ...
I believe ...	Don't ...
If you ... ,	What's more, ...
In my opinion, ...	If you agree, ...
Please ...	

4 Connect to Me

Have you ever done something without thinking about what will happen?
When I ...., I ....
Then ....

Chapter 3 25

1 Draw lines to show which things are connected in the story. Then complete.

The children match the pictures of objects which are connected in the story, then complete the sentences about them. Elicit answers.

Answers

Lines drawn between: people + frogs/mosquitoes; frogs + snakes/mosquitoes; mosquitoes + chemicals; fish + chemicals

1 The mosquitoes are eaten by the frogs. **2** The frogs are killed by the people. **3** The frogs are eaten by the snakes. **4** The people are bitten by the mosquitoes. **5** The fish are destroyed by the chemicals.

2 Complete.

The children complete the sentences using the phrases supplied. Elicit answers.

Answers

1 In my opinion **2** I believe **3** Don't **4** If you do this

3 Persuade Amazu not to kill the frogs. Write a letter in your notebook. Use the Story Creator.

Use the **Story Creator** prompts to elicit ideas. The children write a letter in their notebook persuading Amazu not to kill the frogs, then compare with a friend. Have children read out their texts for the class.

4 Connect to Me

Elicit examples of a time the children have done something without thinking about what will happen. (e.g. *buying something that is too expensive, then not having enough money to buy other things*) The children write their own response, then compare with a friend. Elicit responses.

Cooler: Persuade the teacher

Tell the children you are not sure if you are going to give them homework or not today. Have them work in pairs to think of reasons not to have homework. Encourage them to use the phrases in the **Writing Tools** box. Elicit suggestions. Then decide if they persuaded you! (Do this on a day when you were not going to give homework anyway!)

Competency Focus

Me: Critical Literacy

The children use critical literacy skills to reflect on the story and the characters and how this story relates to other true stories.

Presentation Kit • For SB Activity 4, have children use *Highlighter* to identify persuasive sentences with *If* in the Reader story.

- TIP Give children the opportunity to be your assistant! Ask a child to be responsible for choosing the relevant buttons (e.g. to go to the next activity or *Answer Key*).
- If you haven't already, show Oral Storytelling Video 3 (a different story on a related theme).

Teacher's Resource Center • If you haven't already, print out Oral Storytelling Video Worksheet 3 to do the support activities.

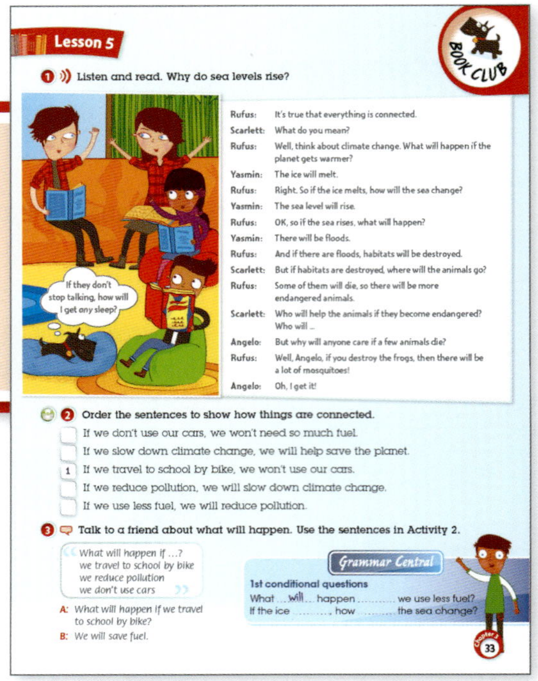
Lesson 5

BOOK CLUB

1 Listen and read. Why do sea levels rise?

Rufus: It's true that everything is connected.
Scarlett: What do you mean?
Rufus: Well, think about climate change. What will happen if the planet gets warmer?
Yasmin: The ice will melt.
Rufus: Right. So if the ice melts, how will the sea change?
Yasmin: The sea level will rise.
Rufus: OK, so if the sea rises, what will happen?
Yasmin: There will be floods.
Rufus: And if there are floods, habitats will be destroyed.
Scarlett: But if habitats are destroyed, where will the animals go?
Rufus: Some of them will die, so there will be more endangered animals.
Scarlett: Who will help the animals if they become endangered? Who will ...
Angelo: But why will anyone care if a few animals die?
Rufus: Well, Angelo, if you destroy the frogs, then there will be a lot of mosquitoes!
Angelo: Oh, I get it!

2 Order the sentences to show how things are connected.
- [ ] If we don't use our cars, we won't need so much fuel.
- [ ] If we slow down climate change, we will help save the planet.
- [1] If we travel to school by bike, we won't use our cars.
- [ ] If we reduce pollution, we will slow down climate change.
- [ ] If we use less fuel, we will reduce pollution.

3 Talk to a friend about what will happen. Use the sentences in Activity 2.

What will happen if ...?
we travel to school by bike
we reduce pollution
we don't use cars

A: What will happen if we travel to school by bike?
B: We will save fuel.

Grammar Central
1st conditional questions
What ...will... happen .... we use less fuel?
If the ice ...., how .... the sea change?

Chapter 3 33

Grammar and Reading

Lesson objectives: ask and answer questions using the 1st conditional
Key grammar: 1st conditional questions
Secondary language: *rise, habitat, endangered*
Materials: Class CD; Grammar Worksheet 3B [TRC printout] (optional)

Warmer: Condition or result?

Write on the board *If we take care of our planet, our lives will be better.* Ask the children *In this sentence, which is the result, and which is the condition?* (If *for the condition*, will *for the result*) Read out the half-sentences from the Lesson 3 Warmer in random order and for each one have the children respond: they sit down and say *Condition* or stand up and say *Result*.

1 1.23 Listen and read. Why do sea levels rise?

- Play the CD. The children listen and read along. Ask *Does Rufus think everything is connected?* (*yes*)
- Play the CD again and ask *Why do sea levels rise?* (*because the ice melts*)

2 Order the sentences to show how things are connected.

- Have one child read out the first sentence in the chain of events.
- The children order the sentences, then compare with a friend.
- Elicit answers.

Answers

2 If we don't ... **5** If we slow ... **1** If we travel ...
4 If we reduce ... **3** If we use ...

Grammar Central

1st conditional questions

Have the children complete the grammar examples. Elicit answers. Then elicit when we use 1st conditional questions. (*to ask about things which are possible in the present or future*) The children write more examples in their notebook. See also the Grammar Reference sections in the Student Book (p. 99) and Activity Book (p. 98) for further explanation and practice.

Grammar Central Answers: will, if, melts, will

AB Answers Activity 2: 1 b **2** f **3** c **4** a **5** d **6** e

3 Talk to a friend about what will happen. Use the sentences in Activity 2.

- Ask *What will happen if we turn off the lights more often?* Elicit the results. (e.g. *we will save electricity*)
- Have the children continue the activity in pairs with the prompts supplied and the Activity 2 sentences.
- Have pairs perform their dialogue for the class.

Optional activity: What will happen if ...?

Have the children work in pairs. Each pair writes a question at the top of a piece of paper, starting *What will happen if ...* This can be about anything they like. Each pair passes their paper to another pair and receives one. They then write an answer to the *What will happen if ...?* question. Repeat this activity for a few minutes, then ask pairs to read their favorite questions and answers.

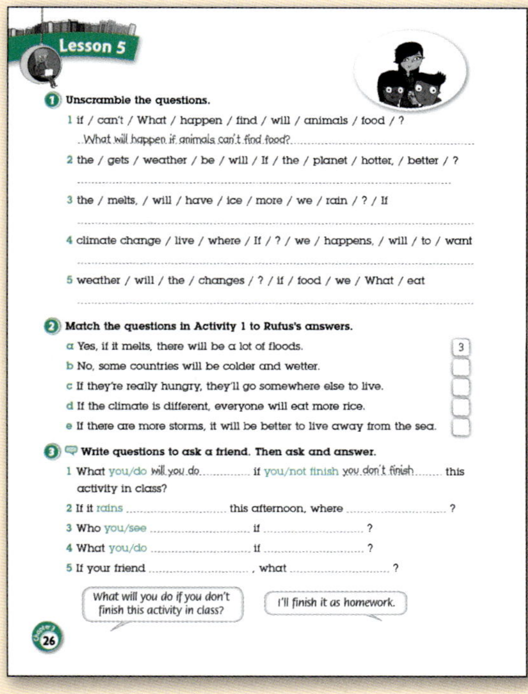

Lesson 5

1 Unscramble the questions.

1 if / can't / What / happen / find / will / animals / food / ?

What will happen if animals can't find food?

2 the / gets / weather / be / will / If / the / planet / hotter, / better / ?

3 the / melts, / will / have / ice / more / we / rain / ? / If

4 climate change / live / where / If / ? / we / happens, / will / to / want

5 weather / will / the / changes / ? / if / food / we / What / eat

2 Match the questions in Activity 1 to Rufus's answers.

a Yes, if it melts, there will be a lot of floods. 3

b No, some countries will be colder and wetter.

c If they're really hungry, they'll go somewhere else to live.

d If the climate is different, everyone will eat more rice.

e If there are more storms, it will be better to live away from the sea.

3 Write questions to ask a friend. Then ask and answer.

1 What you/do will you do .... if you/not finish you don't finish .... this activity in class?

2 If it rains .... this afternoon, where .... ?

3 Who you/see .... if .... ?

4 What you/do .... if .... ?

5 If your friend .... , what .... ?

What will you do if you don't finish this activity in class?

I'll finish it as homework.

26

1 Unscramble the questions.

The children write out the scrambled questions correctly. Elicit answers.

Answers

1 What will happen if animals can't find food?
2 If the planet gets hotter, will the weather be better?
3 If the ice melts, will we have more rain?
4 If climate change happens, where will we want to live?
5 What food will we eat if the weather changes?

2 Match the questions in Activity 1 to Rufus's answers.

For each answer, the children write the number of the question in Activity 1. Elicit responses.

Answers

a 3 **b** 2 **c** 1 **d** 5 **e** 4

3 Write questions to ask a friend. Then ask and answer.

The children complete the questions using the prompts supplied. Elicit answers. Then they ask and answer the questions with a friend.

Answers

Children's own answers.

Cooler: Play "Disappearing Text"

Play the game with sentences from Student Book Activity 2 (see Games Bank p. 222).

Competency Focus

Learn

The children demonstrate their understanding of the new language by reading the dialogue and completing the activity.

Presentation Kit • Use *Hotspots* and choose the Grammar Central box to enlarge it. Have children use *Highlighter* to identify 1st conditional questions in the SB Activity 1 text.

• Have children use *Pen* to write the answers in AB Activity 2, before you use *Answer Key* to confirm.

Teacher's Resource Center • For extra grammar practice, print out Grammar Worksheet 3B.

Student's Resource Center • The children can use Interactive Grammar 3B at home.

Vocabulary, Listening, and Spelling

Lesson objectives: identify and use vocabulary of ocean transportation; practice spelling words with the *k* sound
Key vocabulary: *broke down, cargo ship, chemicals, containers, currents, factory, port, storm*
Secondary language: *float, enormous*
Materials: Class CD; pictures for Key vocabulary (Warmer); sets of large cards with *c/k/ck/ch* (Cooler)

Lesson 6

1 Listen and circle on the map. Where were the toys found?

2 Listen again and order the sentences.

- ☐ Strong **currents** took them to the USA, Alaska, Japan, Australia, and South America.
- ☐ The **cargo ship** left the **port** in Hong Kong.
- ☐ The boxes **broke down** and the plastic ducks floated far across the ocean.
- ☐ Twelve enormous **containers** fell into the ocean.
- 1 A **factory** in Hong Kong made thousands of plastic toys.
- ☐ They will take years to break down and will leave **chemicals** in the ocean.
- ☐ There was a **storm** in the ocean.

3 Talk to a friend and retell the story. Use the words in the text.

A: *What happened?*
B: *The toys left the port in Hong Kong in a cargo ship.*

Spelling Central

Circle the words with a *k* sound. Write the words in the chart. Can you add more *k* sound words?

c	k	ck	ch
container			

34

Warmer: Pre-teach vocabulary

Pre-teach the vocabulary by showing pictures, or draw images on the board. Alternatively, give definitions. Tell the class to stand. Ask questions using each of the words, e.g. *Does a cargo ship go on the sea?* The children raise their hand for *yes* or sit down for *no*.

1 1.24 Listen and circle on the map. Where were the toys found?

- Play the CD. Have the children listen and look at the map.
- Play the CD again, and have the children circle all the places the toys were found.
- Ask *Where were the toys found?* (*USA, Alaska, Japan, Australia, South America, Europe*)

Audioscript

A toy factory in Hong Kong made colorful plastic bath toys. They were going to sell the toys in stores in the USA.
The toys left the port in Hong Kong in a cargo ship in 1992. While the ship was sailing across the Pacific Ocean, there was a terrible storm. Twelve big containers fell into the ocean and opened up when they hit the water. Boxes of toys floated out of them. The ship then sailed to Tacoma in Washington State, in the USA.
The boxes made of cardboard broke down slowly in the water, and thousands of yellow plastic ducks floated away. There were blue turtles and green frogs, too! They traveled far across the ocean in strong currents.
Years later, yellow ducks were found on beaches in the USA. Other ducks, turtles, and frogs traveled to Alaska, Japan, Australia, and South America. And some were found in Europe, too.
Many are still swimming around the world! It's a funny story, but it's serious, too. The plastic toys will take years to break down and they will leave chemicals in the ocean. These chemicals will harm animals that eat them.

2 1.24 Listen again and order the sentences.

- Play the CD again. The children listen and number the sentences in the order they hear them.
- Elicit answers.

Answers

6, 2, 5, 4, 1, 7, 3

3 Talk to a friend and retell the story. Use the words in the text.

- Choose two children to read the example dialogue. Elicit other examples using words from the text.
- The children practice in pairs.
- Have pairs perform a dialogue for the class.

Spelling Central

Words with a *k* sound

Have the children repeat *container* after you, paying attention to the *k* sound. They find the words with that sound on the page and complete the chart. They then add other words in each category. (e.g. *colorful*; *kangaroo*; *back*; *stomach*) Elicit the more usual pronunciation of *ch*. (*the sound in chair*)

Answers

c: container, circle, currents, America, cargo, plastic, across, factory, Can
k: Alaska, broke, Kong, take, break
ck: ducks
ch: chemicals

Optional activity: Play "Collocations"

Play the game with collocations from the lesson, e.g. *strong—currents, the ship—left the port, break—down, across—the ocean, plastic—toys*, etc. (see Games Bank p. 222).

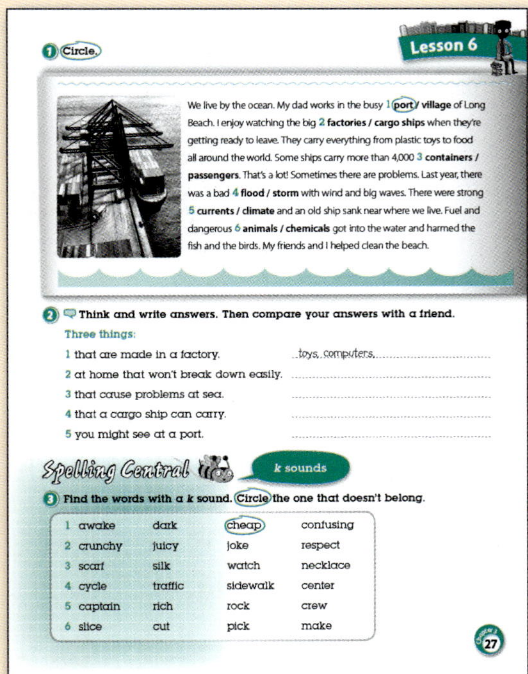

Lesson 6

1 Circle.

We live by the ocean. My dad works in the busy 1 **port / village** of Long Beach. I enjoy watching the big 2 **factories / cargo ships** when they're getting ready to leave. They carry everything from plastic toys to food all around the world. Some ships carry more than 4,000 3 **containers / passengers**. That's a lot! Sometimes there are problems. Last year, there was a bad 4 **flood / storm** with wind and big waves. There were strong 5 **currents / climate** and an old ship sank near where we live. Fuel and dangerous 6 **animals / chemicals** got into the water and harmed the fish and the birds. My friends and I helped clean the beach.

2 Think and write answers. Then compare your answers with a friend.

Three things:
1 that are made in a factory. toys, computers,
2 at home that won't break down easily.
3 that cause problems at sea.
4 that a cargo ship can carry.
5 you might see at a port.

Spelling Central — *k* sounds

3 Find the words with a *k* sound. Circle the one that doesn't belong.

1	awake	dark	cheap	confusing
2	crunchy	juicy	joke	respect
3	scarf	silk	watch	necklace
4	cycle	traffic	sidewalk	center
5	captain	rich	rock	crew
6	slice	cut	pick	make

27

1 Circle.

The children complete the text by circling the correct option from the two given each time. Elicit answers.

Answers

1 port **2** cargo ships **3** containers **4** storm **5** currents **6** chemicals

2 Think and write answers. Then compare your answers with a friend.

The children write items for each description. They compare answers with a friend. Elicit ideas.

Answers (suggested)

Any three for each prompt:

1 toys/computers/furniture/food, etc.
2 plastic bottles/bags/toys/cans/food containers, etc.
3 storms/currents/waves/chemicals/wind, etc.
4 toys/wood/computers/clothes/plants, etc.
5 ships/containers/lifeboats/life jackets, etc.

3 Find the words with a *k* sound. Circle the one that doesn't belong.

To practice the **Spelling Central** feature, the children read the words aloud and circle the one in each group that does not have a *k* sound. Elicit answers.

Answers

1 cheap **2** juicy **3** watch **4** center **5** rich **6** slice

Cooler: Hold it up

Give each child four cards, each with *c*, *k*, *ck*, or *ch* in big letters. Call out words from **Spelling Central** and have the children hold up the appropriate card.

Competency Focus

Collaborate and Communicate

The children work together to share their ideas on the topic, incorporating the new vocabulary.

Presentation Kit • Use Vocabulary Tool 3B to pre-teach key vocabulary. Use *Slideshow* to introduce the words and *Picture Dictionary* to review/test.

- Have children use *Highlighter* to identify *k* sound words in the SB Activity 2 text. Have different children use *Pen* to write in more *k* sound words in the Spelling Central chart.

Student's App • Encourage the children to play the games on their smartphone/tablet. Ask them to record their scores to compare in the next lesson.

CLIL: Science—Effects of plastic

Lesson objective: find out about the effects of plastic on the environment
Materials: CLIL Graphic Organizer 3 [TRC printout] (optional)

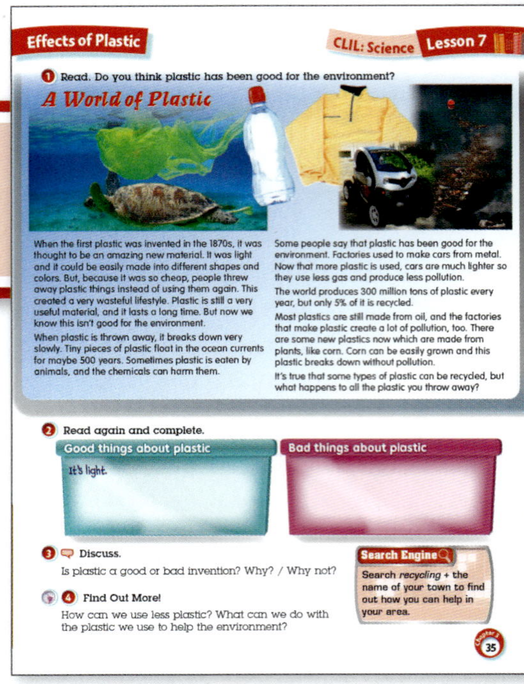
Effects of Plastic — CLIL: Science — Lesson 7

1 Read. Do you think plastic has been good for the environment?

A World of Plastic

When the first plastic was invented in the 1870s, it was thought to be an amazing new material. It was light and it could be easily made into different shapes and colors. But, because it was so cheap, people threw away plastic things instead of using them again. This created a very wasteful lifestyle. Plastic is still a very useful material, and it lasts a long time. But now we know this isn't good for the environment.

When plastic is thrown away, it breaks down very slowly. Tiny pieces of plastic float in the ocean currents for maybe 500 years. Sometimes plastic is eaten by animals, and the chemicals can harm them.

Some people say that plastic has been good for the environment. Factories used to make cars from metal. Now that more plastic is used, cars are much lighter so they use less gas and produce less pollution.

The world produces 300 million tons of plastic every year, but only 5% of it is recycled.

Most plastics are still made from oil, and the factories that make plastic create a lot of pollution, too. There are some new plastics now which are made from plants, like corn. Corn can be easily grown and this plastic breaks down without pollution.

It's true that some types of plastic can be recycled, but what happens to all the plastic you throw away?

2 Read again and complete.

Good things about plastic	Bad things about plastic
It's light.	

3 Discuss.
Is plastic a good or bad invention? Why? / Why not?

4 Find Out More!
How can we use less plastic? What can we do with the plastic we use to help the environment?

Search Engine
Search *recycling* + the name of your town to find out how you can help in your area.

35

Warmer: Board race

Divide the class into two groups and the board into two halves. Write *Plastic* on the board. Give one child in each group a board pen. The children have two minutes to write as many items as possible that are made of plastic. Each new word must be written by a different child and only one child from each team can stand up at a time. Count the words and check spelling at the end.

1 Read. Do you think plastic has been good for the environment?

- Have the children read the article quickly and then discuss the answer to the question with a friend.
- Ask *Do you think plastic has been good for the environment?* Invite opinions from children and ask for class agreement.

2 Read again and complete.

- Have the children find and underline the sentence in the text that mentions that plastic is light. (*It was light and it could be easily made into different shapes and colors*—lines 2–4.) Point out that the sentence can be expressed as *It's light*. Elicit more basic information that can be taken from it. (*different shapes and colors*)
- Have them continue to find and underline good and bad things about plastic and summarize them in the chart. The children compare with a friend.
- Elicit answers.

Answers

Good: It's light. It can easily be made into different shapes and colors. It's cheap/useful. It lasts a long time. Cars are lighter so they use less gas. Some types of plastic can be recycled. You can make plastic from corn.
Bad: It isn't good for the environment. It breaks down very slowly. It is eaten by animals. The chemicals can harm plants and animals. The factories that make plastic create a lot of pollution.

3 Discuss.

- Have a child read out the discussion question.
- Have the children talk about their ideas in small groups, then share ideas as a class.

4 Find Out More!

- The children research how we can use less plastic and what we can do with the plastic we use to help the environment. The **Search Engine** feature gives support on where to look. The children will need to complete this research before doing the follow-up activity in the Activity Book. (It could be set as homework.)

Optional activity: Scan the text

To help the children practice the skill of scanning (and to focus on key phrases), read out the beginning of some phrases to elicit what follows, e.g. *Plastic was invented … in the 1870s. It could be easily made … into different shapes and colors.*, etc.

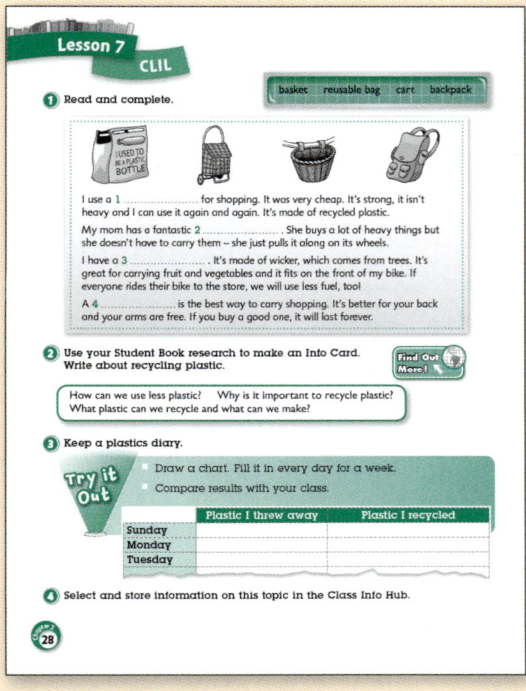
Lesson 7 CLIL

1 Read and complete.

basket reusable bag cart backpack

I use a 1 .... for shopping. It was very cheap. It's strong, it isn't heavy and I can use it again and again. It's made of recycled plastic.

My mom has a fantastic 2 .... She buys a lot of heavy things but she doesn't have to carry them – she just pulls it along on its wheels.

I have a 3 .... It's made of wicker, which comes from trees. It's great for carrying fruit and vegetables and it fits on the front of my bike. If everyone rides their bike to the store, we will use less fuel, too!

A 4 .... is the best way to carry shopping. It's better for your back and your arms are free. If you buy a good one, it will last forever.

2 Use your Student Book research to make an Info Card. Write about recycling plastic. Find Out More!

How can we use less plastic? Why is it important to recycle plastic? What plastic can we recycle and what can we make?

3 Keep a plastics diary.

Try it Out
- Draw a chart. Fill it in every day for a week.
- Compare results with your class.

	Plastic I threw away	Plastic I recycled
Sunday		
Monday		
Tuesday		

4 Select and store information on this topic in the Class Info Hub.

Chapter 3 28

1 Read and complete.

The children complete the text using the words supplied. Elicit answers.

Answers

1 reusable bag **2** cart **3** basket **4** backpack

2 Use your Student Book research to make an Info Card. Write about recycling plastic.

Divide the class into groups. Have the children pool the information they learned from their research in the Student Book and the Activity Book. The children write about and illustrate their ideas individually. Have the groups present their Info Cards to the class.

3 Keep a plastics diary.

The children follow the **Try It Out** instructions to keep a plastics diary. After a week, they bring in their diaries and compare with friends.

4 Select and store information on this topic in the Class Info Hub.

Have the children vote for the five most interesting Info Cards and the best plastics diaries. Archive these in your Class Hub (see p. 41) in a folder called **Chapter 3 Recycling Plastic**.

Cooler: Play "Back to the Board"

Play the game with words from Student Book Activity 1 (see Games Bank p. 222).

Competency Focus

Act

The children carry out research to find out about reducing our use of plastic and recycling. This helps them expand their learning and relate it to their world, both inside and outside the classroom.

Presentation Kit • TIP When using the board for "heads-up" teaching, give the children as much opportunity as possible to participate. Ask plenty of questions so they engage with the text. Use *Pointer* on the text as you read it aloud.

- Have different children use *Pen* to write AB Activity 1 answers. Elicit class agreement by a show of hands. Confirm with *Answer Key*.

Teacher's Resource Center • Print out CLIL Graphic Organizer 3 for the children to use in collating their Find Out More! research.

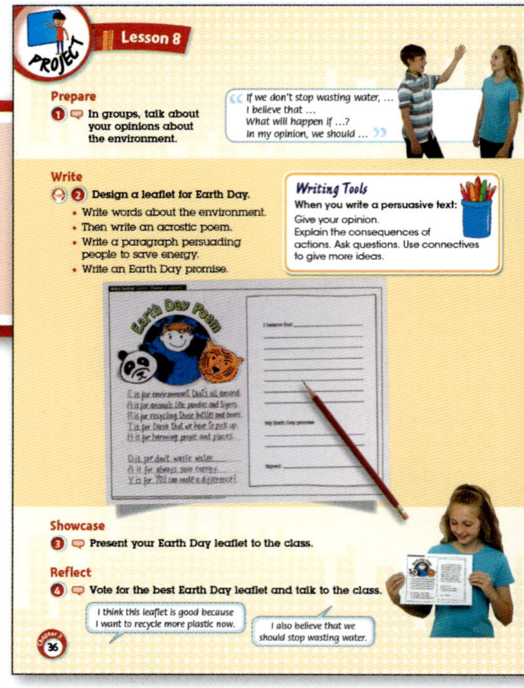
PROJECT
Lesson 8

Prepare

1 In groups, talk about your opinions about the environment.

If we don't stop wasting water, …
I believe that …
What will happen if …?
In my opinion, we should …

Write

2 Design a leaflet for Earth Day.

- Write words about the environment.
- Then write an acrostic poem.
- Write a paragraph persuading people to save energy.
- Write an Earth Day promise.

Writing Tools
When you write a persuasive text:
Give your opinion.
Explain the consequences of actions. Ask questions. Use connectives to give more ideas.

Earth Day Poem

Showcase

3 Present your Earth Day leaflet to the class.

Reflect

4 Vote for the best Earth Day leaflet and talk to the class.

I think this leaflet is good because I want to recycle more plastic now.
I also believe that we should stop wasting water.

Chapter 3 36

Writing Project

Lesson objectives: review language from Chapter 3; design a leaflet for Earth Day and present it to the class
Materials: Writing Template 3 [TRC printout] (optional)

Warmer: Missing vowels

Write key vocabulary items (*recycling*, *pollution*, *endangered*, *energy*, *climate*, *plastic*, *fuel*, *habitat*) on the board, omitting the vowels. The children have to figure out what the words are and write them correctly by putting the vowels in the correct places. Invite children to write in the missing vowels on the board.

Prepare

1 In groups, talk about your opinions about the environment.

- Give the children a model using your opinions about two aspects of the environment—one pessimistic and one optimistic. Introduce them with phrases like *In my opinion* or *I believe*.
- Divide the class into small groups to continue the discussion. Ask them to decide after two minutes if their group is more positive or more negative about the future of the environment.

Write

2 Design a leaflet for Earth Day.

- Have the children read the Earth Day leaflet as a model for their own writing.
- Read the **Writing Tools** box together. Elicit examples of persuasive sentences and suggestions for lines for a new acrostic poem.
- The children prepare an Earth Day leaflet, using the instructions and the model leaflet. They write and illustrate their leaflet, then compare with a friend. Give support as necessary.

Showcase

3 Present your Earth Day leaflet to the class.

- Choose children to read their Earth Day leaflet to the class. Ask the class to listen and figure out what the acrostic words are.

Reflect

4 Vote for the best Earth Day leaflet and talk to the class.

- Have the children comment on which leaflet was the best and why. Have a class vote to identify their favorite.

Optional activity: Memorization

Give the children one minute to look at and try to memorize the acrostic Earth Day poem in the Student Book. Then have them close their books. Read out the first part of each line, e.g. *E is for environment* … and see if they can remember the ending of each line (… *that's all around.*).

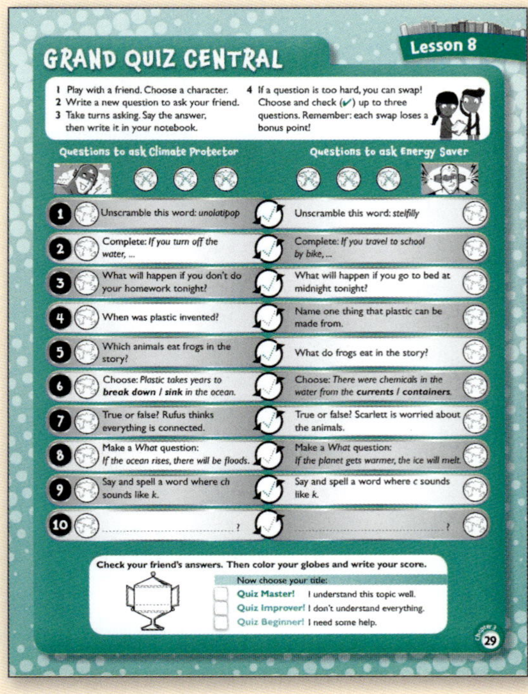
GRAND QUIZ CENTRAL

Lesson 8

1 Play with a friend. Choose a character.
2 Write a new question to ask your friend.
3 Take turns asking. Say the answer, then write it in your notebook.
4 If a question is too hard, you can swap! Choose and check (✔) up to three questions. Remember: each swap loses a bonus point!

	Questions to ask Climate Protector	Questions to ask Energy Saver
1	Unscramble this word: *unolatipop*	Unscramble this word: *stelfilly*
2	Complete: *If you turn off the water, ...*	Complete: *If you travel to school by bike, ...*
3	What will happen if you don't do your homework tonight?	What will happen if you go to bed at midnight tonight?
4	When was plastic invented?	Name one thing that plastic can be made from.
5	Which animals eat frogs in the story?	What do frogs eat in the story?
6	Choose: *Plastic takes years to* **break down / sink** *in the ocean.*	Choose: *There were chemicals in the water from the* **currents / containers**.
7	True or false? Rufus thinks everything is connected.	True or false? Scarlett is worried about the animals.
8	Make a *What* question: *If the ocean rises, there will be floods.*	Make a *What* question: *If the planet gets warmer, the ice will melt.*
9	Say and spell a word where *ch* sounds like *k*.	Say and spell a word where *c* sounds like *k*.
10	..................................?	..................................?

Check your friend's answers. Then color your globes and write your score.

Now choose your title:
- Quiz Master! I understand this topic well.
- Quiz Improver! I don't understand everything.
- Quiz Beginner! I need some help.

Chapter 3 29

Grand Quiz Central

See p. 43 for details of how to take the quiz.

Answers

1 population / lifestyle **2** you will save water *or* you won't waste water / you will save energy *or* you won't waste energy **3** Children's own answers. **4** in the 1870s / oil or corn **5** snakes / mosquitoes or insects **6** break down / containers **7** true / true **8** What will happen if the ocean rises? / What will happen if the planet gets warmer? **9** *any one of:* chemicals, school, archeologist / *any one of:* container, cargo, color **10** Children's own answers.

Cooler: One word at a time

Tell the children you will all discuss your ideas about the environment, but with each person giving just one word of each sentence. Give the first topic, saying *Let's talk about energy*. Start the sentence with *If* … The children add a word each, e.g. *we – save – energy*, etc.). You can help when necessary, or change the direction of the sentence by adding in your own words. When the children come to the natural end of a sentence, ask the class to recall the whole sentence. Repeat with other topics.

Competency Focus

Me

The children invent and write their own leaflet for Earth Day, exploring their imagination and creativity.

Presentation Kit • Choose from Vocabulary Tools 1A–3B to review a vocabulary topic from previous chapters. Have the children raise their hand to vote to select a topic and a way to review it (e.g. *Distort*, *Flash*). Then use *Stopwatch* and give the class one minute to recall all the words in the topic. Repeat with a different topic if you have time.

Teacher's Resource Center • Print out Writing Template 3 to use for the SB writing activity.

Language Review

Lesson objective: review language from Chapter 3
Materials: Class CD

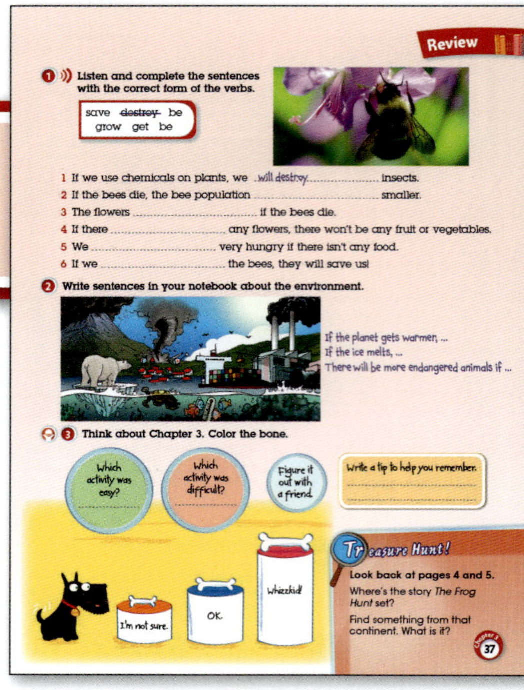

Warmer: Memory test

Tell the children to close their Student Book. Say their "password" to begin today's lesson is to remember the first part of all the lines of the acrostic poem in Lesson 8 (*E is for environment, A is for animals*, etc.) Write the letters vertically. Have the children raise their hand to give a suggestion. Write each correct suggestion on the board.

1 1.25 Listen and complete the sentences with the correct form of the verbs.

- Have the children look at the pictures and read the sentences. They try to guess the complete versions in pairs. Elicit suggestions.
- Play the CD and have the children listen and complete the sentences.
- Play the CD again for the children to listen and check.
- Elicit answers.

Audioscript

Boy: *What will happen if we use chemicals on the plants?*
Woman: *Well, the chemicals will destroy insects you don't want. But they can also harm other creatures. Chemicals will cause bees to die. The bee population will get smaller.*
Boy: *What will happen if all the bees die? I guess there won't be any honey!*
Woman: *No, there won't be any honey. But if all the bees die, the flowers won't grow. Bees help flowers grow. And if there aren't any flowers, there won't be any fruit or vegetables to eat and everyone will be very hungry.*
Boy: *So we need to help the bees!*
Woman: *Yes, if we save the bees, the bees will save us.*

Answers

1 will destroy **2** will be/get **3** won't grow **4** aren't **5** will be/get **6** save

2 Write sentences in your notebook about the environment.

- Elicit sentences from the class using the prompts.
- The children write more sentences in their notebook, then compare their sentences in pairs.

Answers

Children's own answers.

3 Think about Chapter 3. Color the bone.

- Have the children look back at Chapter 3 and color the bone to evaluate their progress (self-evaluation).
- Discuss ideas for remembering difficult words, e.g. note difficult words on a special page in your notebook. The children choose and write a tip in their Student Book.

Treasure Hunt

Ask *Where does the story* The Frog Hunt *take place?* (*Africa*) Have the children look at pp. 4–5 to find something from Africa. (*an African mask*)

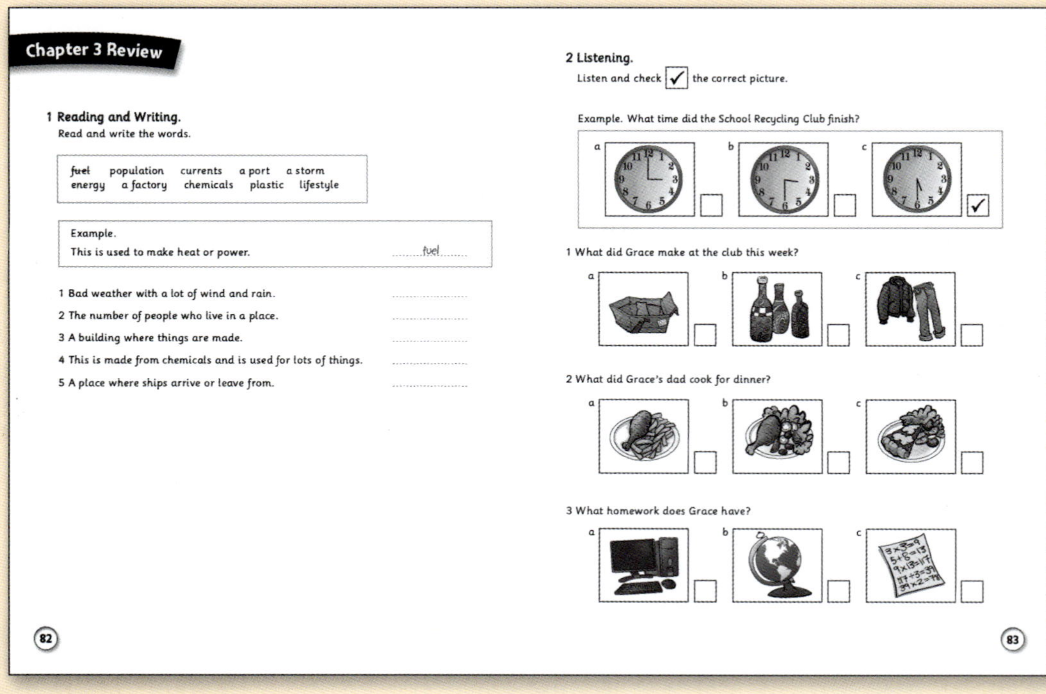

Chapter 3 Review

1 Reading and Writing.
Read and write the words.

~~fuel~~	population	currents	a port	a storm
energy	a factory	chemicals	plastic	lifestyle

Example.
This is used to make heat or power. ......fuel......

1 Bad weather with a lot of wind and rain. ....
2 The number of people who live in a place. ....
3 A building where things are made. ....
4 This is made from chemicals and is used for lots of things. ....
5 A place where ships arrive or leave from. ....

2 Listening.
Listen and check ✓ the correct picture.

Example. What time did the School Recycling Club finish?
a b c ✓

1 What did Grace make at the club this week?
a b c

2 What did Grace's dad cook for dinner?
a b c

3 What homework does Grace have?
a b c

82 83

1 Reading and Writing. Read and write the words.

The children complete the text using the words supplied. Check answers.

Answers

1 a storm **2** population **3** a factory **4** plastic **5** a port

2 2.33 Listening. Listen and check (✓) the correct picture.

The children read the questions. Play the CD twice. They listen and check the correct picture in each section. Check answers.

Answers (Audioscript on p. 223)

1 a **2** b **3** b

Cooler: Play "Tic-Tac-Toe"

Play the game using key words from the chapter to elicit sentences and questions (see Games Bank p. 222).

Competency Focus

Me: Self-evaluation

The children reflect on the chapter, express their personal opinions about their own progress, and look for ways to improve. This encourages them to evaluate and make decisions about what they need to revisit and how they can learn better.

Presentation Kit • Use the drop-down Menu to access the AB Review pages.

Teacher's Resource Center • Print out Test Chapter 3 to use at the end of this lesson. The Test Generator also allows you to create customized tests.

- For the CEYLT (Cambridge YLE) exam preparation activities, there are Speaking prompts available for this chapter.
- Print out Festival Worksheet: New Year's Eve to expand the children's knowledge of celebrations throughout the world.

Chapter 4

Superheroes, Special Powers!

Overview

The children will:

- use critical thinking skills to identify vocabulary relating to special powers.
- talk about what they would do with special powers using the 2nd conditional.
- read and understand a comic book about a superhero.
- ask and answer questions using the 2nd conditional.
- describe animal abilities.
- find out about memory and the brain.
- write a description of a superhero.

Key Vocabulary

Special powers: brave, control minds, intelligent, invisible, secret identity, special power, villains

Animal abilities: amazing, champion, enemies, genius, heart, memory, strong, technique

Key Grammar

2nd conditional

- If I were a superhero, I'd be able to fly.
- If I were invisible, you wouldn't see me.

2nd conditional questions

- If your friend were sick, would you visit him?
- What would you do if your friend were sad?

Reading Skills

Story: *Master Mind Returns*

Genre: comic book

Literacy Development

- use reading skills to understand and predict content
- relate story theme to personal experience
- use adjectives to describe appearance and personality

Functional Language

- Oh, no! I've broken Scarlett's cup! What should I do?
- If I were you, I'd tell Scarlett!
- Yes, you should tell her and then say sorry.

Spelling

Words with *qu*

CLIL: Science—Memory and the brain

The children find out how our brains store memory and how to improve it.

Competency Focus

The children will:

use critical thinking skills to deduce the meaning of new vocabulary. (Lesson 1) predict the content of a story. (Lesson 3)	activate new vocabulary and apply new grammar knowledge. (Lesson 2) apply new grammar rules in a familiar context. (Lesson 5)	work in threes to act out a dialogue. (Lesson 3) work in pairs to talk about which animal they would be. (Lesson 6)	relate the story and story theme to their personal experience. (Lesson 4) write a character description of their superhero. (Lesson 8) evaluate their own progress in the chapter. (Review)	develop an understanding of memory by researching games to improve it. (Lesson 7)

Digital Overview

Presentation Kit

Projectable Student Book, Activity Book, and Reader pages

- Vocabulary Tool 4A: Special powers
- Vocabulary Tool 4B: Animal abilities
- Interactive versions of selected SB and AB activities
- Integrated *Audio* and *Answer Key* for all activities

Teacher's Resource Center

Resources for planning, lesson delivery, and homework

- Class Planner Chapter 4
- Worksheets to print out (including notes and answers):
  - Grammar Worksheet 4A: 2nd conditional
  - Grammar Worksheet 4B: 2nd conditional questions
  - CLIL Graphic Organizer 4
  - Writing Template 4
  - Test Chapter 4
- Test Generator
- Literacy Handbook

Student's Resource Center

Resources for consolidation and practice at home

- Interactive Grammar 4A: 2nd conditional
- Interactive Grammar 4B: 2nd conditional questions
- Vocabulary Tool 4A: Special powers
- Vocabulary Tool 4B: Animal abilities

Student's App

Vocabulary games: Special powers and animal abilities

Superheroes, Special Powers!

Lesson 1

Vocabulary

Lesson objectives: identify and use vocabulary related to special powers
Key vocabulary: *brave, control minds, intelligent, invisible, secret identity, special power, villains*
Materials: Class CD, superhero pictures (Warmer)

Chapter 4 Superheroes, Special Powers! Lesson 1

1 Listen and complete the chart.

FANTASTIC FAMILY

Real Name	Real Person	Secret Identity	Special Power
Miles Jackson	scientist — Susan's husband	Captain Fantastic	He can change the shape of his body
Susan Jackson	.... — Miles' wife	.... Woman	She can ....
Harry Jackson	school boy — Susan and Miles'	The Brain	He can control people's minds.
Tina Jackson	school girl — Susan and Miles'	Invisible Girl	She can ....

2 Listen again and write the words next to the clues.

special power brave invisible control minds intelligent villains ~~secret identity~~

1 Miles is also Captain Fantastic. secret identity
2 He can change shape. ....
3 He knows a lot of information. ....
4 She's never scared. ....
5 He can change their thoughts. ....
6 She can disappear completely. ....
7 Bad people like Doctor Dark. ....

38

Warmer: The best superhero

Show the children a picture of Superman or Batman (or other superheroes), and ask *What do we call people like this?* (*superheroes*) Write a list of all the superheroes they can name on the board and have a class vote on the best superhero. Ask *What do you like about your favorite superhero?* Elicit ideas.

1 1.26 Listen and complete the chart.

- Have the children look at the pictures. Ask *Who are these people? What do you think makes them special?*
- Play the CD. The children listen and complete the chart.
- Elicit answers.

Audioscript

Meet the Fantastic Family … they're not your ordinary family. Most days they look like you or me, but when they're Fantastic, their costumes are yellow. They wear yellow suits and black boots!
Miles Jackson is really two people! Yes, he's a scientist, but he also has a secret identity called Captain Fantastic. Captain Fantastic is a superhero. He has a special power: he can change the shape of his body. He's very intelligent and he knows a lot of information. He's married to Susan Jackson.
Susan is a teacher but, when she isn't teaching, she's a superhero called Bird Woman. She can fly. She's never scared because she's very brave.
Harry Jackson, their son, is a superhero called The Brain because he has a very big brain inside his head. He knows what people are thinking and he can change their thoughts. He can control their minds.
Tina Jackson is Harry's sister. Sometimes you can see her, but sometimes she's invisible and you can't. She's called Invisible Girl. She can disappear completely!
The Fantastic Family wears yellow costumes. Together they fight bad people—villains like Doctor Dark, who's a very bad man.

Answers

Miles Jackson: body
Susan Jackson: teacher, Bird, fly
Harry Jackson: son
Tina Jackson: daughter, disappear

2 1.26 Listen again and write the words next to the clues.

- Play the CD again. The children listen and write the word described in each clue, using the words supplied.
- Elicit answers.

Answers

1 secret identity **2** special power **3** intelligent **4** brave **5** control minds **6** invisible **7** villains

Optional activity: Memory test

Read out one piece of information from the chart, e.g. *Bird Woman*. Elicit a definition. (*Susan Jackson's secret identity*) Divide the class into pairs and have them continue the activity (one child with their Student Book open). The children swap roles after each question.

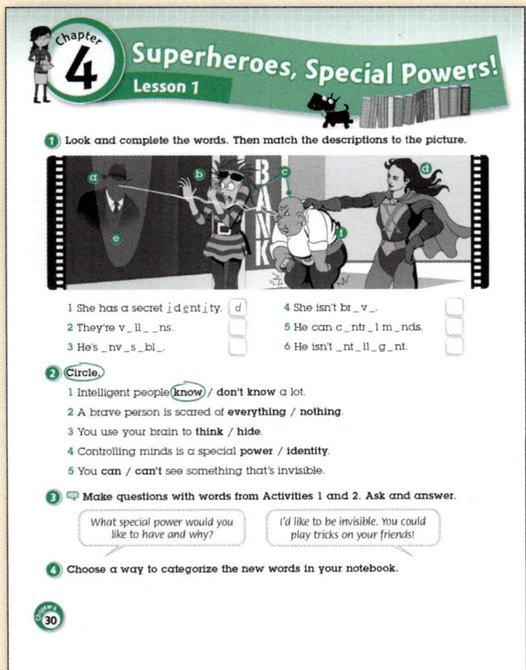
Chapter 4 Superheroes, Special Powers!
Lesson 1

1 Look and complete the words. Then match the descriptions to the picture.

1 She has a secret identity. d
2 They're v_ll_ _ns.
3 He's _nv_s_bl_.
4 She isn't br_v_.
5 He can c_ntr_l m_nds.
6 He isn't _nt_ll_g_nt.

2 Circle.
1 Intelligent people **know** / **don't know** a lot.
2 A brave person is scared of **everything** / **nothing**.
3 You use your brain to **think** / **hide**.
4 Controlling minds is a special **power** / **identity**.
5 You **can** / **can't** see something that's invisible.

3 Make questions with words from Activities 1 and 2. Ask and answer.
What special power would you like to have and why?
I'd like to be invisible. You could play tricks on your friends!

4 Choose a way to categorize the new words in your notebook.

30

1 Look and complete the words. Then match the descriptions to the picture.

The children complete the words in the sentences by writing the missing vowels. Then for each sentence they find the detail it illustrates in the picture, writing the correct letter.

Answers

1 identity d **2** villains c **3** invisible e **4** brave b **5** control minds a **6** intelligent f

2 Circle.

The children complete the sentences by circling the correct option from the two given each time. Elicit answers.

Answers

1 know **2** nothing **3** think **4** power **5** can't

3 Make questions with words from Activities 1 and 2. Ask and answer.

Elicit questions using the words from Activities 1 and 2. The children then make more questions to ask and answer in pairs. Have pairs ask and answer for the class.

4 Choose a way to categorize the new words in your notebook.

Brainstorm appropriate categories, e.g. *good/bad/good and bad, impossible things/possible things, things you'd like to do or be/not like to do or be*. The children choose the best categories for them and list the words in their notebook.

Cooler: Play "Disappearing Words"

Play the game with key vocabulary from the lesson (see Games Bank p. 222).

Competency Focus

Think! Critical Thinking

The children use critical thinking skills to understand the vocabulary by using visual clues and processing the written and spoken forms.

Presentation Kit • Use Vocabulary Tool 4A to pre-teach key vocabulary as an alternative to the critical thinking approach. Use *Slideshow* to introduce the words and *Flash* to review/test.

- Choose *Hotspots* and the Navigation Pane buttons to access *Audio* and *Answer Key*, and view which activities are interactive.
- TIP Most audioscripts appear on the SB page. If they don't, choose the arrow on the *Audio* pop-up to show them.
- TIP Choose *Help* at any time to access FAQs on using the materials.

Grammar

Lesson objective: talk about imagined situations using the 2nd conditional
Key grammar: 2nd conditional
Secondary language: *thieves*
Materials: questionnaire (Warmer); Grammar Worksheet 4A [TRC printout] (optional)

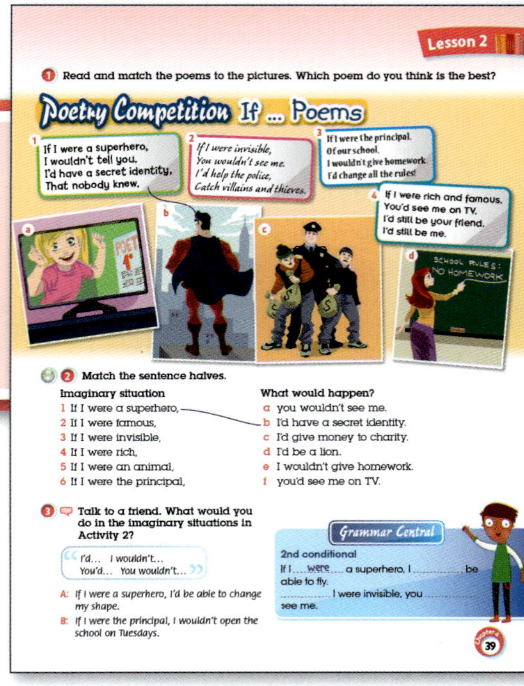
Lesson 2

1 Read and match the poems to the pictures. Which poem do you think is the best?

Poetry Competition If … Poems

1 If I were a superhero,
I wouldn't tell you.
I'd have a secret identity,
That nobody knew.

2 If I were invisible,
You wouldn't see me.
I'd help the police,
Catch villains and thieves.

3 If I were the principal,
Of our school,
I wouldn't give homework.
I'd change all the rules!

4 If I were rich and famous,
You'd see me on TV.
I'd still be your friend,
I'd still be me.

2 Match the sentence halves.

Imaginary situation	What would happen?
1 If I were a superhero,	a you wouldn't see me.
2 If I were famous,	b I'd have a secret identity.
3 If I were invisible,	c I'd give money to charity.
4 If I were rich,	d I'd be a lion.
5 If I were an animal,	e I wouldn't give homework.
6 If I were the principal,	f you'd see me on TV.

3 Talk to a friend. What would you do in the imaginary situations in Activity 2?

"I'd… I wouldn't…
You'd… You wouldn't…"

A: *If I were a superhero, I'd be able to change my shape.*
B: *If I were the principal, I wouldn't open the school on Tuesdays.*

Grammar Central
2nd conditional
If I ...were... a superhero, I .... be able to fly.
.... I were invisible, you .... see me.

Chapter 4 39

Warmer: Find someone who …

Prepare a short questionnaire with prompts to elicit *Do you want to …* ? questions, e.g. *be famous*, *have a superpower*, *be rich*, *live in a different country*, etc. Give each child a copy. Elicit the question to be asked for each prompt. The children then mingle to find a different classmate who answers *yes* to each question.

1 Read and match the poems to the pictures. Which poem do you think is the best?

- Have the children read the poems and match each one to the correct picture.
- Elicit answers. Ask *Which poem do you think is the best?* Elicit responses with reasons.

Answers

1 b **2** c **3** d **4** a

2 Match the sentence halves.

- Ask one child to read out the complete example sentence.
- The children match the sentence halves.
- Nominate one child to (a) read out a complete sentence, (b) ask for a friend's agreement, and (c) nominate another child to do the next sentence.

Answers

1 b **2** f **3** a **4** c **5** d **6** e

Grammar Central

2nd conditional

Have the children complete the grammar examples. Elicit answers. Then elicit the rules for using the 2nd conditional. (If + *simple past to talk about the situation, and* would + *verb to talk about the result.*) The children write more examples in their notebook. See also the Grammar Reference sections in the Student Book (p. 100) and Activity Book (p. 99) for further explanation and practice.

Grammar Central Answers: were, would/'d, If, wouldn't

3 Talk to a friend. What would you do in the imaginary situations in Activity 2?

- Choose two children to read the example dialogue.
- Divide the class into pairs to discuss the situations in Activity 2.
- Have pairs perform a dialogue for the class.

Optional activity: **If I were …**

Read the beginnings of five sentences and have the children write them down, e.g. *If I were a teacher … / If I were at home now …*, etc. Then have the children complete them with their own ideas. When finished, have them work in pairs. They take turns reading out the ending and guessing which beginning it came from.

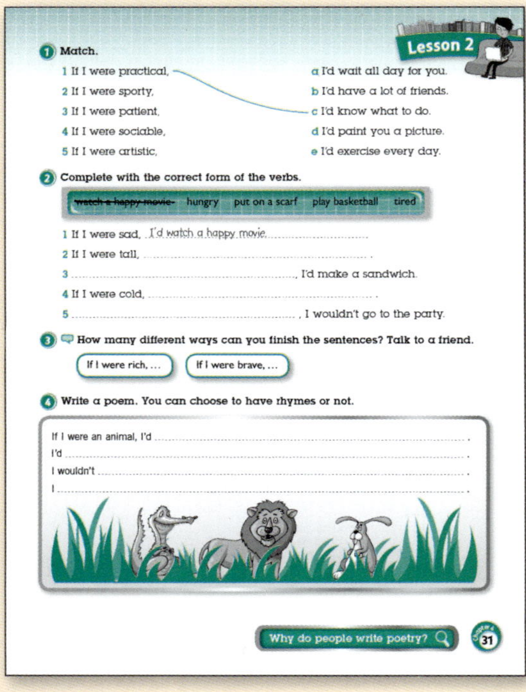

Lesson 2

1 Match.

1 If I were practical,
2 If I were sporty,
3 If I were patient,
4 If I were sociable,
5 If I were artistic,

a I'd wait all day for you.
b I'd have a lot of friends.
c I'd know what to do.
d I'd paint you a picture.
e I'd exercise every day.

2 Complete with the correct form of the verbs.

~~watch a happy movie~~ hungry put on a scarf play basketball tired

1 If I were sad, I'd watch a happy movie.
2 If I were tall, ...
3 ...., I'd make a sandwich.
4 If I were cold, ...
5 ...., I wouldn't go to the party.

3 How many different ways can you finish the sentences? Talk to a friend.

If I were rich, ... If I were brave, ...

4 Write a poem. You can choose to have rhymes or not.

If I were an animal, I'd ....
I'd ....
I wouldn't ....
I ....

Why do people write poetry?

Chapter 4 31

1 Match.

The children match the sentence halves. Elicit answers.

Answers

1 c **2** e **3** a **4** b **5** d

2 Complete with the correct form of the verbs.

The children complete the sentences using the correct form of the verbs supplied. Elicit answers.

Answers

1 I'd watch a happy movie **2** I'd play basketball **3** If I were hungry **4** I'd put on a scarf **5** If I were tired

3 How many different ways can you finish the sentences? Talk to a friend.

Elicit suggestions for completing the sentences. Then the children work in pairs to think up more sentence endings. Elicit responses.

4 Write a poem. You can choose to have rhymes or not.

For support, you could present your own basic poem first, e.g. *If I were an animal, I'd be a lion. I'd run and sleep a lot. I wouldn't eat other animals. I would be friends with everyone.* The children write a poem. Then they compare with a friend. Have children read their poems. Ask *Why do people write poetry?* (*to express themselves, to tell stories, to experiment with rhythm and rhyme*)

Answers

Children's own answers.

Cooler: Read the poems

Have the children read out the Student Book Activity 1 poems around the class, saying one line each. Repeat some of the poems if you have a class of more than 16 children.

Competency Focus

Learn

The children integrate previously acquired vocabulary into new grammar and structure and adapt the language to show an understanding of the topic.

Presentation Kit • Have children write answers to AB Activity 2 on the board using *Pen*. Use *Eraser* to clear and repeat with a few different children, before you use *Answer Key*.

- TIP Position the Navigation Pane on the left or right of the screen, depending on where you want to stand at the board. Choose *Swap sides* to change.

Teacher's Resource Center • For extra grammar practice, print out Grammar Worksheet 4A.

Student's Resource Center • The children can use Interactive Grammar 4A at home.

Reading: Story Extract

Lesson objectives: ask for and give advice; use the title and pictures to predict story content; read the extract from the comic book *Master Mind Returns* (middle)
Functional language: *Oh, no! I've … ! What should I do? If I were you, I'd … ! Yes, you should …*
Secondary language: *Master Mind, get hurt, comic book*
Materials: Class CD

Warmer: Scrambled sentences

Write the following sentences on the board, scrambling the order of the words in each: *There was a cat in a tree. Flying Felicity flew in and saved it. The family was happy again.* The children work in pairs to write the sentences and form a short story. Elicit answers.

Functional language

1 1.27 Listen and read.

- Play the CD. The children listen and read along. Ask *Is Angelo happy?* (*no*) *Why not?* (*He broke Scarlett's cup.*) *Do you think the others have good advice for him?*
- Play the CD again, pausing for them to repeat.
- Divide the class into threes to practice the dialogue.

2 Imagine your friend has done something wrong. Give them advice.

- Two children read the example. Elicit other examples of advice using the prompts supplied.
- The children practice in pairs. Have pairs perform a dialogue for the class.

Before reading

3 Look at the story. Where might you see a story like this?

- Have the children study the story title and pictures. Ask *Where might you see a story like this?* (*comic book*) Ask *Do you often read comic books? Do you like them?*

4 1.28 Read the story extract and answer.

- Play the CD. The children listen and read along. Have them answer question 1. Elicit the answer.
- Play the CD again so they can write their ideas for questions 2 and 3. Encourage them to use reading skills (e.g. using the title, pictures, and context) to infer meaning and make predictions.

- Elicit answers, but do not confirm predictions: explain that they will have to read the story to find out.

Answers

1 He wants Master Mind. **2** Because he wants him to find Neuron. / Children's own answers. **3** Neuron is a villain and Master Mind is a superhero.

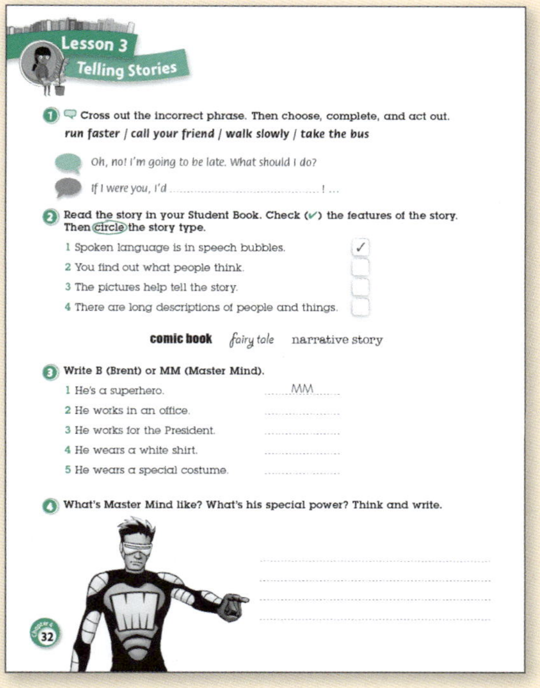
Lesson 3
Telling Stories

1 Cross out the incorrect phrase. Then choose, complete, and act out.
run faster / call your friend / walk slowly / take the bus

Oh, no! I'm going to be late. What should I do?
If I were you, I'd ....! ...

2 Read the story in your Student Book. Check (✓) the features of the story. Then circle the story type.
1 Spoken language is in speech bubbles. ✓
2 You find out what people think.
3 The pictures help tell the story.
4 There are long descriptions of people and things.

comic book *fairy tale* narrative story

3 Write B (Brent) or MM (Master Mind).
1 He's a superhero. MM
2 He works in an office. ....
3 He works for the President. ....
4 He wears a white shirt. ....
5 He wears a special costume. ....

4 What's Master Mind like? What's his special power? Think and write.

32

1 Cross out the incorrect phrase. Then choose, complete, and act out.

The children identify which phrase is incorrect. (*walk slowly*) They then choose one of the others and act out the dialogue in pairs, adapting and extending it. Have pairs act out their dialogue for the class.

2 Read the story in your Student Book. Check (✓) the features of the story. Then circle the story type.

The children read the Student Book story extract again, then check the sentences which describe the story. They then circle the correct story type. Elicit answers.

Answers

✓ *by:* 1, 3; *Circled:* comic book

3 Write B (Brent) or MM (Master Mind).

The children identify whether each sentence describes Brent or Master Mind, writing B or MM as appropriate. Elicit answers.

Answers

1 MM **2** B **3** MM **4** B **5** MM

4 What's Master Mind like? What's his special power? Think and write.

Elicit suggestions on what Master Mind is like and what his special power is. The children write their own ideas, then compare with a friend. Elicit ideas.

Answers

Children's own answers.

Cooler: Bad advice!

Have the children return to the situations in Student Book Activity 1 and 2. Elicit bad advice for the situation in Activity 1. (e.g. *If I were you, I'd hide the cup! You shouldn't tell her! You should say it was someone else!*) Have them act out new versions of the situations with bad advice! Have pairs perform their dialogue for the class.

Competency Focus

Collaborate and Communicate

The children work together to practice, perform, and adapt the new functional language learned.

Think

The children use critical thinking skills to identify the genre of the story by looking at the text and story artwork.

Presentation Kit • Use *Mask* to hide the SB Activity 1 speech bubbles. Elicit and uncover one at a time to confirm. Use *Highlighter* on *I've broken Scarlett's cup.* and *I'd tell Scarlett!*, and elicit different things you could say in this context.

- Use *Mask* to display only Picture 5 of the SB story extract. Ask *Where is this? What is happening? What do you think is going to happen?* Elicit ideas, then uncover the rest of the story extract to confirm.

Master Mind Returns

1
Female editor: What's happening?

2
Neuron: How do I look? Oh, I'm on TV!

3
Neuron: Hello, Washington! It's a beautiful day! Hahaha! If I were you, I would enjoy the sun while you can. Soon, you won't be able to see it—the sky will be black with pollution.

Male editor: What's he talking about? Who is this guy?

4
Neuron: Today I will destroy the chemical factory ... using this little machine I've invented. Aren't I intelligent? And then, if I'm feeling nice, I might wait 24 hours before destroying the city's power station.

5
Female editor: Why is he doing this?

Neuron: Give me Master Mind, and no one will get hurt. Washington isn't big enough for two super brains. Hahaha!

6
Meanwhile …

Brent: No, there isn't much happening at work these days.

Mom: You need a hobby, Brent.

Brent: Excuse me. I have to take this call.

7
Brent: Yes, Mr. President, this is Master Mind. Where is he? I'm on my way.

8
Brent: Sorry, Mom, Dad. They need me at the office. Enjoy your food.

9
MM: It's hard work having a secret identity. I hope I'm not too late.

10
MM: You aren't invisible. I will find you, Neuron. If you look into my eyes, you will soon change your mind.

11
MM: What? Argh! No power!

12
MM: Can I borrow your motorcycle?

Man: Who are you? No, you—

13
Man: —of course you can. Here, take it!

14
MM: NEURON!

15
Neuron: You can't control my mind. Goodbye, Master Mind.

16
MM: I've lost him.

17
Later …

Neuron: Where's Master Mind? If he were really intelligent, he would find me.

18
Neuron: Look, one o'clock. If I were more patient, I'd wait. But I'm not patient!

Peabrain: That isn't very nice …

Neuron: No, Peabrain. We're villains!

19
KABBOOM!

People in street: Aargh!

20
MM: No! I'm too late. How can I trap him? Let me think … Who's Neuron's favorite person?

Girl: Oh! What's happening?

21
Neuron: Where's my mirror? Is my hair OK? Oh! We're on TV again.

22
Neuron: So, now you see how strong and powerful I am. Don't forget … you have 24 hours until I use it again.

MM: Neuron loves … himself!

23
MM: Mr. President. I have a plan ...

24
Later …

President: Neuron, I have to save our city. At ten o'clock tomorrow, I'll give Master Mind to you. The TV crew and newspaper reporters will be here. Everyone around the world will see.

25
Neuron: I'll be famous! If I had more time, I'd get a new costume. I want to look good for the cameras.

26
The next day …

President: Brave people of Washington, it's a sad day for us all.

27
Photographer: Just one picture, please, Mr. Neuron. You, Master Mind, and the President.

28
Neuron: Of course! Let me take off my glasses.

29
MM: I hope you're going to behave and keep your promise, Neuron.

Neuron: If I were nice, I wouldn't be a villain, would I? I would ... help old people cross the road.

30
President: Perfect shot!

31
Later …

Neuron: *I'll be nice now.*

President: Thank you again, Master Mind.

MM: Just doing my job, Sir!

Lesson objective: read and understand the comic book *Master Mind Returns* in the Reader
Materials: Class CD; Reader

Warmer: Story extract summary

Write words from the story extract on the board. Ask the children to number them in the order they appeared in the story. Then elicit a summary of the story extract.

Story Summary

Master Mind, a superhero who controls minds, fights Neuron, a villain who wants to destroy a chemical factory and power station. Master Mind figures out that Neuron's vanity is his weakness and so he is able to defeat the villain.

Theme: identifying what is really important in your life

1.29 While reading

- Have the children look at the pictures in the Reader. Ask *What is Brent's secret?* (*He's a superhero.*)
- Play the CD. The children listen and read along. Ask *What does Master Mind do to Neuron in the end?* (*He changes him from horrible to nice.*)
- Ask questions to check comprehension, e.g. *What does the President say he'll give to Neuron?* (*Master Mind*) *Who helped Master Mind control Neuron's mind?* (*Mr. President and the photographer*)
- Have the class act out the story (see **Story Time**).

After reading: Reflect

Ask questions to give the children the opportunity to think about the issues raised by the story, e.g. *Why did Neuron lose in the end? How did Master Mind think of the plan? Why are these comic book stories so popular?*

Optional activity: Write more dialogue

Have the children look back at the story and suggest new lines of dialogue. Give two examples of your own and ask the children where they belong: *Where are you going, Brent?* (*picture 8*) and *Smile!* (*picture 27*). Have the children write new lines of dialogue. They then tell a friend, who has to say where the new lines belong.

Story Time

Create additional roles

A story like this, which features very little narration, is ideal for acting out in short sections or even as a whole story. Some children prefer not to act out big parts and so can take one of the smaller parts, or you can introduce new, incidental parts.

Reading Strategy

Reader's Theater

In the Reader's Theater strategy, the children collaborate to read aloud a story. It is similar to a role-play, but offers more support because the children read from the page. They can work on their fluency and develop their confidence performing in front of the class.

For additional explanation and activities, see the Literacy Handbook on the Teacher's Resource Center.

Cooler: Who said it?

Read out some lines of dialogue and ask the children if they can remember (without looking in their Reader) who said each one. The children continue the activity in pairs.

Presentation Kit • For the Warmer activity, have children use *Pen* to identify, circle, and number the words in the order they appear in the story.

- Use *Spotlight* to focus on Neuron in Pictures 2, 4, 15, 17, 18, 26, 30, and 31. Elicit what has happened and how he feels each time. Then have children mime being Neuron in different parts of the story. The class guesses which part of the story each child is miming.

Reading Comprehension and Critical Literacy

Lesson objectives: understand and evaluate the story; relate story theme to personal experience; focus on the use of adjectives to give descriptions of characters
Materials: Class CD; Reader; paper for posters

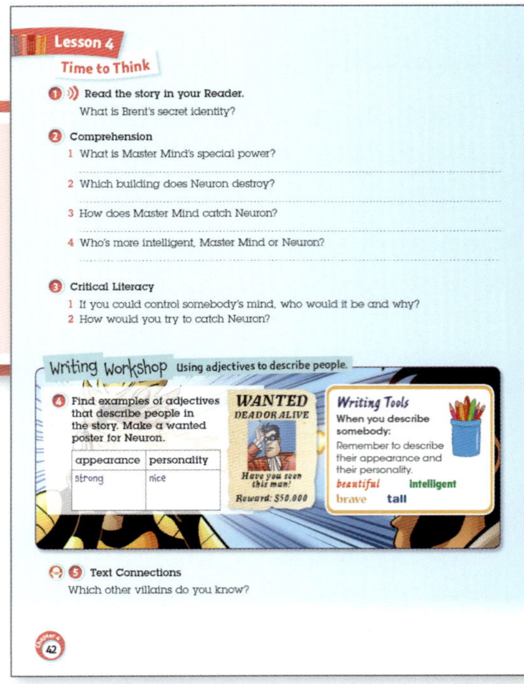
Lesson 4
Time to Think

1 Read the story in your Reader.
What is Brent's secret identity?

2 Comprehension
1 What is Master Mind's special power?
2 Which building does Neuron destroy?
3 How does Master Mind catch Neuron?
4 Who's more intelligent, Master Mind or Neuron?

3 Critical Literacy
1 If you could control somebody's mind, who would it be and why?
2 How would you try to catch Neuron?

Writing Workshop Using adjectives to describe people.

4 Find examples of adjectives that describe people in the story. Make a wanted poster for Neuron.

appearance	personality
strong	nice

Writing Tools
When you describe somebody:
Remember to describe their appearance and their personality.
beautiful intelligent
brave tall

5 Text Connections
Which other villains do you know?

42

Note: Please ensure that your class has read the Reader story before you do this lesson.

Warmer: Mime time

Tell the children you will act out (in mime) one of the events in the story *Master Mind Returns*, e.g. Master Mind is eating dinner. The children have to say what is happening. Then they continue the game in pairs, taking turns miming and saying what is happening.

1 1.29 Read the story in your Reader.

- Have the children read the story. (Alternatively, play the CD and have them read along.)
- Elicit whether the children were correct in their predictions in Lesson 3 Activity 4. Ask *What is Brent's secret identity?* (*the superhero Master Mind*)

2 Comprehension

- The children write answers to the first three questions. Elicit answers.
- Discuss question 4. Ask the children to justify their answers.

Answers

1 He can control people's minds. **2** The chemical factory. **3** He looks into Neuron's eyes using the mirror and controls Neuron's mind. **4** Master Mind.

3 Critical Literacy

- Have the children discuss the answers to the questions with a friend. Elicit answers. Ask the other children if they agree, eliciting reasons. Ask *Do you think it's a good thing to try and control someone's mind?* Thinking about the characters and imagining themselves in their situations helps children engage creatively with the story.

Answers

Children's own answers.

Writing Workshop

Using adjectives to describe people

4 Find examples of adjectives that describe people in the story. Make a wanted poster for Neuron.

Have a child read the poster. Elicit other descriptions, using adjectives from the **Writing Tools** box. The children look back at the story and find more adjectives to write in their notebook. They make a wanted poster for Neuron. Display the posters on the walls for the class to look at them.

Answers

Appearance: strong, invisible, good
Personality: nice, intelligent, patient, powerful, famous, brave
Children's own answers.

5 Text Connections

- Ask *Which other villains do you know?* Elicit ideas and discuss as a class.

Optional activity: **Browse the posters**

Have the children walk around the room looking at their friends' posters from Student Book Activity 4 in more detail. Ask them to look for (a) a good picture, (b) good use of adjectives, and (c) the poster that would get most people's attention. Elicit the best poster.

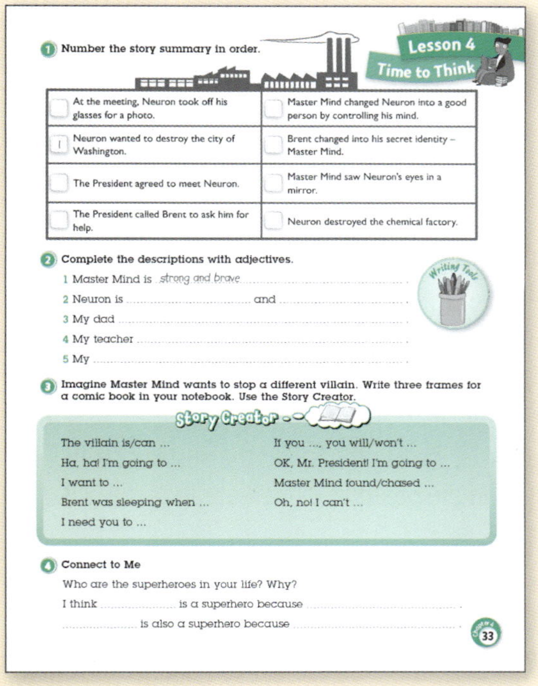

Lesson 4
Time to Think

1 Number the story summary in order.

☐ At the meeting, Neuron took off his glasses for a photo.	☐ Master Mind changed Neuron into a good person by controlling his mind.
1 Neuron wanted to destroy the city of Washington.	☐ Brent changed into his secret identity – Master Mind.
☐ The President agreed to meet Neuron.	☐ Master Mind saw Neuron's eyes in a mirror.
☐ The President called Brent to ask him for help.	☐ Neuron destroyed the chemical factory.

2 Complete the descriptions with adjectives.

1 Master Mind is *strong and brave* ....
2 Neuron is .... and ....
3 My dad ....
4 My teacher ....
5 My ....

Writing Tools

3 Imagine Master Mind wants to stop a different villain. Write three frames for a comic book in your notebook. Use the Story Creator.

Story Creator

The villain is/can ...
Ha, ha! I'm going to ...
I want to ...
Brent was sleeping when ...
I need you to ...
If you ..., you will/won't ...
OK, Mr. President! I'm going to ...
Master Mind found/chased ...
Oh, no! I can't ...

4 Connect to Me

Who are the superheroes in your life? Why?

I think .... is a superhero because ....

.... is also a superhero because ....

Chapter 4 33

1 Number the story summary in order.

The children number the sentences in the correct order to summarize the story. Elicit answers.

Answers

Left-hand column: 6, 1, 5, 2
Right-hand column: 8, 3, 7, 4

2 Complete the descriptions with adjectives.

The children complete the descriptions using appearance and personality adjectives. Elicit answers.

Answers

Children's own answers.

3 Imagine Master Mind wants to stop a different villain. Write three frames for a comic book in your notebook. Use the Story Creator.

Use the **Story Creator** prompts to elicit ideas. The children write and illustrate three comic book frames in their notebook, then compare with a friend. Have children read out and show their texts to the class.

4 Connect to Me

Elicit examples of real superheroes in the children's lives. (e.g. *my mom, my best friend*) The children write their own response, then compare with a friend. Elicit responses.

Cooler: Invent a new ending

Ask the children to imagine that Master Mind's plan did not work. Give them time to imagine what might happen next, then elicit suggestions for a new ending for the story—maybe Neuron wins!

Competency Focus

Me: Critical Literacy

The children use critical literacy skills to reflect on the story and relate it to their own experiences.

Presentation Kit • Display the Reader on the board. Use *Spotlight* to highlight Picture 9. Elicit what happened before and after this. Repeat with Pictures 17 and 26.

- You can move the *Answer Key* pop-up window around the screen to have the activity and the answers side by side.
- For SB Activity 4, have children use *Highlighter* to identify adjectives describing people in the Reader story.
- TIP Choose the SB/AB/Reader button in the Navigation Pane to move easily from one component to another.

Grammar and Reading

Lesson objectives: ask and answer questions using the 2nd conditional
Key grammar: 2nd conditional questions
Secondary language: *cheating, fail*
Materials: Class CD; Grammar Worksheet 4B [TRC printout] (optional)

Lesson 5

BOOK CLUB

1 Listen and read. Do you think Angelo is a good friend?

Angelo: What are you doing?
Yasmin: I'm taking a Superfriend Quiz to find out if I'm a Superfriend.
Angelo: Oh, can I take it, too?
Yasmin: Yes. OK. 1) If your friend were sad, would you a) talk to them, b) buy them some candy, or c) find a new friend?
Angelo: Um, my answer is b. I love candy.
Yasmin: Hm! One point! Question 2) If you saw your friend cheating on an exam, would you a) tell the teacher, b) talk to the friend, or c) say nothing?
Angelo: I'd talk to my friend. Answer b.
Yasmin: Good! Three points! Now, 3) What would you do if your friend were sick? Would you a) send him a text, b) go and visit him, or c) buy him a gift.
Angelo: I'd just wait for him to get better.
Yasmin: Zero points! Angelo, you should go and visit him.
Angelo: But then I might get sick, too!

2 Read the quiz questions and give 1, 2, or 3 "Superfriend" points.

4 What would you do if your friend gave you a T-shirt you didn't like?
a I'd say, "Thank you but I don't like it."
b I'd wear it every day.
c I'd wear it when I saw my friend.

5 If your friend failed the science exam, what would you do?
a I'd say, "Don't worry."
b I'd laugh.
c I'd say, "Can I help you with science?"

6 What would you do if your friend bought some new sneakers the same as yours?
a I'd say, "That's cool! We have the same sneakers."
b I'd buy some different sneakers.
c I wouldn't wear my sneakers.

3 Ask and answer the Superfriend Quiz questions. Talk to a friend.

A: *What would you do if your friends were sick?*
B: *I'd talk to them.*

Grammar Central
2nd conditional questions
If your friend ...were... sick, ... you visit him?
What .... you do if your friend .... sad?

Chapter 4 43

Warmer: Definitions

Write on the board *p, s, p, s, a* (as prompts for *practical, sporty, patient, sociable, artistic*). Give the children a definition of each adjective, e.g. *This adjective describes a person who gets on well with people.* (*sociable*) Then ask *Which of these adjectives do you think describes a good friend? Why?*

1 1.30 Listen and read. Do you think Angelo is a good friend?

- Play the CD. The children listen and read along. Ask *Do you think Angelo is a good friend?* Elicit answers with reasons.
- Explain the concept of "Superfriend" points: an answer that someone who is not a good friend at all wins only one point, an answer a good friend would give wins two points, and an answer a very good friend would give wins three points. Play the CD again, pausing after each set of options. Ask the children if they agree or disagree with the answers.

2 Read the quiz questions and give 1, 2, or 3 "Superfriend" points.

- Have the children read quiz questions 4, 5, and 6. They decide which answer should score 1, 2, or 3 "Superfriend" points.
- Elicit answers, writing these and the answers to 1–3 in Activity 1 on the board as a reference for Activity 3.

Answers

4 a 1 point **b** 3 points **c** 2 points
5 a 2 points **b** 1 point **c** 3 points
6 a 3 points **b** 1 or 2 points **c** 1 or 2 points

Grammar Central

2nd conditional questions

Have the children complete the grammar examples. Elicit answers. Then elicit when we use 2nd conditional questions. (*to ask about imagined situations*) The children write more examples in their notebook. See also the Grammar Reference sections in the Student Book (p. 100) and Activity Book (p. 99) for further explanation and practice.

Grammar Central Answers: were, would, would, were

3 Ask and answer the Superfriend Quiz questions. Talk to a friend.

- Have the children read the Activity 1 dialogue again and choose their own answers for questions 1, 2, and 3. They then do the same for questions 4, 5, and 6 in Activity 2.

- Have the children compare answers with a friend. Ask them to try to find a question where they have a different answer. Then they count individually how many points they scored.
- Ask the children to raise their hands for the appropriate score.
  7 points or fewer: Bad friends!
  8–12 points: Good friends!
  13–18 points: Superfriends! Have them report back to the class on the questions that were answered differently.

Optional activity: Superstudent!

Have the children work in groups of four to write two quiz questions. The questions are to find out if someone is a Superstudent. When finished, invite four children to the front of the class. Each group asks their questions to the four children. The class then decides who gave the most "superstudent" answer.

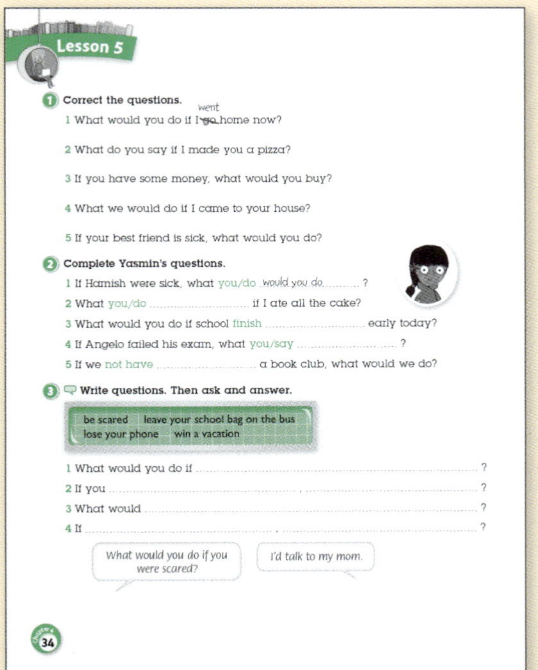
Lesson 5

1 Correct the questions.

1 What would you do if I ~~go~~ went home now?

2 What do you say if I made you a pizza?

3 If you have some money, what would you buy?

4 What we would do if I came to your house?

5 If your best friend is sick, what would you do?

2 Complete Yasmin's questions.

1 If Hamish were sick, what you/do would you do ?

2 What you/do .... if I ate all the cake?

3 What would you do if school finish .... early today?

4 If Angelo failed his exam, what you/say .... ?

5 If we not have .... a book club, what would we do?

3 Write questions. Then ask and answer.

be scared   leave your school bag on the bus
lose your phone   win a vacation

1 What would you do if .... ?

2 If you ...., ... ?

3 What would .... ?

4 If ...., ... ?

Chapter 4 34

1 Correct the questions.

The children identify and cross out the grammatical error in each question, and write in the correction. Elicit answers.

Answers

1 ~~go~~ went **2** ~~do~~ would **3** ~~have~~ had **4** ~~we would~~ would we **5** ~~is~~ were

2 Complete Yasmin's questions.

The children complete the questions using the prompts supplied. Elicit answers.

Answers

1 would you do **2** would you do **3** finished **4** would you say **5** didn't have

3 Write questions. Then ask and answer.

The children write questions using the prompts supplied. Then they ask and answer the questions in pairs. Elicit answers.

Answers

Children's own answers.

Cooler: Class mingle

Have the children write their favorite question from this lesson (in the Student Book or Activity Book) on a slip of paper and mingle to ask and answer. After speaking to each friend, they swap questions, then continue using the new question to ask and answer. Elicit any interesting questions and answers they heard.

Competency Focus

Learn

The children demonstrate their understanding of the new language by reading the dialogue and completing the activity.

Presentation Kit • Display the SB page. Use *Highlighter* to show the 2nd conditional questions in SB Activity 1.

- Have children use *Pen* to write their answers to AB Activity 2. Ask the class to confirm.
- TIP Use *Eraser* to undo any highlighting or writing on the screen if you want to repeat a task or have different children answer.

Teacher's Resource Center • For extra grammar practice, print out Grammar Worksheet 4B.

Student's Resource Center • The children can use Interactive Grammar 4B at home.

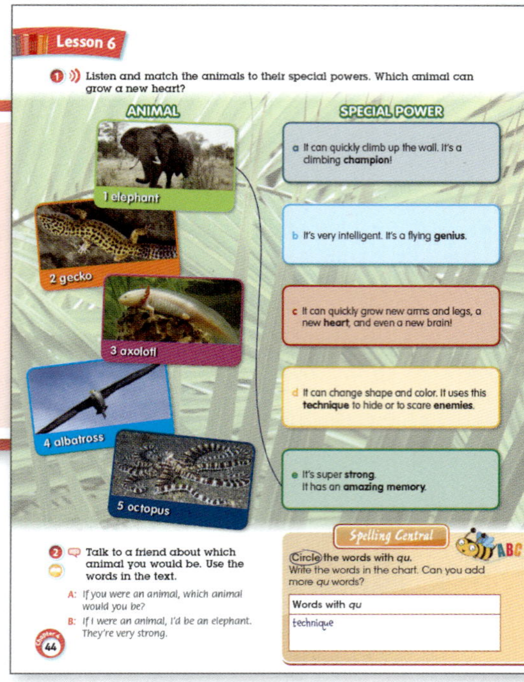

Vocabulary, Listening, and Spelling

Lesson objectives: identify and use vocabulary related to animal abilities; practice spelling words with *qu*

Key vocabulary: *amazing, champion, enemies, genius, heart, memory, strong, technique*

Secondary language: *gecko, albatross, axolotl*

Materials: Class CD

Warmer: Pre-teach vocabulary

Pre-teach the vocabulary by giving definitions or sentences showing them in context, e.g. *If you can remember everything, you have a good memory.* Repeat the definitions/sentences, stopping before the key vocabulary word to elicit it from the class.

1 1.31 Listen and match the animals to their special powers. Which animal can grow a new heart?

- Play the CD. The children listen for the special powers. *Ask Which animal can grow a new heart?* (*the axolotl*)
- Play the CD again for the children to listen and match.

Audioscript

These animals all have surprising special powers.
1 Elephants are super strong! They're the strongest mammals in the world and can move heavy trees with their trunks. They could carry 130 people. People say elephants never forget. It's true that elephants can remember faces. They build up this memory over many years so they can tell a friendly face from an enemy. The older the elephant, the better memory it has!
2 If this gecko were a superhero, it would be Spiderman! Yes, these small lizards are better at climbing than other animals. They're climbing champions! They can climb quickly up a wall made of glass or metal using invisible hairs on their feet.
3 This strange animal is an axolotl. It lives quietly in the water. It doesn't look like a superhero, but it has an amazing power. If it lost a leg, it would grow a new one! An axolotl can even grow a new heart in its body and a new brain! Now that's really smart!
4 Now, we know that birds can fly, but this albatross can fly around the world in about 45 days! That's quick! Albatrosses use the wind to help them fly for thousands of kilometers without stopping. They have intelligent brains, too, to help them find their way (like a compass). The albatross is a flying genius!
5 The Mimic Octopus has eight legs like a squid, but it has an unusual special power. It can change its shape and color to look like other animals. It uses this technique to hide from sharks and other enemies or to frighten them.

Answers

1 e **2** a **3** c **4** b **5** d

2 Talk to a friend about which animal you would be. Use the words in the text.

- Have a child ask you the example question. Answer using the model given, but with a different animal, e.g. *If I were an animal, I'd be a gecko. I love climbing!*
- Have the children continue the activity in pairs, taking turns asking and answering.
- Have children say which animal they would like to be and why.

Spelling Central

Words with *qu*

Have the children find *qu* words on the page and complete the chart. They then add other *qu* words. (e.g. *quietly, square, quiz, mosquito*)

Answers

technique, quickly

Optional activity: Invent a super animal!

The children draw and name a new animal which is a combination of two different animals. They write about its powers. They show and describe their animal in groups.

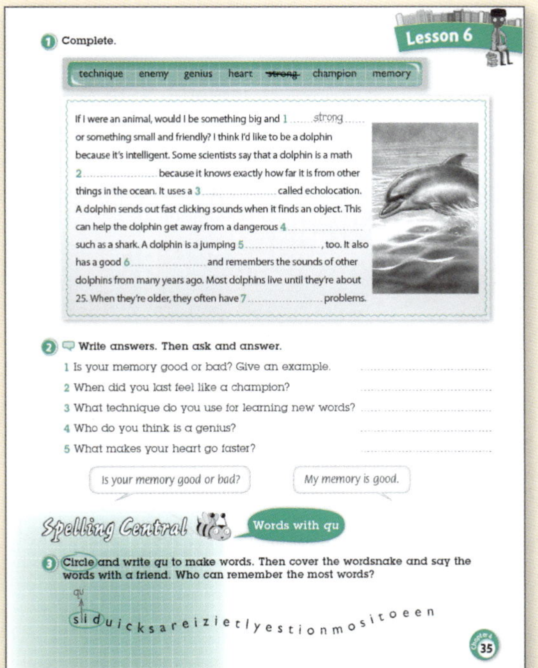

Lesson 6

1 Complete.

technique enemy genius heart ~~strong~~ champion memory

If I were an animal, would I be something big and 1 ...strong... or something small and friendly? I think I'd like to be a dolphin because it's intelligent. Some scientists say that a dolphin is a math 2 .... because it knows exactly how far it is from other things in the ocean. It uses a 3 .... called echolocation. A dolphin sends out fast clicking sounds when it finds an object. This can help the dolphin get away from a dangerous 4 .... such as a shark. A dolphin is a jumping 5 ...., too. It also has a good 6 .... and remembers the sounds of other dolphins from many years ago. Most dolphins live until they're about 25. When they're older, they often have 7 .... problems.

2 Write answers. Then ask and answer.

1 Is your memory good or bad? Give an example. ....
2 When did you last feel like a champion? ....
3 What technique do you use for learning new words? ....
4 Who do you think is a genius? ....
5 What makes your heart go faster? ....

Is your memory good or bad?

My memory is good.

Spelling Central — Words with qu

3 Circle and write qu to make words. Then cover the wordsnake and say the words with a friend. Who can remember the most words?

qu

siduicksareizietlyestionmositoeen

Chapter 4 35

1 Complete.

The children complete the text using the words supplied. Elicit answers.

Answers

1 strong **2** genius **3** technique **4** enemy **5** champion **6** memory **7** heart

2 Write answers. Then ask and answer.

The children write their own answers to the questions. Then they ask and answer the questions in pairs. Invite pairs to ask and answer for the class.

Answers

Children's own answers.

3 Circle and write *qu* to make words. Then cover the wordsnake and say the words with a friend. Who can remember the most words?

To practice the **Spelling Central** feature, the children identify the different words in the wordsnake, adding *qu* in the appropriate place to complete the word each time. Elicit answers. Then they cover the wordsnake and compete with a friend to remember as many *qu* words as possible.

Answers

squid, quick, square, quiz, quietly, question, mosquito, queen

Cooler: *qu* sentences

Challenge the children to write one sentence including as many *qu* words as they can. They swap sentences with a friend to check spelling. Elicit sentences.

Competency Focus

Collaborate and Communicate

The children work together to share their ideas on the topic, incorporating the new vocabulary.

Presentation Kit • Use Vocabulary Tool 4B to pre-teach key vocabulary. Use *Slideshow* to introduce the words and *Find the Pairs* to review/test.

- Use *Stopwatch* to set a time limit for the SB Spelling Central activity. Have children use *Highlighter* to identify *qu* words on the page, and *Pen* to complete the chart.
- To give feedback on the Cooler activity, ask children to write their sentences containing as many *qu* words as possible in *Notepad*. Have the class check and correct any errors.

CLIL: Science—Memory and the brain

Lesson objective: find out how our brains store memory and how to improve it

Materials: CLIL Graphic Organizer 4 [TRC printout] (optional)

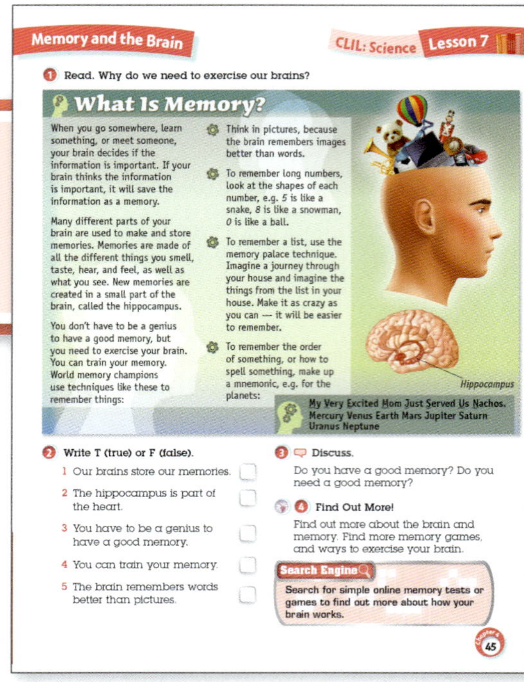

Memory and the Brain — CLIL: Science — Lesson 7

1 Read. Why do we need to exercise our brains?

What Is Memory?

When you go somewhere, learn something, or meet someone, your brain decides if the information is important. If your brain thinks the information is important, it will save the information as a memory.

Many different parts of your brain are used to make and store memories. Memories are made of all the different things you smell, taste, hear, and feel, as well as what you see. New memories are created in a small part of the brain, called the hippocampus.

You don't have to be a genius to have a good memory, but you need to exercise your brain. You can train your memory. World memory champions use techniques like these to remember things:

- Think in pictures, because the brain remembers images better than words.
- To remember long numbers, look at the shapes of each number, e.g. *5* is like a snake, *8* is like a snowman, *0* is like a ball.
- To remember a list, use the memory palace technique. Imagine a journey through your house and imagine the things from the list in your house. Make it as crazy as you can — it will be easier to remember.
- To remember the order of something, or how to spell something, make up a mnemonic, e.g. for the planets:

My Very Excited Mom Just Served Us Nachos.
Mercury Venus Earth Mars Jupiter Saturn Uranus Neptune

Hippocampus

2 Write T (true) or F (false).

1 Our brains store our memories.
2 The hippocampus is part of the heart.
3 You have to be a genius to have a good memory.
4 You can train your memory.
5 The brain remembers words better than pictures.

3 Discuss.

Do you have a good memory? Do you need a good memory?

4 Find Out More!

Find out more about the brain and memory. Find more memory games, and ways to exercise your brain.

Search Engine

Search for simple online memory tests or games to find out more about how your brain works.

Chapter 4 45

Warmer: Memory test 1

Write on the board *Can you remember what you had for lunch two days ago?* Have the children mingle and ask the same question. Ask the children *Is it more difficult to remember things that happened a long time ago?*

1 Read. Why do we need to exercise our brains?

- Have the children read the text about memory. Ask *Why do we need to exercise our brains?* (*to have a good memory*)

2 Write T (true) or F (false).

- Have the children scan the text to find the information to answer the first question. (*true—Many different parts of your brain are used to make and store memories. lines 8–10*) Point out the technique of looking for important words from the question and then reading carefully to find the answer.
- The children do the activity using this technique, writing T (true) or F (false) for each statement.
- Elicit answers.

Answers

1 T **2** F **3** F **4** T **5** F

3 Discuss.

- Have a child read out the discussion questions.
- Have the children talk about their ideas in small groups, then share ideas as a class.

4 Find Out More!

- The children research the brain, memory, and memory games. The **Search Engine** feature gives support on where to look. The children will need to complete this research before doing the follow-up activity in the Activity Book. (It could be set as homework.)

Optional activity: The "memory palace"

Write a list of words (*kangaroo, basketball, superhero, pencil case, carrots, swimming pool, newspaper, graffiti, wings, candle*) on the board. Give the children two minutes to read the list and imagine the items using the memory palace technique. Erase the list and have the children work in pairs to remember the list.

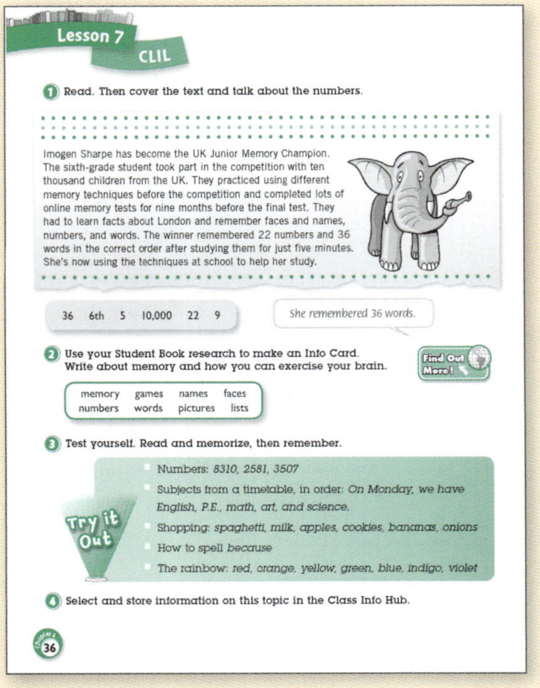

Lesson 7
CLIL

1 Read. Then cover the text and talk about the numbers.

Imogen Sharpe has become the UK Junior Memory Champion. The sixth-grade student took part in the competition with ten thousand children from the UK. They practiced using different memory techniques before the competition and completed lots of online memory tests for nine months before the final test. They had to learn facts about London and remember faces and names, numbers, and words. The winner remembered 22 numbers and 36 words in the correct order after studying them for just five minutes. She's now using the techniques at school to help her study.

36 6th 5 10,000 22 9

She remembered 36 words.

2 Use your Student Book research to make an Info Card. Write about memory and how you can exercise your brain.

Find Out More!

memory games names faces
numbers words pictures lists

3 Test yourself. Read and memorize, then remember.

Try it Out

- Numbers: *8310, 2581, 3507*
- Subjects from a timetable, in order: *On Monday, we have English, P.E., math, art, and science.*
- Shopping: *spaghetti, milk, apples, cookies, bananas, onions*
- How to spell *because*
- The rainbow: *red, orange, yellow, green, blue, indigo, violet*

4 Select and store information on this topic in the Class Info Hub.

Chapter 4 36

1 Read. Then cover the text and talk about the numbers.

The children read the text. Then they discuss the number prompts in pairs, recalling facts from the text. Elicit responses.

2 Use your Student Book research to make an Info Card. Write about memory and how you can exercise your brain.

Divide the class into groups. Have the children pool the information they learned from their research in the Student Book and the Activity Book. The children write about and illustrate their ideas individually. Have the groups present their Info Cards to the class.

3 Test yourself. Read and memorize, then remember.

The children follow the **Try It Out** instructions. They try to memorize the facts given, then test each other in pairs. Elicit which they found easiest/hardest. Elicit which techniques they used, referring back to the Student Book as necessary.

4 Select and store information on this topic in the Class Info Hub.

Have the children vote for the five most interesting Info Cards. Archive these in your Class Hub (see p. 41) in a folder called **Chapter 4 Memory**.

Cooler: Memory test 2

Test the children on how well they have remembered their "memory palace" list from the Optional activity. They work individually to write as many words as they can remember. The first child to remember all the words wins. If you did not do the Optional Activity, it can replace the Cooler activity here.

Competency Focus

Act

The children carry out research to find out about the brain and memory. This helps them expand their learning and relate it to their world, both inside and outside the classroom.

Presentation Kit • Use the SB for an alternative "heads-up" introduction to the topic (Activity 1 point 1). Use *Pointer* on the text as you read it aloud.

- As support for less confident children, you could elicit findings orally before AB Activity 2. Use *Highlighter* on the word bank options (*memory*, *games*, etc.), one at a time, to elicit information and ideas from the class.

Teacher's Resource Center • Print out CLIL Graphic Organizer 4 for the children to use in collating their Find Out More! research.

Writing Project

Lesson objectives: review language from Chapter 4; write a description of a superhero and present it to the class
Materials: Writing Template 4 [TRC printout] (optional)

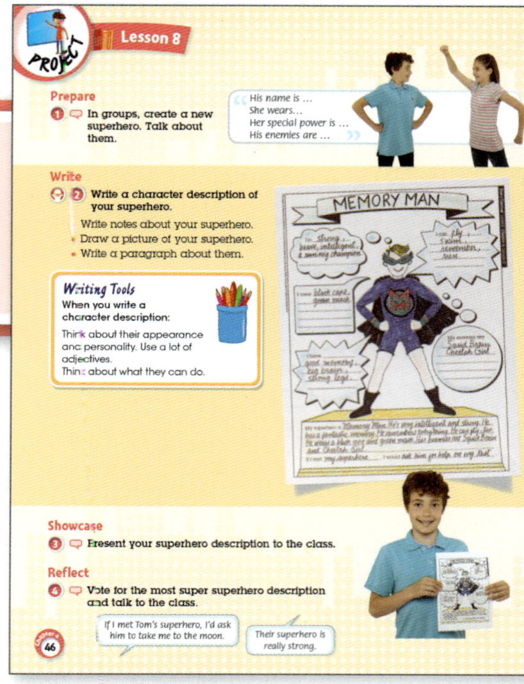
Lesson 8
Prepare
1 In groups, create a new superhero. Talk about them.
His name is …
She wears…
Her special power is …
His enemies are …
Write
2 Write a character description of your superhero.
Write notes about your superhero.
Draw a picture of your superhero.
Write a paragraph about them.
Writing Tools
When you write a character description:
Think about their appearance and personality. Use a lot of adjectives.
Think about what they can do.
MEMORY MAN
Showcase
3 Present your superhero description to the class.
Reflect
4 Vote for the most super superhero description and talk to the class.
If I met Tom's superhero, I'd ask him to take me to the moon.
Their superhero is really strong.
46

Warmer: Play "Back to the Board"

Play the game with key vocabulary from Chapter 4 (see Games Bank p. 222).

Prepare

1 In groups, create a new superhero. Talk about them.

- Tell the children they will create a new superhero with special powers, a costume, enemies, and a secret identity. Divide the class into groups of four children. Give them a few minutes to discuss and decide on the details of their superhero.
- Elicit ideas.

Write

2 Write a character description of your superhero.

- Have the children look at the example. Ask for examples of what to include for a good description.
- Read the **Writing Tools** box together and have the children make notes about their superhero. They then write and illustrate their text following the model in the book. Give support as necessary.

Showcase

3 Present your superhero description to the class.

- Choose children to read their superhero description to the class. Ask the class to listen to see which superheroes have similar powers.

Reflect

4 Vote for the most super superhero description and talk to the class.

- Have the children comment on which superhero was the best and why. Have a class vote to identify their favorite.

Optional activity: Invent a villain

The children create the same information about the villains who are their superheroes' enemies. Then the children can browse the descriptions and pictures and decide which villain is the best match for each superhero.

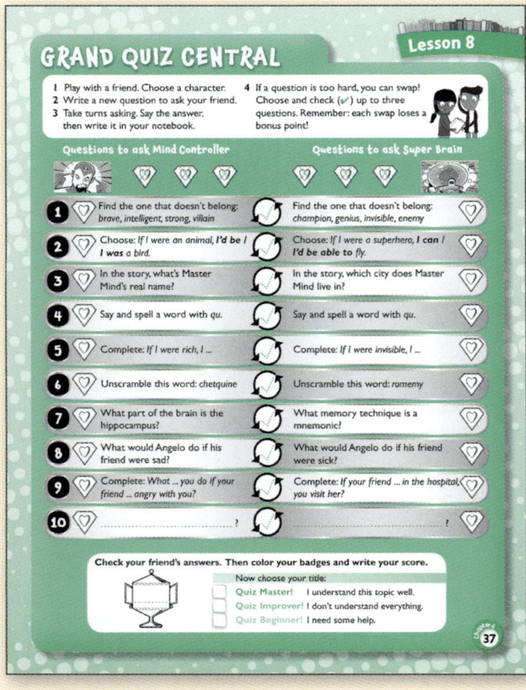

GRAND QUIZ CENTRAL

Lesson 8

1 Play with a friend. Choose a character.
2 Write a new question to ask your friend.
3 Take turns asking. Say the answer, then write it in your notebook.
4 If a question is too hard, you can swap! Choose and check (✓) up to three questions. Remember: each swap loses a bonus point!

	Questions to ask Mind Controller	Questions to ask Super Brain
1	Find the one that doesn't belong: *brave, intelligent, strong, villain*	Find the one that doesn't belong: *champion, genius, invisible, enemy*
2	Choose: *If I were an animal,* ***I'd be / I was*** *a bird.*	Choose: *If I were a superhero,* ***I can / I'd be able to*** *fly.*
3	In the story, what's Master Mind's real name?	In the story, which city does Master Mind live in?
4	Say and spell a word with *qu*.	Say and spell a word with *qu*.
5	Complete: *If I were rich, I …*	Complete: *If I were invisible, I …*
6	Unscramble this word: *chetquine*	Unscramble this word: *romemy*
7	What part of the brain is the hippocampus?	What memory technique is a mnemonic?
8	What would Angelo do if his friend were sad?	What would Angelo do if his friend were sick?
9	Complete: *What … you do if your friend … angry with you?*	Complete: *If your friend … in the hospital, … you visit her?*
10	………………………………?	………………………………?

Check your friend's answers. Then color your badges and write your score.

Now choose your title:
- Quiz Master! I understand this topic well.
- Quiz Improver! I don't understand everything.
- Quiz Beginner! I need some help.

37

Grand Quiz Central

See p. 43 for details of how to take the quiz.

Answers

1 villain / invisible **2** I'd be / I'd be able to **3** Brent / Washington **4** Any word with *qu*, e.g. squid, mosquito **5** If I were rich, I would + verb / If I were invisible, I would + verb **6** technique / memory **7** where memories are created / when you remember the order of things using the first letters of each word **8** He would buy them some candy. / He would wait for them to get better. **9** would, were / were **10** Children's own answers.

Cooler: Play "Change the Text"

Play the game with the text about Memory Man from Student Book Activity 2 (see Games Bank p. 222).

Competency Focus

Me

The children write a character description of their own superhero, exploring their imagination and creativity.

Presentation Kit • Use *Stopwatch* to give the children one minute to study the SB Prepare box. Use *Mask* to cover the text. Elicit and uncover the sentence openings one at a time. Ask different children to complete the sentence with a correct ending. Elicit class agreement.

- TIP Use *Notepad* to log the results of the class vote in SB Activity 4. Involve the children in collating and writing the results.

Teacher's Resource Center • Print out Writing Template 4 to use for the SB writing activity.

Language Review

Lesson objective: review language from Chapter 4
Materials: Class CD

Review

1 Listen and correct the sentences.

If she were a superhero, ...

1 ... she wouldn't have a secret identity. she would have a secret identity.
2 ... she would be a student at night.
3 ... she would be able to fly.
4 ... she would wear a special costume to make her fly.
5 ... she wouldn't have a very good memory.
6 ... she would be able to control her enemy's body.

2 What would you do if you saw this? Write sentences in your notebook about the pictures.

If I saw somebody drop money / steal / cheat, ...

3 Think about Chapter 4. Color the bone.

Which activity was easy?
Which activity was difficult?
Figure it out with a friend.
Write a tip to help you remember.
I'm not sure.
OK.
Whizzkid!

Treasure Hunt!

Look back at pages 4 and 5.
Which city does Neuron want to destroy?
Find something from that country. What is it?

Chapter 4 47

Warmer: Play "Board Pelmanism"

Play the game with half words/phrases, e.g. *secret—identify, super—hero, vil—lain, invis—ible, Presi—dent, alba—tross, mem—ory, scare—enemies, special—power* (see Games Bank p. 222).

1 1.32 Listen and correct the sentences.

- Have the children look at the sentences. Ask *What do you think we're going to listen to?* Elicit ideas about the content of the recording.
- Play the CD. The children listen and correct the sentences.
- Play the CD again for the children to check their answers.
- Elicit answers.

Audioscript

If I were a superhero, I would have a secret identity. I would be a student in the day and a superhero at night. I would be brave and have a lot of amazing powers. I wouldn't be able to fly, but I would wear a special costume to make me invisible. I would have an enormous brain and an amazing memory, so I would be a genius student, too. And I would be able to control my enemy's mind. So watch out! I know what you're thinking! I would use my special powers to help people. I wouldn't want to rule the world—I would just want to save it!

Answers

1 she would have a secret identity. **2** she would be a student in the day. / she would be a superhero at night. **3** she wouldn't be able to fly. **4** she would wear a special costume to make her invisible. **5** she would have an amazing memory. **6** she would be able to control her enemy's mind.

2 What would you do if you saw this? Write sentences in your notebook about the pictures.

- Elicit what is happening in the pictures.
- Elicit sentences for the first picture.
- The children write sentences in their notebook and compare their sentences in pairs.
- Elicit responses.

Answers

Children's own answers.

3 Think about Chapter 4. Color the bone.

- Have the children look back at Chapter 4 and color the bone to evaluate their progress (self-evaluation).
- Discuss ideas for more effective listening, e.g. underline key words in questions before you listen and predict what you are going to hear. The children choose and write a tip in their Student Book.

Treasure Hunt

Ask *Which city does Neuron want to destroy?* (*Washington*) *Which country is it in?* (*the USA*) Have the children look at pp. 4–5 to find something from the USA. (*the Statue of Liberty*)

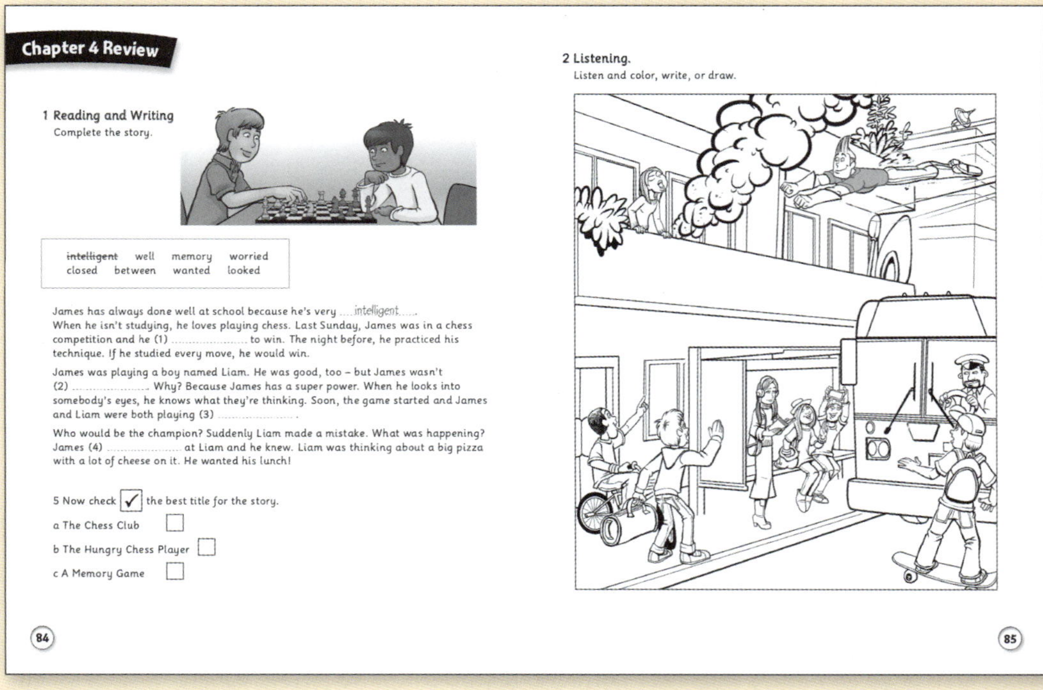

Chapter 4 Review

1 Reading and Writing
Complete the story.

~~intelligent~~ well memory worried
closed between wanted looked

James has always done well at school because he's very ....intelligent......
When he isn't studying, he loves playing chess. Last Sunday, James was in a chess competition and he (1) .... to win. The night before, he practiced his technique. If he studied every move, he would win.

James was playing a boy named Liam. He was good, too – but James wasn't (2) .... Why? Because James has a super power. When he looks into somebody's eyes, he knows what they're thinking. Soon, the game started and James and Liam were both playing (3) ....

Who would be the champion? Suddenly Liam made a mistake. What was happening? James (4) .... at Liam and he knew. Liam was thinking about a big pizza with a lot of cheese on it. He wanted his lunch!

5 Now check ✓ the best title for the story.

a The Chess Club ☐

b The Hungry Chess Player ☐

c A Memory Game ☐

84

2 Listening.
Listen and color, write, or draw.

85

1 Reading and Writing. Complete the story.

The children complete the text using the words supplied and choose the best title. Check answers.

Answers

1 wanted **2** worried **3** well **4** looked
b The Hungry Chess Player

2 2.34 Listening. Listen and color, write, or draw.

Play the CD twice. The children listen and color, write, or draw the objects according to the recording. Check answers.

Answers (Audioscript on p. 223)

Boy on skateboard: hat colored blue
Sports bag: STAR written on it
Suitcase drawn beside woman at bus stop
Girl's phone: colored red
Bus number written: X70

Cooler: Class quiz

Have the children look back at Chapter 4 and write five questions on the content for their friends. They ask and answer questions with a friend, then choose the best five to ask another pair.

Competency Focus

Me: Self-evaluation

The children reflect on the chapter, express their personal opinions about their own progress, and look for ways to improve. This encourages them to evaluate and make decisions about what they need to revisit and how they can learn better.

Presentation Kit • Use the drop-down Menu to access the AB Review pages.

Teacher's Resource Center • Print out Test Chapter 4 to use at the end of this lesson. The Test Generator also allows you to create customized tests.

• For the CEYLT (Cambridge YLE) exam preparation activities on the AB page, choose *Audio* to access the recordings.

Student's App • Encourage the children to play the games on their smartphone/tablet. Have a class vote on which of the three games they played is their favorite.

Chapter 5

Powerful Earth

Overview

The children will:

- use critical thinking skills to identify natural disaster vocabulary and ocean exploration.
- talk about actions at a time before a past event using the past perfect.
- read and understand a Greek myth about a legend.
- ask and answer questions using the past perfect and present perfect.
- identify and use ocean exploration vocabulary.
- find out about tsunamis.
- write a newspaper article about a disaster.

Key Vocabulary

Natural disasters: disaster, erupt, flood, hurricane, protect, shake, tsunami, warnings
Shipwrecks and ocean exploration: coast, damage, inland, scuba divers, shipwreck, underwater

Key Grammar

Past perfect

- There had been an earthquake under the ocean before the tsunami hit.
- Some people hadn't had time to leave their houses before the floods.

Past perfect and present perfect questions

- Have you ever been to Spain?
- Had you heard of Plato before you read that story?

Reading Skills

Story: *The Legend of the Lost Island*
Genre: Greek myth

Literacy Development

- use reading skills to understand and predict content
- relate story theme to personal experience
- use alliteration to highlight language

Functional Language

- Did you enjoy the movie yesterday?
- Yes, it was great. I hadn't seen a good movie for a long time.

Spelling

Compound nouns

CLIL: Geography—Tsunamis

The children find out about tsunamis.

Competency Focus

The children will:

- use critical thinking skills to deduce the meaning of new vocabulary. (Lesson 1)
- predict the content of a story. (Lesson 3)

- activate new vocabulary and apply new grammar knowledge. (Lesson 2)
- apply new grammar rules in a familiar context. (Lesson 5)

- work in pairs to act out a dialogue. (Lesson 3)
- work in pairs to talk about famous shipwrecks. (Lesson 6)

- relate the story and story theme to their personal experience. (Lesson 4)
- write a newspaper article. (Lesson 8)
- evaluate their own progress in the chapter. (Review)

- develop an understanding of natural disasters by carrying out research. (Lesson 7)

Digital Overview

Presentation Kit

Projectable Student Book, Activity Book, and Reader pages

- Vocabulary Tool 5A: Natural disasters
- Vocabulary Tool 5B: Shipwrecks and ocean exploration
- Oral Storytelling Video 5: *A Gift from the Beach*
- Interactive versions of selected SB and AB activities
- Integrated *Audio* and *Answer Key* for all activities

Teacher's Resource Center

Resources for planning, lesson delivery, and homework

- Class Planner Chapter 5
- Worksheets to print out (including notes and answers):
  - Grammar Worksheet 5A: Past perfect
  - Grammar Worksheet 5B: Past perfect and present perfect questions
  - Oral Storytelling Video Worksheet 5: *A Gift from the Beach*
  - CLIL Graphic Organizer 5
  - Writing Template 5
  - Test Chapter 5 and Mid-year Test
- Test Generator
- Literacy Handbook

Student's Resource Center

Resources for consolidation and practice at home

- Interactive Grammar 5A: Past perfect
- Interactive Grammar 5B: Past perfect and present perfect questions
- Vocabulary Tool 5A: Natural disasters
- Vocabulary Tool 5B: Shipwrecks and ocean exploration
- Oral Storytelling Video 5: *A Gift from the Beach*

Student's App

Vocabulary games: Natural disasters and shipwrecks/ocean exploration

Watch the Oral Storytelling Video

Chapter 5

Powerful Earth

Lesson 1

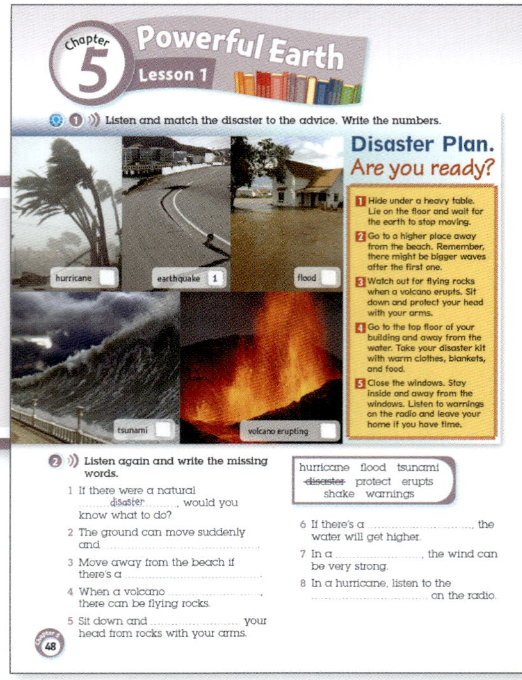
Chapter 5 Powerful Earth
Lesson 1

1 Listen and match the disaster to the advice. Write the numbers.

hurricane [ ] earthquake [1] flood [ ] tsunami [ ] volcano erupting [ ]

Disaster Plan. Are you ready?

1 Hide under a heavy table. Lie on the floor and wait for the earth to stop moving.

2 Go to a higher place away from the beach. Remember, there might be bigger waves after the first one.

3 Watch out for flying rocks when a volcano erupts. Sit down and protect your head with your arms.

4 Go to the top floor of your building and away from the water. Take your disaster kit with warm clothes, blankets, and food.

5 Close the windows. Stay inside and away from the windows. Listen to warnings on the radio and leave your home if you have time.

2 Listen again and write the missing words.

hurricane flood tsunami ~~disaster~~ protect erupts shake warnings

1 If there were a natural ...disaster..., would you know what to do?
2 The ground can move suddenly and ....
3 Move away from the beach if there's a ....
4 When a volcano ...., there can be flying rocks.
5 Sit down and .... your head from rocks with your arms.
6 If there's a ...., the water will get higher.
7 In a ...., the wind can be very strong.
8 In a hurricane, listen to the .... on the radio.

Chapter 5 48

Vocabulary

Lesson objectives: identify and use vocabulary for natural disasters
Key vocabulary: *disaster, erupt, flood, hurricane, protect, shake, tsunami, warnings*
Materials: Class CD

Warmer: Play "Vocabulary Ping-Pong"

Divide the class into two teams. Give the topic: *weather*. The teams name as many words connected with that topic as possible, taking turns saying a word. The first team to repeat a word or take longer than five seconds to play is out and the other team wins a point. Start a new game of ping-pong with a different topic.

1 1.33 Listen and match the disaster to the advice. Write the numbers.

- Have the children look at the pictures. Ask *What can you see happening? What do we call these situations?* (*natural disasters*)
- Play the CD. The children listen and match the disasters to the advice by writing the correct numbers.
- Elicit answers.

Audioscript

Disaster Plan—Are you ready? If there were a natural disaster, would you know what to do? When there's an earthquake, the ground can move suddenly and shake. If you're inside, hide under a heavy table and lie on the floor. If you're outside, move away from buildings. Lie on the ground and wait for the earth to stop moving after the earthquake. A tsunami carries a lot of water and has very big waves. Move away from the beach if there's a tsunami and go to a higher place. Remember, there might be bigger waves behind the first one. When a volcano erupts, there can be flying rocks. Close the windows and doors; bring animals inside. Then, sit down and protect your head from rocks with your arms.
If there's a flood, the water will get higher so go to the top floor of your building away from the water. Take your disaster kit. You might need warm clothes, blankets, and food.
In a hurricane, the wind can be very strong. Go inside. Close the windows. Then stay away from them because the wind might break the glass. Listen to the warnings on the radio and only leave your home if you have time.
Remember, it's unusual for very bad things to happen because of the weather, but it's better to be ready.

Answers

hurricane 5, earthquake 1, flood 4, tsunami 2, volcano erupting 3

2 1.33 Listen again and write the missing words.

- Play the CD again. The children listen and complete the sentences using the words supplied.
- Elicit answers.

Answers

1 disaster **2** shake **3** tsunami **4** erupts **5** protect **6** flood **7** hurricane **8** warnings

Optional activity: Picture dictation

Slowly read the following text aloud: *Draw three houses. Each house has five windows and a door. On the roof of one of the houses there are two people and a dog. Draw two trees on the right. At the top of the picture draw some clouds. The clouds are gray and it's raining a lot. Around the houses there is water. The water is touching the top windows of the house.* Ask the children what they think the disaster was. (*tsunami/flood/hurricane*) Repeat the description again and have the children draw. They compare their pictures and find differences.

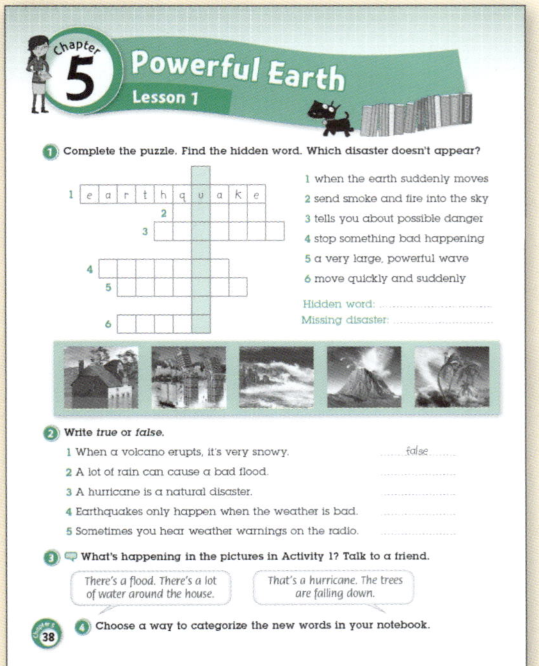
Chapter 5 Powerful Earth
Lesson 1

1 Complete the puzzle. Find the hidden word. Which disaster doesn't appear?

1 e a r t h q u a k e

1 when the earth suddenly moves
2 send smoke and fire into the sky
3 tells you about possible danger
4 stop something bad happening
5 a very large, powerful wave
6 move quickly and suddenly

Hidden word: ……
Missing disaster: ……

2 Write *true* or *false*.

1 When a volcano erupts, it's very snowy. ……false……
2 A lot of rain can cause a bad flood. ……
3 A hurricane is a natural disaster. ……
4 Earthquakes only happen when the weather is bad. ……
5 Sometimes you hear weather warnings on the radio. ……

3 What's happening in the pictures in Activity 1? Talk to a friend.

There's a flood. There's a lot of water around the house.
That's a hurricane. The trees are falling down.

4 Choose a way to categorize the new words in your notebook.

Chapter 5 38

1 Complete the puzzle. Find the hidden word. Which disaster doesn't appear?

The children use the clues to complete the puzzle and find the hidden word on the colored squares. Then they compare the pictures to the clues and write the missing disaster. Elicit answers.

Answers

1 earthquake **2** erupt **3** warning **4** protect **5** tsunami **6** shake
Hidden word: hurricane
Missing disaster: flood

2 Write *true* or *false*.

The children write true or false for each sentence. Elicit answers.

Answers

1 false **2** true **3** true **4** false **5** true

3 What's happening in the pictures in Activity 1? Talk to a friend.

The children talk in pairs about what they can see in the disaster pictures in Activity 1. Elicit ideas.

4 Choose a way to categorize the new words in your notebook.

Brainstorm appropriate categories, e.g. *nouns/verbs, common/not common, happens in my country/does not happen in my country.* The children choose the best categories for them and list the words in their notebook.

Answers

Children's own answers.

Cooler: Play "The Spelling Game"

Divide the class into teams. Start spelling the word *flood* aloud. As soon as a child recognizes it, they raise their hand. Ask them to write it on the board. The other teams confirm whether it is correct or not. A correct answer wins a point. If it is incorrect, the team that identifies the error nominates a child to write the word correctly to win a point. Repeat with *hurricane*, *warnings*, *earthquake*, *tsunami*, *disaster*, etc.

Competency Focus

Think! Critical Thinking

The children use critical thinking skills to understand the new vocabulary by using visual clues and processing the written and spoken forms.

Presentation Kit • Use Vocabulary Tool 5A to pre-teach key vocabulary. Use *Slideshow* to introduce the words and *Spotlight* to review/test.

- Play "Kim's Game" with the new vocabulary. *Spotlight* the word bank in SB Activity 2. Have the class read the words aloud. Use *Stopwatch* to give the class one minute to memorize the words, then one minute to recall them. Repeat several times.
- TIP Within *Hotspots*, use the arrows in the Navigation Pane at the bottom of the screen to navigate through the activities.

Grammar

Lesson objective: talk about actions at a time before a past event
Key grammar: past perfect
Secondary language: *northeast, warning*
Materials: Grammar Worksheet 5A [TRC printout] (optional)

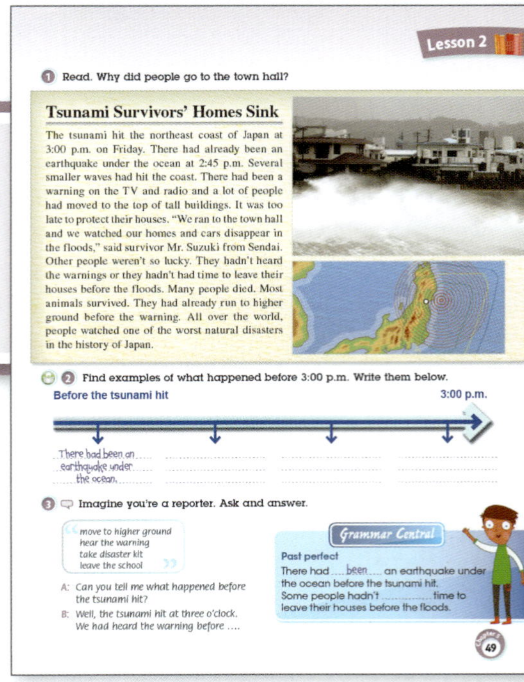
Lesson 2

1 Read. Why did people go to the town hall?

Tsunami Survivors' Homes Sink

The tsunami hit the northeast coast of Japan at 3:00 p.m. on Friday. There had already been an earthquake under the ocean at 2:45 p.m. Several smaller waves had hit the coast. There had been a warning on the TV and radio and a lot of people had moved to the top of tall buildings. It was too late to protect their houses. "We ran to the town hall and we watched our homes and cars disappear in the floods," said survivor Mr. Suzuki from Sendai. Other people weren't so lucky. They hadn't heard the warnings or they hadn't had time to leave their houses before the floods. Many people died. Most animals survived. They had already run to higher ground before the warning. All over the world, people watched one of the worst natural disasters in the history of Japan.

2 Find examples of what happened before 3:00 p.m. Write them below.

Before the tsunami hit — 3:00 p.m.

There had been an earthquake under the ocean.

3 Imagine you're a reporter. Ask and answer.

move to higher ground
hear the warning
take disaster kit
leave the school

A: Can you tell me what happened before the tsunami hit?
B: Well, the tsunami hit at three o'clock. We had heard the warning before ....

Grammar Central
Past perfect
There had ....been.... an earthquake under the ocean before the tsunami hit.
Some people hadn't .... time to leave their houses before the floods.

49

Warmer: Play "Back to the Board"

Play the game with key vocabulary: *hurricane, flood, tsunami, earthquake, disaster, protect, erupt, shake, warnings* (see Games Bank p. 222).

1 Read. Why did people go to the town hall?

- Have the children look at the pictures. Ask *What is happening? What can you see?*
- Ask *What sort of text is this? A letter? A newspaper article? An email?* (*a newspaper article*)
- Ask *Why did people go to the town hall?* (*because it was a tall building*) Elicit answers.

2 Find examples of what happened before 3:00 p.m. Write them below.

- Elicit what happened at 3:00 p.m. (*The tsunami hit the coast of Japan.*)
- Draw the children's attention to the sentence *There had already been an earthquake under the ocean at 2.45 p.m.* which gives the example answer.
- Have the children use this example to find at least three more things that happened before 3:00 p.m.
- Elicit answers.

Answers (suggested)

There had been an earthquake under the ocean. + *any three of:* Several smaller waves had hit the coast. / There had been a warning on TV and the radio. / A lot of people had moved to the top of tall buildings. / Some people hadn't heard the warnings. / Some people hadn't had time to leave their houses before the floods. / Most animals had run to higher ground.

Grammar Central

Past perfect

Have the children complete the grammar examples. Elicit answers. Then elicit the rules for using the past perfect. (had + *verb tells us about events before the main action*) The children write more examples in their notebook. See also the Grammar Reference sections in the Student Book (p. 100) and Activity Book (p. 100) for further explanation and practice.

Grammar Central Answers: been, had

AB Answers Activity 1: 1 had already found **2** had saved **3** hadn't eaten **4** had drunk **5** hadn't been **6** had already given

3 Imagine you're a reporter. Ask and answer.

- Elicit a response for the first prompt.
- Have the children work in pairs and continue asking and answering about the events before 3:00 p.m.
- Have pairs act out their dialogues for the class.

Optional activity: Play "The Chain Game"

Play the game with the phrase *When I arrived at school this morning, I had already ...* (see Games Bank p. 222).

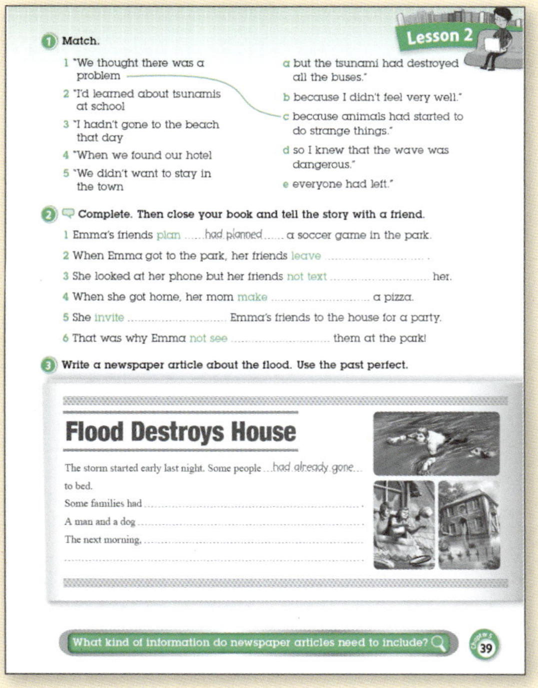
Lesson 2

1 Match.

1 "We thought there was a problem
2 "I'd learned about tsunamis at school
3 "I hadn't gone to the beach that day
4 "When we found our hotel
5 "We didn't want to stay in the town

a but the tsunami had destroyed all the buses."
b because I didn't feel very well."
c because animals had started to do strange things."
d so I knew that the wave was dangerous."
e everyone had left."

2 Complete. Then close your book and tell the story with a friend.

1 Emma's friends plan ......had planned...... a soccer game in the park.
2 When Emma got to the park, her friends leave ....
3 She looked at her phone but her friends not text .... her.
4 When she got home, her mom make .... a pizza.
5 She invite .... Emma's friends to the house for a party.
6 That was why Emma not see .... them at the park!

3 Write a newspaper article about the flood. Use the past perfect.

Flood Destroys House

The storm started early last night. Some people ...had already gone... to bed.
Some families had ....
A man and a dog ....
The next morning, ...
....

What kind of information do newspaper articles need to include?

Chapter 5 39

1 Match.

The children match the sentence halves. Elicit answers.

Answers

1 c **2** d **3** b **4** e **5** a

2 Complete. Then close your book and tell the story with a friend.

The children complete the sentences using the correct form of the verbs given. Elicit answers. Then the children close their book and retell the story in pairs. Invite pairs to say a line of the story each.

Answers

1 had planned **2** had left **3** hadn't texted **4** had made **5** had invited **6** hadn't seen

3 Write a newspaper article about the flood. Use the past perfect.

The children write a newspaper article about the flood using the past perfect. Then they compare with a friend. Ask *What kind of information do newspaper articles need to include?* (*facts/what happened next, times/when it happened, people/who was there*)

Answers

Children's own answers.

Cooler: Play "Disappearing Words"

Play the game with past perfect verbs from the lesson, e.g. *had found*, *had been*, *had hit*, etc. (see Games Bank p. 222).

Competency Focus

Learn

The children integrate previously acquired vocabulary into new grammar and structure, and adapt the language to show an understanding of the topic.

Presentation Kit • Display the AB and use the link in the drop-down Menu to access the corresponding Grammar Reference section at the back.

- Use the AB page to give feedback on activities, using the built-in interactive activity or *Answer Key*, as appropriate.
- TIP With *Answer Key*, you can show the answers all at once or one by one to customize feedback.

Teacher's Resource Center • For extra grammar practice, print out Grammar Worksheet 5A.

Student's Resource Center • The children can use Interactive Grammar 5A at home.

Reading: Story Extract

Lesson objectives: ask and answer about something they had not done for a long time; use the title and pictures to predict story content; read the extract from the Greek myth *The Legend of the Lost Island* (middle)
Functional language: *Did you enjoy …? Yes, it was great. I hadn't seen … for a long time.*
Secondary language: *powers, paradise, feeding, decorated, fountains*
Materials: Class CD

Warmer: Play "Sentence Builders"

Play the game with past perfect sentences, e.g. *There had been an earthquake before the tsunami hit. They had already run to higher ground before the warning.* (see Games Bank p. 222).

Functional language

1 1.34 Listen and read.

- Play the CD. The children listen and read along. Ask *Why is Rufus happy? (He enjoyed the movie.) When was the last time he enjoyed a movie?* (*a long time ago*)
- Play the CD again, pausing for them to repeat.
- Divide the class into pairs to practice the dialogue.

2 Talk to a friend about something you hadn't done for a long time.

- Two children read the example. Elicit other examples of events using the prompts supplied.
- The children practice in pairs. Have pairs perform a dialogue for the class.

Before reading

3 Look at the story. Do you think this is a real place?

- Have the children study the story title and pictures to figure out if the place is real. Elicit ideas.

4 1.35 Read the story extract and answer.

- Play the CD. The children listen and read along. Have them answer question 1. Elicit the answer.
- Play the CD again so they can write their ideas for questions 2 and 3. Encourage them to use reading skills (e.g. using the title, pictures, and context) to infer meaning and make predictions.

- Elicit answers, but do not confirm predictions: explain that they will have to read the story to find out.

Answers

1 He changed it into a paradise with trees, flowers, and wild animals. **2** Children's own answers. **3** It's a Greek myth. / Children's own answers.

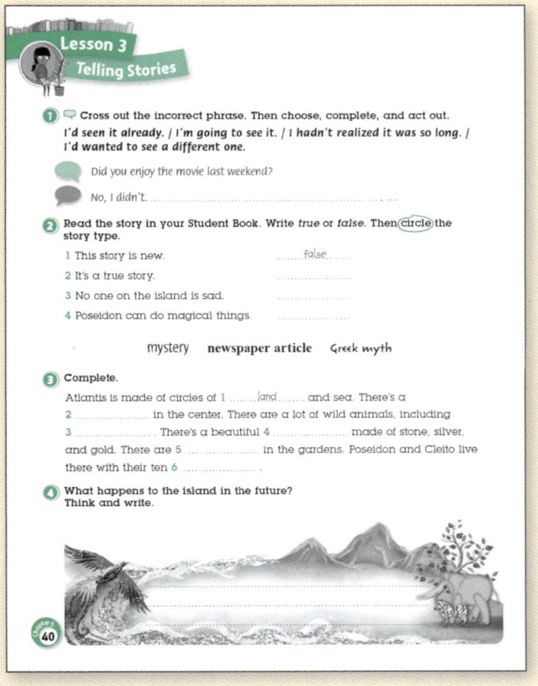
Lesson 3
Telling Stories

1 Cross out the incorrect phrase. Then choose, complete, and act out.
I'd seen it already. / I'm going to see it. / I hadn't realized it was so long. / I'd wanted to see a different one.

Did you enjoy the movie last weekend?
No, I didn't. ....

2 Read the story in your Student Book. Write *true* or *false*. Then circle the story type.
1 This story is new. ......false......
2 It's a true story. ....
3 No one on the island is sad. ....
4 Poseidon can do magical things. ....

mystery newspaper article Greek myth

3 Complete.
Atlantis is made of circles of 1 ......land...... and sea. There's a 2 .... in the center. There are a lot of wild animals, including 3 .... There's a beautiful 4 .... made of stone, silver, and gold. There are 5 .... in the gardens. Poseidon and Cleito live there with their ten 6 ....

4 What happens to the island in the future? Think and write.

40

1 Cross out the incorrect phrase. Then choose, complete, and act out.

The children identify which phrase is incorrect. (*I'm going to see it.*) They then choose one of the other phrases and act out the dialogue in pairs. Encourage them to use what they know to adapt and extend the dialogue. Have pairs act out their dialogue for the class.

2 Read the story in your Student Book. Write *true* or *false*. Then circle the story type.

The children read the Student Book story extract again, then write true or false for each sentence and circle the correct story type. Elicit answers.

Answers

1 false **2** false **3** true **4** true
Circled: Greek myth

3 Complete.

The children complete the text using details from the story extract. Elicit answers.

Answers

1 land **2** mountain **3** elephants/giraffes/zebras/birds **4** palace **5** fountains **6** sons/children

4 What happens to the island in the future? Think and write.

Elicit suggestions on what happens to the island of Atlantis in the future. The children write their own ideas, then compare with a friend. Elicit ideas.

Answers

Children's own answers.

Cooler: Play "Change the Text"

Play the game with a summary of the story extract (see Games Bank p. 222).

Competency Focus

Collaborate and Communicate

The children work together to practice, perform, and adapt the new functional language learned.

Think

The children use critical thinking skills to identify the setting of the story by looking at the text and story artwork.

Presentation Kit • *Mask* the SB Activity 1 speech bubbles. Elicit and uncover individually to confirm. Use *Highlighter* on *enjoy the movie* and the sentence starting *I hadn't seen …*, and elicit different things you could say in this context.

- Display the AB page for Activity 4 feedback. Have children use *Pen* to write their version of what happens to the island in the future. Elicit who in the class had the same response. Use *Eraser* to clear and repeat with children with different ideas.

THE LEGEND OF THE LOST ISLAND

Have you ever heard of Atlantis—the island that sank under the ocean in a storm? The Greek philosopher Plato wrote about the island thousands of years ago. He said an old man told him this tale a long, long time ago …

1
Long ago, when the sky was ruled by Zeus and the oceans were ruled by Poseidon, there was a small rocky island in the middle of the ocean. A few families lived there quietly, until Poseidon visited the island after he had noticed a beautiful girl.

2
He came out of the sea and turned himself into a handsome human and hurried to her house. Her name was Cleito. They soon fell in love and got married on the island.

3
Then, Poseidon used his powers to change the island into a paradise. He created circles of land and circles of sea around the central mountain. There were a lot of trees with fruit, and wild animals, including elephants, lived there happily feeding off the land. Vegetables and flowers grew everywhere.

4
The people built a palace for Poseidon and Cleito. It was made of stone and decorated with silver and gold. There were gardens and fountains. Everyone was happy. Poseidon and Cleito had five pairs of twin sons. The first boy was named Atlas and they named the island after him.

5
Poseidon gave each son one tenth of the island. They lived happily on the island. Poseidon said, "If you take care of the city and protect it, all will be well. But if you don't, there will be a terrible disaster." His sons and the people listened to him: they were good, nice, and smart. They lived in peace together. Poseidon had done his job. He went back to his home under the ocean and slept.

7
But one day, a loud roar woke him up. It was Zeus calling him from the sky. Poseidon rose up from the sea and looked at the island, and saw that it had changed. The people had not taken care of the city—they had ignored his warnings. Buildings had fallen down. The people had started to argue. They had become greedy. They wanted more food. They wanted more silver and gold. They wanted more power. They had started to steal, lie, cheat, and fight. Poseidon was angry. He remembered what he had said about the terrible disaster. The time had come.

8
He stirred the ocean into an enormous wave. It hit the island like a hurricane. The earth shook and it felt like an earthquake. The volcano erupted, and a tsunami flooded the island. The island disappeared under the sea forever.

9
The whole population of Atlantis had disappeared. But had it really disappeared? Some people believe that unusual fish now live in the water and mermaids swim there and rescue humans from drowning. They say the rocks beneath the sea are the remains of the lost city of Atlantis.

Lesson objective: read and understand the Greek myth *The Legend of the Lost Island* in the Reader
Materials: Class CD; Reader; Oral Storytelling Video Worksheet 5 [TRC printout] (optional)

Warmer: What's changed?

Read the story extract aloud, but change key objects so the story becomes a funny adaptation (e.g. *Then Poseidon used his cell phone to change the island into a movie theater.*, etc.). Each time the children hear something different from the original, they say *Stop!* and correct you.

Story Summary

Poseidon, the god of the oceans, turns an island into a paradise for a girl he loves, Cleito. Poseidon asks their children to take care of the island. At first everyone is happy, but the people become greedy and argue. Poseidon is angry and destroys the island with a great wave.

Theme: the importance of taking care of the things you own

1.36 While reading

- Have the children look at the pictures in the Reader. Ask *What happened to Atlantis?* (*A big wave hit it and it sank.*)
- Play the CD. The children listen and read along. Ask *Why did Poseidon destroy the island?* (*because he told the people to take care of the island but they didn't*)
- Ask questions to check comprehension, e.g. *How many children did Poseidon and Cleito have?* (*ten sons*) *What happened to the island at the end of the story?* (*It disappeared under the sea.*)
- The class read the story again with children playing different roles and sharing the narrator's part. Bring the story to life using sound effects (see **Story Time**).

After reading: Reflect

Ask questions to give the children the opportunity to think about the issues raised by the story, e.g. *Do you think Poseidon was right to destroy Atlantis? What do you think we can learn from this story?*

Optional activity: What did Poseidon do?

The children imagine that Poseidon did not destroy the city, but talked to the people. Elicit what he said.

Story Time

Add sound effects

This activity helps the children focus on actions in the story and pay close attention to the text. Have three groups focus on a page each, and decide on sound effects for the actions or events in the story. Then read out the story and have each group make the sound effects to bring the story to life.

Reading Strategy

Persuasive Writing

Persuasive Writing helps the children develop their writing skills in non-fiction tasks. With this strategy, they learn to think and plan carefully before they write, to develop their arguments, and to use language efficiently.

For additional explanation and activities, see the Literacy Handbook on the Teacher's Resource Center.

Cooler: Advice for Atlantis

Have the children imagine they are on the island of Atlantis when the disasters hit, and give advice to the people of Atlantis, e.g. *Lie under a table! Close the windows!*, etc.

Presentation Kit • Explain that sound effects can be used to make storytelling more dramatic (see Story Time). Have children use *Pen* to circle scenes or details in the story for the class to suggest a suitable sound effect.
• Oral Storytelling Video 5 contains a different story on a related theme (*A Gift from the Beach*). Watch and discuss it at the end of the lesson.

Teacher's Resource Center • Print out Oral Storytelling Video Worksheet 5 to get the most out of the video.

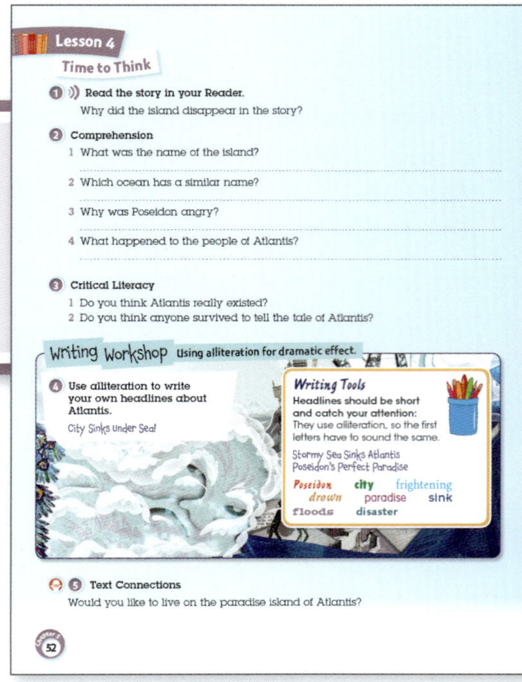
Lesson 4

Time to Think

1 Read the story in your Reader.

Why did the island disappear in the story?

2 Comprehension

1 What was the name of the island?

2 Which ocean has a similar name?

3 Why was Poseidon angry?

4 What happened to the people of Atlantis?

3 Critical Literacy

1 Do you think Atlantis really existed?

2 Do you think anyone survived to tell the tale of Atlantis?

Writing Workshop Using alliteration for dramatic effect.

4 Use alliteration to write your own headlines about Atlantis.

City Sinks Under Sea!

Writing Tools

Headlines should be short and catch your attention: They use alliteration, so the first letters have to sound the same.

Stormy Sea Sinks Atlantis

Poseidon's Perfect Paradise

Poseidon city frightening drown paradise sink floods disaster

5 Text Connections

Would you like to live on the paradise island of Atlantis?

52

Reading Comprehension and Critical Literacy

Lesson objectives: understand and evaluate the story; relate story theme to personal experience; focus on the use of alliteration to catch attention

Materials: Class CD; Reader; Oral Storytelling Video Worksheet 5 [TRC printout] (optional); strips of paper (optional)

Note: Please ensure that your class has read the Reader story before you do this lesson.

Warmer: Play "Tic-Tac-Toe"

Play the game with the children recalling a fact from the story to win a square (see Games Bank p. 222).

1 1.36 Read the story in your Reader.

- Have the children read the story. (Alternatively, play the CD and have them read along.)
- Elicit whether the children were correct in their predictions in Lesson 3 Activity 4. Ask *How did the island disappear in the story?* (*because there was a tsunami*)

2 Comprehension

- The children write answers to the first three questions. Elicit answers.
- Discuss question 4. Ask the children to justify their answers.

Answers

1 Atlantis **2** The Atlantic Ocean **3** Because the people had not taken care of the island/had ignored his warnings. **4** They disappeared. / They became fish and mermaids. / Children's own answers.

3 Critical Literacy

- Have the children discuss the answers to the questions with a friend.
- Elicit ideas and have a class discussion. Encourage the children to give reasons for their opinions. Making comparisons to real life and considering how characters change as the story progresses help readers understand the underlying message of the story.

Answers

Children's own answers.

Writing Workshop

Using alliteration for dramatic effect

4 Use alliteration to write your own headlines about Atlantis.

Have a child read the example. Elicit other alliterative headlines, using words from the **Writing Tools** box. The children write headings about Atlantis in their notebook, then compare with a friend. Encourage them to look in the story for good words to use. Elicit responses.

Answers

Children's own answers.

5 Text Connections

- Ask *Would you like to live on the paradise island of Atlantis?* Elicit ideas and discuss as a class.

Optional activity: Illustrate the headlines

Have the children write their alliterative headlines on strips of paper and stick them around the walls. The children walk around, read the headlines, and draw a picture to illustrate one of them. Collect the pictures and give each child someone else's picture. They now stick the picture with the headline that best suits it.

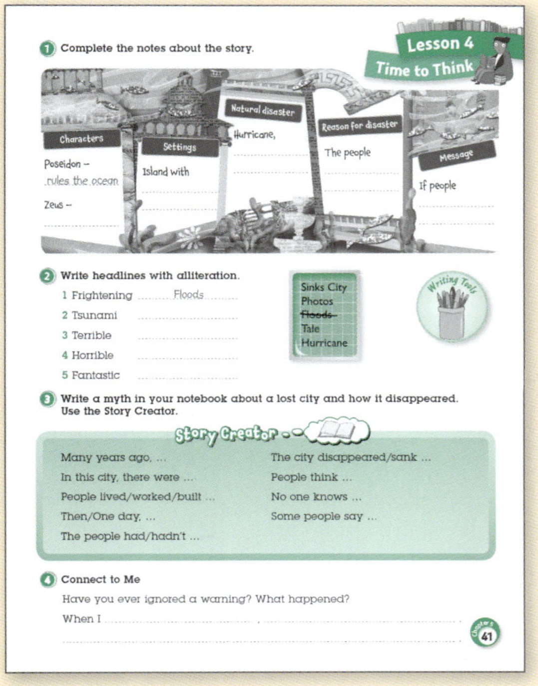

Lesson 4
Time to Think

1 Complete the notes about the story.

Characters	Settings	Natural disaster	Reason for disaster	Message
Poseidon – rules the ocean Zeus –	Island with	Hurricane,	The people	If people

2 Write headlines with alliteration.

1 Frightening Floods
2 Tsunami
3 Terrible
4 Horrible
5 Fantastic

Sinks City
Photos
~~Floods~~
Tale
Hurricane

Writing Tools

3 Write a myth in your notebook about a lost city and how it disappeared. Use the Story Creator.

Story Creator

Many years ago, ...
In this city, there were ...
People lived/worked/built ...
Then/One day, ...
The people had/hadn't ...
The city disappeared/sank ...
People think ...
No one knows ...
Some people say ...

4 Connect to Me

Have you ever ignored a warning? What happened?

When I ...., ...

Chapter 5 41

1 Complete the notes about the story.

The children complete the notes about the story. Elicit answers.

Answers

Characters: Poseidon—rules the ocean; Zeus—rules the sky
Settings: island with mountain, trees, fruit, flowers, animals, etc.
Natural disaster: hurricane, enormous wave, earthquake, volcano, tsunami, floods
Reason for disaster: the people had started to argue/become greedy/steal and lie/cheat and fight
Message: If people are greedy, things will go wrong. / If people lie and fight, they will be unhappy.

2 Write headlines with alliteration.

The children write headlines with alliteration using the words supplied. Elicit answers.

Answers

1 Frightening Floods **2** Tsunami Sinks City **3** Terrible Tale **4** Horrible Hurricane **5** Fantastic Photos

3 Write a myth in your notebook about a lost city and how it disappeared. Use the Story Creator.

Use the **Story Creator** prompts to elicit ideas. The children write a myth in their notebook about a lost city and how it disappeared, then compare with a friend. Have children read out their texts for the class.

4 Connect to Me

Elicit examples of ignoring a warning and the consequences of ignoring it. (e.g. *My friend told me to take an umbrella. I ignored their advice and I ended up getting wet.*) The children write their own response, then compare with a friend.
Elicit responses.

Cooler: Alliteration

Ask one child to say a letter from the alphabet. The letter is to be used for a headline, which must have an adjective, a noun, a verb, and one more word (e.g. *Stormy Sea Sinks Atlantis*). At least three of the words have to start with the same sound. The children work in pairs to write headlines. Elicit ideas. Repeat with more letters.

Competency Focus

Me: Critical Literacy

The children use critical literacy skills to reflect on the story and relate it to their own experiences.

Presentation Kit • Have children use *Pen* to write the answers for SB Activity 2. If the class thinks an answer is wrong, use *Eraser* to clear for another child to write.
• If you haven't already, show Oral Storytelling Video 5 (a different story on a related theme).

Teacher's Resource Center • If you haven't already, print out Oral Storytelling Video Worksheet 5 to do the support activities.

Student's Resource Center • The children can watch Oral Storytelling Video 5 at home with their family.

Grammar and Reading

Lesson objectives: talk about experiences in the recent past and before
Key grammar: past perfect and present perfect questions
Secondary language: *divers, warning, greedy, argue*
Materials: Class CD; pieces of paper with sentence words (Warmer); Grammar Worksheet 5B [TRC printout] (optional); questionnaire (Cooler)

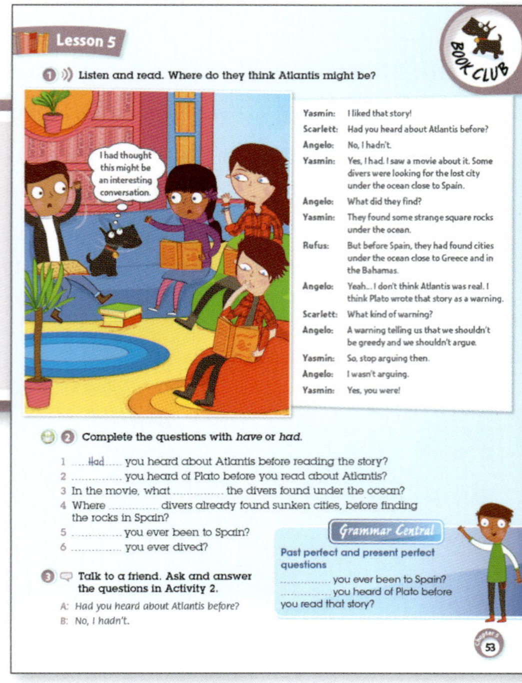
Lesson 5

BOOK CLUB

1 Listen and read. Where do they think Atlantis might be?

Yasmin: I liked that story!
Scarlett: Had you heard about Atlantis before?
Angelo: No, I hadn't.
Yasmin: Yes, I had. I saw a movie about it. Some divers were looking for the lost city under the ocean close to Spain.
Angelo: What did they find?
Yasmin: They found some strange square rocks under the ocean.
Rufus: But before Spain, they had found cities under the ocean close to Greece and in the Bahamas.
Angelo: Yeah... I don't think Atlantis was real. I think Plato wrote that story as a warning.
Scarlett: What kind of warning?
Angelo: A warning telling us that we shouldn't be greedy and we shouldn't argue.
Yasmin: So, stop arguing then.
Angelo: I wasn't arguing.
Yasmin: Yes, you were!

2 Complete the questions with *have* or *had*.

1 ....Had..... you heard about Atlantis before reading the story?
2 .... you heard of Plato before you read about Atlantis?
3 In the movie, what .... the divers found under the ocean?
4 Where .... divers already found sunken cities, before finding the rocks in Spain?
5 .... you ever been to Spain?
6 .... you ever dived?

3 Talk to a friend. Ask and answer the questions in Activity 2.

A: Had you heard about Atlantis before?
B: No, I hadn't.

Grammar Central
Past perfect and present perfect questions
.... you ever been to Spain?
.... you heard of Plato before you read that story?

53

Warmer: Scrambled sentences

Write a key sentence using the past perfect, each word on a separate piece of paper. Invite a group of children to hold up a word each to show the class. The class instructs the children to stand in the correct order to make the sentence. Repeat with different sentences and children.

1 1.37 Listen and read. Where do they think Atlantis might be?

- Play the CD. The children listen and read along. Ask *Had Anglo heard of Atlantis before?* (*no*)
- Play the CD again and ask *Where do they think Atlantis might be?* (*close to Spain, Greece, or the Bahamas*)
- Elicit answers.

Grammar Central

Past perfect and present perfect questions

Have the children complete the grammar examples. Elicit answers. Elicit how we make the two question forms. (*past perfect:* had + *subject* + *past participle*; *present perfect:* have + *subject* + *past participle*) See also the Grammar Reference sections in the Student Book (p. 100) and Activity Book (p. 100) for further explanation and practice.

Grammar Central Answers: Have, Had

AB Answers Activity 2: 1 Have, have **2** Had, had **3** Had, hadn't **4** Had, had **5** Have, haven't

2 Complete the questions with *have* or *had*.

- Using the example sentence, draw a timeline on the board to show where the two events occurred and how the use of *had* talks about before a point in the past, and *have* talks about before now.
- Have the children continue the activity, then compare answers with a friend.
- Elicit answers.

Answers

1 Had **2** Had **3** had **4** had **5** Have **6** Have

3 Talk to a friend. Ask and answer the questions in Activity 2.

- Have children ask you the first and last questions and give your answers, e.g. *Yes, I had, but I hadn't heard it in as much detail before. / No, I haven't, but I'd love to try it one day!*
- Have the children take turns asking and answering in pairs.
- Pairs perform their questions and answers for the class.

Optional activity: Before you were …

Write on the board *met your best friend, learned to ride a bike, learned English, read a book*. Give the children each a number between 2 and 12 and have them write a question using the number as an age, e.g. *Had you learned English before you were eight?* Have the children write the questions in their notebook, then ask and answer with their friends.

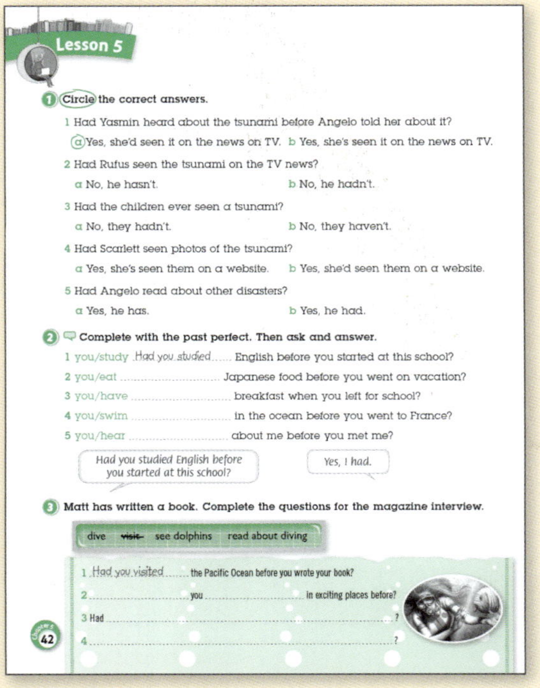
Lesson 5

1 Circle the correct answers.

1 Had Yasmin heard about the tsunami before Angelo told her about it?
(a) Yes, she'd seen it on the news on TV. b Yes, she's seen it on the news on TV.

2 Had Rufus seen the tsunami on the TV news?
a No, he hasn't. b No, he hadn't.

3 Had the children ever seen a tsunami?
a No, they hadn't. b No, they haven't.

4 Had Scarlett seen photos of the tsunami?
a Yes, she's seen them on a website. b Yes, she'd seen them on a website.

5 Had Angelo read about other disasters?
a Yes, he has. b Yes, he had.

2 Complete with the past perfect. Then ask and answer.

1 you/study Had you studied ...... English before you started at this school?
2 you/eat .... Japanese food before you went on vacation?
3 you/have .... breakfast when you left for school?
4 you/swim .... in the ocean before you went to France?
5 you/hear .... about me before you met me?

Had you studied English before you started at this school?
Yes, I had.

3 Matt has written a book. Complete the questions for the magazine interview.

dive ~~visit~~ see dolphins read about diving

1 Had you visited ...... the Pacific Ocean before you wrote your book?
2 .... you .... in exciting places before?
3 Had ....?
4 ....?

Chapter 5 42

1 Circle the correct answers.

The children answer the questions by circling the correct option from the two given each time. Elicit answers.

Answers

1 a **2** b **3** a **4** b **5** b

2 Complete with the past perfect. Then ask and answer.

The children complete the questions using the prompts supplied. Elicit answers. Then they ask and answer the questions in pairs.

Answers

1 Had you studied **2** Had you eaten **3** Had you had **4** Had you swum **5** Had you heard

3 Matt has written a book. Complete the questions for the magazine interview.

The children complete the questions for a magazine interview using the prompts supplied. Then they compare with a friend. Elicit answers.

Answers

1 Had you visited **2** Had, dived **3** Had you read about diving before you wrote your book? **4** Had you seen dolphins before?

Cooler: Find someone who …

Make a simple questionnaire with the title *Find someone who* … and six questions based on activities the children may have done before a certain age, e.g. … *had read a book before they were six*. The children mingle and write a name next to the question if their friends had done the activity. Elicit responses.

Competency Focus

Learn

The children demonstrate their understanding of the new language by reading the dialogue and completing the activity.

Presentation Kit • Have children use *Highlighter* to identify past perfect and present perfect questions in SB Activity 1.

• TIP Give the children as many opportunities as possible to use the digital resources—completing interactive activities, showing answers, writing and drawing on the board, etc. Make a point of encouraging less confident children to participate, because this will help them engage.

Teacher's Resource Center • For extra grammar practice, print out Grammar Worksheet 5B.

Student's Resource Center • The children can use Interactive Grammar 5B at home.

Vocabulary, Listening, and Spelling

Lesson objectives: identify and use vocabulary related to shipwrecks and ocean exploration; practice spelling compound nouns
Key vocabulary: *coast, damage, inland, scuba divers, shipwreck, underwater*
Secondary language: *sink*
Materials: Class CD; pictures for Key vocabulary (Warmer)

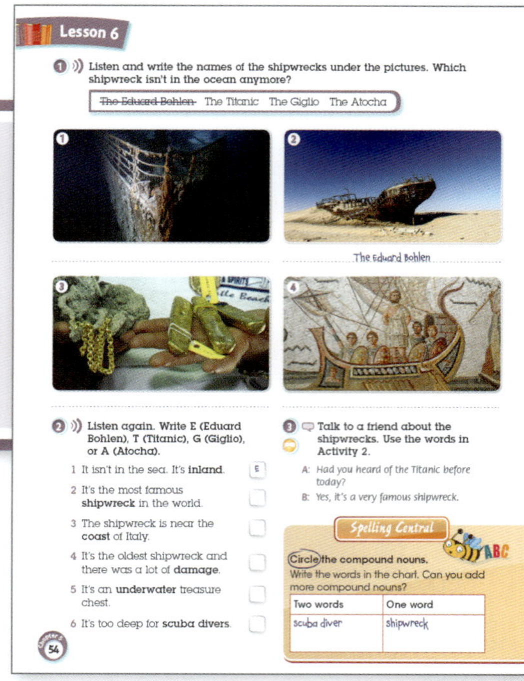
Lesson 6

1 Listen and write the names of the shipwrecks under the pictures. Which shipwreck isn't in the ocean anymore?

~~The Eduard Bohlen~~ The Titanic The Giglio The Atocha

1 .... 2 The Eduard Bohlen 3 .... 4 ....

2 Listen again. Write E (Eduard Bohlen), T (Titanic), G (Giglio), or A (Atocha).

1 It isn't in the sea. It's **inland**. E
2 It's the most famous **shipwreck** in the world.
3 The shipwreck is near the **coast** of Italy.
4 It's the oldest shipwreck and there was a lot of **damage**.
5 It's an **underwater** treasure chest.
6 It's too deep for **scuba divers**.

3 Talk to a friend about the shipwrecks. Use the words in Activity 2.

A: *Had you heard of the Titanic before today?*
B: *Yes, it's a very famous shipwreck.*

Spelling Central

Circle the compound nouns. Write the words in the chart. Can you add more compound nouns?

Two words	One word
scuba diver	shipwreck

Chapter 5 54

Warmer: Pre-teach vocabulary

Pre-teach the vocabulary by showing pictures, or draw icons on the board. Then make sentences for the class to complete, e.g. *A person who can swim down deep in the ocean is a …* (*scuba diver*) *A fish swims …* (*underwater*), etc.

1 1.38 Listen and write the names of the shipwrecks under the pictures. Which shipwreck isn't in the ocean anymore?

- Play the CD. The children listen and label the shipwreck pictures, using the names supplied.
- Play the CD again. Ask *Which shipwreck isn't in the ocean anymore?* (*The* Eduard Bohlen)
- Elicit answers.

Audioscript

***1** The* Eduard Bohlen *is a shipwreck which is not in the ocean. It's in the Namib Desert in southern Africa. The sand and ocean have moved so much that the shipwreck of the* Eduard Bohlen *now lies half a kilometer inland. It's a very strange sight to see a ship in the sand.*
***2** Everyone knows about the* Titanic *disaster. The ship sank in 1912 after hitting an iceberg. The* Titanic *is the most famous shipwreck in the world and it's in the North Atlantic Ocean. It's too deep for scuba divers to reach, but they have sent a robot to photograph the shipwreck. They saw pots, bottles, and shoes.*
***3** The* Giglio *sank over 2,500 years ago. The shipwreck was found by divers in the 1960s near Giglio Island near the coast of Italy. It's the oldest shipwreck in the world. There was a lot of damage but the divers found coins, vases, and musical instruments. These taught them a lot about the ancient civilization called the Etruscans.*
***4** In 1622, around the time that Christopher Columbus sailed to America, a lot of ships sailed from America back to Spain carrying treasure. The* Atocha *was caught in a hurricane, and the heavy treasure made it sink to the bottom very quickly. Scuba divers discovered this underwater treasure chest in 1985. Divers are still searching for treasure today.*

Answers

1 The *Titanic* **2** The *Eduard Bohlen* **3** The *Atocha*
4 The *Giglio*

2 1.38 Listen again. Write E (Eduard Bohlen), T (Titanic), G (Giglio), or A (Atocha).

- Play the CD again. The children listen and write the letters of the correct shipwreck by each description. Then they compare with a friend.
- Elicit answers.

Answers

1 E **2** T **3** G **4** G **5** A **6** T

3 Talk to a friend about the shipwrecks. Use the words in Activity 2.

- Ask two children to read out the example dialogue.
- Have the children discuss the shipwrecks in pairs, using as many words from Activity 2 as possible.
- Have pairs perform a dialogue for the class.

Spelling Central

Compound nouns

Have the children find compound nouns on the page and complete the chart. They then add other words in each category. (e.g. *musical instrument, police officer; kilometer, iceberg*)

Answers

two words: scuba diver, treasure chest
one word: shipwreck, inland, underwater

Optional activity: **One word or two?**

Draw a line down the middle of the board with *One word* on the left and *Two words* on the right. Call out words from **Spelling Central** and other compound nouns the children will know. The children indicate to the left or right side of the board as appropriate.

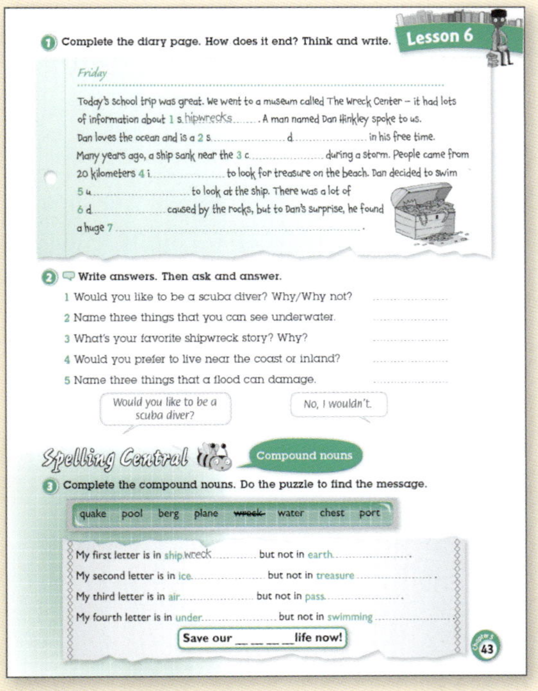

Lesson 6

1 Complete the diary page. How does it end? Think and write.

Friday

Today's school trip was great. We went to a museum called The Wreck Center – it had lots of information about 1 s.hipwrecks........ A man named Dan Hinkley spoke to us. Dan loves the ocean and is a 2 s.................. d.................. in his free time. Many years ago, a ship sank near the 3 c.................. during a storm. People came from 20 kilometers 4 i.................. to look for treasure on the beach. Dan decided to swim 5 u.................. to look at the ship. There was a lot of 6 d.................. caused by the rocks, but to Dan's surprise, he found a huge 7 ....

2 Write answers. Then ask and answer.

1 Would you like to be a scuba diver? Why/Why not? ....
2 Name three things that you can see underwater. ....
3 What's your favorite shipwreck story? Why? ....
4 Would you prefer to live near the coast or inland? ....
5 Name three things that a flood can damage. ....

Would you like to be a scuba diver?
No, I wouldn't.

Spelling Central — Compound nouns

3 Complete the compound nouns. Do the puzzle to find the message.

quake pool berg plane ~~wreck~~ water chest port

My first letter is in ship.wreck.......... but not in earth.................. .
My second letter is in ice.................. but not in treasure.................. .
My third letter is in air.................. but not in pass.................. .
My fourth letter is in under.................. but not in swimming.................. .

Save our __ __ __ __ life now!

Chapter 5 43

1 Complete the diary page. How does it end? Think and write.

The children complete the text by writing in the missing words (the initial letters are supplied as prompts) and their own conclusion to the story. Elicit answers and ideas for the story ending.

Answers

1 shipwrecks **2** scuba diver **3** coast **4** inland **5** underwater **6** damage **7** Children's own answers.

2 Write answers. Then ask and answer.

The children write their own answers to the questions. Then they ask and answer the questions in pairs. Invite pairs to ask and answer for the class.

Answers

Children's own answers.

3 Complete the compound nouns. Do the puzzle to find the message.

To practice the **Spelling Central** feature, the children complete the compound nouns using the words supplied. Elicit answers. Then they figure out what the missing letters in the message are. Elicit answers.

Answers

shipwreck, earthquake; iceberg, treasure chest; airplane, passport; underwater, swimming pool
Message: wildlife

Cooler: Play "Ready, Set, Draw!"

Play the game with key phrases from the lesson, e.g. *He's inland. They're at the coast. She's underwater. I'm a scuba diver! There's a shipwreck. I've found the treasure!* (see Games Bank p. 222).

Competency Focus

Collaborate and Communicate

The children work together to share their ideas on the topic, incorporating the new vocabulary.

Presentation Kit • Use Vocabulary Tool 5B to pre-teach key vocabulary. Use *Slideshow* to introduce the words and *Picture Dictionary* to review/test.

- TIP Show any audioscript that does not appear on the SB page by choosing the arrow on the *Audio* pop-up.
- TIP Use *Stopwatch* to set a time limit for the SB Spelling Central activity.

Student's App • Encourage the children to play the games on their smartphone/tablet. They could do this with a friend as a fun way to review the chapter vocabulary together.

CLIL: Geography—Tsunamis

Lesson objective: find out about tsunamis
Materials: CLIL Graphic Organizer 5 [TRC printout] (optional)

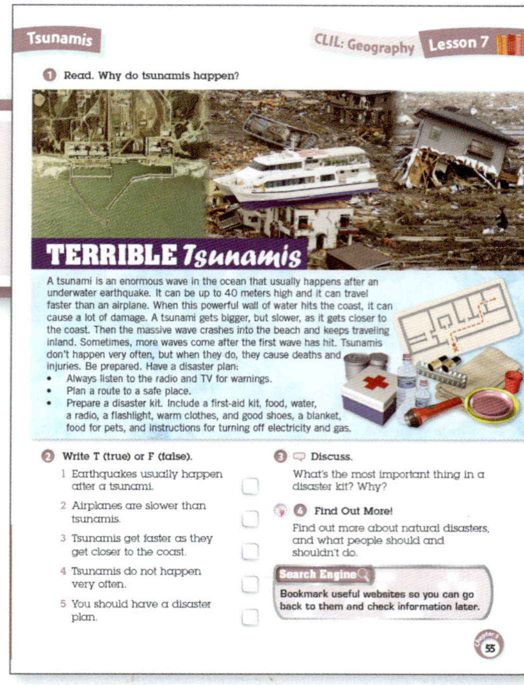
Tsunamis

CLIL: Geography Lesson 7

1 Read. Why do tsunamis happen?

TERRIBLE Tsunamis

A tsunami is an enormous wave in the ocean that usually happens after an underwater earthquake. It can be up to 40 meters high and it can travel faster than an airplane. When this powerful wall of water hits the coast, it can cause a lot of damage. A tsunami gets bigger, but slower, as it gets closer to the coast. Then the massive wave crashes into the beach and keeps traveling inland. Sometimes, more waves come after the first wave has hit. Tsunamis don't happen very often, but when they do, they cause deaths and injuries. Be prepared. Have a disaster plan:

- Always listen to the radio and TV for warnings.
- Plan a route to a safe place.
- Prepare a disaster kit. Include a first-aid kit, food, water, a radio, a flashlight, warm clothes, and good shoes, a blanket, food for pets, and instructions for turning off electricity and gas.

2 Write T (true) or F (false).

1 Earthquakes usually happen after a tsunami.
2 Airplanes are slower than tsunamis.
3 Tsunamis get faster as they get closer to the coast.
4 Tsunamis do not happen very often.
5 You should have a disaster plan.

3 Discuss.

What's the most important thing in a disaster kit? Why?

4 Find Out More!

Find out more about natural disasters, and what people should and shouldn't do.

Search Engine

Bookmark useful websites so you can go back to them and check information later.

Chapter 5 55

Warmer: Brainstorm tsunamis

Write *tsunami* in the middle of the board. Invite children to come to the board and write a word or idea that they associate with a tsunami. Then have the children work in pairs to talk about what they know about tsunamis.

1 Read. Why do tsunamis happen?

- Have the children look at the pictures. Ask *What can you see in these pictures? What's happening?*
- Have the children read the text quickly and find which of the words from the Warmer are present in the text. Elicit the words.
- Ask *Why do tsunamis happen?* (*An underwater earthquake makes an enormous wave.*) Elicit ideas. Ask the class if they agree.

2 Write T (true) or F (false).

- Elicit the answer for the first question, and where the evidence for this is. (*False—A tsunami usually happens after an underwater earthquake. lines 1–2*)
- Have the children write T (true) or F (false) for each sentence, scanning the text for the right section and reading carefully to find the answer.
- Elicit answers, including the correct version of the false sentences.

Answers

1 F **2** T **3** F **4** T **5** T

3 Discuss.

- Have a child read out the discussion question.
- Have the children talk about their ideas in pairs, then share ideas as a class.

4 Find Out More!

- The children research natural disasters and what people should and shouldn't do. The **Search Engine** feature gives support on where to look. The children will need to complete this research before doing the follow-up activity in the Activity Book. (It could be set as homework.)

Optional activity: Plan for a disaster

Ask the children to imagine a warning of a disaster. Write the underlined words on the board as prompts: (a) what a safe place in their town is; (b) what the best route to it is; (c) what is in the disaster kit; (d) where they will get the items; (e) where they will keep the kit. Have the children discuss their plans in pairs. Elicit answers.

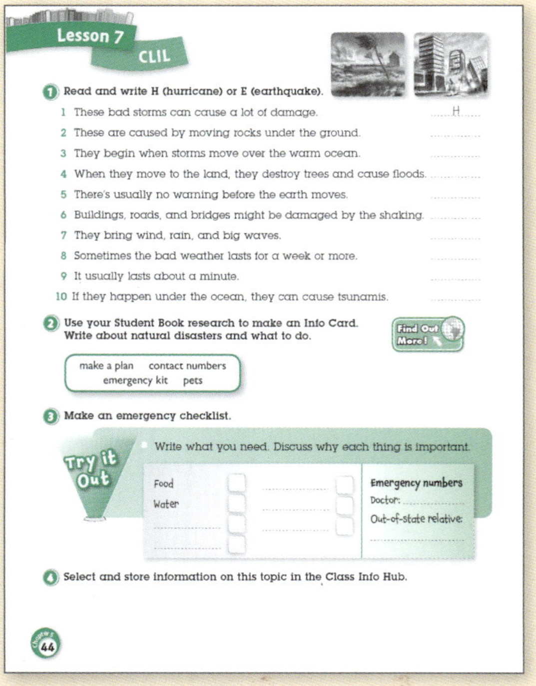
Lesson 7
CLIL

1 Read and write H (hurricane) or E (earthquake).

1 These bad storms can cause a lot of damage. H
2 These are caused by moving rocks under the ground. ......
3 They begin when storms move over the warm ocean. ......
4 When they move to the land, they destroy trees and cause floods. ......
5 There's usually no warning before the earth moves. ......
6 Buildings, roads, and bridges might be damaged by the shaking. ......
7 They bring wind, rain, and big waves. ......
8 Sometimes the bad weather lasts for a week or more. ......
9 It usually lasts about a minute. ......
10 If they happen under the ocean, they can cause tsunamis. ......

2 Use your Student Book research to make an Info Card. Write about natural disasters and what to do.

Find Out More!

make a plan contact numbers emergency kit pets

3 Make an emergency checklist.

Try it Out

Write what you need. Discuss why each thing is important.

Food
Water

Emergency numbers
Doctor: ......
Out-of-state relative: ......

4 Select and store information on this topic in the Class Info Hub.

Chapter 5 44

1 Read and write H (hurricane) or E (earthquake).

The children identify whether each sentence describes a hurricane or an earthquake, writing H or E as appropriate. Elicit answers.

Answers

1 H **2** E **3** H **4** H **5** E **6** E **7** H **8** H **9** E **10** E

2 Use your Student Book research to make an Info Card. Write about natural disasters and what to do.

Divide the class into groups. Have the children pool the information they learned from their research in the Student Book and the Activity Book. The children write about and illustrate their ideas individually. Have the groups present their Info Cards to the class.

Answers

Children's own answers.

3 Make an emergency checklist.

In their groups, the children follow the **Try It Out** instructions to make an emergency checklist. Then they present it to the class.

Answers

Children's own answers.

4 Select and store information on this topic in the Class Info Hub.

Have the children vote for the five most interesting Info Cards. Archive these in your Class Hub (see p. 41) in a folder called **Chapter 5 Natural Disasters**.

Cooler: Play "Disappearing Text"

Play the game with the correct/corrected sentences in Student Book Activity 2 (see Games Bank p. 222).

Competency Focus

Act

The children carry out research to find out about natural disasters. This helps them expand their learning and relate it to their world, both inside and outside the classroom.

Presentation Kit • To extend feedback on SB Activity 2, have children use *Highlighter* to identify the section of the text which gives the answer to each question.

- Have children use *Pen* to write answers to AB Activity 3, each writing one detail. Each time, elicit why the thing listed is important.
- TIP Choose *Help* at any time to access FAQs on using the materials.

Teacher's Resource Center • Print out CLIL Graphic Organizer 5 for the children to use in collating their Find Out More! research.

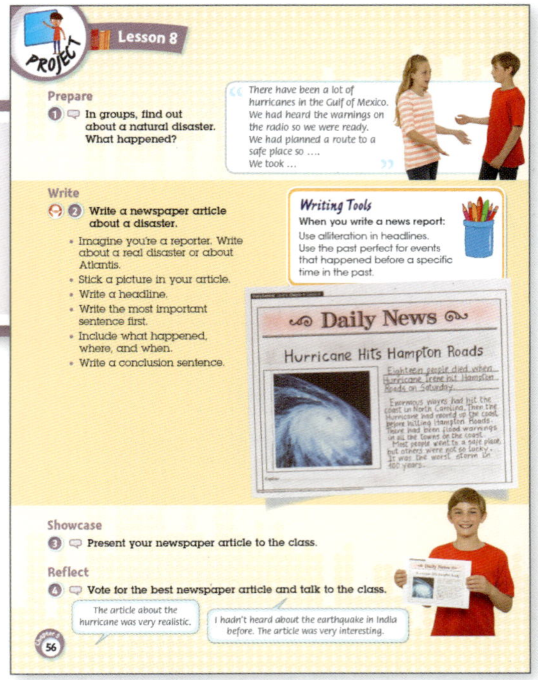

PROJECT

Lesson 8

Prepare

1 In groups, find out about a natural disaster. What happened?

There have been a lot of hurricanes in the Gulf of Mexico. We had heard the warnings on the radio so we were ready. We had planned a route to a safe place so …. We took …

Write

2 Write a newspaper article about a disaster.

- Imagine you're a reporter. Write about a real disaster or about Atlantis.
- Stick a picture in your article.
- Write a headline.
- Write the most important sentence first.
- Include what happened, where, and when.
- Write a conclusion sentence.

Writing Tools

When you write a news report:

Use alliteration in headlines.
Use the past perfect for events that happened before a specific time in the past.

Daily News

Hurricane Hits Hampton Roads

Eighteen people died when Hurricane Irene hit Hampton Roads on Saturday.

Enormous waves had hit the coast in North Carolina. Then the Hurricane had moved up the coast before hitting Hampton Roads. There had been flood warnings in all the towns on the coast.

Most people went to a safe place, but others were not so lucky. It was the worst storm in 400 years.

Showcase

3 Present your newspaper article to the class.

Reflect

4 Vote for the best newspaper article and talk to the class.

The article about the hurricane was very realistic.

I hadn't heard about the earthquake in India before. The article was very interesting.

56

Writing Project

Lesson objectives: review language from Chapter 5; write a newspaper article and present it to the class

Materials: Writing Template 5 [TRC printout] (optional)

Warmer: True or False?

Write a big *TRUE* on one side of the board and a big *FALSE* on the other. Read out sentences about tsunamis adapted from Student Book Lesson 7 Activity 2, e.g. *Tsunamis can be up to 40 meters high.* (*true*) *A tsunami gets faster as it reaches the coast.* (*false*) The children point to true or false as appropriate. If false, ask the children to explain why.

Prepare

1 In groups, find out about a natural disaster. What happened?

- Elicit any natural disasters the children have heard about on the news or radio. Write key words on the board.
- Ask the children to imagine that they were there at the time of the disaster and discuss in groups what happened.
- Elicit ideas.

Write

2 Write a newspaper article about a disaster.

- Have children read the model article aloud, one line each.
- The children then check the model against the **Writing Tools** box. Ask *Does it have all the recommended features?* (*yes*) Elicit the details from the model.
- Have the children write a similar article about a different disaster, or about the island of Atlantis, then compare with a friend. Give support as necessary.

Showcase

3 Present your newspaper article to the class.

- Choose children to read their newspaper article to the class. Ask the class to listen and check they included the recommended features.

Reflect

4 Vote for the best newspaper article and talk to the class.

- Have children comment on which article was the best and why. Have a class vote to identify their favorite.

Optional activity: Vocabulary review

Write up the first letter of each item of key vocabulary from Lessons 1 and 6. Give the children two minutes working in pairs to see how many of the words they can remember. Elicit answers.

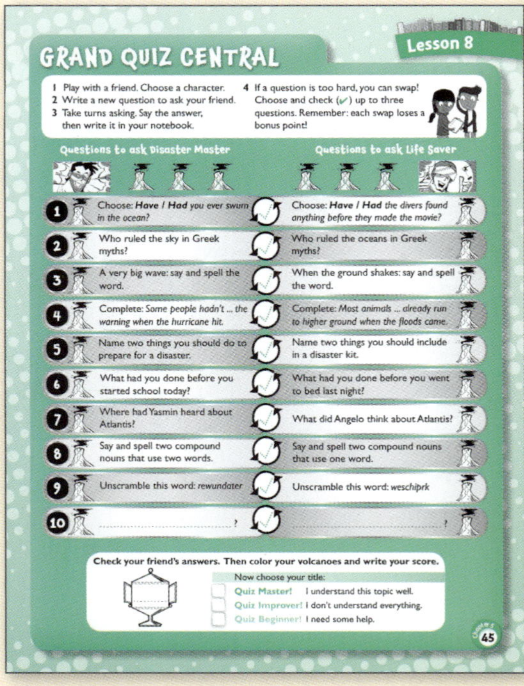

GRAND QUIZ CENTRAL

Lesson 8

1 Play with a friend. Choose a character.
2 Write a new question to ask your friend.
3 Take turns asking. Say the answer, then write it in your notebook.
4 If a question is too hard, you can swap! Choose and check (✓) up to three questions. Remember: each swap loses a bonus point!

	Questions to ask Disaster Master	Questions to ask Life Saver
1	Choose: **Have / Had** *you ever swum in the ocean?*	Choose: **Have / Had** *the divers found anything before they made the movie?*
2	Who ruled the sky in Greek myths?	Who ruled the oceans in Greek myths?
3	A very big wave: say and spell the word.	When the ground shakes: say and spell the word.
4	Complete: *Some people hadn't ... the warning when the hurricane hit.*	Complete: *Most animals ... already run to higher ground when the floods came.*
5	Name two things you should do to prepare for a disaster.	Name two things you should include in a disaster kit.
6	What had you done before you started school today?	What had you done before you went to bed last night?
7	Where had Yasmin heard about Atlantis?	What did Angelo think about Atlantis?
8	Say and spell two compound nouns that use two words.	Say and spell two compound nouns that use one word.
9	Unscramble this word: *rewundater*	Unscramble this word: *weschiprk*
10	……………………?	……………………?

Check your friend's answers. Then color your volcanoes and write your score.

Now choose your title:
- Quiz Master! I understand this topic well.
- Quiz Improver! I don't understand everything.
- Quiz Beginner! I need some help.

45

Grand Quiz Central

See p. 43 for details of how to take the quiz.

Answers

1 Have / Had **2** Zeus / Poseidon **3** tsunami / earthquake **4** heard / had **5** *Any two of:* listen to the radio or TV for warnings, plan a route to a safe place, prepare a disaster kit / *Any two of:* food, water, blankets, a flashlight, shoes, clothes **6** Children's own answers. **7** She'd seen a movie. / He thought it wasn't real. **8** *Any two of:* scuba diver, treasure chest, musical instrument, swimming pool / *Any two of:* shipwreck, underwater, inland, iceberg **9** underwater / shipwreck **10** Children's own answers.

Cooler: Read around the class

Have the children read out the model article from Student Book Activity 2, one word each. Nominate one child to start and decide which direction the text will go around the class. If anyone misses their turn or hesitates too much, they are eliminated. At the end bring everyone back in to read it again, this time seeing how fast they can read the whole text.

Competency Focus

Me

The children write a newspaper article about a disaster. This helps them develop their understanding of how to tell a story clearly, exploring their imagination and creativity.

Presentation Kit • Before the children write, *Mask* the text on the model newspaper article. Pairs look at the headline and picture and discuss what kind of information you would need to give in the article. Elicit ideas. Then uncover the text and have the children compare their own ideas with the model.

Teacher's Resource Center • Print out Writing Template 5 to use for the SB writing activity.

Student's Resource Center • Encourage the children to share Vocabulary Tools 3A–5B at home to reinforce vocabulary learning.

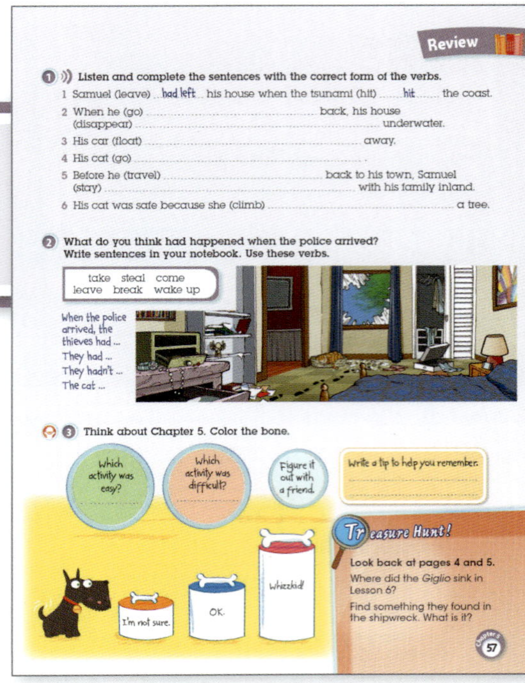
Review

1 Listen and complete the sentences with the correct form of the verbs.

1 Samuel (leave) ... had left ... his house when the tsunami (hit) ... hit ... the coast.
2 When he (go) .... back, his house (disappear) .... underwater.
3 His car (float) .... away.
4 His cat (go) ....
5 Before he (travel) .... back to his town, Samuel (stay) .... with his family inland.
6 His cat was safe because she (climb) .... a tree.

2 What do you think had happened when the police arrived? Write sentences in your notebook. Use these verbs.

take steal come leave break wake up

When the police arrived, the thieves had ...
They had ...
They hadn't ...
The cat ...

3 Think about Chapter 5. Color the bone.

Language Review

Lesson objective: review language from Chapter 5

Materials: Class CD

Warmer: Play "Collocations"

Play the game with key collocations from the chapter, e.g. *natural—disaster, disaster—kit, scuba—divers, warm—clothes*, etc. (see Games Bank p. 222).

1 1.39 Listen and complete the sentences with the correct form of the verbs.

- Before they listen, have the children discuss with a friend what they think will be the correct form of the verbs.
- Play the CD. The children listen and complete.
- Play the CD again for the children to listen and check their answers.
- Elicit answers.

Audioscript

Samuel was lucky. He had already left his house before the tsunami hit the coast. Yesterday he went back to see the damage, but his house had disappeared underwater. His car had floated away in the flood and his cat, Portia, had gone. Samuel had stayed for two nights with his family inland before he traveled back to his home. There was nothing he could do to protect his home and cat. Samuel had decided to leave when he heard a noise. It was his cat, Portia. She had climbed the highest tree in the yard and was waiting for him.

Answers

1 had left / hit **2** went / had disappeared **3** had floated **4** had gone **5** traveled / had stayed **6** had climbed

2 What do you think had happened when the police arrived? Write sentences in your notebook. Use these verbs.

- Elicit suggestions using the prompts.
- Have the children write sentences using the verbs in the box.
- They compare their sentences in pairs.
- Elicit answers.

Answers

Children's own answers.

3 Think about Chapter 5. Color the bone.

- Have the children look back at Chapter 5 and color the bone to evaluate their progress (self-evaluation).
- Discuss ideas for remembering spelling, e.g. spell words aloud. The children choose and write a tip in their Student Book.

Treasure Hunt

Ask *Where was the* Giglio *shipwreck found?* (*near the coast of Italy*) Have the children look at pp. 4–5 to find something found in the shipwreck. (*musical instrument—guitar*)

Chapter 5 Review

1 Reading and Writing.
Read, find, and write the words.

Floods

Floods often happen when ......*there*...... is bad weather. Storms (1) .... a lot of rain and the rivers can't carry all the water away. Hurricanes often (2) .... floods on the coast. The strong winds move across the ocean and make huge waves. When they hit the coast, they damage houses and buildings. Sometimes homes, cars, and animals (3) .... lost. A flash flood is a flood that happens very quickly. When a lot of rain falls in a short time, roads are soon underwater. It can be very dangerous (4) .... there often aren't any warnings. In a recent flood in Italy, 16 people drowned. They (5) .... had time to leave their houses before the rain started. All the cars and buses had floated away in the water.

Example: (there) / it / the

1 brings / bring / brought
2 cause / were / makes
3 is / are / be
4 because / why / so
5 didn't / haven't / hadn't

86

2 Listening.
Listen and match.

87

1 **Reading and Writing. Read, find, and write the words.**

The children complete the text with one of the three words supplied for each blank. Check answers.

Answers

1 bring **2** cause **3** are **4** because **5** hadn't

2 **2.35 Listening. Listen and match.**

Play the CD twice. The children listen and match the names to the people mentioned. Check answers.

Answers (Audioscript on pp. 223–4)

Lines between:
Patrick—boy getting into boat
Alice—girl waving
Daniel—boy shivering
Sonia—girl holding towel
Charlie—boy looking in bag

Competency Focus

Me: Self-evaluation

The children reflect on the chapter, express their personal opinions about their own progress, and look for ways to improve. This encourages them to evaluate and make decisions about what they need to revisit and how they can learn better.

Cooler: Make gapped sentences

Have the children rewrite four of their sentences from Student Book Activity 2, each with a key word missing. They give the version with blanks to a friend for them to complete. They swap back to check.

Presentation Kit • Display the SB page. Choose *Image* in the Navigation Pane to give feedback on Treasure Hunt. Elicit where the *Giglio* sank and ask children to use *Pen* to find and circle something that was found in the shipwreck.

Teacher's Resource Center • Print out Test Chapter 5 and Mid-year Test for the end of this lesson. The Test Generator also allows you to create customized tests.

- For the CEYLT (Cambridge YLE) exam preparation activities on the AB page, choose *Audio* to access the recordings.

Chapter 6

Showtime
Overview

The children will:

- use critical thinking skills to identify performing arts vocabulary.
- talk about recent and unfinished activities using the present perfect progressive.
- read and understand a playscript about a dance school.
- ask and answer questions about recent and unfinished activities using the present perfect progressive.
- identify and use performance and show vocabulary.
- find out about Javanese shadow puppets.
- write a scene for a play.

Key Vocabulary

Performing arts and talents: audition, musical, perform, rehearsal, stage, superstar, talent, voice

Performance and shows: audience, backstage crew, cast, lighting crew, make-up, performance, sets

Key Grammar

Present perfect progressive

- I've been practicing my song for six months.
- I haven't been doing my homework.

Present perfect progressive questions

- What have you been doing?
- How long have you been learning English?
- Has Scarlett been going to rehearsals?

Reading Skills

Story: *Just Dance!*

Genre: playscript

Literacy Development

- use reading skills to understand and predict content
- relate story theme to personal experience
- use playscript writing conventions

Functional Language

- Sorry I'm late. Have you been waiting long?
- No, don't worry. I've only been waiting for five minutes. I've been listening to music.

Spelling

Words with *s* sound (*s*, *ce*, *ss*)

CLIL: Performing arts—Javanese puppet theater

The children find out about puppet theater in Java.

Competency Focus

The children will:

use critical thinking skills to deduce the meaning of new vocabulary. (Lesson 1)	activate new vocabulary and apply new grammar knowledge. (Lesson 2)	work in pairs to act out a dialogue. (Lesson 3)	relate the story and story theme to their personal experience. (Lesson 4)	develop an understanding of traditional performing arts by carrying out research. (Lesson 7)
predict the content of a story. (Lesson 3)	apply new grammar rules in a familiar context. (Lesson 5)	work in pairs to talk about what they would like to be in a show. (Lesson 6)	invent and write a scene for a play. (Lesson 8)	
			evaluate their own progress in the chapter. (Review)	

Digital Overview

Presentation Kit

Projectable Student Book, Activity Book, and Reader pages

- Vocabulary Tool 6A: Performing arts and talents
- Vocabulary Tool 6B: Performance and shows
- Music Video 6: *Thank You, Everyone!*
- Interactive versions of selected SB and AB activities
- Integrated *Audio* and *Answer Key* for all activities

Teacher's Resource Center

Resources for planning, lesson delivery, and homework

- Class Planner Chapter 6
- Worksheets to print out (including notes and answers):
  - Grammar Worksheet 6A: Present perfect progressive
  - Grammar Worksheet 6B: Present perfect progressive questions
  - CLIL Graphic Organizer 6
  - Writing Template 6
  - Test Chapter 6
- Test Generator
- Speaking Assessment: CEYLT
- Literacy Handbook

Student's Resource Center

Resources for consolidation and practice at home

- Interactive Grammar 6A: Present perfect progressive
- Interactive Grammar 6B: Present perfect progressive questions
- Vocabulary Tool 6A: Performing arts and talents
- Vocabulary Tool 6B: Performance and shows
- Music Video 6: *Thank You, Everyone!*

Student's App

Vocabulary games: Performing arts/talents and performance/shows

Watch the Music Video

Chapter 6 Showtime

Lesson 1

Chapter 6 Showtime
Lesson 1

1 Listen and complete the information on the poster.

Calling all SUPERSTARS!

Do you have a talent? Can you sing and dance? Do you want to perform on stage?

Come to an audition for *My School Musical* in the school gym on ....

Or you can send us a video of you and your talent.
You don't need a ...., just you and your voice.
Rehearsals start in May and the show will be in ....

2 Listen again and write the words next to the clues.

~~musical~~ audition perform stage rehearsal voice superstar talent

1 A show with songs. musical
2 To sing and dance, for people to watch and enjoy. ....
3 To be good at something. ....
4 A famous and successful person. ....
5 A real actor stands on a ....
6 It's like a test to decide if you're good enough. ....
7 You use this to talk and sing. ....
8 The time when you practice for a show. ....

Chapter 6 58

Vocabulary

Lesson objectives: identify and use vocabulary for performing arts
Key vocabulary: *audition, musical, perform, rehearsal, stage, superstar, talent, voice*
Materials: Class CD; alphabet pages (Warmer)

Warmer: Play "Entertainment A–Z"

Prepare an answer page for each team (the title *Entertainment* + the alphabet written vertically). Put the class into teams. Give them two minutes to write a word related to entertainment for as many letters of the alphabet as possible. Ask the team with the most words to read their list, then ask other teams to say any other words. A correct answer wins a point. The team with the most points wins.

1 2.2 Listen and complete the information on the poster.

- Play the CD. The children listen and complete the poster.
- Have the children compare answers with a friend. Elicit answers.

Audioscript

Jack: *Hey, Greg, look. They're having auditions for* My School Musical. *I love shows with songs! Listen. "Do you want to perform on stage?"*
Greg: *What do you mean "perform"?*
Jack: *You know, sing and dance, for people to watch and enjoy! You have talent—you're very good at singing, Greg. You have a great voice.*
Greg: *Hm, but I'm not so good at dancing.*
Jack: *Don't worry, Greg. Just go to the audition or send them a video.*
Greg: *When are the auditions?*
Jack: *They're in the gym, on Thursday after school. Don't you want to be a famous and successful person? You could be a superstar! Stand on a stage like a real actor and show them what you can do. The auditions will be like a test—they'll watch you and decide if you're good enough.*
Greg: *But I don't have a costume.*
Jack: *You don't need a costume. Look! It says "Just you and your voice." You use it to talk every day, so use it to sing, too.*
Greg: *When is the show?*
Jack: *The show will be in July, but the rehearsals start in May. So you'll have two months to practice for the show at the rehearsals.*
Greg: *OK, I might fail the audition, but I'll give it a try.*
Jack: *Great. I'm sure you'll get a part.*

Answers

Thursday after school, costume, July

2 2.2 Listen again and write the words next to the clues.

- Play the CD again. The children listen and write the word described in each clue, using the words supplied.
- Elicit answers.

Answers

1 musical **2** perform **3** talent **4** superstar **5** stage **6** audition **7** voice **8** rehearsal

Optional activity: Persuade a friend

Ask *Can you persuade your friend?* Divide the class into pairs. The children take turns trying to persuade their friend to go for an audition and giving reasons not to go.

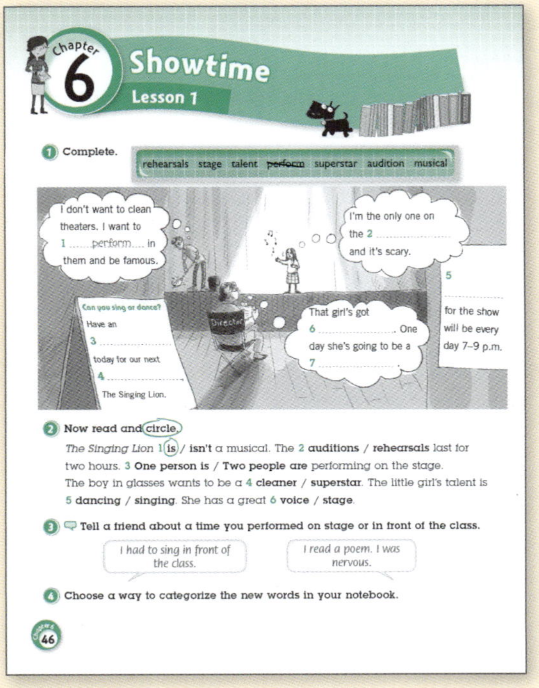
Chapter 6 Showtime
Lesson 1

1 Complete. rehearsals stage talent ~~perform~~ superstar audition musical

2 Now read and circle.

The Singing Lion 1 is / isn't a musical. The 2 **auditions / rehearsals** last for two hours. 3 **One person is / Two people are** performing on the stage. The boy in glasses wants to be a 4 **cleaner / superstar**. The little girl's talent is 5 **dancing / singing**. She has a great 6 **voice / stage**.

3 Tell a friend about a time you performed on stage or in front of the class.

I had to sing in front of the class.

I read a poem. I was nervous.

4 Choose a way to categorize the new words in your notebook.

46

1 Complete.

The children complete the texts using the words supplied. Elicit answers.

Answers

1 perform **2** stage **3** audition **4** musical **5** Rehearsals **6** talent **7** superstar

2 Now read and circle.

The children complete the text by circling the correct option from the two given each time. Elicit answers.

Answers

1 is **2** rehearsals **3** One person is **4** superstar **5** singing **6** voice

3 Tell a friend about a time you performed on stage or in front of the class.

First tell the children about a performing experience of yours, e.g. *I sang a solo once in a school concert. I was so nervous my voice kept disappearing! But everyone applauded!* The children talk in pairs about similar experiences. Elicit responses.

4 Choose a way to categorize the new words in your notebook.

Brainstorm appropriate categories, e.g. *verbs/nouns/adjectives, easy/difficult to spell, alphabetical order.* The children choose the best categories for them and list the words in their notebook.

Answers

Children's own answers.

Cooler: Play "Back to the Board"

Play the game with key vocabulary from the lesson: *musical, audition, perform, stage, rehearsal, voice, superstar, talent,* etc. (see Games Bank p. 222).

Competency Focus

Think! Critical Thinking

The children use critical thinking skills to understand the new vocabulary by using visual clues and processing the written and spoken forms.

Presentation Kit • Use Vocabulary Tool 6A to pre-teach key vocabulary as an alternative to the critical thinking approach. Use *Slideshow* to introduce the words and *Distort* to review/test.

- TIP Use the arrow in the *Audio* pop-up window to see the audioscript for SB Activity 1.
- Have children circle the answers for AB Activity 2, before you use *Answer Key*. Ask the class to confirm each time. Use *Eraser* if an answer is incorrect to give another child a chance to answer correctly.

Grammar

Lesson objective: talk about recent and unfinished activities
Key grammar: present perfect progressive
Secondary language: *costume*
Materials: Grammar Worksheet 6A [TRC printout] (optional)

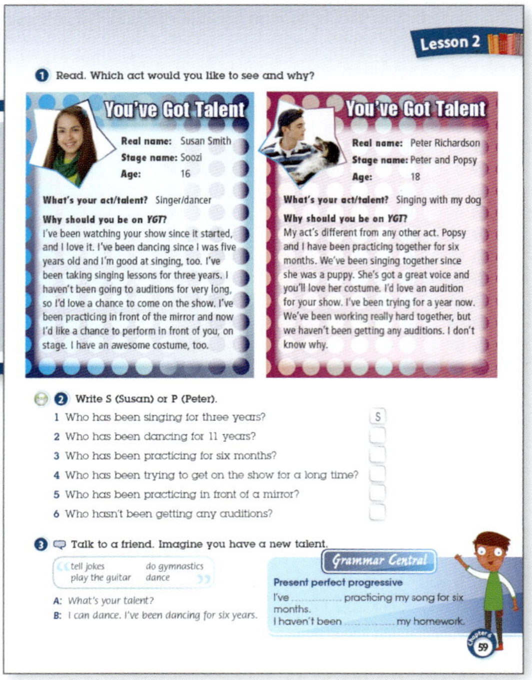
Lesson 2

1 Read. Which act would you like to see and why?

You've Got Talent

Real name: Susan Smith
Stage name: Soozi
Age: 16

What's your act/talent? Singer/dancer

Why should you be on *YGT*?
I've been watching your show since it started, and I love it. I've been dancing since I was five years old and I'm good at singing, too. I've been taking singing lessons for three years. I haven't been going to auditions for very long, so I'd love a chance to come on the show. I've been practicing in front of the mirror and now I'd like a chance to perform in front of you, on stage. I have an awesome costume, too.

You've Got Talent

Real name: Peter Richardson
Stage name: Peter and Popsy
Age: 18

What's your act/talent? Singing with my dog

Why should you be on *YGT*?
My act's different from any other act. Popsy and I have been practicing together for six months. We've been singing together since she was a puppy. She's got a great voice and you'll love her costume. I'd love an audition for your show. I've been trying for a year now. We've been working really hard together, but we haven't been getting any auditions. I don't know why.

2 Write S (Susan) or P (Peter).

1 Who has been singing for three years? S
2 Who has been dancing for 11 years?
3 Who has been practicing for six months?
4 Who has been trying to get on the show for a long time?
5 Who has been practicing in front of a mirror?
6 Who hasn't been getting any auditions?

3 Talk to a friend. Imagine you have a new talent.

tell jokes *do gymnastics*
play the guitar *dance*

A: *What's your talent?*
B: *I can dance. I've been dancing for six years.*

Grammar Central
Present perfect progressive
I've .... practicing my song for six months.
I haven't been .... my homework.

Chapter 6 59

Warmer: When did you ...?

Ask the children a series of *When did you ...?* questions about past actions, e.g. ... *learn to tie your shoes?* ... *have breakfast today?* For each question have them write either their age or a time when they did it. Write the verb phrases on the board as a memory aid. Then have the children compare answers with a friend using complete sentences. Their objective is to find someone with at least three answers the same.

1 Read. Which act would you like to see and why?

- Have the children look at the pictures. Ask *Which act would you like to see and why?*
- Have the children read the two texts and decide.
- They compare their ideas with a friend and then vote by a show of hands for the act they want to see.
- Ask children who voted on each side why they chose that act (or did not choose the other one).

Answers

Children's own answers.

2 Write S (Susan) or P (Peter).

- The children identify who is described in each question, writing S (Susan) or P (Peter) as appropriate.
- Elicit answers.

Answers

1 S **2** S **3** P **4** P **5** S **6** P

Grammar Central

Present perfect progressive

Have the children complete the grammar examples. Elicit answers. Elicit how the present perfect progressive is formed (have + been + –ing) and the period of time (for + *time*). The children write further examples in their notebook. See also the Grammar Reference sections in the Student Book (p. 101) and Activity Book (p. 101) for further explanation and practice.

Grammar Central Answers: been, doing

3 Talk to a friend. Imagine you have a new talent.

- Have two children read out the example dialogue and then have a child ask you the same question. Give your answer, e.g. *I can balance things on my head. I've been balancing things for days!*
- Have the children make dialogues in pairs.
- Have pairs perform a dialogue for the class.

Optional activity: How long?

Elicit how to make sentences from the Warmer (e.g. *I started to learn English five years ago.*) into present perfect progressive sentences (*I've been learning English for five years.*) Have the children work with a friend to make similar sentences. Elicit sentences.

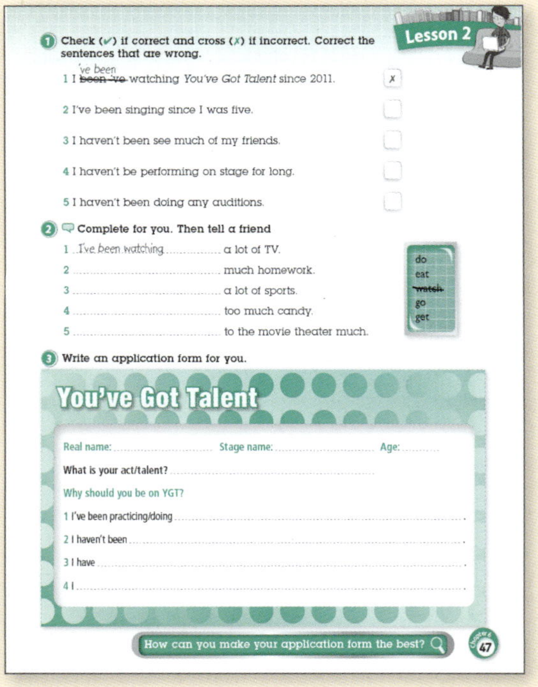
Lesson 2

1 Check (✓) if correct and cross (✗) if incorrect. Correct the sentences that are wrong.

1 I ~~been 've~~ 've been watching *You've Got Talent* since 2011. ✗

2 I've been singing since I was five.

3 I haven't been see much of my friends.

4 I haven't be performing on stage for long.

5 I haven't been doing any auditions.

2 Complete for you. Then tell a friend

1 I've been watching .... a lot of TV.

2 .... much homework.

3 .... a lot of sports.

4 .... too much candy.

5 .... to the movie theater much.

do / eat / ~~watch~~ / go / get

3 Write an application form for you.

You've Got Talent

Real name: .... Stage name: .... Age: ....

What is your act/talent? ....

Why should you be on YGT?

1 I've been practicing/doing ....

2 I haven't been ....

3 I have ....

4 I ....

How can you make your application form the best?

Chapter 6 47

1 Check (✓) if correct and cross (✗) if incorrect. Correct the sentences that are wrong.

The children write a check by sentences which are correct and a cross by those which are incorrect. They then score through the errors in the incorrect sentences and write in the corrections.

Answers

1 ✗ ~~been 've~~/'ve been watching **2** ✓
3 ✗ ~~haven't been see~~/haven't been seeing
4 ✗ ~~haven't be performing~~/haven't been performing **5** ✓

2 Complete for you. Then tell a friend.

The children complete the sentences with their own details. Then they discuss their responses in pairs.

Answers

I've been/I haven't been …
1 watching **2** getting **3** doing **4** eating **5** going

3 Write an application form for you.

The children fill in the application form with their own details. Then they compare with a friend. Ask children to read extracts from their form. Ask *How can you make your application form the best? (give lots of interesting but important information, choose a good stage name, sound friendly and enthusiastic)*

Answers

Children's own answers.

Cooler: Browse the applications

Have the children leave their Activity Book open on their desk on page 47. They walk around the classroom to look at the different applications and choose who they think has the best chance. Ask children to explain which application they chose and why.

Competency Focus

Learn

The children integrate previously acquired vocabulary into new grammar and structure, and adapt the language to show an understanding of the topic.

Presentation Kit • Use *Hotspots* to enlarge the SB Grammar Central box. Use *Highlighter* to identify the present perfect progressive in the SB Activity 1 text.

• TIP When using *Hotspots*, look for *Answer Key* in the Navigation Pane. Choose to show the answers all at once or one by one.

Teacher's Resource Center • For extra grammar practice, print out Grammar Worksheet 6A.

Student's Resource Center • The children can use Interactive Grammar 6A at home.

Reading: Story Extract

Lesson objectives: apologize and accept an apology for lateness; use the title and pictures to predict story content; read the extract from the playscript *Just Dance!* (middle)

Functional language: *Sorry I'm late. Have you been waiting long? No, don't worry. I've only been waiting for ... I've been ...*

Secondary language: *performing arts, ballet dancers, embarrassed*

Materials: Class CD

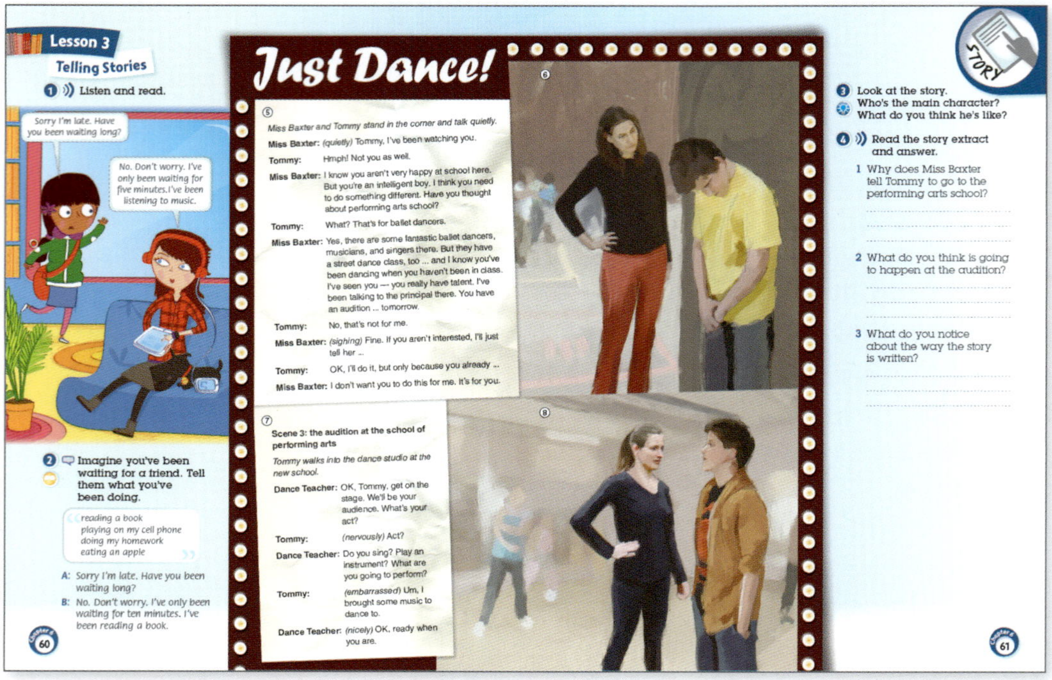

Lesson 3

Telling Stories

1 Listen and read.

2 Imagine you've been waiting for a friend. Tell them what you've been doing.

reading a book
playing on my cell phone
doing my homework
eating an apple

A: Sorry I'm late. Have you been waiting long?
B: No. Don't worry. I've only been waiting for ten minutes. I've been reading a book.

60

Just Dance!

⑤

Miss Baxter and Tommy stand in the corner and talk quietly.

Miss Baxter: *(quietly)* Tommy, I've been watching you.

Tommy: Hmph! Not you as well.

Miss Baxter: I know you aren't very happy at school here. But you're an intelligent boy. I think you need to do something different. Have you thought about performing arts school?

Tommy: What? That's for ballet dancers.

Miss Baxter: Yes, there are some fantastic ballet dancers, musicians, and singers there. But they have a street dance class, too ... and I know you've been dancing when you haven't been in class. I've seen you — you really have talent. I've been talking to the principal there. You have an audition ... tomorrow.

Tommy: No, that's not for me.

Miss Baxter: *(sighing)* Fine. If you aren't interested, I'll just tell her ...

Tommy: OK, I'll do it, but only because you already ...

Miss Baxter: I don't want you to do this for me. It's for you.

⑥

⑦

Scene 3: the audition at the school of performing arts

Tommy walks into the dance studio at the new school.

Dance Teacher: OK, Tommy, get on the stage. We'll be your audience. What's your act?

Tommy: *(nervously)* Act?

Dance Teacher: Do you sing? Play an instrument? What are you going to perform?

Tommy: *(embarrassed)* Um, I brought some music to dance to.

Dance Teacher: *(nicely)* OK, ready when you are.

⑧

STORY

3 Look at the story. Who's the main character? What do you think he's like?

4 Read the story extract and answer.

1 Why does Miss Baxter tell Tommy to go to the performing arts school?

2 What do you think is going to happen at the audition?

3 What do you notice about the way the story is written?

61

Warmer: Missing vowels

Write key sentences from Lesson 2 on the board, e.g. *I've been singing for three years.*, omitting the vowels. The children write the complete sentences. Then invite them to write in the missing vowels on the board.

Functional language

1 2.3 Listen and read.

- Play the CD. The children listen and read along. Ask *Is Yasmin happy?* (*no*) *Is Scarlett annoyed?* (*no*) *How does Yasmin feel at the end?* (*She probably feels better because Scarlett was nice to her.*)
- Play the CD again, pausing for the children to repeat.
- Divide the class into pairs to practice the dialogue.

2 Imagine you've been waiting for a friend. Tell them what you've been doing.

- Choose two children to read the example dialogue. Elicit other examples using the prompts supplied.
- The children practice in pairs, using different times and activities. Have pairs perform a dialogue for the class.

Before reading

3 Look at the story. Who's the main character? What do you think he's like?

- Have the children study the story title and pictures. Ask *Who's the main character?* (*Tommy*) *What do you think he's like?* Elicit ideas.

4 2.4 Read the story extract and answer.

- Play the CD. The children listen and read along. Have them answer question 1. Elicit the answer.

- Play the CD again so they can write their ideas for questions 2 and 3. Encourage them to use reading skills (e.g. using the title, pictures, and context) to infer meaning and make predictions.
- Elicit answers, but do not confirm predictions: explain that they will have to read the story to find out.

Answers

1 She knows he has been dancing. / She knows he isn't very happy at the school. **2** Children's own answers.
3 Children's own answers. / It's a playscript.

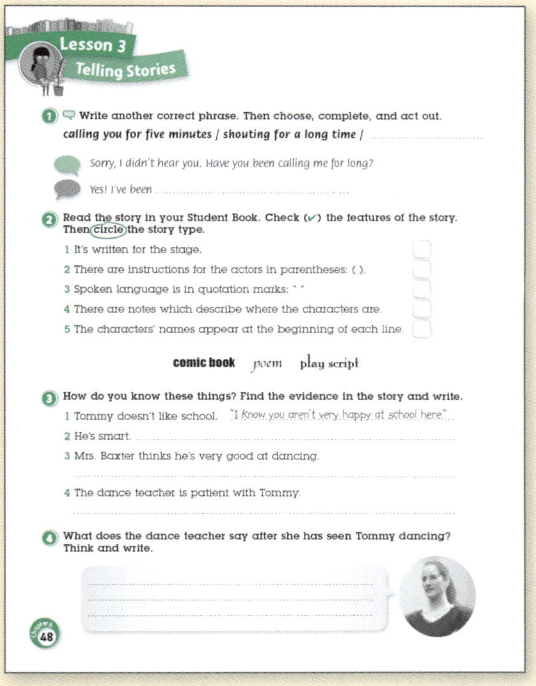

Lesson 3
Telling Stories

1 Write another correct phrase. Then choose, complete, and act out.
calling you for five minutes / shouting for a long time / ....

Sorry, I didn't hear you. Have you been calling me for long?
Yes! I've been ....

2 Read the story in your Student Book. Check (✔) the features of the story. Then circle the story type.
1 It's written for the stage.
2 There are instructions for the actors in parentheses: ( ).
3 Spoken language is in quotation marks: " "
4 There are notes which describe where the characters are.
5 The characters' names appear at the beginning of each line.

comic book poem play script

3 How do you know these things? Find the evidence in the story and write.
1 Tommy doesn't like school. "I know you aren't very happy at school here."
2 He's smart. ....
3 Mrs. Baxter thinks he's very good at dancing. ....
4 The dance teacher is patient with Tommy. ....

4 What does the dance teacher say after she has seen Tommy dancing? Think and write.

Chapter 6 48

1 Write another correct phrase. Then choose, complete, and act out.

Elicit other phrases that could follow *Yes! I've been …* The children choose a phrase and complete the dialogue. They then act it out in pairs. Encourage the children to use what they know to adapt and extend the dialogue. Have pairs act out their dialogue for the class.

2 Read the story in your Student Book. Check (✔) the features of the story. Then circle the story type.

The children read the Student Book story extract again, then check the sentences which describe the story. They circle the story type. Elicit answers.

Answers

✔ *next to:* 1, 2, 4, 5
Circled: playscript

3 How do you know these things? Find the evidence in the story and write.

The children find and write evidence in the story for the statements. Elicit answers.

Answers

1 "I know you aren't very happy at school here."
2 "You're an intelligent boy." **3** "You really have talent."
4 "OK, ready when you are."

4 What does the dance teacher say after she has seen Tommy dancing? Think and write.

Elicit suggestions. The children write their own ideas, then compare with a friend. Elicit ideas.

Answers

Children's own answers.

Cooler: Play "Disappearing Words"

Play the game with words from the chapter (see Games Bank p. 222).

Competency Focus

Collaborate and Communicate

The children work together to practice, perform, and adapt the new functional language learned.

Think

The children use critical thinking skills to identify the text type of the story and the personality of the main character.

Presentation Kit • Use *Mask* to uncover the speech bubbles in SB Activity 1, eliciting what comes next before you uncover each one. Use *Highlighter* on *listening to music*. Elicit different things you could say in this context.

- Use *Spotlight* on the two pictures of Tommy in the story extract. Each time, elicit how he is feeling.
- TIP Choose *Hotspots*. Look at the bottom of the screen in the Navigation Pane to see if an activity is interactive, or has an *Audio* or *Answer Key* button.

Just Dance!

1

Scene 1: in the classroom

Tommy walks quickly into the classroom.

Miss Baxter: Why are you late? Sit down.

Tommy: I was in detention.

Miss Baxter: Stop that noise, stop moving. I'm warning you! If I hear your voice again, I'll send you to the principal's office ... again!

3

Scene 2: in the school yard

Tommy and another boy are fighting in the school yard. Miss Baxter walks over.

Miss Baxter: (*angrily*) Stop! Come with me.

Tommy: No, I'm going ...

Miss Baxter: NOW!

Tommy: OK, OK.

5

Miss Baxter and Tommy stand in the corner and talk quietly.

Miss Baxter: (*quietly*) Tommy, I've been watching you.

Tommy: Hmph! Not you as well.

Miss Baxter: I know you aren't very happy at school here. But you're an intelligent boy. I think you need to do something different. Have you thought about performing arts school?

Tommy: What? That's for ballet dancers.

Miss Baxter: Yes, there are some fantastic ballet dancers, musicians, and singers there. But they have a street dance class, too ... and I know you've been dancing when you haven't been in class. I've seen you—you really have talent. I've been talking to the principal there. You have an audition ... tomorrow.

Tommy: No, that's not for me.

Miss Baxter: (*sighing*) Fine. If you aren't interested, I'll just tell her ...

Tommy: OK, I'll do it, but only because you already ...

Miss Baxter: I don't want you to do this for me. It's for you.

7

Scene 3: the audition at the school of performing arts

Tommy walks into the dance studio at the new school.

Dance Teacher: OK, Tommy, get on the stage. We'll be your audience. What's your act?

Tommy: (*nervously*) Act?

Dance Teacher: Do you sing? Play an instrument? What are you going to perform?

Tommy: (*embarrassed*) Um, I brought some music to dance to.

Dance Teacher: (*nicely*) OK, ready when you are.

9

Tommy dances.

Dance Teacher: You're very good. You can come to the school, but you have to practice and study hard. You'll still have classes, it's not only dancing. If you fail any subject, you'll have to leave. OK?

11

Scene 4: Tommy's house

Dad: My son, a dancer!

Mom: But Arnie, he doesn't like his school now. He might enjoy this new school, and they said he was good at dancing.

Dad: I guess so.

13

Scene 5: school of performing arts hallway

Tommy and Omar are arguing at the lockers.

Tommy: (*angrily*) Hey, that's mine!

Omar: (*more angrily*) Get out of here, new kid. You can't just ...

Tommy: (*loudly*) Oh, yeah?

Dance Teacher: Don't fight. ... DANCE!

Tommy: What?

Dance Teacher: Dance off! Everyone, in the gym, now!

15

Scene 6: in the gym

The audience cheers and claps. Omar dances first.

Boy in audience: Come on, Omar!

Girl in audience: I wish I could dance like that.

Tommy dances.

Omar: (*surprised*) Not bad. Go, Tommy!

17

The audience cheers loudly.

Omar: Nice work! You're a superstar, new kid.

Dance Teacher: OK. That was actually your audition for the school musical next year. You both have parts. Rehearsals start next semester.

19

They leave the gym and go back to class.

Tommy: (*excitedly*) Man, I *love* this place!

Lesson objective: read and understand the playscript *Just Dance!* in the Reader
Materials: Class CD; Reader

Warmer: True or False?

Write a big *TRUE* on one side of the board and a big *FALSE* on the other. Read out sentences about the story extract, e.g. *Tommy is a good dancer.* (*true*) *Tommy loves school.* (*false*) The children point to true or false as appropriate. If false, ask the children to explain why.

Story Summary

Tommy is a disruptive high school student. Miss Baxter sets up an audition at a performing arts school for him. Tommy dances well at his audition and gets a place. Despite initial problems in the new school, Tommy also gets a place in the school musical.

Theme: the importance of pursuing your own dreams

2.5 While reading

- Have the children look at the pictures in the Reader. Ask *Is Tommy good at dancing?* (*yes*)
- Play the CD. The children listen and read along. Ask *Does Tommy feel differently about things at the end?* (*Yes—he's happy and positive and he loves his new school.*)
- Ask questions to check comprehension, e.g. *What does Tommy have to do at his new school?* (*practice and study hard*) *When do rehearsals start?* (*next semester*)
- Have the class read the story aloud in groups, following/adapting the stage directions (see **Story Time**).

After reading: Reflect

Ask questions to give the children the opportunity to think about the issues raised by the story, e.g. *Why do you think Tommy didn't like his old school? Do you think people all need the same type of education? What special activity would you like to study at school?*

Optional activity: Difficult situations

Summarize the story, pausing for the children to complete, e.g. *Tommy wasn't … at school. He was always …*

Story Time

Following stage directions

A script like this with stage directions is ideal for the children to think about their tone of voice or volume when acting out the story. Have the children say the lines first in a neutral tone, and then change the effect of the scene by following different directions, e.g. *angrily, quietly, sighing, embarrassed*, etc.

Reading Strategy

Story Map

Using a story map helps the children identify the characters of a story and the parts of the plot, as well as the setting, problem, and solution. A basic story map focuses on the main parts of the story (beginning, middle, and end).

For additional explanation and activities, see the Literacy Handbook on the Teacher's Resource Center.

Cooler: Learn your lines

Give the children one minute to memorize Tommy's lines on Reader p. 30. They close their Reader. Read the parts of Miss Baxter and the Dance Teacher to elicit what Tommy says next.

Presentation Kit • Use *Hotspots* to show the Reader story one enlarged picture at a time as you play *Audio*.

- For the Warmer, have children use *Highlighter* to identify in the story extract the text that shows whether each statement you make is true or false.
- Use *Spotlight* to focus on the story pictures in the Reader one at a time to elicit a summary of the story.

Reading Comprehension and Critical Literacy

Lesson objectives: understand and evaluate the story; relate story theme to personal experience; focus on the use of stage directions to say how the characters say or do things

Materials: Class CD; Reader

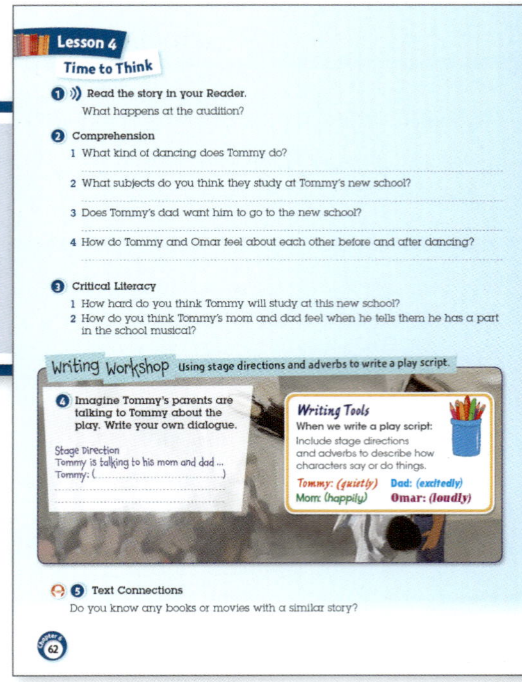
Lesson 4

Time to Think

1 Read the story in your Reader.
What happens at the audition?

2 Comprehension
1 What kind of dancing does Tommy do?
2 What subjects do you think they study at Tommy's new school?
3 Does Tommy's dad want him to go to the new school?
4 How do Tommy and Omar feel about each other before and after dancing?

3 Critical Literacy
1 How hard do you think Tommy will study at this new school?
2 How do you think Tommy's mom and dad feel when he tells them he has a part in the school musical?

Writing Workshop Using stage directions and adverbs to write a play script.

4 Imagine Tommy's parents are talking to Tommy about the play. Write your own dialogue.

Stage Direction
Tommy is talking to his mom and dad ...
Tommy: (.....................)

Writing Tools
When we write a play script:
Include stage directions and adverbs to describe how characters say or do things.
Tommy: (quietly) Dad: (excitedly)
Mom: (happily) Omar: (loudly)

5 Text Connections
Do you know any books or movies with a similar story?

62

Note: Please ensure that your class has read the Reader story before you do this lesson.

Warmer: Name the characters

Have the children work in pairs to list the characters from the Reader story without looking in their books. Ask children to write them on the board. Then have the class check in their Reader. (*Tommy, Miss Baxter, Dance Teacher, Dad, Mom, Omar, Boy in audience, Girl in audience*)

1 2.5 Read the story in your Reader.

- Have the children read the story. (Alternatively, play the CD and have them read along.)
- Elicit whether the children were correct in their predictions in Lesson 3 Activity 4. Ask *What happens at the audition?* (*Tommy dances well./The teacher offers him a place at the school.*)

2 Comprehension

- The children write answers to the first three questions. Elicit answers.
- Discuss question 4. Ask the children to justify their answers.

Answers

1 Street dancing. **2** Children's own answers.
3 No, he doesn't. / No, he isn't sure about it.
4 *Before:* They don't like each other. / They fight.
After: They like each other.

3 Critical Literacy

- Have the children discuss the answers to the questions with a friend.
- Elicit ideas and have a class discussion. Encourage the children to give reasons for their opinions. Empathizing with the characters and their situations helps children engage creatively with the story.

Answers

Children's own answers.

Writing Workshop

Using stage directions and adverbs to write a playscript

4 Imagine Tommy's parents are talking to Tommy about the play. Write your own dialogue.

Have a child read the playscript. Elicit other things to include, using the stage directions and adverbs from the **Writing Tools** box. The children write a dialogue in their notebook, then compare with a friend. Elicit responses.

Answers

Children's own answers.

5 Text Connections

- Ask *Do you know any books or movies with a similar story?* Elicit ideas and discuss as a class.

Optional activity: More stage directions

Have the children look back at *The Tomb of the Ancient Dog* and *Master Mind Returns* in their Reader. They decide where they would insert stage directions for movements or how to say things if the story were a script. Elicit ideas.

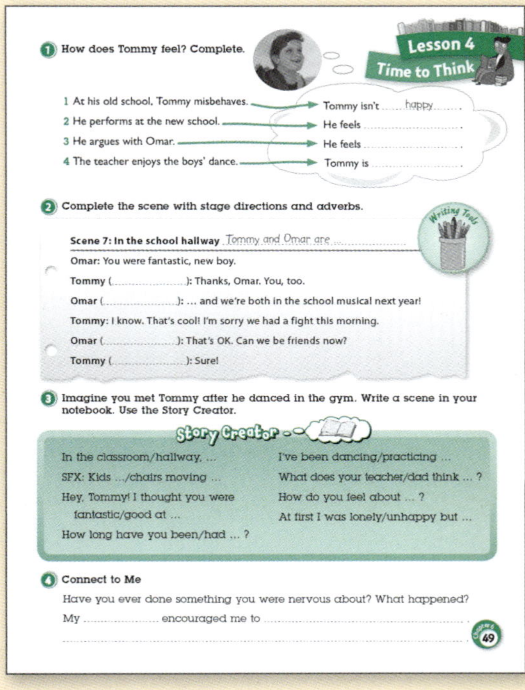

Lesson 4
Time to Think

1 How does Tommy feel? Complete.

1 At his old school, Tommy misbehaves. → Tommy isn't ...happy... .
2 He performs at the new school. → He feels ....
3 He argues with Omar. → He feels ....
4 The teacher enjoys the boys' dance. → Tommy is ....

2 Complete the scene with stage directions and adverbs.

Writing Tools

Scene 7: In the school hallway Tommy and Omar are ....
Omar: You were fantastic, new boy.
Tommy (...............): Thanks, Omar. You, too.
Omar (...............): ... and we're both in the school musical next year!
Tommy: I know. That's cool! I'm sorry we had a fight this morning.
Omar (...............): That's OK. Can we be friends now?
Tommy (...............): Sure!

3 Imagine you met Tommy after he danced in the gym. Write a scene in your notebook. Use the Story Creator.

Story Creator

In the classroom/hallway, ...
SFX: Kids .../chairs moving ...
Hey, Tommy! I thought you were fantastic/good at ...
How long have you been/had ... ?
I've been dancing/practicing ...
What does your teacher/dad think ... ?
How do you feel about ... ?
At first I was lonely/unhappy but ...

4 Connect to Me

Have you ever done something you were nervous about? What happened?
My .... encouraged me to ....
....

Chapter 6 49

1 How does Tommy feel? Complete.

The children write adjectives to complete the descriptions of Tommy at different points in the story. Elicit answers.

Answers

1 happy **2** nervous/embarrassed **3** angry **4** proud

2 Complete the scene with stage directions and adverbs.

The children complete the scene, writing in stage directions and adverbs. Elicit answers.

Answers (suggested)

talking and smiling; excitedly, happily, nicely, happily

3 Imagine you met Tommy after he danced in the gym. Write a scene in your notebook. Use the Story Creator.

Use the **Story Creator** prompts to elicit ideas. The children write a new scene in their notebook, describing their conversation with Tommy after he danced in the gym, then compare with a friend. Have children read out their scenes for the class.

4 Connect to Me

Elicit examples of events that make the children nervous. (e.g. *an audition, meeting new people*) The children write their own response, then compare with a friend. Elicit responses.

Cooler: Say it different ways

Write the following sentences on the board:

1 Tommy, I've been watching you.
2 I brought some music to dance to.
3 My son, a dancer!

Elicit how people say things in the story (*angrily, quietly, sighing, nervously, embarrassed, nicely, loudly, surprised, excitedly*). Have the children say each line when you call out a number and an adverb/adjective, e.g. *Number 3—angrily!* The children continue the activity in pairs.

Competency Focus

Me: Critical Literacy

The children use critical literacy skills to reflect on the story and relate it to their own experiences.

Presentation Kit • Have children use *Highlighter* to identify examples of playscript features in the Reader story for SB Activity 4.

- TIP Use *Stopwatch* to make activities more fun and challenging. For the Warmer, you could set a time limit and ask the pair with the most characters to write them for the class to confirm.
- TIP You can move the *Answer Key* pop-up window to show the answers by the activity. Hold the cursor over the colored band at the top of the window.

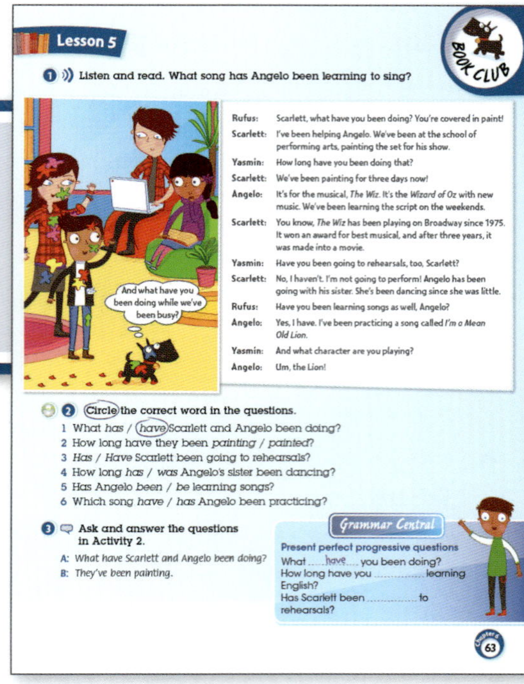

Lesson 5

BOOK CLUB

1 Listen and read. What song has Angelo been learning to sing?

Rufus: Scarlett, what have you been doing? You're covered in paint!
Scarlett: I've been helping Angelo. We've been at the school of performing arts, painting the set for his show.
Yasmin: How long have you been doing that?
Scarlett: We've been painting for three days now!
Angelo: It's for the musical, *The Wiz*. It's the *Wizard of Oz* with new music. We've been learning the script on the weekends.
Scarlett: You know, *The Wiz* has been playing on Broadway since 1975. It won an award for best musical, and after three years, it was made into a movie.
Yasmin: Have you been going to rehearsals, too, Scarlett?
Scarlett: No, I haven't. I'm not going to perform! Angelo has been going with his sister. She's been dancing since she was little.
Rufus: Have you been learning songs as well, Angelo?
Angelo: Yes, I have. I've been practicing a song called *I'm a Mean Old Lion*.
Yasmin: And what character are you playing?
Angelo: Um, the Lion!

2 Circle the correct word in the questions.

1 What *has* / *have* Scarlett and Angelo been doing?
2 How long have they been *painting* / *painted*?
3 *Has* / *Have* Scarlett been going to rehearsals?
4 How long *has* / *was* Angelo's sister been dancing?
5 Has Angelo *been* / *be* learning songs?
6 Which song *have* / *has* Angelo been practicing?

3 Ask and answer the questions in Activity 2.

A: *What have Scarlett and Angelo been doing?*
B: *They've been painting.*

Grammar Central

Present perfect progressive questions
What ....have.... you been doing?
How long have you .... learning English?
Has Scarlett been .... to rehearsals?

Chapter 6 63

Grammar and Reading

Lesson objectives: ask and answer about recent and unfinished activities
Key grammar: present perfect progressive questions
Secondary language: *rehearsals*
Materials: Class CD; Grammar Worksheet 6B [TRC printout] (optional)

Warmer: Play "The Chain Game"

Play the game with *When our school put on a musical, . . .* (see Games Bank p. 222).

1 2.6 Listen and read. What song has Angelo been learning to sing?

- Have the children look at the picture. Ask *What do you think Scarlett and Angelo have been doing?* (*painting*)
- Play the CD. The children listen and read along. Ask *What song has Angelo been learning to sing?* (I'm a Mean Old Lion)
- Play the CD again, pausing after key phrases (especially questions with *have you been –ing*). Have the children repeat the phrases.

2 Circle the correct word in the questions.

- Draw the children's attention to the completed example. Elicit why it is the correct answer. (*"Scarlett and Angelo" is plural—you use "have" with plural*)
- The children complete the sentences by circling the correct word from the two options.
- Elicit answers.

Answers

1 have **2** painting **3** Has **4** has **5** been **6** has

Grammar Central

Present perfect progressive questions

Have the children complete the grammar examples. Elicit answers. Elicit how present perfect progressive questions are formed. (*question words* + have/has + *subject* + *been* + *verb* + –ing) The children write further examples in their notebook. See also the Grammar Reference sections in the Student Book (p. 101) and Activity Book (p. 101) for further explanation and practice.

Grammar Central Answers: have, been, going

AB Answers Activity 2: 1 have you been playing **2** have you been singing **3** been painting **4** Have you been … for long?

3 Ask and answer the questions in Activity 2.

- Have the children work in pairs to ask and answer the questions. You can raise the challenge a little by having the child answering keep their book closed.
- Invite pairs to ask and answer for the class.

Optional activity: Write story questions

Have the children write questions about the Reader story, e.g. *What happened after Tommy and Omar argued in the hallway?* Have the children write questions and then ask a friend their questions. Elicit questions for the class to answer.

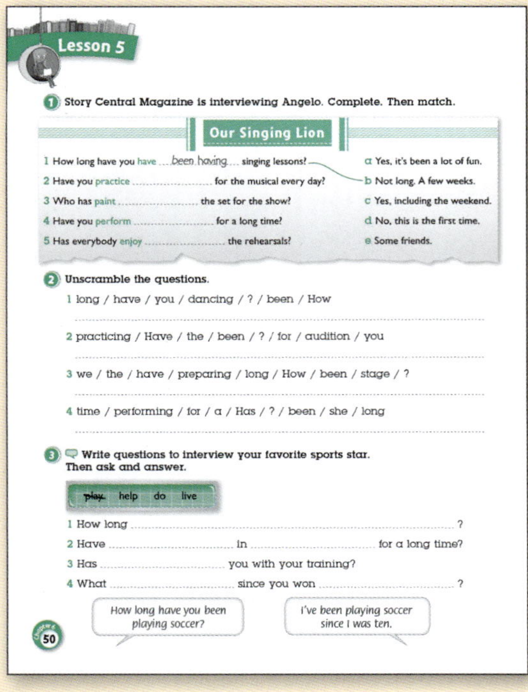

Lesson 5

1 Story Central Magazine is interviewing Angelo. Complete. Then match.

Our Singing Lion

1 How long have you have ...been having... singing lessons? — a Yes, it's been a lot of fun.
2 Have you practice .... for the musical every day? — b Not long. A few weeks.
3 Who has paint .... the set for the show? — c Yes, including the weekend.
4 Have you perform .... for a long time? — d No, this is the first time.
5 Has everybody enjoy .... the rehearsals? — e Some friends.

2 Unscramble the questions.

1 long / have / you / dancing / ? / been / How
2 practicing / Have / the / been / ? / for / audition / you
3 we / the / have / preparing / long / How / been / stage / ?
4 time / performing / for / a / Has / ? / been / she / long

3 Write questions to interview your favorite sports star. Then ask and answer.

~~play~~ help do live

1 How long .... ?
2 Have .... in .... for a long time?
3 Has .... you with your training?
4 What .... since you won .... ?

How long have you been playing soccer?

I've been playing soccer since I was ten.

50

1 Story Central Magazine is interviewing Angelo. Complete. Then match.

The children complete the interview questions using the verb prompts supplied. Then they match the completed questions and answers. Elicit responses.

Answers

1 been having b, **2** been practicing c, **3** been painting e, **4** been performing d, **5** been enjoying a

2 Unscramble the questions.

The children write out the correct versions of the questions. Elicit responses.

Answers

1 How long have you been dancing? **2** Have you been practicing for the audition? **3** How long have we been preparing the stage? **4** Has she been performing for a long time?

3 Write questions to interview your favorite sports star. Then ask and answer.

The children write questions to interview their favorite sports star using the prompts supplied. Then they ask and answer in pairs, taking turns playing the part of the interviewer and the sports star. Elicit answers.

Answers

1 have you been playing **2** you been living, Children's own answer **3** anyone been helping **4** have you been doing, Children's own answer

Cooler: Play "Disappearing Text"

Play the game with questions from the lesson (see Games Bank p. 222).

Competency Focus

Learn

The children demonstrate their understanding of the new language by reading the dialogue and completing the activity.

Presentation Kit • Have children identify key language in SB Activity 1, using *Highlighter* to show the present perfect progressive questions.

- TIP Display the AB and use the link in the drop-down Menu to access the corresponding Grammar Reference section at the back.
- Give feedback on AB activities using *Answer Key* (Activities 1 and 3) or the built-in interactive activity (Activity 2).

Teacher's Resource Center • For extra grammar practice, print out Grammar Worksheet 6B.

Student's Resource Center • The children can use Interactive Grammar 6B at home.

Lesson 6

1 Listen and sing. Who's involved in putting on a show?

SONG

Thank You, Everyone!

The cast would like to say thank you,
To the backstage crew.
For doing our hair and make-up,
We say a big thank you!

Has everyone been working?
Through the night and day.
Sewing costumes, painting sets,
Practicing lines and what to say.

Thank you to the musicians,
And the lighting crew.
The performance wouldn't be possible,
If we didn't have you.

But most of all we thank you,
For coming to watch our show.
If there weren't an audience,
There wouldn't be a show...

2 Talk to a friend about what you'd like to be. Use the words in the song.

A: Would you like to be in a show?
B: Yes, I'd like to be a singer.

Spelling Central

Circle the words with *s* sounds in the song.

Write the words in the chart. Can you add more words?

s	*ce*	*ss*
backstage		

Chapter 6 64

Vocabulary, Song, and Spelling

Lesson objectives: identify and use vocabulary connected to performance and shows; practice spelling words with *s* sound (*s, ce, ss*)

Key vocabulary: *audience, backstage crew, cast, lighting crew, make-up, performance, sets*

Secondary language: *sewing, costumes*

Materials: Class CD

Warmer: Pre-teach vocabulary

Pre-teach the vocabulary using mimes. Call out the words for the class to do the appropriate mime. Then make sentences for the class to complete, e.g. *The people who act in a play are the … (cast). The people who make sure you can see everything on stage are the … (lighting crew).*

1 2.7 Listen and sing. Who's involved in putting on a show?

- Play the CD. The children listen and read along. Ask *Who's involved in putting on a show?* (*cast, backstage crew, musicians, lighting crew, audience*)
- Play the CD again for the children to sing along.

2 Talk to a friend about what you'd like to be. Use the words in the song.

- Divide the class into pairs. Read the example with the class. Then have them talk about what they would like to be.
- Elicit responses. Encourage the children to give reasons for their choices.

Spelling Central

Words with *s* sound

Write *first, nice, glass* on the board. Ask the children what sound all the words have. (*s*) Ask *What letters can make this sound?* (*s, ce, ss*) Have the children find words with *s, ce*, and *ss* on the page and complete the chart. They then add other words in each category. (e.g. *sister, superstar, dance, sentence; class, lesson*—but not *has* or *musicians*)

Answers

s: backstage, cast, say, sewing, costumes, sets, most
ce: performance, audience
ss: possible

Optional activity: Mime time

Write key vocabulary from **Spelling Central** on small pieces of paper (one word per piece). Take one word yourself, and mime it for the class so they can guess what it is. Invite children to come to the front of the class and give them a word to mime for the others to guess and spell.

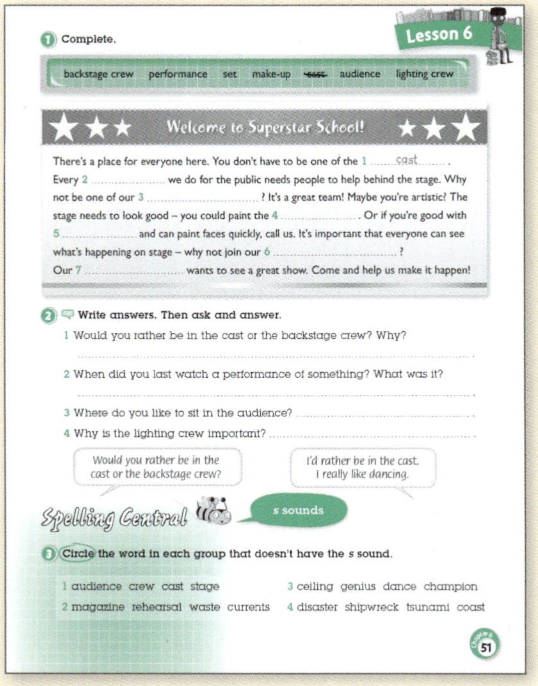
Lesson 6

1 Complete.

backstage crew · performance · set · make-up · ~~cast~~ · audience · lighting crew

Welcome to Superstar School!

There's a place for everyone here. You don't have to be one of the 1 ....cast.... . Every 2 .... we do for the public needs people to help behind the stage. Why not be one of our 3 ....? It's a great team! Maybe you're artistic? The stage needs to look good – you could paint the 4 .... Or if you're good with 5 .... and can paint faces quickly, call us. It's important that everyone can see what's happening on stage – why not join our 6 ....? Our 7 .... wants to see a great show. Come and help us make it happen!

2 Write answers. Then ask and answer.

1 Would you rather be in the cast or the backstage crew? Why?

2 When did you last watch a performance of something? What was it?

3 Where do you like to sit in the audience?

4 Why is the lighting crew important?

Would you rather be in the cast or the backstage crew?

I'd rather be in the cast. I really like dancing.

Spelling Central — s sounds

3 Circle the word in each group that doesn't have the s sound.

1 audience crew cast stage

2 magazine rehearsal waste currents

3 ceiling genius dance champion

4 disaster shipwreck tsunami coast

51

1 Complete.

The children complete the text using the words supplied. Elicit answers.

Answers

1 cast **2** performance **3** backstage crew **4** set **5** make-up **6** lighting crew **7** audience

2 Write answers. Then ask and answer.

The children write their own answers to the questions. Then they ask and answer the questions in pairs. Invite pairs to ask and answer for the class.

Answers

Children's own answers.

3 Circle the word in each group that doesn't have the *s* sound.

To practice the **Spelling Central** feature, the children read the words aloud and circle the one in each group that does not have the *s* sound. Elicit answers.

Answers

1 crew **2** magazine **3** champion **4** shipwreck

Cooler: Sing and mime

2.7

Play the CD again from Student Book Activity 1. Have the children sing the song and mime actions for all the key words in the song.

Competency Focus

Collaborate and Communicate

The children work together to share their ideas on the topic, incorporating the new vocabulary.

Presentation Kit • Use Vocabulary Tool 6B to pre-teach key vocabulary. Use *Slideshow* to introduce the words and *Find the Pairs* to review/test.

• Choose Music Video 6 and encourage the children to sing along, using the graphic lyrics on screen. Pause *Video* for the children to continue singing. Monitor to check the children are participating and identify any who are struggling.

Student's Resource Center • Remind the children they can access Music Video 6 at home to practice the song.

CLIL: Performing arts—Javanese shadow puppets

Lesson objective: find out about puppet theater in Java

Materials: a puppet (Warmer); magazines with famous people, cardboard, glue (Cooler); CLIL Graphic Organizer 6 [TRC printout] (optional)

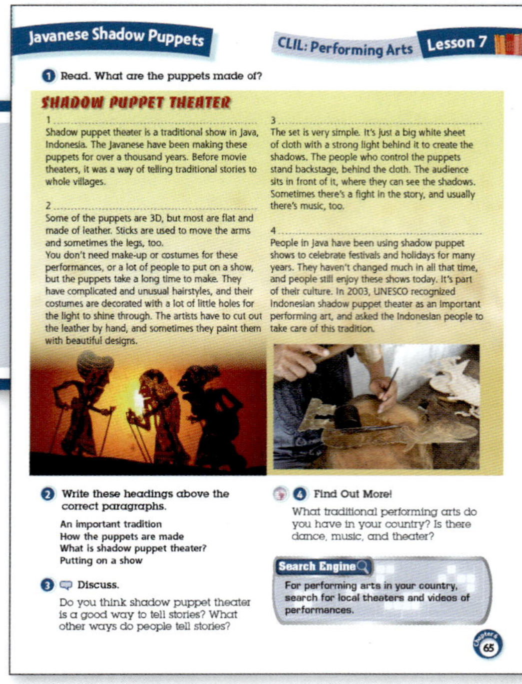

Javanese Shadow Puppets

CLIL: Performing Arts Lesson 7

1 Read. What are the puppets made of?

SHADOW PUPPET THEATER

1 ....

Shadow puppet theater is a traditional show in Java, Indonesia. The Javanese have been making these puppets for over a thousand years. Before movie theaters, it was a way of telling traditional stories to whole villages.

2 ....

Some of the puppets are 3D, but most are flat and made of leather. Sticks are used to move the arms and sometimes the legs, too.
You don't need make-up or costumes for these performances, or a lot of people to put on a show, but the puppets take a long time to make. They have complicated and unusual hairstyles, and their costumes are decorated with a lot of little holes for the light to shine through. The artists have to cut out the leather by hand, and sometimes they paint them with beautiful designs.

3 ....

The set is very simple. It's just a big white sheet of cloth with a strong light behind it to create the shadows. The people who control the puppets stand backstage, behind the cloth. The audience sits in front of it, where they can see the shadows. Sometimes there's a fight in the story, and usually there's music, too.

4 ....

People in Java have been using shadow puppet shows to celebrate festivals and holidays for many years. They haven't changed much in all that time, and people still enjoy these shows today. It's part of their culture. In 2003, UNESCO recognized Indonesian shadow puppet theater as an important performing art, and asked the Indonesian people to take care of this tradition.

2 Write these headings above the correct paragraphs.

An important tradition
How the puppets are made
What is shadow puppet theater?
Putting on a show

3 Discuss.

Do you think shadow puppet theater is a good way to tell stories? What other ways do people tell stories?

4 Find Out More!

What traditional performing arts do you have in your country? Is there dance, music, and theater?

Search Engine

For performing arts in your country, search for local theaters and videos of performances.

Chapter 6 65

Warmer: Brainstorm puppets

Show the children your puppet (this can be a proper puppet or something as simple as a sock with two craft eyes stuck on). Ask *Do you know any other puppets?* Then have the children work in pairs to list famous puppets (e.g. *Pinocchio*, the Muppets, Sesame Street characters, etc.). Invite children to describe the puppets to the class.

1 Read. What are the puppets made of?

- Have the children look at the pictures and talk to a friend about what they can see.
- Have the children read the text quickly. Ask *What are the puppets made of?* (*leather*)
- Elicit any other information the children found out when they read the text.

2 Write these headings above the correct paragraphs.

- Elicit the best heading for paragraph 1 (*What is shadow puppet theater?*) and reasons why.
- Have the children write the heading for each paragraph, then compare with a friend.
- Elicit answers.

Answers

1 What is shadow puppet theater? **2** How the puppets are made **3** Putting on a show **4** An important tradition

3 Discuss.

- Have a child read out the discussion question.
- Have the children talk about their ideas in pairs, then share ideas as a class.

4 Find Out More!

- The children research traditional performing arts in their own country (e.g. dance, music, theater). The **Search Engine** feature gives support on where to look. The children will need to complete this research before doing the follow-up activity in the Activity Book. (It could be set as homework.)

Optional activity: A puppet show

Have the children look back at the first six stories in the Reader and decide which would make a good puppet show. The children discuss what would and would not be a good choice with a friend, e.g. Icarus *would be a good choice because the actions can be shown as shadows.* Invite pairs to share their ideas with the class.

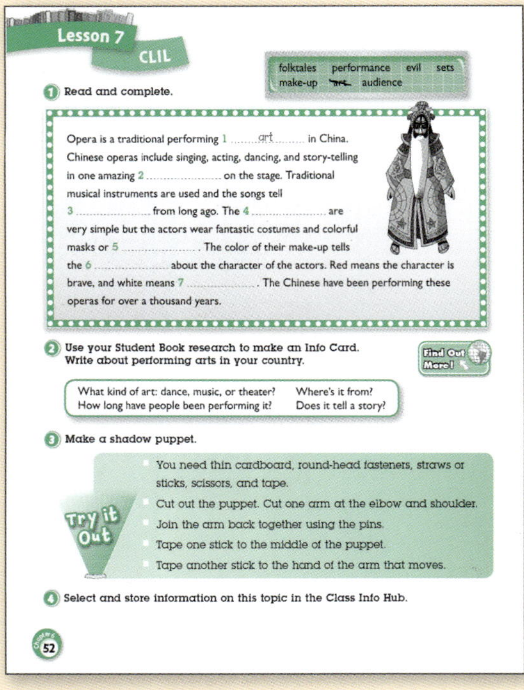

Lesson 7 CLIL

folktales performance evil sets make-up ~~art~~ audience

1 Read and complete.

Opera is a traditional performing 1 ......art...... in China. Chinese operas include singing, acting, dancing, and story-telling in one amazing 2 .... on the stage. Traditional musical instruments are used and the songs tell 3 .... from long ago. The 4 .... are very simple but the actors wear fantastic costumes and colorful masks or 5 .... The color of their make-up tells the 6 .... about the character of the actors. Red means the character is brave, and white means 7 .... The Chinese have been performing these operas for over a thousand years.

2 Use your Student Book research to make an Info Card. Write about performing arts in your country.

Find Out More!

What kind of art: dance, music, or theater? Where's it from?
How long have people been performing it? Does it tell a story?

3 Make a shadow puppet.

Try it Out

- You need thin cardboard, round-head fasteners, straws or sticks, scissors, and tape.
- Cut out the puppet. Cut one arm at the elbow and shoulder.
- Join the arm back together using the pins.
- Tape one stick to the middle of the puppet.
- Tape another stick to the hand of the arm that moves.

4 Select and store information on this topic in the Class Info Hub.

Chapter 6 52

1 Read and complete.

The children complete the text using the words supplied. Elicit answers.

Answers

1 art **2** performance **3** folktales **4** sets **5** make-up **6** audience **7** evil

2 Use your Student Book research to make an Info Card. Write about performing arts in your country.

Divide the class into groups. Have the children pool the information they learned from their research in the Student Book and the Activity Book. The children write about and illustrate their ideas individually. Have the groups present their Info Cards to the class.

3 Make a shadow puppet.

In their groups, the children follow the **Try It Out** instructions to make a shadow puppet. Give support as necessary. Have the groups show their shadow puppets to the class.

4 Select and store the information on this topic in the Class Info Hub.

Have the children vote for the five most interesting Info Cards. Archive these and the best of the shadow puppets in your Class Hub (see p. 41) in a folder called **Chapter 6 Performing Arts**.

Cooler: Magazine puppets

Have the children cut out famous people from magazines and stick them on thin cardboard to make a puppet each. The children then work in pairs to ask and answer questions about their famous person, using their puppet to answer the questions.

Competency Focus

Act

The children carry out research to find out about Javanese shadow puppets. This helps them expand their learning and relate it to their world, both inside and outside the classroom.

Presentation Kit • Remember—do not be afraid to turn off the screen! Children benefit from variety of pace and focus—sometimes you will want to work just with books or without prompts. Work the materials into your teaching in the way that suits you.

- As support for less confident children, use *Highlighter* on the AB Activity 2 word bank prompts to elicit ideas from the class.

Teacher's Resource Center • Print out CLIL Graphic Organizer 6 for the children to collate their Find Out More! research.

Writing Project

Lesson objectives: review language from Chapter 6; write another scene for the play and present it to the class
Materials: Writing Template 6 [TRC printout] (optional)

PROJECT Lesson 8

Prepare

1 In groups, talk about what you think will happen next in the Reader story.

Write

2 Write another scene for the play.

- Write about what happens before the school musical starts.
- Continue the scene. Think about these questions:
  What happens next?
  Does Tommy dance well?
  Who's in the audience?
  How does he feel at the end?

Writing Tools
When you write a play script:
Write stage directions in the present tense.
Write the character's name, then a colon (:), then the dialogue.
Include sound effects (SFX).

Showcase

3 Perform your scene for the class.

Reflect

4 Vote for the best scene and talk to the class.

66

Warmer: Play "Ready, Set, Draw!"

Play the game with key vocabulary: *cast, audience, make-up, lighting, puppets, shadow* (see Games Bank p. 222).

Prepare

1 In groups, talk about what you think will happen next in the Reader story.

- Have the children remember what happened at the end of the story. (*Tommy had a part in the school musical and was very excited.*) Have a child read out the sentence openings supplied. Elicit a few ideas about what will happen next in the story. Encourage the children to think about potential problems as well as good things that might happen.
- Have the children discuss their ideas in groups, then share with the class.

Write

2 Write another scene for the play.

- Have the children read the model scene. Draw their attention to the conventions of script writing in the **Writing Tools** box and have them circle examples in the model scene.
- Have the children discuss possible variations on the model with a friend. They then write a scene individually and compare with a different friend. Give support as necessary.

Showcase

3 Perform your scene for the class.

- Choose children to perform their scene for the class. Ask the class to listen and guess the stage directions.

Reflect

4 Vote for the best scene and talk to the class.

- Have the children comment on which scene was the best (considering the funniest, best acting, best dialogue, etc.) and why. Have a class vote to identify their favorite.

Optional activity: Adapt a story

Have the children choose a scene from one of the stories in the Reader and adapt it as a script. A story with a lot of dialogue already written is easier, but a story with less dialogue is more of a challenge for stronger students. Have children act out their adaptation for the class.

GRAND QUIZ CENTRAL

Lesson 8

1 Play with a friend. Choose a character.
2 Write a new question to ask your friend.
3 Take turns asking. Say the answer, then write it in your notebook.
4 If a question is too hard, you can swap! Choose and check (✓) up to three questions. Remember: each swap loses a bonus point!

	Questions to ask Superstar	Questions to ask Dance Champion
1	Complete: *I haven't ... learning to play the piano for long.*	Complete: *I've been ... my homework for an hour.*
2	Unscramble this word: *itaudino*	Unscramble this word: *slhearare*
3	Why are Scarlett and Angelo covered in paint?	What character is Angelo playing in the musical?
4	How long have you been learning English?	How long have you been living in your house?
5	Which country is Java in?	What are Javanese puppets made of?
6	Say and spell two words with *ss*.	Say and spell two words with *ce* that sounds like *s*.
7	Complete: *How long ... you been sitting in this classroom?*	Complete: *How long has your friend ... taking this quiz?*
8	What does Omar call Tommy at the end of the story?	What type of school do Tommy and Omar go to in the story?
9	Find the one that doesn't belong: *crew, cast, audience, stage*	Find the one that doesn't belong: *backstage, set, perform, lights*
10	............................?	............................?

Check your friend's answers. Then color your masks and write your score.

Now choose your title:
Quiz Master! I understand this topic well.
Quiz Improver! I don't understand everything.
Quiz Beginner! I need some help.

Chapter 6 53

Grand Quiz Central

See p. 43 for details of how to take the quiz.

Answers

1 been / doing **2** audition / rehearsal **3** They've been painting the set. / He's the lion. **4** Children's own answers: I've been learning / living … for/since … **5** Indonesia / leather **6** *Any two of:* possible, lesson, class, grass, etc. / *Any two of:* science, dance, performance, audience, etc. **7** have / been **8** Superstar / Performing Arts school **9** stage / perform **10** Children's own answers.

Cooler: Act out the scene

The children take turns acting out the model scene from Student Book Activity 2. There are three parts (Tommy, Omar, and the Teacher) but other children can provide the sound effects!

Competency Focus

Me

The children invent and write another scene for the play they have read, exploring their imagination and creativity.

Presentation Kit • Have children use *Highlighter* to identify examples in the model text of the key features of the writing task: stage direction, speaker, dialogue, sound effects.

- TIP You can position the Navigation Pane on the left or right of the screen, depending on where you want to stand. Choose *Swap sides* to change.

Teacher's Resource Center • Print out Writing Template 6 for the SB writing activity.

Student's Resource Center • Encourage the children to share Vocabulary Tools 6A–6B at home to reinforce vocabulary learning.

Language Review

Lesson objective: review language from Chapter 6
Materials: Class CD

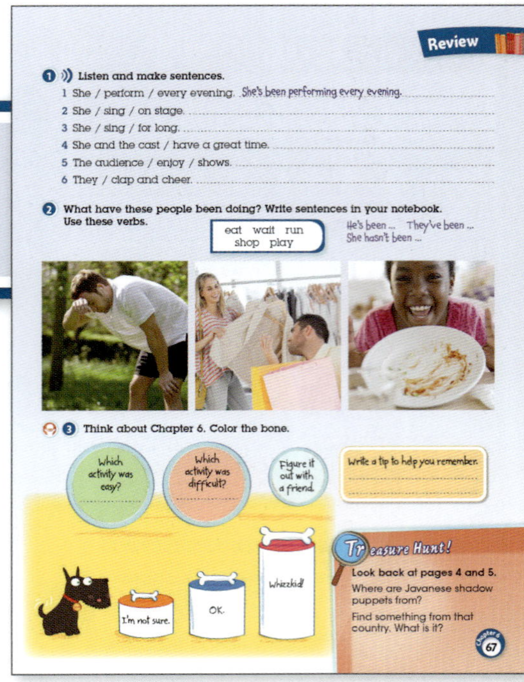
Review

1 Listen and make sentences.
1 She / perform / every evening. She's been performing every evening.
2 She / sing / on stage.
3 She / sing / for long.
4 She and the cast / have a great time.
5 The audience / enjoy / shows.
6 They / clap and cheer.

2 What have these people been doing? Write sentences in your notebook. Use these verbs.
eat wait run shop play
He's been ... They've been ... She hasn't been ...

3 Think about Chapter 6. Color the bone.
Which activity was easy?
Which activity was difficult?
Figure it out with a friend.
Write a tip to help you remember.
I'm not sure.
OK.
Whizzkid!

Treasure Hunt!
Look back at pages 4 and 5.
Where are Javanese shadow puppets from?
Find something from that country. What is it?
67

Warmer: Play "Board Pelmanism"

Play the game with key collocations from this chapter, e.g. *perform/on stage*, *practicing in front/of the mirror*, *performing/arts*, etc. (see Games Bank p. 222).

1 2.8 Listen and make sentences.

- Have the children read the prompts. Ask *What do you think we're going to hear about?* (*someone talking about preparing for a show*)
- Play the CD twice. The children listen and complete the sentences. Elicit answers.

Audioscript

Kate: *I'm so tired.*
Anna: *What have you been doing, Kate?*
Kate: *I've been performing every evening this week. The theater is my new home!*
Anna: *What's the performance?*
Kate: *It's a musical. It's playing for one month. I've been singing on stage in front of hundreds of people.*
Anna: *Wow! Have you been singing for long?*
Kate: *No! I've been singing for about a year.*
Anna: *What's the cast like?*
Kate: *The actors are great. They've been having a great time.*
Anna: *Has the audience been enjoying the shows?*
Kate: *Yes, everyone has been clapping and cheering. People have been saying great things about it! Who knows, we might be on Broadway one day!*

Answers

1 She's been performing every evening.
2 She's been singing on stage.
3 She hasn't been singing for long.
4 She and the cast have been having a great time.
5 The audience has been enjoying the shows.
6 They've been clapping and cheering.

2 What have these people been doing? Write sentences in your notebook. Use these verbs.

- Have the children look at the pictures and say what they can see.
- Elicit what the person in the first picture has been doing. (*He's been running/playing sports/doing exercise.*)
- The children write sentences in their notebook, then compare their sentences in pairs.

Answers

Children's own answers.

3 Think about Chapter 6. Color the bone.

- Have the children look back at Chapter 6 and color the bone to evaluate their progress (self-evaluation).
- Discuss ideas for staying motivated, e.g. listen to songs you like in English and learn the words. The children choose and write a tip in their Student Book.

Treasure Hunt

Ask *Which country are Javanese shadow puppets from?* (*Indonesia*) Have the children look at pp. 4–5 to find something from Indonesia. (*a puppet*)

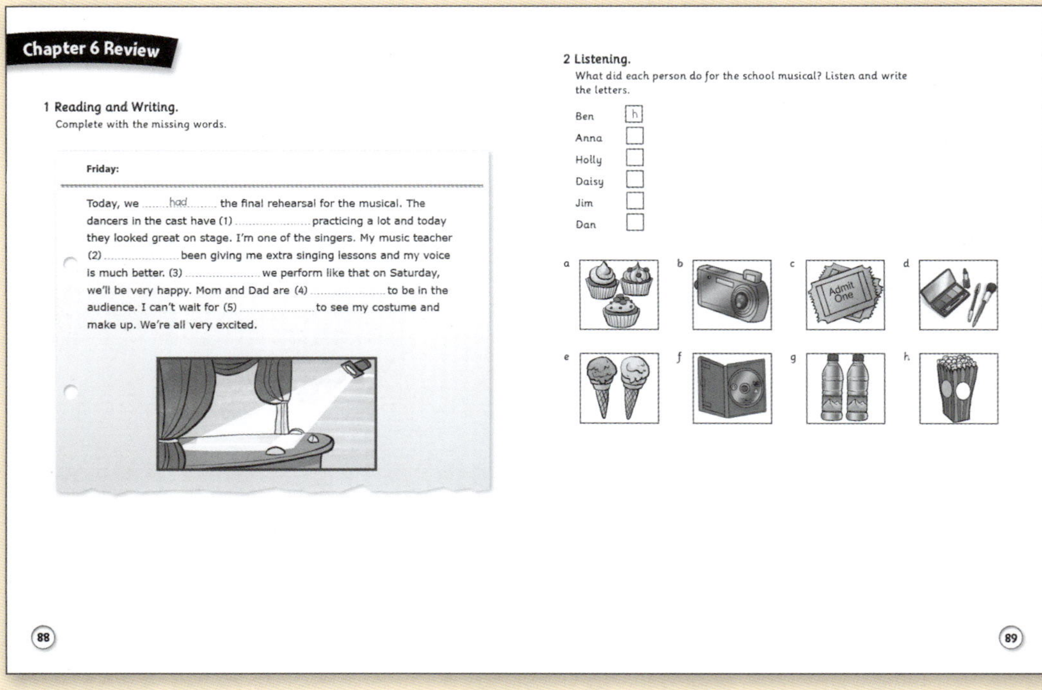
Chapter 6 Review

1 Reading and Writing.
Complete with the missing words.

Friday:

Today, we ....had........ the final rehearsal for the musical. The dancers in the cast have (1) .... practicing a lot and today they looked great on stage. I'm one of the singers. My music teacher (2) .... been giving me extra singing lessons and my voice is much better. (3) .... we perform like that on Saturday, we'll be very happy. Mom and Dad are (4) .... to be in the audience. I can't wait for (5) .... to see my costume and make up. We're all very excited.

2 Listening.
What did each person do for the school musical? Listen and write the letters.

Ben h
Anna
Holly
Daisy
Jim
Dan

a b c d e f g h

88 89

1 Reading and Writing. Complete with the missing words.

The children read and complete the text. Check answers.

Answers

1 been **2** has **3** If **4** going **5** them

2 2.36 Listening. What did each person do for the school musical? Listen and write the letters.

Play the CD twice. The children write the letter of the correct object for each person. Check answers.

Answers (Audioscript on p. 224)

Anna d, Holly c, Daisy a, Jim g, Dan b

Competency Focus

Me: Self-evaluation

The children reflect on the chapter, express their personal opinions about their own progress, and look for ways to improve. This encourages them to evaluate and make decisions about what they need to revisit and how they can learn better.

Cooler: Visualization

Have the children close their eyes. Say *Imagine you are in the theater in the last 20 minutes before the show. Now you're backstage. What are people doing? What can you see around you? What can you hear? How do people feel? Now go into the audience. What are they talking about? How do the people feel?* Then have the children open their eyes and tell a friend what they imagined.

Teacher's Resource Center • Print out Test Chapter 6 to use at the end of this lesson. The Test Generator also allows you to create customized tests.

- For the CEYLT (Cambridge YLE) exam preparation activities, there are Speaking prompts available for this chapter.

Student's App • Encourage the children to play the games on their smartphone/tablet. Ask them to record their scores to compare in the next lesson.

Chapter 7 Fantastic Friends

Overview

The children will:

- use critical thinking skills to identify vocabulary related to social life.
- talk about activities that relate to the person doing them using reflexive pronouns.
- read and understand a true story about an unusual friendship.
- talk about doing things differently using comparative adverbs.
- identify and use adjectives to describe personality and feelings.
- find out about the health benefits of smiling.
- write a true story about friendship.

Reading Skills

Story: *An Unusual Friendship*
Genre: true story

Literacy Development

- use reading skills to understand and predict content
- relate story theme to personal experience
- use facts and opinions to make a story interesting

Key Vocabulary

Social life: be alone, be interested in, be introduced, be invited, get along with, hang out, have a social life, join in
Personality: cheerful, good sense of humor, lazy, lonely, miserable, personality, shy

Functional Language

- Can I help you carry those books?
- It's OK, thanks. I can do it myself.

Spelling

Words with *gh*

CLIL: Science—Health benefits of smiling

The children find out how smiling can positively influence our health.

Key Grammar

Reflexive pronouns

- We're happy with ourselves.
- He introduced himself.

Comparative adverbs

- You could listen more carefully when people are talking.
- There are always things you could do better.

Competency Focus

The children will:

- use critical thinking skills to deduce the meaning of new vocabulary. (Lesson 1)
- predict the content of a story. (Lesson 3)

- activate new vocabulary and apply new grammar knowledge. (Lesson 2)
- apply new grammar rules in a familiar context. (Lesson 5)

- work in pairs to act out a dialogue. (Lesson 3)
- work in pairs to describe their personality. (Lesson 6)

- relate the story and story theme to their personal experience. (Lesson 4)
- write a true story about friendship. (Lesson 8)
- evaluate their own progress in the chapter. (Review)

- develop an understanding of how the brain works by carrying out research. (Lesson 7).

Digital Overview

Presentation Kit

Projectable Student Book, Activity Book, and Reader pages

- Vocabulary Tool 7A: Social life
- Vocabulary Tool 7B: Personality adjectives and feelings
- Oral Storytelling Video 7: *Christian the Lion*
- Interactive versions of selected SB and AB activities
- Integrated *Audio* and *Answer Key* for all activities

Teacher's Resource Center

Resources for planning, lesson delivery, and homework

- Class Planner Chapter 7
- Worksheets to print out (including notes and answers):
  - Grammar Worksheet 7A: Reflexive pronouns
  - Grammar Worksheet 7B: Comparative adverbs
  - Oral Storytelling Video Worksheet 7: *Christian the Lion*
  - CLIL Graphic Organizer 7
  - Writing Template 7
  - Festival Worksheet: International Children's Book Day
  - Test Chapter 7
- Test Generator
- Literacy Handbook

Student's Resource Center

Resources for consolidation and practice at home

- Interactive Grammar 7A: Reflexive pronouns
- Interactive Grammar 7B: Comparative adverbs
- Vocabulary Tool 7A: Social life
- Vocabulary Tool 7B: Personality adjectives and feelings
- Oral Storytelling Video 7: *Christian the Lion*

Student's App

Vocabulary games: Social life and personality adjectives/feelings

Watch the Oral Storytelling Video

Chapter 7 Fantastic Friends

Lesson 1

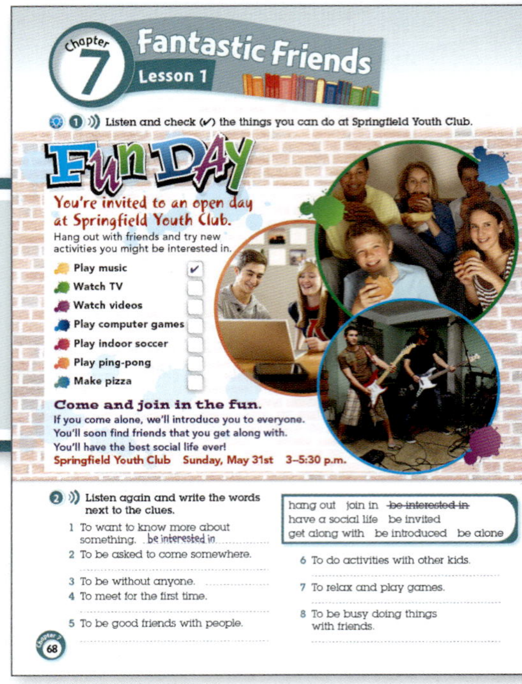
Chapter 7 Fantastic Friends
Lesson 1

1 Listen and check (✔) the things you can do at Springfield Youth Club.

FUN DAY

You're invited to an open day at Springfield Youth Club.

Hang out with friends and try new activities you might be interested in.

- Play music ✔
- Watch TV
- Watch videos
- Play computer games
- Play indoor soccer
- Play ping-pong
- Make pizza

Come and join in the fun.

If you come alone, we'll introduce you to everyone.
You'll soon find friends that you get along with.
You'll have the best social life ever!
Springfield Youth Club Sunday, May 31st 3–5:30 p.m.

2 Listen again and write the words next to the clues.

hang out join in ~~be interested in~~ have a social life be invited get along with be introduced be alone

1 To want to know more about something. be interested in
2 To be asked to come somewhere.
3 To be without anyone.
4 To meet for the first time.
5 To be good friends with people.
6 To do activities with other kids.
7 To relax and play games.
8 To be busy doing things with friends.

68

Vocabulary

Lesson objectives: identify and use vocabulary related to social life
Key vocabulary: *be alone, be interested in, be introduced, be invited, get along with, hang out, have a social life, join in*
Materials: Class CD; alphabet pages (Warmer)

Warmer: Play "Free-time A–Z"

Prepare an answer page for each team (the title *Free-time activities* and the alphabet written vertically). Put the class into teams. Give them two minutes to write a free-time activity or item related to an activity for as many letters of the alphabet as possible. Ask the team with the most words to read their list, then ask other teams to say any other words. A correct answer wins a point. The team with the most points wins.

1 2.9 Listen and check (✔) the things you can do at Springfield Youth Club.

- Have the children look at the pictures. Ask *What can you see happening?*
- Play the CD. The children listen and check the activities you can do at the youth club.
- Elicit answers.

Audioscript

Youth worker: *Are you interested in the Springfield Youth Club? Would you like to know more about it?*
Boy: *Um, yes, but I haven't been invited.*
YW: *We're asking everyone to come to the fun day. Look. "You're invited."*
Boy: *Hm …*
YW: *You don't need to come with friends or anyone. If you're alone, that's OK. You'll meet people who like the same things as you. You'll be introduced to people.*
Boy: *That sounds good.*
YW: *Yes, you'll find people that you get along with, and soon you'll make good friends. What are you interested in? What do you like?*
Boy: *I like music and I'd like to know more about the guitar.*
YW: *That's great! You can join in with the other kids who play musical instruments.*
Boy: *OK. Is there a TV?*
YW: *We don't have a TV, but we have three new computers. You can watch videos and play computer games.*
Boy: *Oh, and I like playing soccer.*
YW: *That's great. You can play soccer on the field behind the club. You can't play it indoors, but we have a ping-pong table inside.*
Boy: *It sounds fun. I get bored when I'm alone.*
YW: *OK, well, come to the fun day. If you like it, you can hang out at the club after school or on the weekend. You can relax, play games, and things like that. There isn't a kitchen at the club so you have to bring your own food.*
Boy: *Sounds cool.*
YW: *You'll have a great social life. You'll be so busy doing things with friends. You won't ever be bored or alone again!*

Answers

✔ *next to:* play music, watch videos, play computer games, play ping-pong

2 2.9 Listen again and write the words next to the clues.

- Play the CD again. The children listen and write the words described in each clue, using the words supplied.
- Elicit answers.

Answers

1 be interested in **2** be invited **3** be alone **4** be introduced **5** get along with **6** join in **7** hang out **8** have a social life

Optional activity: Complete the sentences

Read the following sentence to the children and ask them to guess the missing word: *Last weekend I was ______ to my cousin's birthday party.* (*invited*) Have the children write similar sentences secretly. In pairs they read their sentences to each other, replacing the word with a "beep." Their friend guesses the missing word.

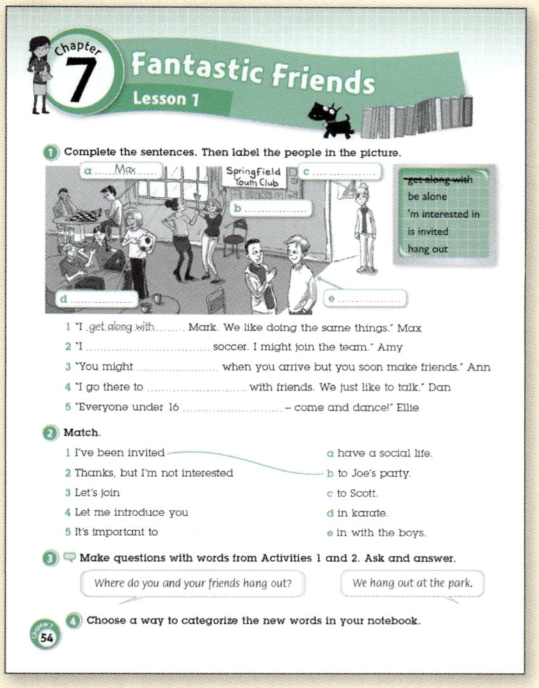
Chapter 7 Fantastic Friends
Lesson 1

1 Complete the sentences. Then label the people in the picture.

a Max
b ....
c ....
d ....
e ....

Springfield Youth Club

~~get along with~~
be alone
'm interested in
is invited
hang out

1 "I get along with .... Mark. We like doing the same things." Max
2 "I .... soccer. I might join the team." Amy
3 "You might .... when you arrive but you soon make friends." Ann
4 "I go there to .... with friends. We just like to talk." Dan
5 "Everyone under 16 .... – come and dance!" Ellie

2 Match.

1 I've been invited — a have a social life.
2 Thanks, but I'm not interested — b to Joe's party.
3 Let's join — c to Scott.
4 Let me introduce you — d in karate.
5 It's important to — e in with the boys.

3 Make questions with words from Activities 1 and 2. Ask and answer.

Where do you and your friends hang out?
We hang out at the park.

4 Choose a way to categorize the new words in your notebook.

Chapter 7 54

1 Complete the sentences. Then label the people in the picture.

The children complete the sentences using the phrases supplied. Elicit answers. Then they use the information in the completed sentences to label the people in the picture. Elicit answers.

Answers

1 get along with **2** 'm interested in **3** be alone **4** hang out **5** is invited

a Max **b** Ellie **c** Ann **d** Amy **e** Dan

2 Match.

The children match the sentence halves. Elicit answers.

Answers

1 b **2** d **3** e **4** c **5** a

3 Make questions with words from Activities 1 and 2. Ask and answer.

Elicit a few questions using words from Activities 1 and 2. The children make questions to ask and answer in pairs. Have pairs ask and answer for the class.

4 Choose a way to categorize the new words in your notebook.

Brainstorm appropriate categories, e.g. *things you do/don't do, with friends/without friends, easy to do/difficult to do.* The children choose the best categories for them and list the words in their notebook.

Cooler: Play "Disappearing Words"

Play the game with key vocabulary from the lesson (see Games Bank p. 222).

Competency Focus

Think! Critical Thinking

The children use critical thinking skills to understand the new vocabulary by using visual clues and processing the written and spoken forms.

Presentation Kit • Use Vocabulary Tool 7A to pre-teach key vocabulary as an alternative to the critical thinking approach. Use *Slideshow* to introduce the words and *Flash* to review/test.

- TIP Use the arrow in the *Audio* pop-up window to see the audioscript for SB Activity 1.
- TIP Give children the opportunity to be your assistant! Choose a child to be responsible for choosing the relevant buttons (e.g. to go to the next activity or *Answer Key*).

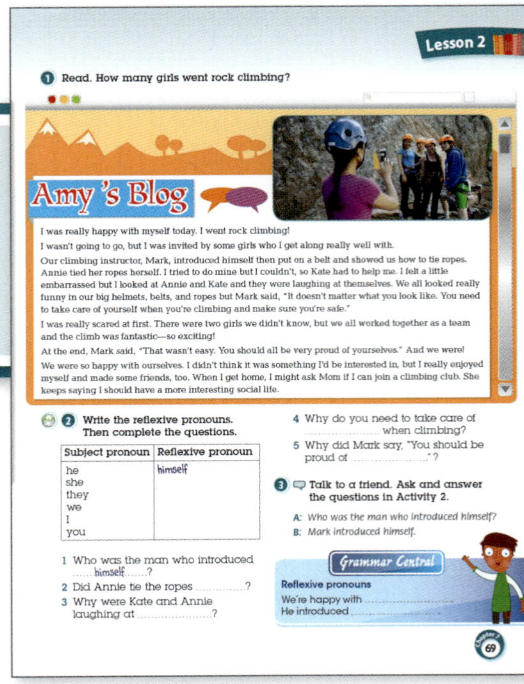
Lesson 2

1 Read. How many girls went rock climbing?

Amy 's Blog

I was really happy with myself today. I went rock climbing!

I wasn't going to go, but I was invited by some girls who I get along really well with.

Our climbing instructor, Mark, introduced himself then put on a belt and showed us how to tie ropes. Annie tied her ropes herself. I tried to do mine but I couldn't, so Kate had to help me. I felt a little embarrassed but I looked at Annie and Kate and they were laughing at themselves. We all looked really funny in our big helmets, belts, and ropes but Mark said, "It doesn't matter what you look like. You need to take care of yourself when you're climbing and make sure you're safe."

I was really scared at first. There were two girls we didn't know, but we all worked together as a team and the climb was fantastic—so exciting!

At the end, Mark said, "That wasn't easy. You should all be very proud of yourselves." And we were!

We were so happy with ourselves. I didn't think it was something I'd be interested in, but I really enjoyed myself and made some friends, too. When I get home, I might ask Mom if I can join a climbing club. She keeps saying I should have a more interesting social life.

2 Write the reflexive pronouns. Then complete the questions.

Subject pronoun	Reflexive pronoun
he	himself
she	
they	
we	
I	
you	

1 Who was the man who introduced ......himself......?
2 Did Annie tie the ropes ....?
3 Why were Kate and Annie laughing at ....?
4 Why do you need to take care of .... when climbing?
5 Why did Mark say, "You should be proud of ...."?

3 Talk to a friend. Ask and answer the questions in Activity 2.

A: *Who was the man who introduced himself?*
B: *Mark introduced himself.*

Grammar Central
Reflexive pronouns
We're happy with ....
He introduced ....

Chapter 7 69

Grammar

Lesson objective: using reflexive pronouns
Key grammar: reflexive pronouns
Secondary language: *rock climbing, instructor, ropes, helmets*
Materials: Grammar Worksheet 7A [TRC printout] (optional)

Warmer: Discussion

Write on the board *What was the last thing that you bought for your mother? How often do you talk to your best friend? Do you usually laugh at jokes? Are you proud of your friends?* Have the children discuss their answers in pairs. Leave the questions on the board to use in the Optional activity.

1 Read. How many girls went rock climbing?

- Have the children look at the picture. Ask *What is happening? Would you like to do this?*
- The children read the text. Ask *How many girls went rock climbing?* (*five*)

Grammar Central

Reflexive pronouns

Have the children complete the grammar examples. Elicit answers. Elicit how we treat the object when it is the same as the subject (*with* –self/–selves). Point out that this sometimes helps emphasize the fact that no one else is involved, e.g. *Anna did it herself.* The children write further examples in their notebook. See also the Grammar Reference sections in the Student Book (p. 102) and Activity Book (p. 102) for further explanation and practice.

Grammar Central Answers: ourselves, himself

AB Answers Activity 1: 1 herself **2** ourselves **3** himself **4** yourselves **5** themselves **6** myself

2 Write the reflexive pronouns. Then complete the questions.

- Have the children scan the text for the first reflexive pronoun. (*myself*) Ask *Which subject pronoun does it go with?* (*I*)
- Have the children scan the text and complete the chart.
- Elicit answers.

Answers

Reflexive pronouns: himself, herself, themselves, ourselves, myself, yourself/yourselves

1 himself **2** herself **3** themselves **4** yourself **5** yourselves

3 Talk to a friend. Ask and answer the questions in Activity 2.

- Have a pair of children read out the example question and answer.
- Then have the children work in pairs to ask and answer the questions.
- Elicit answers.

Optional activity: Change the questions

Have the children look again at the questions on the board (from the Warmer). Tell them they need to change the questions to refer to themselves. Elicit an example, e.g. *What was the last thing you bought for yourself?* Have the children ask and answer the new questions in pairs.

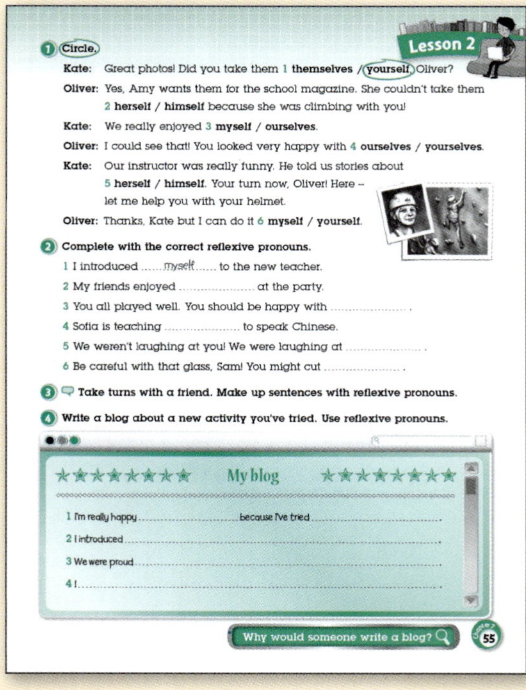
Lesson 2

1 Circle.

Kate: Great photos! Did you take them 1 **themselves / yourself**, Oliver?

Oliver: Yes, Amy wants them for the school magazine. She couldn't take them 2 **herself / himself** because she was climbing with you!

Kate: We really enjoyed 3 **myself / ourselves**.

Oliver: I could see that! You looked very happy with 4 **ourselves / yourselves**.

Kate: Our instructor was really funny. He told us stories about 5 **herself / himself**. Your turn now, Oliver! Here – let me help you with your helmet.

Oliver: Thanks, Kate but I can do it 6 **myself / yourself**.

2 **Complete with the correct reflexive pronouns.**

1 I introduced ......myself...... to the new teacher.
2 My friends enjoyed .... at the party.
3 You all played well. You should be happy with ....
4 Sofia is teaching .... to speak Chinese.
5 We weren't laughing at you! We were laughing at ....
6 Be careful with that glass, Sam! You might cut ....

3 **Take turns with a friend. Make up sentences with reflexive pronouns.**

4 **Write a blog about a new activity you've tried. Use reflexive pronouns.**

My blog

1 I'm really happy .... because I've tried ....
2 I introduced ....
3 We were proud ....
4 I ....

Why would someone write a blog?

Chapter 7 55

1 Circle.

The children complete the dialogue by circling the correct option from the two given each time. Elicit answers.

Answers

1 yourself **2** herself **3** ourselves **4** yourselves **5** himself **6** myself

2 Complete with the correct reflexive pronouns.

The children complete the sentences using the correct reflexive pronouns. Elicit answers.

Answers

1 myself **2** themselves **3** yourselves **4** herself **5** ourselves **6** yourself

3 Take turns with a friend. Make up sentences with reflexive pronouns.

The children work in pairs, taking turns making up a sentence with a reflexive pronoun. They can adapt the sentences in Activities 1 and 2 or use their own ideas.

4 Write a blog about a new activity you've tried. Use reflexive pronouns.

The children write their blog. Then they compare with a friend. Elicit responses. Ask *Why would someone write a blog?* (*to talk about an interest in a new activity / to write about a personal experience*)

Answers

Children's own answers.

Cooler: Play "Pronoun Ping-Pong"

Divide the class into two teams. The teams take turns saying a sentence featuring a reflexive pronoun. If a team makes a mistake or takes longer than ten seconds to play, the other team wins a point. The team with the most points wins.

Competency Focus

Learn

The children integrate previously acquired vocabulary into new grammar and structure, and adapt the language to show an understanding of the topic.

Presentation Kit • TIP As you monitor the children's progress, use *Notepad* to keep a note of weaknesses in vocabulary, grammar, or pronunciation so you can review in later lessons.

• TIP The interactive activities in the SB and AB can be done again and again, giving different children the chance to participate. Choose *Reset* within *Answer Key* to clear the answers.

Teacher's Resource Center • For extra grammar practice, print out Grammar Worksheet 7A.

Student's Resource Center • The children can use Interactive Grammar 7A at home.

Reading: Story Extract

Lesson objectives: offer to help and politely refuse help; use the title and pictures to predict story content; read the extract from the true story *An Unusual Friendship* (beginning)
Functional language: *Can I help you …? It's OK, thanks. I can do it myself.*
Secondary language: *wandering, orphan, vets, rescue*
Materials: Class CD

Warmer: Missing vowels

Write key sentences from Lesson 2 on the board, e.g. *They were proud of themselves. He walked by himself.*, etc., omitting the vowels. The children write the complete sentences. Then invite children to write in the missing vowels on the board.

Functional language

1 2.10 Listen and read.

- Play the CD. The children listen and read along. Ask *What does Yasmin want to do?* (*help carry the books*) *Does Scarlett need help?* (*no*)
- Play the CD again, pausing for them to repeat.
- Divide the class into pairs to practice the dialogue.

2 Imagine your friend needs help. Offer to help them.

- Choose two children to read the example dialogue. Elicit other examples of offering to help using the prompts supplied. Encourage the children to also use *Thank you, that's really nice of you!*
- The children practice in pairs. Have pairs perform a dialogue for the class.

Before reading

3 Look at the story. Who do you think had an unusual friendship?

- Have the children study the story title and pictures. Ask *Who do you think had an unusual friendship?* (*children's own answers / an elephant*) Elicit ideas.

4 2.11 Read the story extract and answer.

- Play the CD. The children listen and read along. Have them answer question 1. Elicit the answer.

- Play the CD again so they can write their ideas for questions 2 and 3. Encourage them to use reading skills (e.g. using the title, pictures, and context) to infer meaning and make predictions.
- Elicit answers, but do not confirm predictions: explain that they will have to read the story to find out.

Answers

1 It was an orphan. / Its mother had died. **2** Children's own answers. **3** Children's own answers.

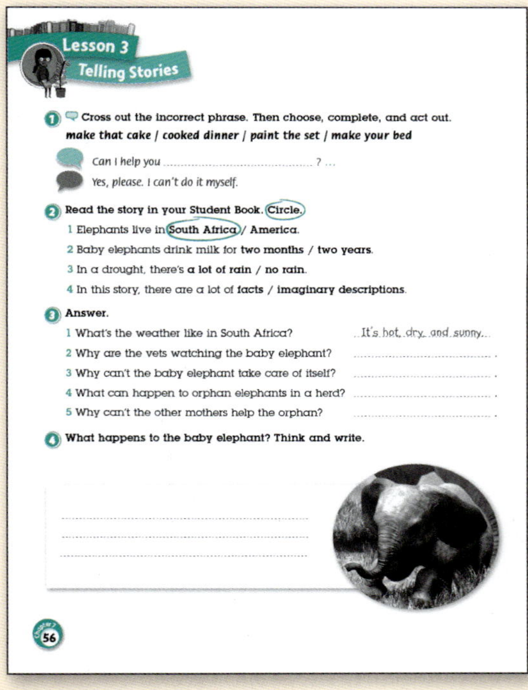

Lesson 3
Telling Stories

1 Cross out the incorrect phrase. Then choose, complete, and act out.
make that cake / cooked dinner / paint the set / make your bed

Can I help you .... ? ...
Yes, please. I can't do it myself.

2 Read the story in your Student Book. Circle.
1 Elephants live in South Africa / America.
2 Baby elephants drink milk for **two months / two years**.
3 In a drought, there's **a lot of rain / no rain**.
4 In this story, there are a lot of **facts / imaginary descriptions**.

3 Answer.
1 What's the weather like in South Africa? It's hot, dry, and sunny.
2 Why are the vets watching the baby elephant? ....
3 Why can't the baby elephant take care of itself? ....
4 What can happen to orphan elephants in a herd? ....
5 Why can't the other mothers help the orphan? ....

4 What happens to the baby elephant? Think and write.

56

1 Cross out the incorrect phrase. Then choose, complete, and act out.

The children identify which phrase is incorrect. (*cooked dinner*) They then choose one of the other phrases and act out the dialogue in pairs. Encourage them to use what they know to adapt and extend the dialogue. Have pairs act out their dialogue for the class.

2 Read the story in your Student Book. Circle.

The children read the Student Book story extract again, then complete the sentences by circling the correct option from the two given each time. Elicit answers.

Answers

1 South Africa **2** two years **3** no rain **4** facts

3 Answer.

The children write answers to the questions about the story extract. Elicit answers.

Answers

1 It's hot, dry, and sunny. **2** Its mother had fallen down a cliff and died. **3** It was only 6 months old (and elephants need their mother's milk for two years). **4** Sometimes another mother might take care of an orphan. **5** They can't help because there has been a drought and they need to take care of themselves and their own babies.

4 What happens to the baby elephant? Think and write.

Elicit suggestions. The children write their own ideas, then compare with a friend. Elicit ideas.

Answers

Children's own answers.

Cooler: Play "Change the Text"

Play the game with a summary of the story extract (see Games Bank p. 222).

Competency Focus

Collaborate and Communicate

The children work together to practice, perform, and adapt the new functional language learned.

Think

The children use critical thinking skills to identify the setting of the story by looking at the text and story artwork.

Presentation Kit • *Mask* the speech bubbles in SB Activity 1. Elicit what is happening in the picture and what Yasmin and Scarlett might be saying.

- *Mask* the story extract text. Elicit answers to SB Activities 3 and 4 orally, with the children looking at the pictures only. Then, use *Eraser* to reveal the text and play the story extract audio. Have the children write their answers. Elicit if they changed their predictions.
- TIP Choose *Help* at any time for FAQs on using the materials.

AN UNUSUAL FRIENDSHIP

1
One hot, dry, sunny day in South Africa, a baby elephant was wandering alone. It was an orphan. Its mother had fallen down a cliff and died. The baby was only six months old, and young elephants need their mother's milk for two years. The little elephant wasn't old enough to take care of itself.

2
Vets from a nearby game reserve watched the young elephant from a distance. Elephants are interesting animals. Sometimes another mother elephant in the herd might take care of an orphan and feed it herself. But there was a drought—it hadn't rained for months and none of the elephants could help. They didn't have much milk and they needed to take care of themselves and their own babies first.

3
Each day, the little elephant was getting weaker and was alone. It was walking more and more slowly, and the vets were very worried. The situation was getting worse. After a week, they decided to rescue it.

4
They took the young elephant to the animal hospital, but it was very hungry and thin. The keepers named him Themba, which means hope. Themba was frightened and miserable after losing his mother. At first, he didn't drink anything. After a while, he started to drink water, but he still wouldn't drink milk. His health was getting worse and the keepers didn't know what to do. If Themba didn't feed himself soon, he wouldn't survive.

5
Elephants are social animals and live in herds in the wild. So one day, a keeper thought to himself that Themba might be lonely and need a friend. A sheep named Albert, who came from a nearby farm, was brought to live with Themba. When Albert was introduced to Themba, they didn't get along. Albert was shy, and Themba wasn't interested in having a friend. Albert was scared of Themba and hid behind a gate.

6
But Themba reached out gently through the gate to touch the sheep with his trunk, and Albert became braver. The next day, Albert was bored so he came out to look around. Soon, the two animals started to play together. They walked along with Themba's trunk on Albert's woolly back. Three days later, Themba started to drink milk. The keepers and vets were very happy. The little elephant was more cheerful, and his chances of living were getting better.

7
As time passed, the two animals became good friends. They played and slept together. Albert copied everything Themba did. If Themba ate leaves from a tree, Albert would join in and eat the same food. Every day, the keepers watched the two best friends hanging out together around the reserve. Slowly, Themba became healthier, happier, and stronger.

8
This true story happened in 2008 at the Shamwari Game Reserve, and shows how an unusual friendship really helped save this small elephant's life.

Lesson objective: read and understand the true story *An Unusual Friendship* in the Reader
Materials: Class CD; Reader; papers with animal words (Cooler); Oral Storytelling Video Worksheet 7 [TRC printout] (optional)

Warmer: My friends and family

Have the children work in small groups to list the things they like about their friends and family. Elicit responses, e.g. *They make me laugh.* Then they discuss how they would feel if they were always on their own. Elicit responses.

Story Summary

Themba, an orphaned baby elephant, was weak. Keepers introduced him to a sheep named Albert, so that he had company. Themba was not interested and Albert was shy, but soon they become good friends and Themba grew stronger.

Theme: the importance of recognizing that we can still be friends even though we are different

2.12 While reading

- Have the children look at the pictures in the Reader. Ask *What happened when Albert the sheep came to the animal hospital?* (*He became friends with Themba.*)
- Play the CD. The children listen and read along. Ask *How did Albert feel about Themba at first?* (*He was scared of him.*)
- Ask questions to check comprehension, e.g. *Who thought Themba might be lonely?* (*a vet*) *What did they think Themba might need?* (*a friend*) *How did Themba change?* (*He became healthier, happier, and stronger.*)
- Have the class read the story again in groups of five, with one child asking *Why?* after each section. The groups discuss why things happen (see **Story Time**).

After reading: Reflect

Ask questions to give the children the opportunity to think about the issues raised by the story, e.g. *Why do you think Albert and Themba weren't friends at first? What helped them become friends? Why is friendship important?*

Optional activity: Role-play

Have the children work in pairs to write a dialogue between Albert and Themba to go with Picture 6 of the story. Have pairs read out their dialogue for the class.

Story Time

Why?

When a story features complex interaction (e.g. *vets/elephants/sheep*), asking *Why?* at the end of each section can prompt useful discussion. Use this technique to help the children focus on the triggers and motivations for the main events.

Reading Strategy

Paired Reading

This involves the children reading aloud to each other in pairs. Less fluent readers learn from more fluent readers, and gain confidence reading to just one person. It is also a mutually beneficial strategy when readers of the same skills level work together.

For additional explanation and activities, see the Literacy Handbook on the Teacher's Resource Center.

Cooler: Choose an animal

Write animals on separate pieces of paper, e.g. *parrot*, *hamster*, *cat*, *giraffe*, etc., and give one to each child. The children mingle to find another animal that would make a good friend. Elicit ideas with reasons.

Presentation Kit • Use *Hotspots* to focus on each picture in turn to elicit a short summary of the story from different children.
- Oral Storytelling Video 7 contains a different story on a related theme (*Christian the Lion*). Watch and discuss it together at the end of the lesson.

Teacher's Resource Center • Print out Oral Storytelling Video Worksheet 7 to help you get the most out of the video.

Student's Resource Center • The children can watch Oral Storytelling Video 7 at home with their family.

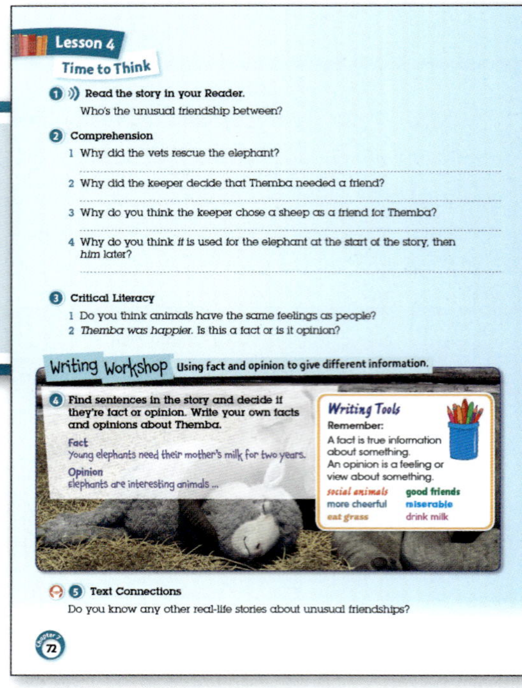
Lesson 4

Time to Think

1 Read the story in your Reader.

Who's the unusual friendship between?

2 Comprehension

1 Why did the vets rescue the elephant?

2 Why did the keeper decide that Themba needed a friend?

3 Why do you think the keeper chose a sheep as a friend for Themba?

4 Why do you think *it* is used for the elephant at the start of the story, then *him* later?

3 Critical Literacy

1 Do you think animals have the same feelings as people?

2 *Themba was happier.* Is this a fact or is it opinion?

Writing Workshop Using fact and opinion to give different information.

4 Find sentences in the story and decide if they're fact or opinion. Write your own facts and opinions about Themba.

Fact

Young elephants need their mother's milk for two years.

Opinion

Elephants are interesting animals ...

Writing Tools

Remember:

A fact is true information about something.

An opinion is a feeling or view about something.

social animals good friends

more cheerful miserable

eat grass drink milk

5 Text Connections

Do you know any other real-life stories about unusual friendships?

Chapter 7 72

Reading Comprehension and Critical Literacy

Lesson objectives: understand and evaluate the story; relate story theme to personal experience; focus on the difference between fact and opinion

Materials: Class CD; Reader; Oral Storytelling Video Worksheet 7 [TRC printout] (optional)

Note: Please ensure that your class has read the Reader story before you do this lesson.

Warmer: Play "Tic-Tac-Toe"

Play the game with the children recalling a fact from the story to win a square (see Games Bank p. 222).

1 2.12 Read the story in your Reader.

- Have the children read the story. (Alternatively, play the CD and have them read along.)
- Elicit whether the children were correct in their predictions in Lesson 3 Activity 4. Ask *Who's the unusual friendship between?* (*the baby elephant and a sheep*)

2 Comprehension

- The children write answers to the first three questions. Elicit answers.
- Discuss question 4. Ask the children to justify their answers.

Answers

1 Because they were worried about the elephant. / Because the elephant was sick / getting weaker. **2** Because he thought Themba was lonely. / Because elephants are social animals. **3** Children's own answers. / Because, like elephants, sheep live in herds. **4** Children's own answers. / Because we know the elephant later. / Because he has some human feelings in the story.

3 Critical Literacy

- Have the children discuss the answers to the questions with a friend.
- Elicit ideas and have a class discussion. Encourage the children to distinguish between what they know to be true (fact) and what they think (opinion). Have them relate the story to their own feelings when giving their opinion. Analyzing the story in this way helps develop critical literacy.

Answers

Children's own answers.

Writing Workshop

Using fact and opinion to give different information

4 Find sentences in the story and decide if they're fact or opinion. Write your own facts and opinions about Themba.

Have a child read the examples. Elicit other facts and opinions, using the prompts in the **Writing Tools** box. The children look back at the story and find more facts and opinions. They write them in their notebook, then compare with a friend. Elicit responses.

Answers

Children's own answers.

5 Text Connections

- Ask *Do you know any other real-life stories about unusual friendships?* Elicit ideas and discuss as a class.

Optional activity: Fact or opinion?

Write the following themes on the board: *snakes, soccer,* [*name of children's country*], *the USA, vegetables*. Tell the children they can choose one or two themes and write two facts and two opinions about each in their notebook. Have children read out sentences for the class to decide if they are fact or opinion.

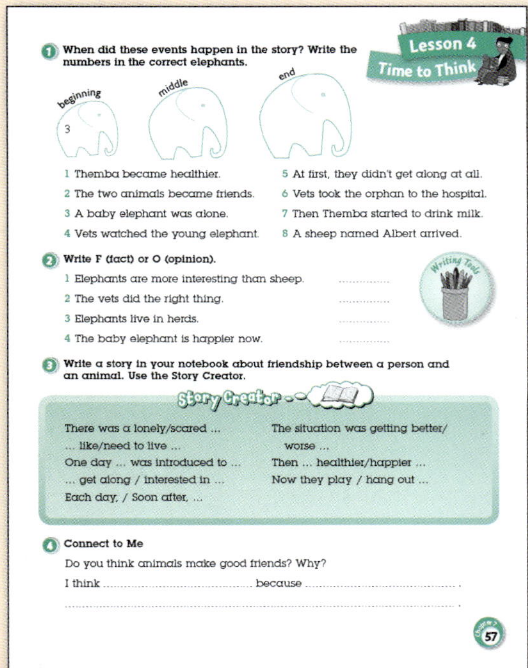

Lesson 4
Time to Think

1 When did these events happen in the story? Write the numbers in the correct elephants.

beginning — 3 | middle | end

1 Themba became healthier.
2 The two animals became friends.
3 A baby elephant was alone.
4 Vets watched the young elephant.
5 At first, they didn't get along at all.
6 Vets took the orphan to the hospital.
7 Then Themba started to drink milk.
8 A sheep named Albert arrived.

2 Write F (fact) or O (opinion).

1 Elephants are more interesting than sheep. ....
2 The vets did the right thing. ....
3 Elephants live in herds. ....
4 The baby elephant is happier now. ....

Writing Tools

3 Write a story in your notebook about friendship between a person and an animal. Use the Story Creator.

Story Creator

There was a lonely/scared ...
... like/need to live ...
One day ... was introduced to ...
... get along / interested in ...
Each day, / Soon after, ...

The situation was getting better/worse ...
Then ... healthier/happier ...
Now they play / hang out ...

4 Connect to Me

Do you think animals make good friends? Why?

I think .... because ....

57

1 When did these events happen in the story? Write the numbers in the correct elephants.

The children write the number of the sentences in the correct elephants, depending on whether the event described happened at the beginning, in the middle, or at the end of the story. Elicit answers.

Answers

beginning: 3, 4
middle: 5, 6, 8
end: 1, 2, 7

2 Write F (fact) or O (opinion).

The children identify whether each sentence expresses a fact or an opinion, writing F or O as appropriate. Elicit answers.

Answers

1 O **2** O **3** F **4** F

3 Write a story in your notebook about friendship between a person and an animal. Use the Story Creator.

Use the **Story Creator** prompts to elicit ideas. The children write a story in their notebook about friendship between a person and an animal, then compare with a friend. Have children read out their texts for the class.

4 Connect to Me

Elicit examples of animals making good friends. (e.g. *a guide dog*) The children write their own response, then compare with a friend. Elicit responses.

Cooler: True or False?

Write a big *TRUE* on one side of the board and a big *FALSE* on the other. Read out sentences about the Reader story, e.g. *The story took place in South Africa.* (*true*) *The elephant was named Albert.* (*false*) The children point to true or false as appropriate. If false, ask the children to explain why.

Competency Focus

Me: Critical Literacy

The children use critical literacy skills to reflect on the story and relate it to their own experiences.

Presentation Kit • Use *Mask* to cover the Reader story. Move the black area around to reveal random details and elicit what is happening.

- TIP Use the arrows in the Navigation Pane to navigate to previous or later lessons. Within *Hotspots*, use the arrows to navigate through the activities.
- If you haven't already, show Oral Storytelling Video 7 (a different story on a related theme).

Teacher's Resource Center • If you haven't already, print out Oral Storytelling Video Worksheet 7 to do the support activities.

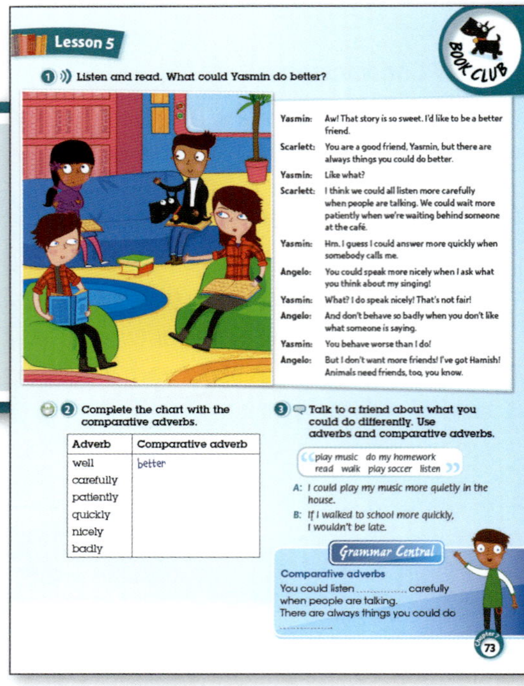

Lesson 5

BOOK CLUB

1 Listen and read. What could Yasmin do better?

Yasmin: Aw! That story is so sweet. I'd like to be a better friend.
Scarlett: You are a good friend, Yasmin, but there are always things you could do better.
Yasmin: Like what?
Scarlett: I think we could all listen more carefully when people are talking. We could wait more patiently when we're waiting behind someone at the café.
Yasmin: Hm. I guess I could answer more quickly when somebody calls me.
Angelo: You could speak more nicely when I ask what you think about my singing!
Yasmin: What? I do speak nicely! That's not fair!
Angelo: And don't behave so badly when you don't like what someone is saying.
Yasmin: You behave worse than I do!
Angelo: But I don't want more friends! I've got Hamish! Animals need friends, too, you know.

2 Complete the chart with the comparative adverbs.

Adverb	Comparative adverb
well	better
carefully	
patiently	
quickly	
nicely	
badly	

3 Talk to a friend about what you could do differently. Use adverbs and comparative adverbs.

play music do my homework read walk play soccer listen

A: I could play my music more quietly in the house.
B: If I walked to school more quickly, I wouldn't be late.

Grammar Central
Comparative adverbs
You could listen .... carefully when people are talking.
There are always things you could do ....

Chapter 7 73

Grammar and Reading

Lesson objectives: ask and answer about doing things differently
Key grammar: comparative adverbs
Secondary language: *behave*
Materials: Class CD; Grammar Worksheet 7B [TRC printout] (optional); words for sentences on paper (Cooler)

Warmer: What are they like?

Write the following adjectives on the board: *shy*, *lonely*, *kind*, *happy*, *patient*, *careful*, *friendly*, *smart*, *nervous*. Have the children decide in pairs which adjectives describe the elephant, the sheep, or the vets from the Reader story, and why. Elicit answers.

1 2.13 Listen and read. What could Yasmin do better?

- Play the CD. The children listen and read along. Ask *Who would like to be a better friend?* (*Yasmin*)
- Play the CD again and ask *What could Yasmin do better?* (*She could listen more carefully, wait more patiently, answer more quickly, speak more nicely, not behave so badly.*)
- Elicit answers.

Grammar Central

Comparative adverbs

Have the children complete the grammar examples. Elicit answers. Elicit how we form comparative adverbs. (more + –ly or *irregular forms* better/worse) The children write further examples in their notebook. See also the Grammar Reference sections in the Student Book (p. 102) and Activity Book (p. 102) for further explanation and practice.

Grammar Central Answers: more, better

2 Complete the chart with the comparative adverbs.

- Have the children find *better* in the dialogue. Write on the board *She does it ____, but she could do it better.* and ask the children to complete the sentence to show the relation between *well* and *better*.
- Have the children complete the chart, referring to the dialogue to check their answers.
- Elicit answers.

Answers

Comparative adverb: better, more carefully, more patiently, more quickly, more nicely, worse

3 Talk to a friend about what you could do differently. Use adverbs and comparative adverbs.

- Choose two children to read the example dialogue.
- Divide the class into pairs to practice the dialogue using the prompts supplied and their own ideas. Have pairs perform for the class.

Optional activity: Act it out adverbs

Write on the board verbs in one column and adjectives in another column, e.g. *sing*, *walk*; *well*, *badly*, etc. Have the children choose a combination for you to act out, e.g. *sing badly*. Act it out, but not very badly. Ask *Am I singing badly enough?* and encourage the children to say *No! Sing worse!* Have the children continue the activity in pairs.

Lesson 5

1 Complete with comparative adverbs.

I don't know. I think there are a lot of things Yasmin and her friends could do 1 good ......better...... They should watch me 2 careful .... ! I wait 3 patient .... than Rufus for my food even when I'm very hungry. I sometimes eat 4 loud .... than they do but that's because I'm a dog. I can run 5 quick .... than all of them and when they're sad I can look 6 nice .... at them. That's why they all love me.

2 Write sentences with comparative adverbs. Then tell a friend: true or false for you?

1 I / play tennis / bad / than you

I play tennis worse than you.

2 You / speak / loud / when / you / wear earphones

....

3 I / play music / quiet / when / I / do my homework

....

4 I / always / speak / nice / to my pet than to my brother

....

5 You / learn English / quick / than me

....

You speak more loudly when you're wearing earphones. That's true.

Yes. Sometimes it's very funny.

3 Write about you. Use comparative adverbs.

1 I cook better when ....

2 I read more .... when ....

3 I don't listen ....

4 I ....

Chapter 7 58

1 Complete with comparative adverbs.

The children complete the text using the comparative adverb of the adjective prompts supplied. Elicit answers.

Answers

1 better **2** more carefully **3** more patiently **4** more loudly **5** more quickly **6** more nicely

2 Write sentences with comparative adverbs. Then tell a friend: true or false for you?

The children use the prompts given to write sentences with comparative adverbs. They then discuss and compare the sentences with a friend, saying whether they are true or false for them. Elicit answers.

Answers

1 I play tennis worse than you. **2** You speak more loudly when you're wearing/you wear earphones. **3** I play music more quietly when I'm doing/I do my homework.
4 I always speak more nicely to my pet than to my brother.
5 You learn/You're learning English more quickly than me.

3 Write about you. Use comparative adverbs.

The children write about themselves using comparative adverbs. Then they compare with a friend. Elicit responses.

Answers

Children's own answers.

Cooler: Scrambled sentences

Write out the sentences from Activity Book Activity 2 on pieces of paper, one word per paper. Invite a group of children to the front of the class and hand out the words for one sentence (one word to each child). They hold their words to show the class. The other children tell them to move to the correct positions to make complete sentences. Repeat with different sentences and children.

Competency Focus

Learn

The children demonstrate their understanding of the new language by reading the dialogue and completing the activity.

Presentation Kit • TIP Children love to be involved in using the digital resources. Give them as many opportunities as possible—completing interactive activities or showing answers, as well as writing and drawing on the board in more open-ended tasks. Make a point of encouraging less confident children to participate, because this will help them engage.

Teacher's Resource Center • For extra grammar practice, print out Grammar Worksheet 7B.

Student's Resource Center • The children can use Interactive Grammar 7B at home.

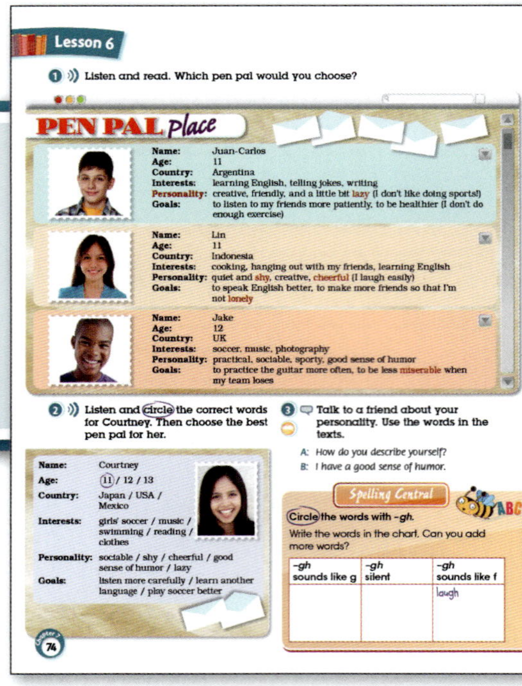
Lesson 6

1 Listen and read. Which pen pal would you choose?

PEN PAL place

Name: Juan-Carlos
Age: 11
Country: Argentina
Interests: learning English, telling jokes, writing
Personality: creative, friendly, and a little bit lazy (I don't like doing sports!)
Goals: to listen to my friends more patiently, to be healthier (I don't do enough exercise)

Name: Lin
Age: 11
Country: Indonesia
Interests: cooking, hanging out with my friends, learning English
Personality: quiet and shy, creative, cheerful (I laugh easily)
Goals: to speak English better, to make more friends so that I'm not lonely

Name: Jake
Age: 12
Country: UK
Interests: soccer, music, photography
Personality: practical, sociable, sporty, good sense of humor
Goals: to practice the guitar more often, to be less miserable when my team loses

2 Listen and circle the correct words for Courtney. Then choose the best pen pal for her.

Name: Courtney
Age: 11 / 12 / 13
Country: Japan / USA / Mexico
Interests: girls' soccer / music / swimming / reading / clothes
Personality: sociable / shy / cheerful / good sense of humor / lazy
Goals: listen more carefully / learn another language / play soccer better

3 Talk to a friend about your personality. Use the words in the texts.

A: How do you describe yourself?
B: I have a good sense of humor.

Spelling Central

Circle the words with -gh.
Write the words in the chart. Can you add more words?

-gh sounds like g	-gh silent	-gh sounds like f
		laugh

Chapter 7 74

Vocabulary, Listening, and Spelling

Lesson objectives: identify and use adjectives to describe personality and feelings; practice spelling words with *gh*
Key vocabulary: *cheerful, good sense of humor, lazy, lonely, miserable, personality, shy*
Secondary language: *photography*
Materials: Class CD

Warmer: Pre-teach vocabulary

Pre-teach the vocabulary using definitions. Then make sentences for the class to complete, e.g. *A person who is on their own can feel …* (*lonely*). *A person who is very sad is …* (*miserable*)., etc.

1 2.14 Listen and read. Which pen pal would you choose?

- Have the children look at the pictures of the pen pals. Elicit their first impressions, then play the CD. The children listen and read along to check if their impressions were right. Elicit responses.
- Play the CD again and ask *Which pen pal would you choose?* Elicit responses. Ask for a show of hands to see who is the favorite.

Answers

Children's own answers.

2 2.15 Listen and circle the correct words for Courtney. Then choose the best pen pal for her.

- Have the children look at the picture of Courtney and say what kind of personality they think she has.
- Play the CD. The children listen and circle the correct information in her profile.
- Play the CD again for the children to confirm or complete their answers.
- Elicit answers.

Audioscript

My name is Courtney and I'm from the USA. I'm 11 years old and I'm looking for a pen pal. It can be a boy or a girl about my age. I'm interested in girls' soccer, music, and clothes. I'd like someone who comes from a different culture and speaks a different language.
My personality? Well, I'm pretty sociable, I like hanging out with friends, and I think I have a good sense of humor. I have a lot of friends so I'm never lonely. I'm pretty cheerful. I'm not miserable very often. It'd be great if they have video calling, too, so we could communicate more easily. My goals are to listen more carefully at school and to play soccer better.

Answers

Circled: 11; USA; girls' soccer, music, clothes; sociable, good sense of humor, cheerful; listen more carefully, play soccer better

3 Talk to a friend about your personality. Use the words in the texts.

- Have a child ask you the question in the example. Give your model answer, e.g. *I'm usually cheerful, but I sometimes get a little miserable when I have a lot of work! I'm a little bit lazy! I'm sociable and I think I have a good sense of humor.*
- Have the children take turns asking and answering in pairs. Ask if any children would like to share their answers with the class. Ask if the others agree!

Spelling Central

Words with *gh*

Have the children find words with *gh* on the page and complete the chart. They then add other words in each category. (e.g. *ghost, spaghetti; eight, right; cough*)

Answers

gh (sounds like g): – *gh (silent):* –
gh (sounds like f): laugh, enough

Optional activity: My best friend

Have the children draw and make a profile picture of their best friend including all the information from the examples in the book. Elicit responses.

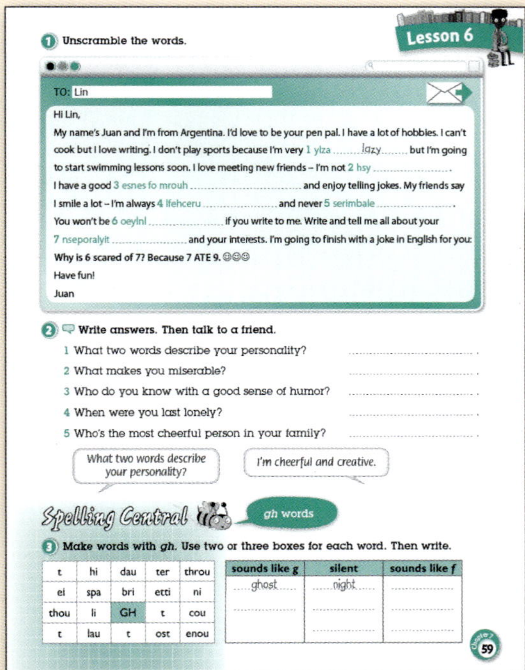
1 Unscramble the words.

Lesson 6

TO: Lin

Hi Lin,

My name's Juan and I'm from Argentina. I'd love to be your pen pal. I have a lot of hobbies. I can't cook but I love writing. I don't play sports because I'm very 1 ylza ....lazy........ but I'm going to start swimming lessons soon. I love meeting new friends – I'm not 2 hsy .... I have a good 3 esnes fo mrouh .... and enjoy telling jokes. My friends say I smile a lot – I'm always 4 lfehceru .... and never 5 serimbale .... You won't be 6 oeylnl .... if you write to me. Write and tell me all about your 7 nseporalyit .... and your interests. I'm going to finish with a joke in English for you: Why is 6 scared of 7? Because 7 ATE 9. ☺☺☺

Have fun!

Juan

2 Write answers. Then talk to a friend.

1 What two words describe your personality? ....
2 What makes you miserable? ....
3 Who do you know with a good sense of humor? ....
4 When were you last lonely? ....
5 Who's the most cheerful person in your family? ....

What two words describe your personality?

I'm cheerful and creative.

Spelling Central – *gh* words

3 Make words with *gh*. Use two or three boxes for each word. Then write.

t	hi	dau	ter	throu
ei	spa	bri	etti	ni
thou	li	GH	t	cou
t	lau	t	ost	enou

sounds like g	silent	sounds like f
ghost	night	

Chapter 7 59

1 Unscramble the words.

The children complete the text by unscrambling and writing the words. Elicit answers.

Answers

1 lazy **2** shy **3** sense of humor **4** cheerful **5** miserable **6** lonely **7** personality

2 Write answers. Then talk to a friend.

The children write their own answers. They ask and answer in pairs. Invite pairs to perform for the class.

Answers

Children's own answers.

3 Make words with *gh*. Use two or three boxes for each word. Then write.

To practice the **Spelling Central** feature, the children make words using one or two different letter blocks in the grid + *gh*. They write the words in the correct column, depending on how *gh* is pronounced. Elicit answers.

Answers

sounds like g: ghost, spaghetti
silent (any three of): night, daughter, high, through, eight, bright, thought, light
sounds like f (any three of): cough, laugh, enough

Cooler: Play "Sentence Builders"

Play the game with sentences/questions featuring words from **Spelling Central** (see Games Bank p. 222).

Competency Focus

Collaborate and Communicate

The children work together to share their ideas on the topic, incorporating the new vocabulary.

Presentation Kit • Use Vocabulary Tool 7B to pre-teach key vocabulary. Use *Slideshow* to introduce the words and *Picture Dictionary* to review/test.

• TIP Have children use *Pen* to complete the chart in AB Activity 3, before using *Answer Key* to give feedback.

Student's App • Encourage the children to play the games on their smartphone/tablet. They could do this with a friend as a fun way to review the chapter vocabulary.

CLIL: Science—Health benefits of smiling

Lesson objective: find out how smiling can positively influence our health
Materials: CLIL Graphic Organizer 7 [TRC printout] (optional)

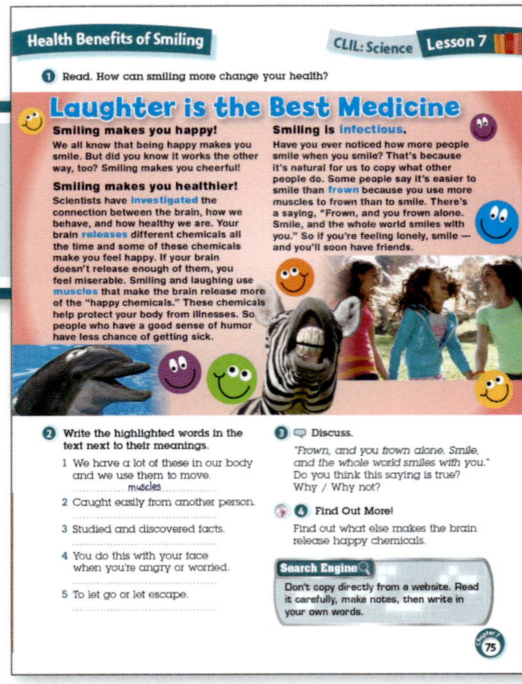

Health Benefits of Smiling

CLIL: Science Lesson 7

1 Read. How can smiling more change your health?

Laughter is the Best Medicine

Smiling makes you happy!
We all know that being happy makes you smile. But did you know it works the other way, too? Smiling makes you cheerful!

Smiling makes you healthier!
Scientists have **investigated** the connection between the brain, how we behave, and how healthy we are. Your brain **releases** different chemicals all the time and some of these chemicals make you feel happy. If your brain doesn't release enough of them, you feel miserable. Smiling and laughing use **muscles** that make the brain release more of the "happy chemicals." These chemicals help protect your body from illnesses. So people who have a good sense of humor have less chance of getting sick.

Smiling is infectious.
Have you ever noticed how more people smile when you smile? That's because it's natural for us to copy what other people do. Some people say it's easier to smile than **frown** because you use more muscles to frown than to smile. There's a saying, "Frown, and you frown alone. Smile, and the whole world smiles with you." So if you're feeling lonely, smile — and you'll soon have friends.

2 Write the highlighted words in the text next to their meanings.
1 We have a lot of these in our body and we use them to move. muscles
2 Caught easily from another person.
3 Studied and discovered facts.
4 You do this with your face when you're angry or worried.
5 To let go or let escape.

3 Discuss.
"Frown, and you frown alone. Smile, and the whole world smiles with you." Do you think this saying is true? Why / Why not?

4 Find Out More!
Find out what else makes the brain release happy chemicals.

Search Engine
Don't copy directly from a website. Read it carefully, make notes, then write in your own words.

Chapter 7 75

Warmer: Ranking activities

Elicit from the children nine activities that they usually do during the week. These can include sports, studying, etc. Add in one of your own: smiling. Have the children work in pairs to decide which they think are best for our health. Have two pairs read out their lists. Ask the children where they put smiling on their lists.

1 Read. How can smiling more change your health?

- Have the children look at the images and ask what they can see and what the people are doing.
- Ask *How can smiling more change your health?* Have the children read the text and find the answer to the question. (*When you smile, your brain releases chemicals that help protect your body from illnesses.*)
- Ask if they would now change the position of smiling in their ranking from the Warmer.

2 Write the highlighted words in the text next to their meanings.

- Draw the children's attention to the example answer. Have them show some muscles!
- The children write the word for each definition, choosing from the blue words in Activity 1.
- Elicit answers.

Answers

1 muscles **2** infectious **3** investigated **4** frown **5** releases

3 Discuss.

- Have a child read out the discussion question.
- Have the children talk about their ideas in pairs, then share ideas as a class.

4 Find Out More!

- The children research what else makes the brain release happy chemicals. The **Search Engine** feature gives support on where to look. The children will need to complete this research before doing the follow-up activity in the Activity Book. (It could be set as homework.)

Optional activity: Play "Back to the Board"

Play the game with key vocabulary: *good sense of humor, lazy, miserable, personality, shy, cheerful, lonely* (see Games Bank p. 222).

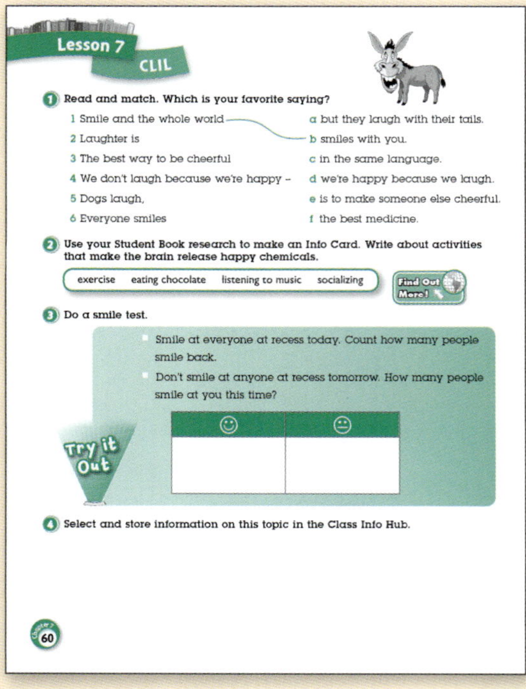
Lesson 7
CLIL

1 Read and match. Which is your favorite saying?

1 Smile and the whole world	a but they laugh with their tails.
2 Laughter is	b smiles with you.
3 The best way to be cheerful	c in the same language.
4 We don't laugh because we're happy –	d we're happy because we laugh.
5 Dogs laugh,	e is to make someone else cheerful.
6 Everyone smiles	f the best medicine.

2 Use your Student Book research to make an Info Card. Write about activities that make the brain release happy chemicals.

exercise eating chocolate listening to music socializing

Find Out More!

3 Do a smile test.

Try it Out

- Smile at everyone at recess today. Count how many people smile back.
- Don't smile at anyone at recess tomorrow. How many people smile at you this time?

4 Select and store information on this topic in the Class Info Hub.

Chapter 7 60

1 Read and match. Which is your favorite saying?

The children match the sentence halves. Elicit answers. Find out with a show of hands which is their favorite saying.

Answers

1 b **2** f **3** e **4** d **5** a **6** c

2 Use your Student Book research to make an Info Card. Write about activities that make the brain release happy chemicals.

Divide the class into groups. Have the children pool the information they learned from their research in the Student Book and the Activity Book. The children write about and illustrate their ideas individually. Have the groups present their Info Cards to the class.

3 Do a smile test.

Discuss the **Try It Out** instructions on doing a smile test. The children carry out the test and report back to the class in the next lesson. Share and discuss results.

4 Select and store information on this topic in the Class Info Hub.

Have the children vote for the five most interesting Info Cards. Archive these in your Class Hub (see p. 41) in a folder called **Chapter 7 Happy Chemicals**.

Cooler: Play "Disappearing Text"

Play the game with key sentences from the Student Book Activity 1 text, e.g. *We all know that being happy makes you smile.* (see Games Bank p. 222).

Competency Focus

Act

The children carry out research to find out about what makes the brain release happy chemicals. This helps them expand their learning and relate it to their world, both inside and outside the classroom.

Presentation Kit • TIP You could store a website link in *Notepad* so that you can illustrate how to implement the Search Engine advice.

- TIP When using the board for "heads-up" teaching, remember to give the children as much opportunity as possible to participate. Ask plenty of questions so they engage with the topic. Use *Pointer* to help them follow the text as children read it aloud.

Teacher's Resource Center • Print out CLIL Graphic Organizer 7 for the children to collate their Find Out More! research.

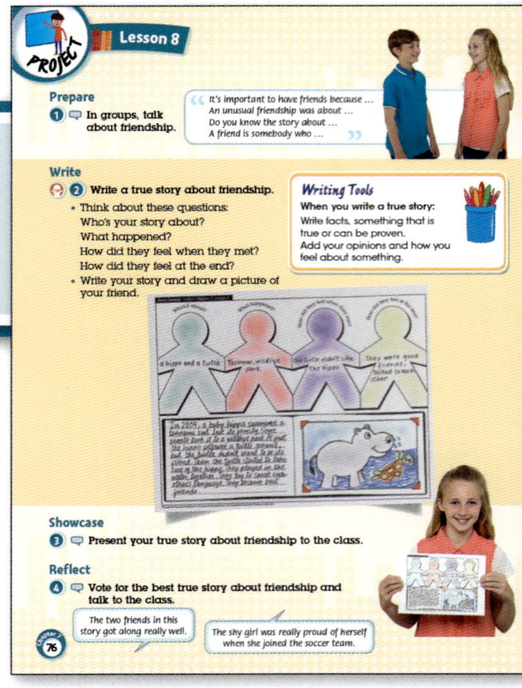
PROJECT
Lesson 8

Prepare

1 In groups, talk about friendship.

It's important to have friends because ...
An unusual friendship was about ...
Do you know the story about ...
A friend is somebody who ...

Write

2 Write a true story about friendship.

- Think about these questions:
  Who's your story about?
  What happened?
  How did they feel when they met?
  How did they feel at the end?
- Write your story and draw a picture of your friend.

Writing Tools
When you write a true story:
Write facts, something that is true or can be proven.
Add your opinions and how you feel about something.

Showcase

3 Present your true story about friendship to the class.

Reflect

4 Vote for the best true story about friendship and talk to the class.

The two friends in this story got along really well.
The shy girl was really proud of herself when she joined the soccer team.

Chapter 7
76

Writing Project

Lesson objectives: review language from Chapter 7; write a story and present it to the class

Materials: Writing Template 7 [TRC printout] (optional)

Warmer: Your friends

Tell the children to think of all the friends they have had over their life. Was there one a little bit different or that was/ is very special, e.g. a pet, a best friend, a friend they met on vacation, etc.? Have them compare their friends in pairs.

Prepare

1 In groups, talk about friendship.

- Have the children look at the example sentence openings and ask them what kind of information is given. (*why friends are important, an example of an unusual friendship, a story about friends, a definition of a friend*) Then they discuss these in small groups.
- Ask the groups to share what they discussed.

Write

2 Write a true story about friendship.

- Have the children read the story as a model for their own writing.
- Ask *Why are there two sets of details?* (*notes for preparing / the full story*)
- Read the **Writing Tools** box together. Elicit examples of facts and opinions.
- The children make notes and write a story about friendship. They can illustrate their work and then compare with a friend. Remind them to include facts and opinions.

Showcase

3 Present your true story about friendship to the class.

- Choose children to read their true story to the class. Ask the class to listen for the facts and the opinions. Elicit examples of both.

Reflect

4 Vote for the best true story about friendship and talk to the class.

- Have the children comment on which story was the best and why. Have a class vote to identify their favorite.

Optional activity: Just facts

Have the children rewrite the story of the hippo and the tortoise (the model story in Student Book Activity 2) so that it only contains facts. Ask them if they think the story is interesting like this, or if they prefer it with opinions included.

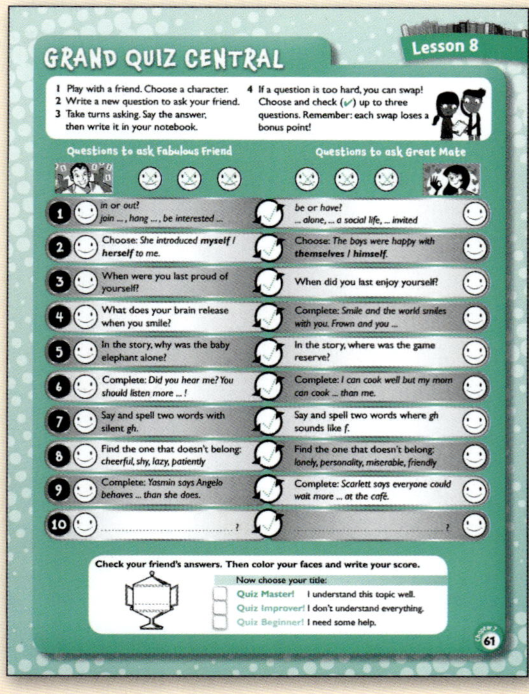
GRAND QUIZ CENTRAL

Lesson 8

1 Play with a friend. Choose a character.
2 Write a new question to ask your friend.
3 Take turns asking. Say the answer, then write it in your notebook.
4 If a question is too hard, you can swap! Choose and check (✓) up to three questions. Remember: each swap loses a bonus point!

	Questions to ask Fabulous Friend	Questions to ask Great Mate
1	in or out? *join ... , hang ... , be interested ...*	be or have? *... alone, ... a social life, ... invited*
2	Choose: *She introduced* ***myself / herself*** *to me.*	Choose: *The boys were happy with* ***themselves / himself.***
3	When were you last proud of yourself?	When did you last enjoy yourself?
4	What does your brain release when you smile?	Complete: *Smile and the world smiles with you. Frown and you ...*
5	In the story, why was the baby elephant alone?	In the story, where was the game reserve?
6	Complete: *Did you hear me? You should listen more ... !*	Complete: *I can cook well but my mom can cook ... than me.*
7	Say and spell two words with silent *gh*.	Say and spell two words where *gh* sounds like *f*.
8	Find the one that doesn't belong: *cheerful, shy, lazy, patiently*	Find the one that doesn't belong: *lonely, personality, miserable, friendly*
9	Complete: *Yasmin says Angelo behaves ... than she does.*	Complete: *Scarlett says everyone could wait more ... at the café.*
10	....?	....?

Check your friend's answers. Then color your faces and write your score.

Now choose your title:
Quiz Master! I understand this topic well.
Quiz Improver! I don't understand everything.
Quiz Beginner! I need some help.

Chapter 7 61

Grand Quiz Central

See p. 43 for details of how to take the quiz.

Answers

1 in, out, in / be, have, be **2** herself / themselves **3** Children's own answers: I was proud of myself / enjoyed myself when ... **4** (happy) chemicals / frown alone **5** because its mother had died *or* it was an orphan / in South Africa **6** carefully / better **7** *Any two of:* thought, eight, right, daughter, high, etc. / *Any two of:* laugh, enough, cough **8** patiently / personality **9** worse / patiently **10** Children's own answers.

Cooler: A word at a time

Have the children tell the story of the hippo and the tortoise around the class, one word each. You can insert words when you want to redirect the story or make the sentence more challenging.

Competency Focus

Me

The children write a true story about friendship. This helps them develop their understanding of how important friendships are to them.

Presentation Kit • Have children use *Highlighter* to identify examples in the model text of the key features of the writing task: facts and opinions.

- Have the children vote to select a topic from Vocabulary Tools 4A–7B and a way to review it (e.g. *Distort*, *Flashcard*).
- Use *Stopwatch* to give them one minute to recall all the words in the topic. Repeat with a different topic if you have time.

Teacher's Resource Center • Print out Writing Template 7 to use for the SB writing activity.

Language Review

Lesson objective: review language from Chapter 7
Materials: Class CD; pieces of paper with questions (Cooler)

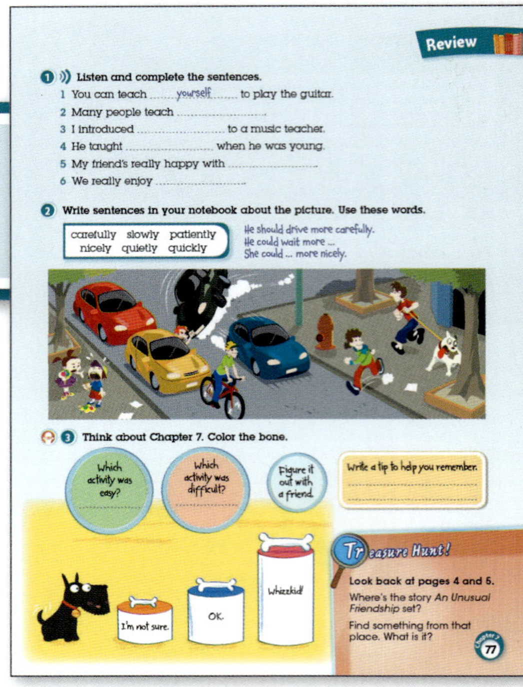

Review

1 Listen and complete the sentences.

1 You can teach ......yourself...... to play the guitar.
2 Many people teach ....
3 I introduced .... to a music teacher.
4 He taught .... when he was young.
5 My friend's really happy with ....
6 We really enjoy ....

2 Write sentences in your notebook about the picture. Use these words.

carefully slowly patiently nicely quietly quickly

He should drive more carefully.
He could wait more ...
She could ... more nicely.

3 Think about Chapter 7. Color the bone.

Which activity was easy?
Which activity was difficult?
Figure it out with a friend.
Write a tip to help you remember.

I'm not sure.
OK.
Whizzkid!

Treasure Hunt!

Look back at pages 4 and 5.
Where's the story *An Unusual Friendship* set?
Find something from that place. What is it?

Chapter 7 77

Warmer: Play "Collocations"

Play the game with collocations from Chapter 7, e.g. *get along/with your friends*, *have a social/life*, etc. (see Games Bank p. 222).

1 2.16 Listen and complete the sentences.

- Have the children look at the sentences and talk with a friend to predict the answers.
- Play the CD and have the children listen and complete the sentences.
- Play the CD again for the children to confirm or complete their answers.
- Elicit answers.

Audioscript

I found a website that said you could teach yourself to play the guitar in a week. Many people teach themselves, but I was too lazy and didn't practice. I'm really shy, but I introduced myself to a music teacher at school and asked him to teach me. He taught himself to play when he was young and took some lessons, too. My friend was interested in joining in so now she comes to the classes, too, so I'm not so lonely. She can play really well now and is really happy with herself. We're not the best musicians in the world, but our teacher is cheerful and has a great sense of humor. We get along with him well and really enjoy ourselves.

Answers

1 yourself **2** themselves **3** myself **4** himself **5** herself **6** ourselves

2 Write sentences in your notebook about the picture. Use these words.

- Elicit a sentence using one of the adverbs supplied, e.g. *They could wait more patiently.*
- The children write sentences in their notebook and compare their sentences in pairs.

Answers

Children's own answers.

3 Think about Chapter 7. Color the bone.

- Have the children look back at Chapter 7 and color the bone to evaluate their progress (self-evaluation).
- Discuss ideas for remembering vocabulary, e.g. spend five minutes every day reading new word lists. The children choose and write a tip in their Student Book.

Treasure Hunt

Ask *Where is the story* An Unusual Friendship *set?* (*South Africa*) Have the children look at pp. 4–5 to find an animal from South Africa. (*a lion*)

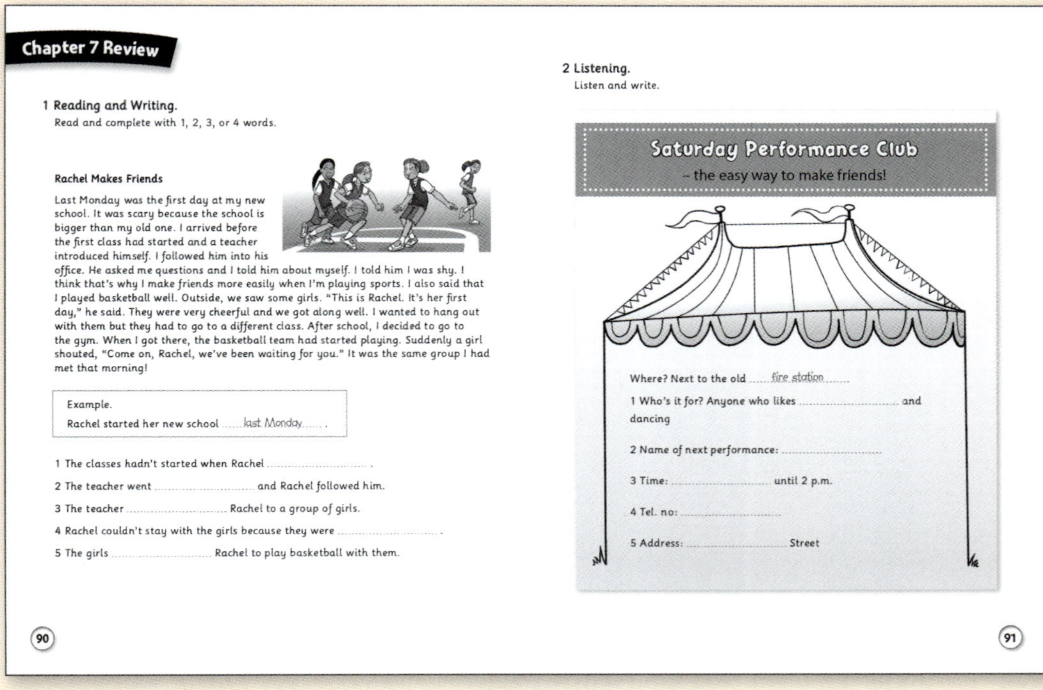

Chapter 7 Review

1 Reading and Writing.
Read and complete with 1, 2, 3, or 4 words.

Rachel Makes Friends

Last Monday was the first day at my new school. It was scary because the school is bigger than my old one. I arrived before the first class had started and a teacher introduced himself. I followed him into his office. He asked me questions and I told him about myself. I told him I was shy. I think that's why I make friends more easily when I'm playing sports. I also said that I played basketball well. Outside, we saw some girls. "This is Rachel. It's her first day," he said. They were very cheerful and we got along well. I wanted to hang out with them but they had to go to a different class. After school, I decided to go to the gym. When I got there, the basketball team had started playing. Suddenly a girl shouted, "Come on, Rachel, we've been waiting for you." It was the same group I had met that morning!

Example.
Rachel started her new school ......last Monday...... .

1 The classes hadn't started when Rachel ....
2 The teacher went .... and Rachel followed him.
3 The teacher .... Rachel to a group of girls.
4 Rachel couldn't stay with the girls because they were ....
5 The girls .... Rachel to play basketball with them.

90

2 Listening.
Listen and write.

Saturday Performance Club
– the easy way to make friends!

Where? Next to the old ......fire station......
1 Who's it for? Anyone who likes .... and dancing
2 Name of next performance: ....
3 Time: .... until 2 p.m.
4 Tel. no: ....
5 Address: .... Street

91

1 Reading and Writing. Read and complete with 1, 2, 3, or 4 words.

The children read the text and complete the sentences. Point out that each answer requires one, two, three, or four words. Check answers.

Answers

1 arrived **2** into his office **3** introduced **4** in a different class **5** wanted/invited

2 2.37 Listening. Listen and write.

The children read the notice. Play the CD twice. They listen and write an answer for each prompt. Check answers.

Answers (Audioscript on p. 224)

1 singing **2** Big Top **3** 10 a.m. **4** 576 246 6902 **5** Market

Competency Focus

Me: Self-evaluation

The children reflect on the chapter, express their personal opinions about their own progress, and look for ways to improve. This encourages them to evaluate and make decisions about what they need to revisit and how they can learn better.

Cooler: Class mingle

Give each child a question on a slip of paper related to the chapter content, e.g. *What's the best way to make yourself happy? What would you like to do better?*, etc. The children mingle with their friends, ask and answer questions, and then swap questions and continue talking to other children.

Presentation Kit • Use *Answer Key* to give feedback on AB Chapter Review activities.
- Print out Festival Worksheet: International Children's Book Day to expand the children's knowledge of celebrations throughout the world.

Teacher's Resource Center • Print out Test Chapter 7 to use at the end of this lesson. The Test Generator also allows you to create customized tests.
- For the CEYLT (Cambridge YLE) exam preparation activities on the AB page, choose *Audio* to access the recordings.

Chapter 8 Social Network Overview

The children will:

- use critical thinking skills to identify technology and Internet vocabulary.
- talk about and focus on past events using the past passive.
- read and understand a modern detective story about a stolen painting.
- talk about how to use the Internet.
- ask and answer questions using the past passive.
- identify and use vocabulary for socializing online.
- find out about online safety.
- write a text poem or micro story.

Key Vocabulary

Technology and the Internet: click, connect, key in, network, password, settings, smartphone, social networking, website
Socializing online: blog, logged in, go viral, post, search online, share, socializing, upload, video

Key Grammar

Past passive

- The video was watched at 9:00 a.m.
- The pictures were taken by people all over the world.

Past passive questions

- Who were they written by?
- Who was it stolen by?
- Was it changed?
- Were they saved?

Reading Skills

Story: *The Stolen Painting*
Genre: modern detective story

Literacy Development

- use reading skills to understand and predict content
- relate story theme to personal experience
- use abbreviated text language

Functional Language

- That's a cool picture!
- Thanks! It was taken on vacation last year.
- Who took it?
- Oh, I took it myself!

Spelling

Words with *sh* sound
(*sh*, *ti*, *ci*)

CLIL: Social sciences—Online safety

The children find out how to be safe when using cell phones, email, and the Internet.

Competency Focus

The children will:

- use critical thinking skills to deduce the meaning of new vocabulary. (Lesson 1)
- predict the content of a story. (Lesson 3)

- activate new vocabulary and apply new grammar knowledge. (Lesson 2)
- apply new grammar rules in a familiar context. (Lesson 5)

- work in pairs to talk about their pictures. (Lesson 3)
- work in pairs to talk about how they use the Internet. (Lesson 6)

- relate the story and story theme to their personal experience. (Lesson 4)
- invent and write a poem or a micro story. (Lesson 8)
- evaluate their own progress in the chapter. (Review)

- develop an understanding of online safety by carrying out research. (Lesson 7)

Digital Overview

Presentation Kit

Projectable Student Book, Activity Book, and Reader pages

- Vocabulary Tool 8A: Technology and the Internet
- Vocabulary Tool 8B: Socializing online
- Music Video 8: *Text Poetry*
- Interactive versions of selected SB and AB activities
- Integrated *Audio* and *Answer Key* for all activities

Teacher's Resource Center

Resources for planning, lesson delivery, and homework

- Class Planner Chapter 8
- Worksheets to print out (including notes and answers):
  - Grammar Worksheet 8A: Past passive
  - Grammar Worksheet 8B: Past passive questions
  - CLIL Graphic Organizer 8
  - Writing Template 8
  - Test Chapter 8
- Test Generator
- Literacy Handbook

Student's Resource Center

Resources for consolidation and practice at home

- Interactive Grammar 8A: Past passive
- Interactive Grammar 8B: Past passive questions
- Vocabulary Tool 8A: Technology and the Internet
- Vocabulary Tool 8B: Socializing online
- Music Video 8: *Text Poetry*

Student's App

Vocabulary games: Technology/the Internet and Socializing online

Watch the Music Video

Chapter 8

Social Network

Lesson 1

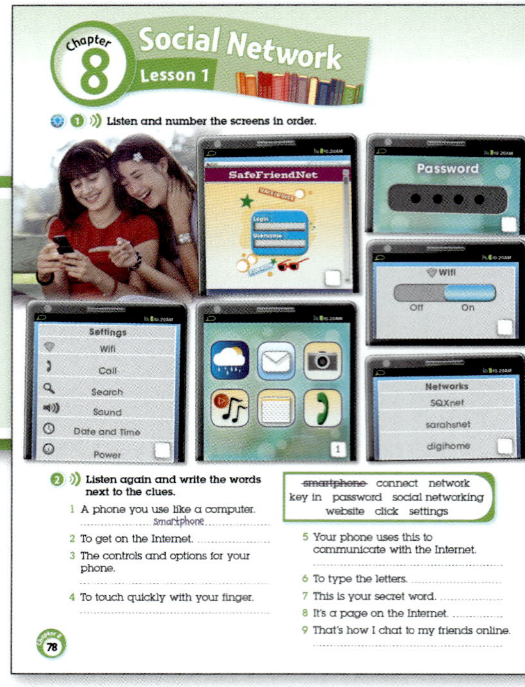

Chapter 8 Social Network
Lesson 1

1 Listen and number the screens in order.

SafeFriendNet
Password
Wifi
Off On
Settings
Wifi
Call
Search
Sound
Date and Time
Power
Networks
SQXnet
sarahsnet
digihome

2 Listen again and write the words next to the clues.

~~smartphone~~ connect network key in password social networking website click settings

1 A phone you use like a computer. smartphone
2 To get on the Internet.
3 The controls and options for your phone.
4 To touch quickly with your finger.
5 Your phone uses this to communicate with the Internet.
6 To type the letters.
7 This is your secret word.
8 It's a page on the Internet.
9 That's how I chat to my friends online.

78

Vocabulary

Lesson objectives: identify and use technology and Internet vocabulary
Key vocabulary: *click, connect, key in, network, password, settings, smartphone, social networking, website*
Materials: Class CD

Warmer: Brainstorm technology

Have the children work with a friend to remember all the things they use regularly that can be called technology. They write a list. Elicit answers, asking children to write each item on the board. When all answers have been given, ask which pair found the most items.

1 2.17 Listen and number the screens in order.

- Have the children look at the pictures. Ask *What can you see on each screen?*
- Play the CD and have the children number the screens in the order they hear them.
- Elicit answers.

Audioscript

Girl 1: *I have this new cell phone, but I don't know how to use it.*
Girl 2: *Oh, it's a smartphone! You can use it like a computer and connect to the Internet. Look on your Home screen first. Go to Settings— these are like the controls and options for your phone. This is where you can turn things on and off. It's this symbol here. When you go into Settings, click on Wifi— just touch it quickly with your finger.*
Girl 1: *OK. It says "off" on the Wifi screen.*
Girl 2: *OK, turn it on. That's the blue button at the right of the screen. Now you're on your Networks screen. Choose a network—look, these names on the list here. Your phone uses this to communicate with the Internet. When you've chosen your network, key in the password. Yes, type the letters for your secret word here. That's it! Now you can look at the Internet. Which website are you looking for? Which page on the Internet do you want?*
Girl 1: *My social networking site. That's how I chat to my classmates online. Look, I can send you a message.*
Girl 2: *But I'm sitting here. You can chat to me now!*

Answers

SafeFriendNet social networking site 6, Password 5, Wifi 3, Settings 2, Home screen (with icons) 1, Networks 4

2 2.17 Listen again and write the words next to the clues.

- Play the CD again. The children listen and write the word described in each clue, using the words supplied.
- Elicit answers.

Answers

1 smartphone **2** connect **3** settings **4** click **5** network **6** key in **7** password **8** website **9** social networking

Optional activity: One long sentence

Have the children work in pairs to write one sentence which includes as many of the vocabulary items from the Activity 2 box as possible. Remind the children that they need to use conjunctions like *and, but, so, because*, etc. Have pairs read their sentences out.

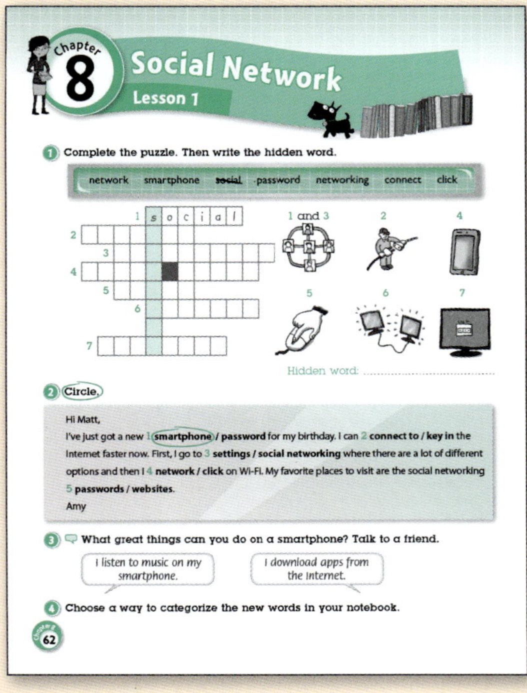
Chapter 8
Social Network
Lesson 1

1 Complete the puzzle. Then write the hidden word.

network smartphone ~~social~~ password networking connect click

1 s o c i a l

1 and 3 2 4 5 6 7

Hidden word: ....

2 Circle.

Hi Matt,
I've just got a new 1 smartphone / password for my birthday. I can 2 connect to / key in the Internet faster now. First, I go to 3 settings / social networking where there are a lot of different options and then I 4 network / click on Wi-Fi. My favorite places to visit are the social networking 5 passwords / websites.
Amy

3 What great things can you do on a smartphone? Talk to a friend.

I listen to music on my smartphone.
I download apps from the Internet.

4 Choose a way to categorize the new words in your notebook.

Chapter 8 62

1 Complete the puzzle. Then write the hidden word.

The children complete the puzzle using the picture prompts. They identify and write the hidden word shown on the colored squares. Elicit answers.

Answers

1 & 3 social networking **2** connect **4** smartphone
5 click **6** network **7** password
Hidden word: settings

2 Circle.

The children complete the text by circling the correct option from the two given each time. Elicit answers.

Answers

1 smartphone **2** connect to **3** settings **4** click **5** websites

3 What great things can you do on a smartphone? Talk to a friend.

The children discuss in pairs the different things you can do on a smartphone. Elicit ideas.

4 Choose a way to categorize the new words in your notebook.

Brainstorm appropriate categories, e.g. *nouns/verbs, I do/I don't do, do at home/do in class.* The children choose the best categories for them and list the words in their notebook.

Answers

Children's own answers.

Cooler: Play "Disappearing Words"

Play the game with words from the lesson (see Games Bank p. 222).

Competency Focus

Think! Critical Thinking

The children use critical thinking skills to understand the new vocabulary by using visual clues and processing the written and spoken forms.

Presentation Kit • Use Vocabulary Tool 8A to pre-teach key vocabulary as an alternative to the critical thinking approach. Use *Slideshow* to introduce the words and *Spotlight* to review/test.

- TIP Use the arrow in the *Audio* pop-up window to see the audioscript for SB Activity 1.
- Have children use *Highlighter* to identify the nouns and *Pen* to circle the verbs in the word bank in SB Activity 2.

Grammar

Lesson objectives: talk about events using the past passive
Key grammar: past passive
Secondary language: *review*, *upload*
Materials: Grammar Worksheet 8A [TRC printout] (optional)

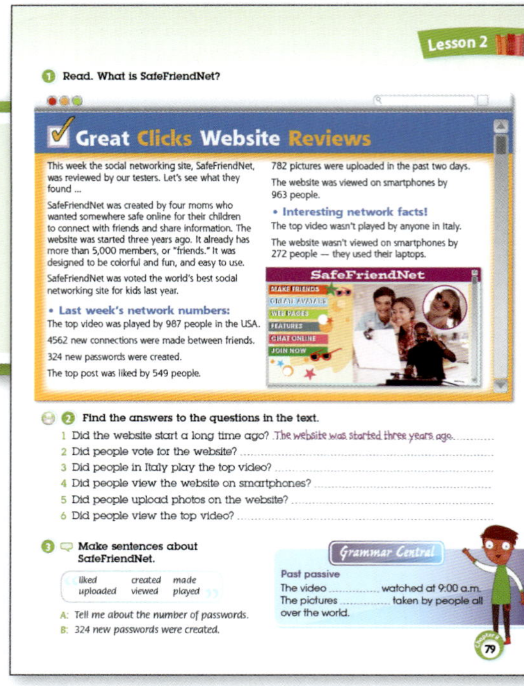

Lesson 2

1 Read. What is SafeFriendNet?

Great Clicks Website Reviews

This week the social networking site, SafeFriendNet, was reviewed by our testers. Let's see what they found ...

SafeFriendNet was created by four moms who wanted somewhere safe online for their children to connect with friends and share information. The website was started three years ago. It already has more than 5,000 members, or "friends." It was designed to be colorful and fun, and easy to use.

SafeFriendNet was voted the world's best social networking site for kids last year.

• Last week's network numbers:

The top video was played by 987 people in the USA.

4562 new connections were made between friends.

324 new passwords were created.

The top post was liked by 549 people.

782 pictures were uploaded in the past two days.

The website was viewed on smartphones by 963 people.

• Interesting network facts!

The top video wasn't played by anyone in Italy.

The website wasn't viewed on smartphones by 272 people — they used their laptops.

2 Find the answers to the questions in the text.

1 Did the website start a long time ago? The website was started three years ago.
2 Did people vote for the website?
3 Did people in Italy play the top video?
4 Did people view the website on smartphones?
5 Did people upload photos on the website?
6 Did people view the top video?

3 Make sentences about SafeFriendNet.

liked created made uploaded viewed played

A: *Tell me about the number of passwords.*
B: *324 new passwords were created.*

Grammar Central

Past passive

The video .... watched at 9:00 a.m.
The pictures .... taken by people all over the world.

79

Warmer: What happened?

Elicit a variety of different things, verbs, and people and write these on the board, e.g. *walk*, *write*; *movie*, *song*; *doctor*, *actor*, etc. Then ask the children to think of sentences using this information and the present passive. They do not have to be true sentences, e.g. *Songs are written by doctors!*

1 Read. What is SafeFriendNet?

- Have the children look at the image. Ask what they think it shows.
- Have the children read the text and find the answer to the question.
- Ask *What is SafeFriendNet?* (*a social networking site*)

2 Find the answers to the questions in the text.

- Have the children scan the text and find the location of the information that gives the first two answers. (*lines 6–7, 10–11*)
- The children write answers to the questions using the past passive.
- Elicit answers.

Answers

1 The website was started three years ago. **2** It was voted the world's best social networking site for kids (last year). **3** The top video wasn't played by anyone in Italy. **4** The website was viewed on smartphones by 963 people. **5** 782 photos were uploaded in the past two days. **6** The top video was played by 987 people in the USA.

Grammar Central

Past passive

Have the children complete the grammar examples. Elicit answers. Elicit why the past passive is used. (*to focus on a past action and not on who did the action*) The children write further examples in their notebook. See also the Grammar Reference sections in the Student Book (p. 102) and Activity Book (p. 103) for further explanation and practice.

Grammar Central Answers: was, were

AB Answers Activity 1: 1 The Internet was invented by Tim Berners-Lee. **2** The gold medal was won by Mexico. **3** *Matilda* was written by Roald Dahl. **4** The pictures were uploaded by Abby. **5** They were rescued by the lifeboat crew.

3 Make sentences about SafeFriendNet.

- Have two children read out the example. Then the children work in pairs using the prompts supplied.
- Have children make questions for the class and challenge the class to answer with their books closed.

Optional activity: Listen and write

Choose three key sentences from the text which use a past passive. Say them aloud twice. Have the children close their eyes and listen. Say the sentences again for the children to note down key words only. Then have them rewrite the sentences in small groups. Dictate the sentences and have different children write them, a word at a time, on the board. The groups check their answers.

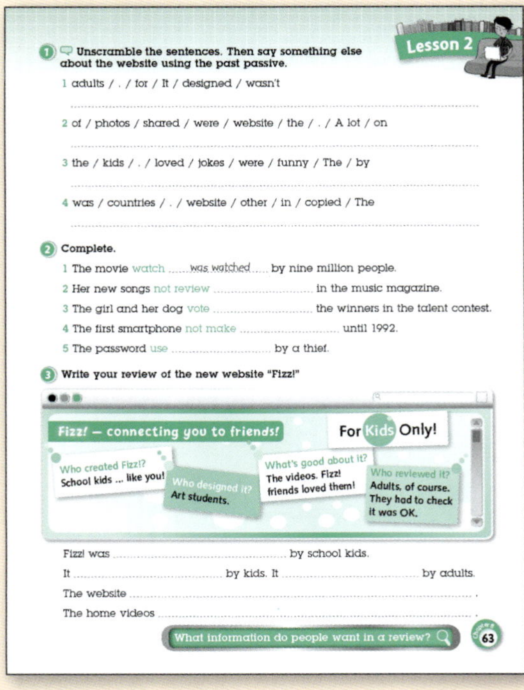

Lesson 2

1 Unscramble the sentences. Then say something else about the website using the past passive.

1 adults / . / for / It / designed / wasn't

2 of / photos / shared / were / website / the / . / A lot / on

3 the / kids / . / loved / jokes / were / funny / The / by

4 was / countries / . / website / other / in / copied / The

2 Complete.

1 The movie watch ...... was watched ..... by nine million people.
2 Her new songs not review .... in the music magazine.
3 The girl and her dog vote .... the winners in the talent contest.
4 The first smartphone not make .... until 1992.
5 The password use .... by a thief.

3 Write your review of the new website "Fizz!"

Fizz! was .... by school kids.
It .... by kids. It .... by adults.
The website ....
The home videos ....

What information do people want in a review?

63

1 Unscramble the sentences. Then say something else about the website using the past passive.

The children write out the sentences correctly. Elicit answers. Then they make up more statements about the website described in the sentences using the past passive. Elicit ideas.

Answers

1 It wasn't designed for adults. **2** A lot of photos were shared on the website. **3** The funny jokes were loved by the kids. **4** The website was copied in other countries.

2 Complete.

The children complete the sentences by writing the past passive form of the verb prompts given. Elicit answers.

Answers

1 was watched **2** weren't reviewed **3** were voted **4** wasn't made **5** was used

3 Write your review of the new website "Fizz!"

The children write a review of the new website "Fizz!" using the prompts supplied. Then they compare with a friend. Elicit responses. Ask *What information do people want in a review? (clear, concise, factual information that answers questions such as "Who made it?" and "Who is it for?"; personal opinion)*

Answers

Children's own answers.

Cooler: Play "Back to the Board"

Play the game with key vocabulary: *smartphone, connect, network, key in, password, social networking, website, click, settings* (see Games Bank p. 222).

Ask the children to bring in a picture of themselves. This can be a photograph or on their cell phone, if you do not mind them bringing phones to class.

Competency Focus

Learn

The children integrate previously acquired vocabulary into new grammar and structure, and adapt the language to show an understanding of the topic.

Presentation Kit • When you are focusing on the new structure in SB Grammar Central, have children use *Highlighter* to identify the past passive in SB Activity 1.

• TIP As you monitor the children's progress, use *Notepad* to keep a note of weaknesses in vocabulary, grammar, or pronunciation so you can review in later lessons.

Teacher's Resource Center • For extra grammar practice, print out Grammar Worksheet 8A.

Student's Resource Center • The children can use Interactive Grammar 8A at home.

Reading: Story Extract

Lesson objectives: talk about photos; use the title and pictures to predict story content; read the extract from the modern detective story *The Stolen Painting* (beginning)
Functional language: *That's a cool picture! Thanks! It was taken ... Who took it? Oh, I took it myself!*
Secondary language: *a joke*
Materials: Class CD; children's own photos

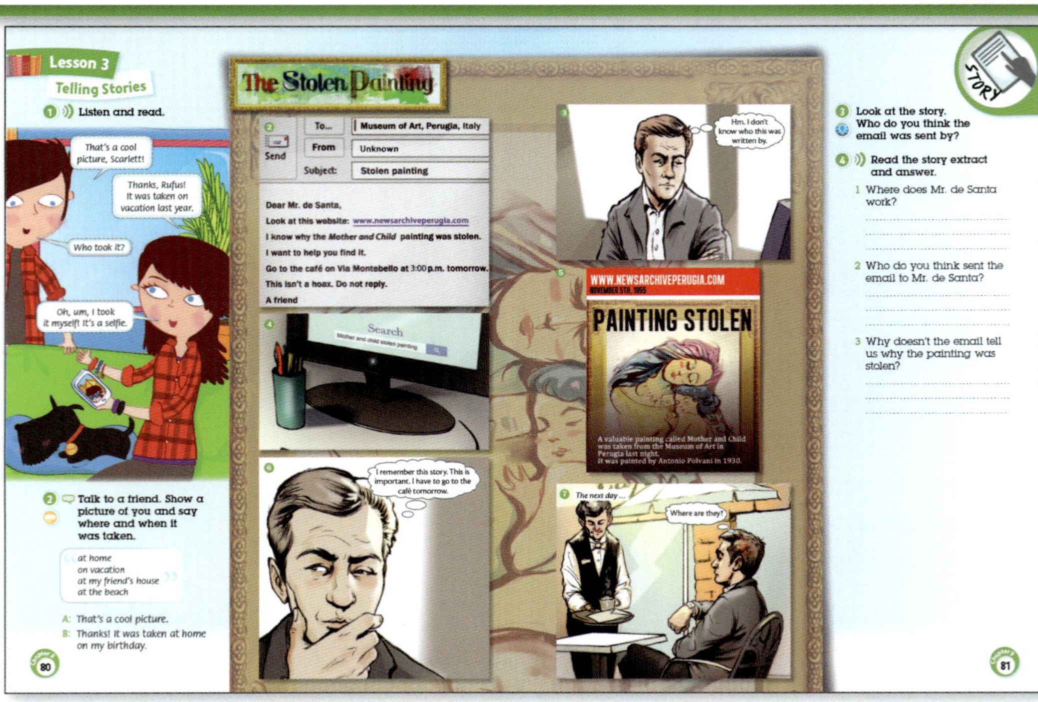

Warmer: Play "Sentence Builders"

Play the game with past passive sentences: *It was stolen by a person. It was hidden by someone.* (see Games Bank p. 222).

Functional language

1 2.18 Listen and read.

- Play the CD. The children listen and read along. Ask *Why is Scarlett happy?* (*because Rufus likes her photo*)
- Play the CD again, pausing for them to repeat.
- Divide the class into pairs to practice the dialogue.

2 Talk to a friend. Show a picture of you and say where and when it was taken.

- Choose two children to read the example dialogue. Elicit other examples using the prompts supplied.
- The children practice in pairs, using photos or pictures on their phone (if allowed). If the children do not have photos to show, they can imagine ones they have taken. Have pairs perform a dialogue for the class.

Before reading

3 Look at the story. Who do you think the email was sent by?

- Have the children study the story title and pictures to try to figure out who the email was sent by. Ask *Who do you think the email was sent by?* Elicit ideas.

Answers

Children's own answers.

4 2.19 Read the story extract and answer.

- Play the CD. The children listen and read along. Have them answer question 1. Elicit the answer.
- Play the CD again so they can write their ideas for questions 2 and 3. Encourage them to use reading skills (e.g. using the title, pictures, and context) to infer meaning and make predictions.

- Elicit answers, but do not confirm predictions: explain that they will have to read the story to find out.

Answers

1 At the Museum of Art (in Perugia, Italy) **2** Children's own answers. **3** Children's own answers.

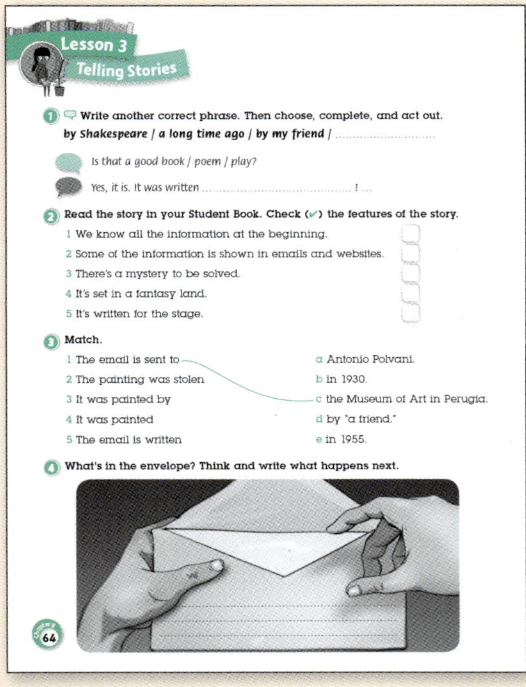

Lesson 3
Telling Stories

1 Write another correct phrase. Then choose, complete, and act out.
by Shakespeare / a long time ago / by my friend / ....

Is that a good book / poem / play?

Yes, it is. It was written .... ! ...

2 Read the story in your Student Book. Check (✓) the features of the story.

1 We know all the information at the beginning. ☐
2 Some of the information is shown in emails and websites. ☐
3 There's a mystery to be solved. ☐
4 It's set in a fantasy land. ☐
5 It's written for the stage. ☐

3 Match.

1 The email is sent to — a Antonio Polvani.
2 The painting was stolen — b in 1930.
3 It was painted by — c the Museum of Art in Perugia.
4 It was painted — d by "a friend."
5 The email is written — e in 1955.

4 What's in the envelope? Think and write what happens next.

64

1 Write another correct phrase. Then choose, complete, and act out.

Elicit other phrases that could follow *It was written* ... The children choose a phrase and complete the dialogue. They then act it out in pairs. Encourage the children to use what they know to adapt and extend the dialogue. Have pairs act out their dialogue for the class.

2 Read the story in your Student Book. Check (✓) the features of the story.

The children read the Student Book story extract again, then check the sentences that describe the story. Elicit answers.

Answers

✓ *by:* 2, 3

3 Match.

The children match the sentence halves. Elicit answers.

Answers

1 c **2** e **3** a **4** b **5** d

4 What's in the envelope? Think and write what happens next.

Elicit suggestions on what is in the envelope. The children write their own ideas, then compare with a friend. Elicit ideas.

Answers

Children's own answers.

Cooler: Play "Text Bingo"

2.19

Have the children close their books. Write on the board 12 words (*museum, stolen, website, café, joke, friend, written, valuable, taken, remember, important, where*). Ask the children to choose the six words that they think they will hear first in the story and write them in a 3 x 2 grid. Play the CD. When the children hear the words they chose, they cross them out. The first child to cross out all six shouts *Bingo!*

Competency Focus

Collaborate and Communicate

The children work together to practice, perform, and adapt the new functional language learned.

Think

The children use critical thinking skills to identify the setting of the story by looking at the text and story artwork.

Presentation Kit • Before doing SB Activity 3, have children use *Pen* to circle in the story extract the three different ways Mr. de Santa obtains information about the painting (*email, Internet/website, envelope*).

- TIP Give children the opportunity to be your assistant! Select a child to be responsible for choosing the relevant buttons (e.g. to go to the next activity).
- TIP Choose the SB/AB button in the Navigation Pane to move from one component to another.

The Stolen Painting

2 *To: Museum of Art, Perugia, Italy*
From: Unknown
Subject: Stolen painting
Dear Mr. de Santa,
Look at this website: www.newsarchiveperugia.com
I know why the Mother and Child *painting was stolen. I want to help you find it. Go to the café on Via Montebello at 3:00 p.m. tomorrow.*
This isn't a hoax. Do not reply.
A friend

3 **Mr. de Santa:** *Hm. I don't know who this was written by.*

5 *www.newsarchiveperugia.com*
November 5th, 1955
PAINTING STOLEN
A valuable painting called Mother and Child *was taken from the Museum of Art in Perugia last night. It was painted by Antonio Polvani in 1930.*

6 **de S:** *I remember this story. This is important. I have to go to the café tomorrow.*

7 The next day …
de S: *Where are they?*

8 *Password: the artist*

9 *Enter Password: POLVANI*

10 *Keep this smartphone. Follow instructions. Go 2 airport tonight.*

11 **de S:** Ha! You have to be joking!

12 **Sender:** *Do u want the painting?*

14 **de S:** *What do u want?*
Sender: *Nothing. I'm not thief. Painting belongs 2 museum. But if u go 2 police, I will destroy it …*
de S: *OK. I'll go*

15 *Passenger Mr. Carlo de Santa*
From: Perugia
To: Verona
Your next flight VRN 2784
Departure time 8:50 p.m.

16 **de S:** Giulia, I need to tell you something …

17 **Giulia:** Who was it sent by?
de S: I don't know, but I think I believe them.
Giulia: It might not be safe. You don't know if it's the real painting.

18 **de S:** I have to find out.
Giulia: Text me to tell me what happens. Let me know you're OK. Take care of yourself.

19 That evening …

20 *Rent Car. Registration number: VR 993RA. Parking lot C. Blue car.*

22 **Sat nav:** You've arrived at your destination.
de S: Hm. It looks like I'm staying here tonight.

23 **de S:** I'd like a room please. My name is …
Receptionist: Mr. de Santa! We've been expecting you. Your room was booked yesterday. Room 17.

24 **Receptionist:** Find the Palazzo network and then key in the password Palazzo1 to connect to the WiFi. Access is free.
de S: Thanks.

25 *@ Hotel Palazzo. Tired + going 2 bed.*

26 The next morning …
TEXT MESSAGE: UNKNOWN

27 *Take bus 2 Via Vitruvio.*

28 *Turn left + walk along river.*
Find package under bridge.
Don't open til U R @ hotel.

30 *I know painting in safe hands. Now throw phone into river.*
de S: What?

33 *The woman in the painting is my mother. The child is me. She died soon after I was born. I didn't want to be a thief—I wanted to keep my mother close to me. The museum wouldn't sell the painting, so I had to steal it. This is the only picture I have of her. I don't need it anymore. Please forgive me.*

34 *Found painting!!! It had been left under bridge + was wrapped in old cloth. Letter was hidden inside. Coming back now.*

35 Later, in Perugia …
News anchor: A missing painting was returned to the Perugia Museum of Art today. The picture was painted by Antonio Polvani, and is of an unknown woman and her baby.

36 **News anchor:** In other news, the billionaire Giovanni Rocca died this afternoon. He was taken to the hospital last night after a long illness. Rocca was born in 1930 …

37 Back in Verona …
Man: Goodbye, Grandpa. Everything was done just as you wanted.

Lesson objective: read and understand the modern detective story *The Stolen Painting* in the Reader
Materials: Class CD; Reader

Warmer: The stolen painting

Elicit what the children remember about the stolen painting. Ask *Who is in the painting? What do they look like? What's their hair like?*, etc. Have the children take turns describing it to a friend and sketching what they describe. They compare to see if their paintings are similar. They then compare with the version in the Reader.

Story Summary

Mr. de Santa, a museum curator, is sent a mysterious email about a stolen painting. He follows the clues and finds the painting. The boy in the painting had stolen it many years ago, but then wanted to return it because he was dying, so he instructed his grandson to carry out his wishes.

Theme: it is never too late to do the right thing.

2.20 While reading

- Have the children look at the pictures in the Reader. Ask *How does Mr. de Santa get clues about where the painting is?* (*on a cell phone*)
- Play the CD. The children listen and read along. Ask *Who was sending the messages and instructions?* (*Giovanni Rocca's grandson*)
- Ask questions to check comprehension, e.g. *Where was the painting taken from?* (*the Museum of Art*) *How did Mr. de Santa get the cell phone?* (*from the waiter*)
- Have the class read the story aloud, with the children acting out the roles of Mr. de Santa, Giulia, grandson, receptionist, news anchor, and narrator.

After reading: Reflect

Ask questions to give the children the opportunity to think about the issues raised by the story, e.g. *Was it right to steal the painting? Why?/Why not? Did the man do the right thing by returning the painting?*

Optional activity: Who said it?

Say lines of dialogue from the story to elicit who said or wrote it. The children continue the activity in pairs.

Story Time

In their shoes

In a story like this, there are many points where you can ask *What would you do? What should he do?*, or give multiple choice options. Encouraging the children to think carefully about choices and motivations helps them become more involved in the story.

Reading Strategy

Making Inferences

Making inferences is essential in understanding the plot and what role each character plays. It is particularly useful when trying to solve a mystery. It requires readers to use their own knowledge and apply critical and visual reading skills.

For additional explanation and activities, see the Literacy Handbook on the Teacher's Resource Center.

Cooler: Mime time

Put the class into groups. The children mime an action from the story for the rest of the group to guess, e.g. *He's reading the email. He's arriving at the hotel.*, etc.

Presentation Kit • Use *Hotspots* to show the Reader story one enlarged picture at a time as you play *Audio*. Before moving on each time, elicit what is going to happen next.

• TIP You can move the *Answer Key* pop-up window around the screen to have the activity and the answers side by side. Hold the cursor over the colored band at the top of the window.

Reading Comprehension and Critical Literacy

Lesson objectives: understand and evaluate the story; relate story theme to personal experience; focus on the use of key words and symbols

Materials: Class CD; Reader; small slips of paper, box for paper text messages (Cooler)

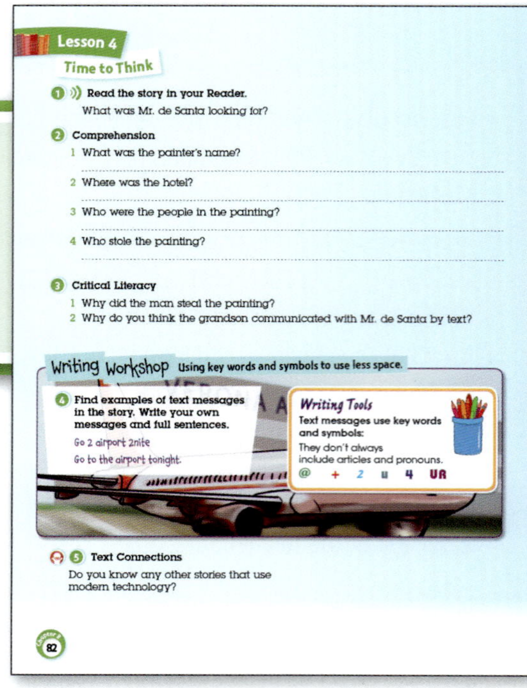
Lesson 4

Time to Think

1 Read the story in your Reader.
What was Mr. de Santa looking for?

2 Comprehension
1 What was the painter's name?
2 Where was the hotel?
3 Who were the people in the painting?
4 Who stole the painting?

3 Critical Literacy
1 Why did the man steal the painting?
2 Why do you think the grandson communicated with Mr. de Santa by text?

Writing Workshop Using key words and symbols to use less space.

4 Find examples of text messages in the story. Write your own messages and full sentences.
Go 2 airport 2nite
Go to the airport tonight.

Writing Tools
Text messages use key words and symbols:
They don't always include articles and pronouns.
@ + 2 u 4 UR

5 Text Connections
Do you know any other stories that use modern technology?

82

Note: Please ensure that your class has read the Reader story before you do this lesson.

Warmer: Talk about texting

Write on the board *How many texts do you send a day/week? What do you text about? Do you use abbreviations (e.g. "u" for "you")? Do you think people should call instead of texting?* Have the children discuss their answers in pairs. Elicit answers and opinions.

1 2.20 Read the story in your Reader.

- Have the children read the story. (Alternatively, play the CD and have them read along.)
- Elicit whether the children were correct in their predictions in Lesson 3 Activity 4. Ask *What was Mr. de Santa looking for?* (*the missing painting*)

2 Comprehension

- The children write answers to the first three questions. Elicit answers.
- Discuss question 4. Ask the children to justify their answers.

Answers

1 Antonio Polvani **2** In Verona. **3** The baby was Giovanni Rocca and the woman was his mother. **4** Giovanni Rocca

3 Critical Literacy

- Have the children discuss the answers to the questions with a friend.
- Elicit ideas, inviting discussion by the class. Encourage the children to consider the reasoning behind the actions of the characters and to decide if they agree with the behavior. Engaging with broader issues like this helps children engage constructively with the story.

Answers

1 Children's own answers. / Giovanni Rocca stole the painting because it was the only picture he had of his mother.

2 Children's own answers. / Because he didn't want Mr. de Santa to know who he was / he wanted to protect his grandfather.

Writing Workshop

Using key words and symbols to use less space

4 Find examples of text messages in the story. Write your own messages and full sentences.

Have a child read the messages. Elicit other ways to use less space, using symbols, letters, and numbers from the **Writing Tools** box. Ask *Can you find any text messages in the story?* The children write their own messages and sentences in their notebook, then compare with a friend. Elicit responses.

Answers

Children's own answers.

5 Text Connections

- Ask *Do you know any other stories that use modern technology?* Elicit ideas and discuss as a class.

Answers

Children's own answers.

Optional activity: Abbreviations

Write *2day I saw u …* on the board and ask if the children know what it means (*Today I saw you …*). Have the children work in pairs to write a very short story in 150 characters. Elicit examples.

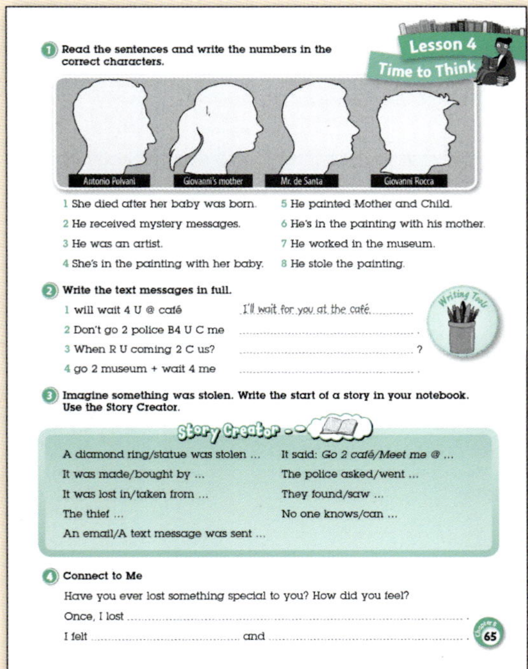

Lesson 4
Time to Think

1 Read the sentences and write the numbers in the correct characters.

Antonio Polvani | Giovanni's mother | Mr. de Santa | Giovanni Rocca

1 She died after her baby was born.
2 He received mystery messages.
3 He was an artist.
4 She's in the painting with her baby.
5 He painted Mother and Child.
6 He's in the painting with his mother.
7 He worked in the museum.
8 He stole the painting.

2 Write the text messages in full.

1 will wait 4 U @ café ..I'll wait for you at the café.........
2 Don't go 2 police B4 U C me ....
3 When R U coming 2 C us? .... ?
4 go 2 museum + wait 4 me ....

Writing Tools

3 Imagine something was stolen. Write the start of a story in your notebook. Use the Story Creator.

Story Creator

A diamond ring/statue was stolen … | It said: *Go 2 café/Meet me @ …*
It was made/bought by … | The police asked/went …
It was lost in/taken from … | They found/saw …
The thief … | No one knows/can …
An email/A text message was sent …

4 Connect to Me

Have you ever lost something special to you? How did you feel?
Once, I lost ....
I felt .... and ....

Chapter 8 65

1 Read the sentences and write the numbers in the correct characters.

The children write the number of each sentence in the picture of the correct character. Elicit answers.

Answers

Antonio Polvani: 3, 5; *Giovanni's mother:* 1, 4; *Mr. de Santa:* 2, 7; *Giovanni Rocca:* 6, 8

2 Write the text messages in full.

The children write out the text messages in full. Elicit answers.

Answers

1 I'll wait for you at the café. **2** Don't go to the police before you see me. **3** When are you coming to see us? **4** Go to the museum and wait for me.

3 Imagine something was stolen. Write the start of a story in your notebook. Use the Story Creator.

Use the **Story Creator** prompts to elicit ideas. The children write the beginning of a story in their notebook about something that was stolen, then compare with a friend. Have children read out their texts for the class.

4 Connect to Me

Elicit examples of things that the children have lost that were special to them (e.g. a souvenir from a special vacation) and how it made them feel. The children write their own response, then compare with a friend. Elicit responses.

Cooler: Paper text messages

Give the children a small piece of paper. Have them write a message at the top (an invitation or a request). Then they put the paper back in a box and take another. They continue adding to the conversations by answering or adding a new question. After a few minutes, ask some children to read out their message conversations.

Competency Focus

Me: Critical Literacy

The children use critical literacy skills to reflect on the story and relate it to their own experiences.

Presentation Kit • Have the children work in pairs to discuss the events of the story in the order they happened. Use *Mask* to conceal the Reader. Elicit what happened in the story, uncovering part of the story after each contribution to see if the children are correct.

- Have children write their answers to AB Activity 2, before you use *Answer Key* to confirm.
- TIP With *Answer Key*, you can show the answers all at once or one by one to customize feedback.

Lesson 5

BOOK CLUB

1 Listen and read. What is the clue to the password?

Angelo: So, was the painting stolen by Giovanni Rocca?
Yasmin: Yes, it was.
Angelo: And who were the texts sent by?
Yasmin: They were sent by his grandson.
Angelo: It was a good story. When was it written?
Scarlett: I don't know but it can't be very old, because people didn't use to have smartphones.
Yasmin: I'll look it up. Oh, no! What's the password on this computer?
Scarlett: I can't remember. The password was changed last week.
Yasmin: Really? Why was it changed?
Angelo: Because Rufus thought it wasn't safe.
Yasmin: And what was it changed to?
Scarlett: I don't know, but look … there's a note here. It says *Password: the dog*.
Angelo: Oh, yes! Rufus changed the password to *Hamish*.

2 Write the questions with the same meanings.

1 Did Giovanni Rocca steal the painting?
Was the painting stolen by Giovanni Rocca?
2 Who sent the texts?
3 When did somebody write that story?
4 Why did somebody change the password?
5 What did somebody change it to?

3 Talk to a friend. Ask and answer the questions in Activity 2.

A: *Was the painting stolen by Giovanni Rocca?*
B: *Yes, it was stolen by him.*

Grammar Central

Past passive questions
Who were they written by?
Who .... it stolen by?
Was .... changed?
Were .... saved?

83

Grammar and Reading

Lesson objectives: ask and answer questions using the past passive
Key grammar: past passive questions
Secondary language: *change a password*
Materials: Class CD; Grammar Worksheet 8B [TRC printout] (optional)

Warmer: Missing vowels

Write on the board some of the key sentences from the Reader story, omitting the vowels. The children write the complete sentences. Then invite children to write in the missing vowels on the board.

1 2.21 Listen and read. What is the clue to the password?

- Play the CD. The children listen and read along. Elicit who changed the password. (*Rufus*)
- Play the CD again and have the children listen and read. Ask *What is the clue to the password?* (*the dog*)

Grammar Central

Past passive questions

Have the children complete the grammar examples. Elicit answers. Ask when we use past passive questions. (*to find out about a past action or who did the action*) The children write further examples in their notebook. See also the Grammar Reference sections in the Student Book (p. 102) and Activity Book (p. 103) for further explanation and practice.

Grammar Central Answers: were, was, it, they

AB Answers Activity 2: **1** What was taken? **2** When was it stolen? **3** Was the crime discovered by Lady Green? **4** Were the windows left open? **5** Who was seen near the library?

2 Write the questions with the same meanings.

- Draw the children's attention to the example question and elicit why it is correct. (*It asks about the same action, but asks what happened to the painting, rather than what Giovanni did.*)
- Have the children rewrite the questions using the past passive, then compare with a friend.
- Elicit answers.

Answers

1 Was the painting stolen by Giovanni Rocca? **2** Who were the texts sent by? **3** When was that story written? **4** Why was the password changed? **5** What was it changed to?

3 Talk to a friend. Ask and answer the questions in Activity 2.

- Have two children read out the example question and answer.
- Have the children take turns asking and answering the questions in Activity 2.
- Invite pairs to ask and answer for the class.

Optional activity: More passive questions

Elicit previous topics in Story Central 6, e.g. *Tutankhamun's tomb*, *the* Titanic, *yarn bombing*, *plastic*, etc. Elicit past passive questions about one of the topics, e.g. *Who was the elephant rescued by?* Have the children make similar questions to ask and answer with a friend.

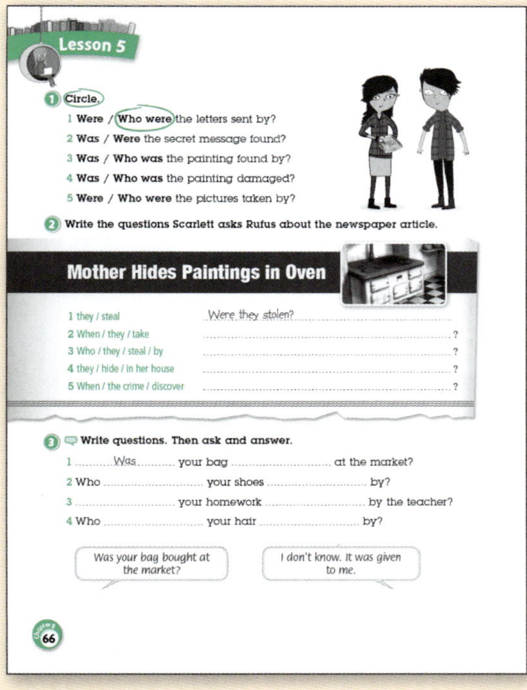
Lesson 5

1 Circle.

1 Were / Who were the letters sent by?
2 Was / Were the secret message found?
3 Was / Who was the painting found by?
4 Was / Who was the painting damaged?
5 Were / Who were the pictures taken by?

2 Write the questions Scarlett asks Rufus about the newspaper article.

Mother Hides Paintings in Oven

1 they / steal ......Were they stolen?......
2 When / they / take ....?
3 Who / they / steal / by ....?
4 they / hide / in her house ....?
5 When / the crime / discover ....?

3 Write questions. Then ask and answer.

1 ......Was...... your bag .... at the market?
2 Who .... your shoes .... by?
3 .... your homework .... by the teacher?
4 Who .... your hair .... by?

Was your bag bought at the market?
I don't know. It was given to me.

66

1 Circle.

The children complete the questions by circling the correct option from the two given each time. Elicit answers.

Answers

1 Who were **2** Was **3** Who was **4** Was **5** Who were

2 Write the questions Scarlett asks Rufus about the newspaper article.

The children write the questions using the prompts supplied. Elicit the questions.

Answers

1 Were they stolen? **2** When were they taken? **3** Who were they stolen by? **4** Were they hidden in her house? **5** When was the crime discovered?

3 Write questions. Then ask and answer.

The children write questions using the past passive and their own ideas. Elicit answers. Then they ask and answer in pairs. Have pairs perform for the class.

Answers

1 Was + children's own answers **2** were + children's own answers **3** Was + children's own answers **4** was + children's own answers

Cooler: Play "Tic-Tac-Toe"

Play the game with children asking or answering a past passive question to win a square (see Games Bank p. 222).

Competency Focus

Learn

The children demonstrate their understanding of the new language by reading the dialogue and completing the activity.

Presentation Kit • Have children use *Highlighter* to identify the past passive questions in SB Activity 1 (don't forget the one from Hamish in the picture!).

• Have children use *Pen* to write the answers to AB Activities 2 and 3. If the class disagrees, use *Eraser* to clear for another child to write. Confirm answers using *Answer Key*.

Teacher's Resource Center • For extra grammar practice, print out Grammar Worksheet 8B.

Student's Resource Center • The children can use Interactive Grammar 8B at home.

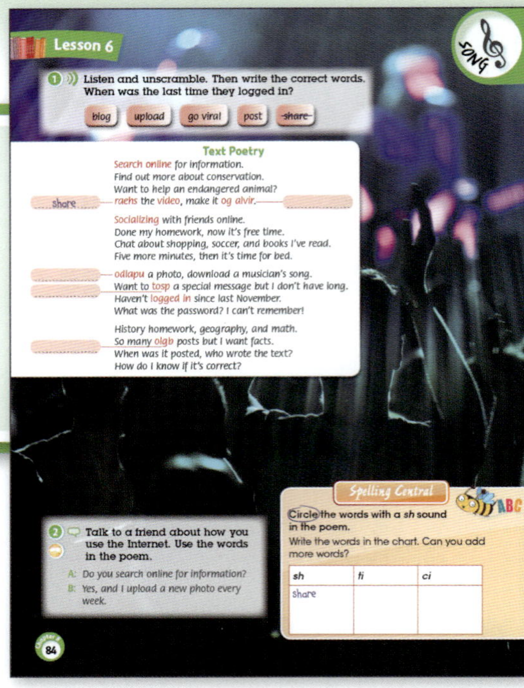

Vocabulary, Song, and Spelling

Lesson objectives: identify and use vocabulary to talk about socializing online; practice spelling words with a *sh* sound
Key vocabulary: *blog, logged in, go viral, post, search online, share, socializing, upload, video*
Secondary language: *chat, download, password*
Materials: Class CD

Warmer: Pre-teach vocabulary

Pre-teach vocabulary by saying the words in context, e.g. *I like to spend time talking to my friends—I like to socialize with them.* Then write the words on the board. Give definitions and ask children to circle the correct word on the board.

1 2.22 Listen and unscramble. Then write the correct words. When was the last time they logged in?

- Play the CD and have the children listen. Explain that *Want to help* in the third line sounds like *Wanna help* because this how it is pronounced in informal American English. Ask *When was the last time they logged in?* (*last November*)
- The children unscramble the words. Elicit answers.
- Play the CD again for the children to sing along.

Answers

share, go viral, Upload, post, blog

2 Talk to a friend about how you use the Internet. Use the words in the poem.

- Have two children read the example to the class. Then divide the class into pairs and have them talk about how they use the Internet.

Spelling Central

Words with *sh* sound

Write *vacation, shadow, special* on the board. Ask *What sound is in all the words?* (*sh*) Underline the letters *ti*, *sh*, and *ci* and point out that these combinations often have the sound *sh*. Have the children find words with *sh*, *ti*, *ci* pronounced *sh* on the page and complete the chart. They then add other words in each category. (e.g. *shark, she*; *action, information*; *sociable, delicious*)

Answers

sh: share, shopping
ti: information, conservation
ci: socializing, musician, special

Optional activity: Test each other

Write on the board: *Yesterday I took a great picture of my cat and I __________ it to my page.* Ask the children what the missing word is. (*uploaded*) Have the children write five more sentences with gaps in their notebook, then swap with a friend to complete.

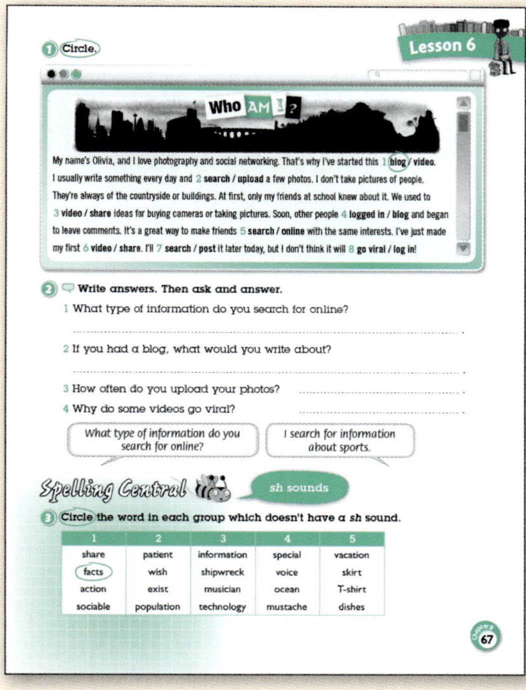
1 Circle.

Lesson 6

Who AM I?

My name's Olivia, and I love photography and social networking. That's why I've started this 1 **blog / video**. I usually write something every day and 2 **search / upload** a few photos. I don't take pictures of people. They're always of the countryside or buildings. At first, only my friends at school knew about it. We used to 3 **video / share** ideas for buying cameras or taking pictures. Soon, other people 4 **logged in / blog** and began to leave comments. It's a great way to make friends 5 **search / online** with the same interests. I've just made my first 6 **video / share**. I'll 7 **search / post** it later today, but I don't think it will 8 **go viral / log in**!

2 **Write answers. Then ask and answer.**

1 What type of information do you search for online?

2 If you had a blog, what would you write about?

3 How often do you upload your photos?

4 Why do some videos go viral?

What type of information do you search for online?

I search for information about sports.

Spelling Central — *sh* sounds

3 **Circle the word in each group which doesn't have a *sh* sound.**

1	2	3	4	5
share	patient	information	special	vacation
facts	wish	shipwreck	voice	skirt
action	exist	musician	ocean	T-shirt
sociable	population	technology	mustache	dishes

Chapter 8 67

1 Circle.

The children complete the text by circling the correct option from the two given each time. Elicit answers.

Answers

1 blog **2** upload **3** share **4** logged in **5** online **6** video **7** post **8** go viral

2 Write answers. Then ask and answer.

The children write their own answers to the questions. Then they ask and answer the questions in pairs. Invite pairs to ask and answer for the class.

Answers

Children's own answers.

3 Circle the word in each group which doesn't have a *sh* sound.

To practice the **Spelling Central** feature, the children read the words aloud and circle the one in each group that does not have a *sh* sound. Elicit answers.

Answers

1 facts **2** exist **3** technology **4** voice **5** skirt

Cooler: Spelling Bee

Have a spelling bee with the words from **Spelling Central**. Call out a word and have a child spell it out. Ask the class to decide if it is correct. Continue with other children and other words.

Competency Focus

Collaborate and Communicate

The children work together to share their ideas on the topic, incorporating the new vocabulary.

Presentation Kit • Use Vocabulary Tool 8B to pre-teach key vocabulary. Use *Slideshow* to introduce the words and *Find the Pairs* to practice.

• For SB Activity 1, choose Music Video 8 and encourage the children to sing along, using the graphic lyrics on screen. Pause *Video* for the children to continue singing. Monitor to check they are participating and identify any who are struggling.

Student's Resource Center • Remind the children they can access Music Video 8 at home to show their family and practice the song.

CLIL: Social sciences—Online safety

Lesson objective: find out about how to be safe when using cell phones, email, and the Internet
Materials: CLIL Graphic Organizer 8 [TRC printout] (optional)

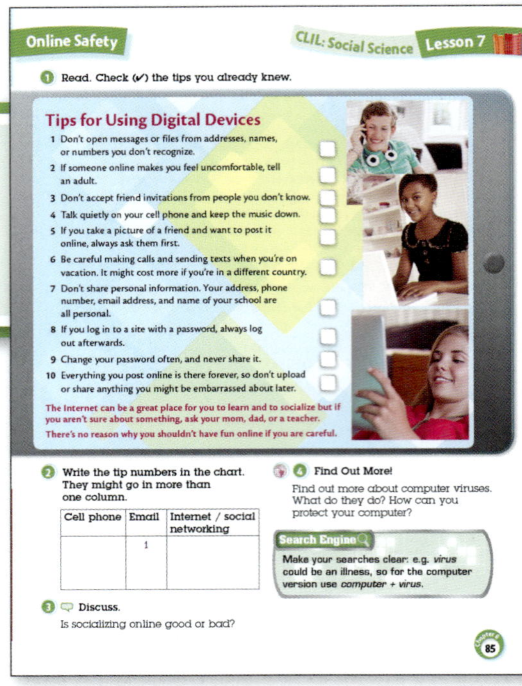
Online Safety

CLIL: Social Science Lesson 7

1 Read. Check (✔) the tips you already knew.

Tips for Using Digital Devices

1 Don't open messages or files from addresses, names, or numbers you don't recognize.
2 If someone online makes you feel uncomfortable, tell an adult.
3 Don't accept friend invitations from people you don't know.
4 Talk quietly on your cell phone and keep the music down.
5 If you take a picture of a friend and want to post it online, always ask them first.
6 Be careful making calls and sending texts when you're on vacation. It might cost more if you're in a different country.
7 Don't share personal information. Your address, phone number, email address, and name of your school are all personal.
8 If you log in to a site with a password, always log out afterwards.
9 Change your password often, and never share it.
10 Everything you post online is there forever, so don't upload or share anything you might be embarrassed about later.

The Internet can be a great place for you to learn and to socialize but if you aren't sure about something, ask your mom, dad, or a teacher.
There's no reason why you shouldn't have fun online if you are careful.

2 Write the tip numbers in the chart. They might go in more than one column.

Cell phone	Email	Internet / social networking
	1	

3 Discuss.
Is socializing online good or bad?

4 Find Out More!
Find out more about computer viruses. What do they do? How can you protect your computer?

Search Engine
Make your searches clear: e.g. *virus* could be an illness, so for the computer version use *computer + virus*.

Chapter 8 85

Warmer: Using the Internet

Write two headings on the board: *GOOD* and *BAD*. Have the children decide with a friend on three good and three bad aspects of the Internet. Ask for suggestions from the class.

1 Read. Check (✔) the tips you already knew.

- Have the children read quickly through the article and count how many of their ideas from the Warmer are included in the article. Ask *Which tips did you already know?* Elicit answers by a show of hands for each one.

2 Write the tip numbers in the chart. They might go in more than one column.

- Elicit from the children where the first two tips belong.
- Have the children write the numbers in the correct column. Point out that there might be more than one answer for each statement. Draw a similar chart on the board and invite children to come and write each number in the right place.
- Elicit answers.

Answers (suggested)

Cell phone: 4, 5, 6, 7, 9
Email: 1, 7
Internet / social networking: 2, 3, 5, 7, 8, 9, 10

3 Discuss.

- Have a child read out the discussion questions.
- Have the children talk about their ideas in small groups, then share ideas as a class.

4 Find Out More!

- The children research computer viruses and how you can protect your computer from them. The **Search Engine** feature gives support on where to look. The children will need to complete this research before doing the follow-up activity in the Activity Book. (It could be set as homework.)

Optional activity: Ranking advice

Have the children choose the five most important pieces of advice. They compare with a friend and try to cut down their two lists into one list of five. Finally, have each pair compare with another pair to try to arrive at a final decision on the top five pieces of advice. Elicit answers.

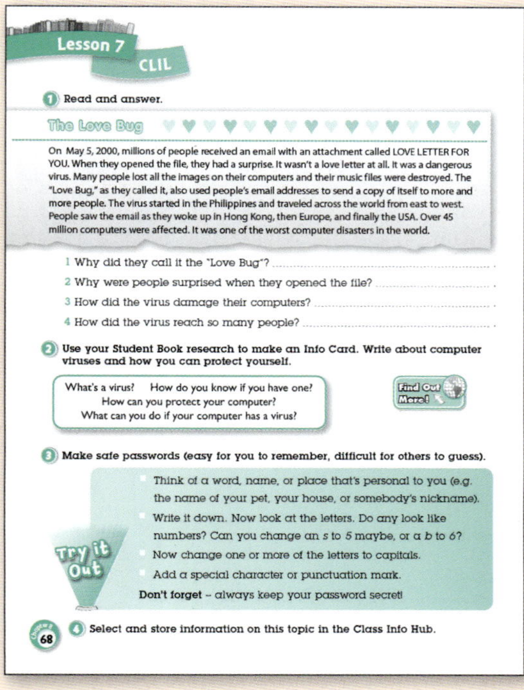
Lesson 7
CLIL

1 Read and answer.

The Love Bug

On May 5, 2000, millions of people received an email with an attachment called LOVE LETTER FOR YOU. When they opened the file, they had a surprise. It wasn't a love letter at all. It was a dangerous virus. Many people lost all the images on their computers and their music files were destroyed. The "Love Bug," as they called it, also used people's email addresses to send a copy of itself to more and more people. The virus started in the Philippines and traveled across the world from east to west. People saw the email as they woke up in Hong Kong, then Europe, and finally the USA. Over 45 million computers were affected. It was one of the worst computer disasters in the world.

1 Why did they call it the "Love Bug"? ....
2 Why were people surprised when they opened the file? ....
3 How did the virus damage their computers? ....
4 How did the virus reach so many people? ....

2 Use your Student Book research to make an Info Card. Write about computer viruses and how you can protect yourself.

What's a virus? How do you know if you have one? How can you protect your computer? What can you do if your computer has a virus?

Find Out More!

3 Make safe passwords (easy for you to remember, difficult for others to guess).

Try it Out

- Think of a word, name, or place that's personal to you (e.g. the name of your pet, your house, or somebody's nickname).
- Write it down. Now look at the letters. Do any look like numbers? Can you change an *s* to *5* maybe, or a *b* to *6*?
- Now change one or more of the letters to capitals.
- Add a special character or punctuation mark.

Don't forget – always keep your password secret!

4 Select and store information on this topic in the Class Info Hub.

68

1 Read and answer.

The children read the text and answer the questions. Elicit answers.

Answers

1 Because the attachment was called "Love letter for you". **2** Because the attachment was a virus. **3** It destroyed the images and music files on their computers. **4** It accessed people's email addresses and sent itself to more and more computers.

2 Use your Student Book research to make an Info Card. Write about computer viruses and how you can protect yourself.

Divide the class into groups. Have the children pool the information they learned from their research in the Student Book and the Activity Book. The children write about and illustrate their ideas individually. Have the groups present their Info Cards to the class.

3 Make safe passwords (easy for you to remember, difficult for others to guess).

The children follow the **Try It Out** instructions to make a safe password. They compare with a friend and give each other advice on how their passwords could be stronger. Then they make a second password, which they keep secret.

4 Select and store information on this topic in the Class Info Hub.

Have the children vote for the five most interesting Info Cards. Archive these in your Class Hub (see p. 41) in a folder called **Chapter 8 Computer Viruses**.

Cooler: A safe password?

Write on the board *Dumbl3dore / ImagineDragonZ / M3li$$aCr@zy / S@cr@mento*. Ask the children to look at these passwords and decide which is the safest and why, using the advice from Activity Book Activity 3). (*M3li$$aCr@zy—it uses capitals and small letters, numbers and symbols, and is 12 letters long.*)

Competency Focus

Act

The children carry out research to find out about computer viruses and online protection. This helps them expand their learning and relate it to their world, both inside and outside the classroom.

Presentation Kit • Ask true/false questions about the SB text. Elicit answers and have children use *Highlighter* to identify the phrase in the text which confirms the answer each time.

• Extend the Cooler activity by having children use *Notepad* to invent a password. The class votes by a show of hands whether each password is safe or not.

Teacher's Resource Center • Print out CLIL Graphic Organizer 8 for the children to use in collating their Find Out More! research.

Writing Project

Lesson objectives: review language from Chapter 8; write a text poem or a micro story and present it to the class
Materials: Writing Template 8 [TRC printout] (optional)

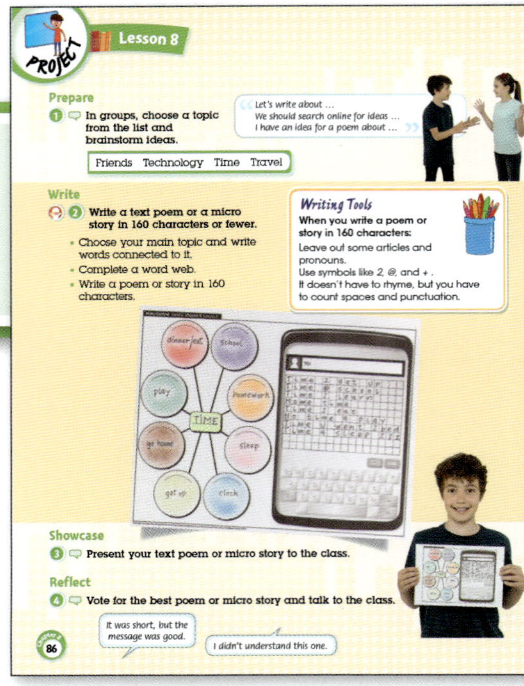
Lesson 8

PROJECT

Prepare

1 In groups, choose a topic from the list and brainstorm ideas.

Let's write about …
We should search online for ideas …
I have an idea for a poem about …

Friends Technology Time Travel

Write

2 Write a text poem or a micro story in 160 characters or fewer.

- Choose your main topic and write words connected to it.
- Complete a word web.
- Write a poem or story in 160 characters.

Writing Tools
When you write a poem or story in 160 characters:
Leave out some articles and pronouns.
Use symbols like 2, @, and + .
It doesn't have to rhyme, but you have to count spaces and punctuation.

Showcase

3 Present your text poem or micro story to the class.

Reflect

4 Vote for the best poem or micro story and talk to the class.

It was short, but the message was good.
I didn't understand this one.

86

Warmer: Play "Rhyme Ping-Pong"

Divide the class into two teams. Say a word. The teams take turns saying words that rhyme with it. The first team to repeat a word or take longer than five seconds to play is out and the other team wins a point. Start a new game of ping-pong with a different word.

Prepare

1 In groups, choose a topic from the list and brainstorm ideas.

- Tell the children the aim of today's lesson: to write a text poem or a micro story (maximum 160 characters). Have the children work in small groups to discuss which topic they should use and how they could make it into one of the pieces of writing.

Write

2 Write a text poem or a micro story in 160 characters or fewer.

- Have the children read the example as a model for their own writing.
- Read the **Writing Tools** box together. Elicit the words that have been left out or changed. (left out: *It's (time) … / There's (no time) …*; changed: *at/@, to/2, for/4, you/U*)
- The children make a poem or story in 160 characters, using abbreviations, symbols, numbers, etc., and omitting some pronouns and articles. Have them compare with a friend. Support as necessary.

Showcase

3 Present your text poem or micro story to the class.

- Choose children to read their text poem or micro story to the class. Ask the class to listen for where they think there are abbreviations or symbols.

Reflect

4 Vote for the best poem or micro story and talk to the class.

- Have children comment on which story was the best and why. Have a class vote to identify their favorite.

Optional activity: Read aloud

Have the children stick their poems or micro stories to the walls of the classroom and then walk around in pairs, reading the poems and stories aloud. This reinforces the sound–symbol connection and also any rhymes that were used.

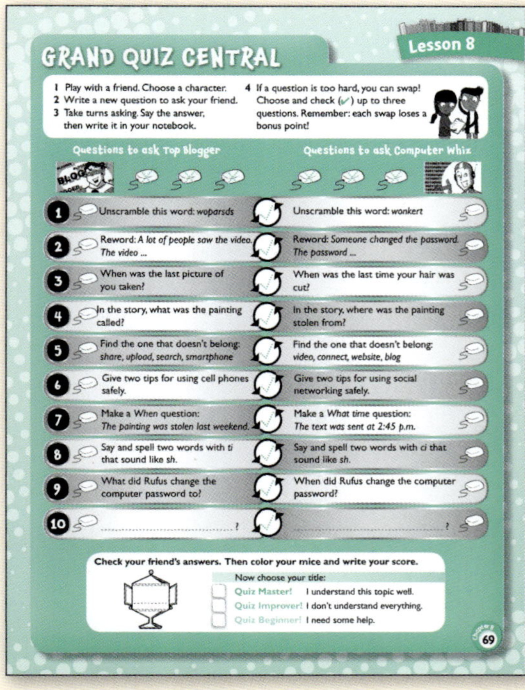

GRAND QUIZ CENTRAL

Lesson 8

1 Play with a friend. Choose a character.
2 Write a new question to ask your friend.
3 Take turns asking. Say the answer, then write it in your notebook.
4 If a question is too hard, you can swap! Choose and check (✓) up to three questions. Remember: each swap loses a bonus point!

Questions to ask Top Blogger	Questions to ask Computer Whiz
1 Unscramble this word: *woparsds*	Unscramble this word: *wonkert*
2 Reword: *A lot of people saw the video. The video ...*	Reword: *Someone changed the password. The password ...*
3 When was the last picture of you taken?	When was the last time your hair was cut?
4 In the story, what was the painting called?	In the story, where was the painting stolen from?
5 Find the one that doesn't belong: *share, upload, search, smartphone*	Find the one that doesn't belong: *video, connect, website, blog*
6 Give two tips for using cell phones safely.	Give two tips for using social networking safely.
7 Make a *When* question: *The painting was stolen last weekend.*	Make a *What time* question: *The text was sent at 2:45 p.m.*
8 Say and spell two words with *ti* that sound like *sh*.	Say and spell two words with *ci* that sound like *sh*.
9 What did Rufus change the computer password to?	When did Rufus change the computer password?
10 ....?	....?

Check your friend's answers. Then color your mice and write your score.

Now choose your title:
- Quiz Master! I understand this topic well.
- Quiz Improver! I don't understand everything.
- Quiz Beginner! I need some help.

Chapter 8 69

Grand Quiz Central

See p. 43 for details of how to take the quiz.

Answers

1 password / network **2** was seen by a lot of people. / was changed (by someone). **3** Children's own answers: It was taken … / It was cut … **4** *Mother and Child* / The Museum of Art (in Perugia) **5** smartphone / connect **6** Talk quietly on your cell phone., Be careful making calls and sending texts when you're on vacation., etc. / If someone online makes you feel uncomfortable, tell an adult., Don't share personal information., etc. **7** When was the painting stolen? / What time was the text sent? **8** *Any two of:* information, patient, audition, nationality / *Any two of:* social, delicious, sociable **9** Hamish / last week **10** Children's own answers.

Cooler: Play "The Chain Game"

Play the game starting with *Yesterday, I used my cell phone to* … (see Games Bank p. 222).

Competency Focus

Me

The children write a text poem or micro story. This helps develop their understanding of text language conventions.

Presentation Kit • Have children use *Highlighter* to identify in the model text poem examples of the poem features shown in the Writing Tools box.

• TIP Use *Notepad* to log the results of the class vote in SB Activity 4. Involve the children in tallying the results and writing the scores.

Teacher's Resource Center • Print out Writing Template 8 to use for the SB writing activity.

Student's Resource Center • Encourage the children to share Vocabulary Tools 6A–8B at home to reinforce vocabulary learning.

Language Review

Lesson objective: review language from Chapter 8
Materials: Class CD

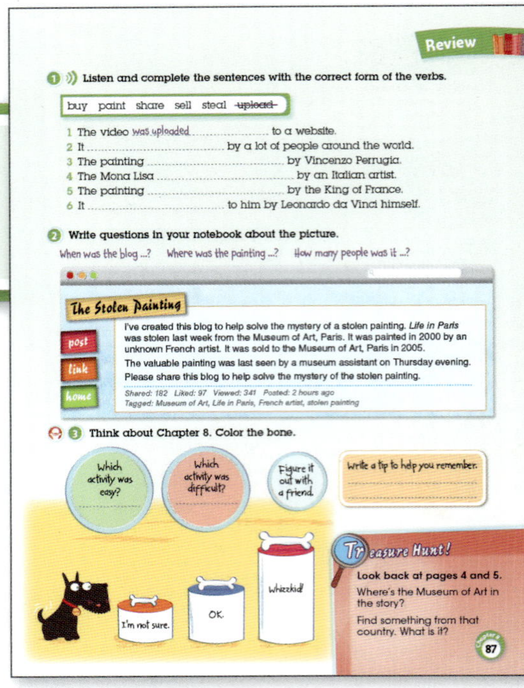

Review

1 Listen and complete the sentences with the correct form of the verbs.

buy paint share sell steal ~~upload~~

1 The video was uploaded .... to a website.
2 It .... by a lot of people around the world.
3 The painting .... by Vincenzo Perrugia.
4 The Mona Lisa .... by an Italian artist.
5 The painting .... by the King of France.
6 It .... to him by Leonardo da Vinci himself.

2 Write questions in your notebook about the picture.

When was the blog ...? Where was the painting ...? How many people was it ...?

The Stolen Painting

post
link
home

I've created this blog to help solve the mystery of a stolen painting. *Life in Paris* was stolen last week from the Museum of Art, Paris. It was painted in 2000 by an unknown French artist. It was sold to the Museum of Art, Paris in 2005.

The valuable painting was last seen by a museum assistant on Thursday evening.

Please share this blog to help solve the mystery of the stolen painting.

Shared: 182 Liked: 97 Viewed: 341 Posted: 2 hours ago
Tagged: Museum of Art, Life in Paris, French artist, stolen painting

3 Think about Chapter 8. Color the bone.

Which activity was easy?
Which activity was difficult?
Figure it out with a friend.
Write a tip to help you remember.

I'm not sure.
OK.
Whizzkid!

Treasure Hunt!

Look back at pages 4 and 5.
Where's the Museum of Art in the story?
Find something from that country. What is it?

87

Warmer: Play "I Spy"

Play the game with vocabulary from the chapter. Model the game, using *I spy with my little eye something beginning with "s."* to elicit *smartphone*. The children continue the game in pairs.

1 2.23 Listen and complete the sentences with the correct form of the verbs.

- Have the children look at the sentences and the words supplied.
- Play the CD. The children listen and complete the sentences using the past passive.
- Give the children one minute to compare with a friend and then play the CD again. The children listen to complete or confirm their answers.
- Elicit answers.

Audioscript

I logged in to a website today and watched a video online about the Mona Lisa. *I keyed in the words "famous stolen paintings" and this post appeared in the search results. The video was uploaded a few days ago and was watched and shared by a lot of people around the world. The* Mona Lisa *painting was taken from a museum in Paris in 1911. After it was stolen, the painting became really famous. It was found again two years later. The thief, Vincenzo Peruggia, thought the painting should be in Italy because it was painted by the Italian artist Leonardo da Vinci. But Peruggia didn't know that the picture was sold to the King of France by Leonardo himself. It was an interesting video, but I don't think it will go viral.*

Answers

1 was uploaded **2** was shared **3** was stolen
4 was painted **5** was bought **6** was sold

2 Write questions in your notebook about the picture.

- Elicit an example question using one of the prompts.
- The children write sentences in their notebook using the prompts and the information.
- Elicit answers.

Answers

Children's own answers.

3 Think about Chapter 8. Color the bone.

- Have the children look back at Chapter 8 and color the bone to evaluate their progress (self-evaluation).
- Discuss ideas for using examples, e.g. write words in sentences to help you remember them. The children choose and write a tip in their Student Book.

Treasure Hunt

Ask *Where's the Museum of Art in the story?* (*Perugia, Italy*) Have the children look at pp. 4–5 to find something from Italy. (*a bowl of pasta*)

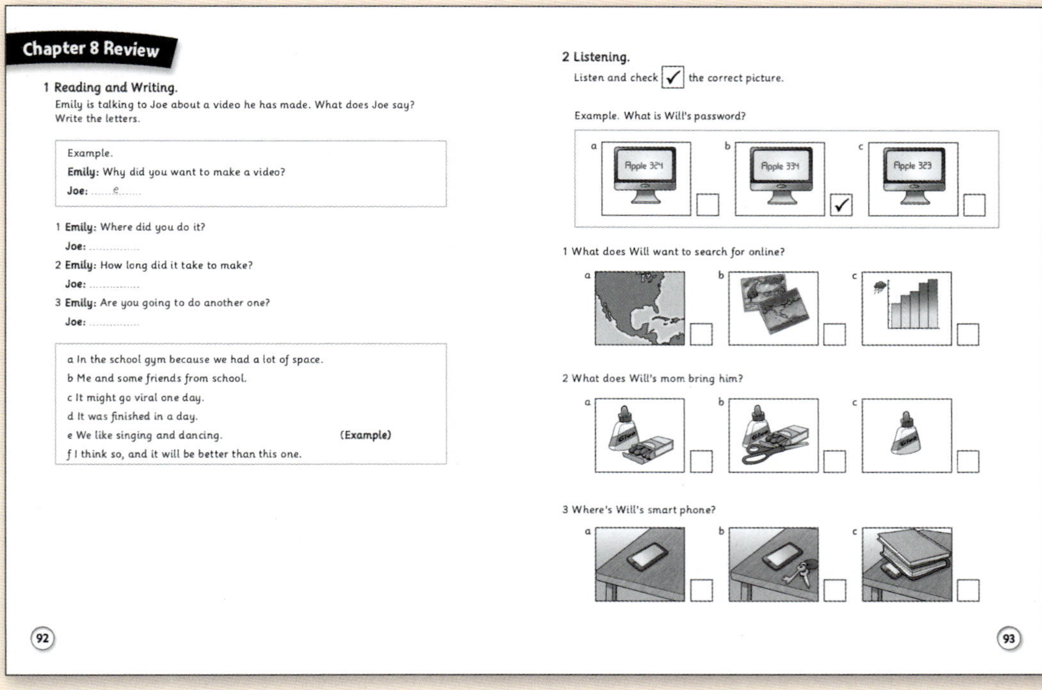

Chapter 8 Review

1 Reading and Writing.
Emily is talking to Joe about a video he has made. What does Joe say? Write the letters.

Example.
Emily: Why did you want to make a video?
Joe: ......e......

1 Emily: Where did you do it?
Joe: ....
2 Emily: How long did it take to make?
Joe: ....
3 Emily: Are you going to do another one?
Joe: ....

a In the school gym because we had a lot of space.
b Me and some friends from school.
c It might go viral one day.
d It was finished in a day.
e We like singing and dancing. (Example)
f I think so, and it will be better than this one.

2 Listening.
Listen and check ✓ the correct picture.

Example. What is Will's password?
a Apple 324 b Apple 334 ✓ c Apple 323

1 What does Will want to search for online?
a b c

2 What does Will's mom bring him?
a b c

3 Where's Will's smart phone?
a b c

92 93

1 Reading and Writing. Emily is talking to Joe about a video he has made. What does Joe say? Write the letters.

The children read the questions and write the letter for the appropriate response each time. Check answers.

Answers

1 a **2** d **3** f

2 2.38 **Listening. Listen and check (✓) the correct picture.**

The children read the questions. Play the CD twice. They listen and check the correct picture in each section. Check answers.

Answers (Audioscript on p. 224)

1 b **2** a **3** c

Competency Focus

Me: Self-evaluation

The children reflect on the chapter, express their personal opinions about their own progress, and look for ways to improve. This encourages them to evaluate and make decisions about what they need to revisit and how they can learn better.

Cooler: Make crazy sentences

Elicit passive sentences, e.g. *The Harry Potter books …* (*were written by J.K. Rowling*). *The Americas …* (*were discovered by Columbus*). *The island of Java …* (*was formed by a volcano*). *Atlantis …* (*was destroyed by Poseidon*). Help with verbs and write the sentences on the board. Then, have the children use the sentences to make crazy sentences, e.g. *The Harry Potter books were formed by a volcano!*

Presentation Kit • Use the drop-down Menu to access the AB Review pages.

Teacher's Resource Center • Print out Test Chapter 8 to use at the end of this lesson. The Test Generator also allows you to create customized tests.

• For the CEYLT (Cambridge YLE) exam preparation activities on the AB page, choose *Audio* to access the recordings.

Student's App • Encourage the children to play the games on their smartphone/tablet. Ask them to record their scores to compare in the next lesson.

Chapter 9

High Flyers

Overview

The children will:

- use critical thinking skills to identify business vocabulary.
- talk about someone's job using different tenses.
- read and understand a modern fairy tale about a successful entrepreneur.
- talk about preferences using *prefer ... to* / *would rather ... than.*
- describe and talk about the future and personal goals.
- find out about young entrepreneurs.
- write an autobiography.

Key Vocabulary

Entrepreneurs and business: apply, boss, career, company, entrepreneur, interview, product, set up, successful
Future goals: achieve, follow, free, goals, hopes, idea, millionaire, succeed

Key Grammar

Different tenses

- It takes four years. (simple present)
- I liked art. (simple past)
- I had always enjoyed art. (past perfect)
- The movies have been successful. (present perfect)
- I've been working here since then. (present perfect progressive)
- I'm going to stay here for a long time. (*going to* for future)
- The models are made of clay. (present passive)

prefer ... to, would rather ... than

- I prefer books to screens.
- I'd rather take a bath than take a shower.
- I'd rather read a book than watch a movie.

Reading Skills

Story: *A Fairy Tale Life*
Genre: modern fairy tale

Literacy Development

- use reading skills to understand and predict content
- relate story theme to personal experience
- use time phrases to order events chronologically

Functional Language

- Would you like a career in movies?
- No way! But I'd like a career in fashion.

Spelling

Words with *ei* or *ie*

CLIL: Social sciences—Young entrepreneurs

The children find out about successful young businesspeople.

Competency Focus

The children will:

use critical thinking skills to deduce the meaning of new vocabulary. (Lesson 1)	activate new vocabulary and apply new grammar knowledge. (Lesson 2)	work in pairs to act out a dialogue. (Lesson 3)	relate the story and story theme to their personal experience. (Lesson 4)	develop an understanding of successful new ideas by carrying out research. (Lesson 7)
predict the content of a story. (Lesson 3)	apply new grammar rules in a familiar context. (Lesson 5)	work in pairs to talk about future goals. (Lesson 6)	write their autobiography. (Lesson 8)	
			evaluate their own progress in the chapter. (Review)	

Digital Overview

Presentation Kit

Projectable Student Book, Activity Book, and Reader pages

- Vocabulary Tool 9A: Entrepreneurs and business
- Vocabulary Tool 9B: Future goals
- Oral Storytelling Video 9: *Achilles, the Great Greek Warrior*
- Music Video 9: *Life is a Journey*
- Interactive versions of selected SB and AB activities
- Integrated *Audio* and *Answer Key* for all activities

Teacher's Resource Center

Resources for planning, lesson delivery, and homework

- Class Planner Chapter 9
- Worksheets to print out (including notes and answers):
  - Grammar Worksheet 9A: Using different tenses
  - Grammar Worksheet 9B: *prefer … to / would rather … than*
  - Oral Storytelling Video Worksheet 9: *Achilles, the Great Greek Warrior*
  - CLIL Graphic Organizer 9
  - Writing Template 9
  - Test Chapter 9 and End-of-year Test
- Test Generator
- Speaking Assessment: CEYLT
- Literacy Handbook

Student's Resource Center

Resources for consolidation and practice at home

- Interactive Grammar 9A: Using different tenses
- Interactive Grammar 9B: *prefer … to / would rather … than*
- Vocabulary Tool 9A: Entrepreneurs and business
- Vocabulary Tool 9B: Future goals
- Oral Storytelling Video 9: *Achilles, the Great Greek Warrior*
- Music Video 9: *Life is a Journey*

Student's App

Vocabulary games: Entrepreneurs/business and future goals

Watch the Music Video

Chapter 9

High Flyers

Lesson 1

Chapter 9 High Flyers Lesson 1

1 Listen and complete the form for Sophie.

Are you a young entrepreneur?

Do you have a good brain for **business**? Could you **set up a successful company**?

We're looking for teenagers who are 16 or older for our next show.

To apply, click on the link below and complete the form.

Successful people will be invited to an interview.

APPLY

Name: Sophie
Age:
Company name:
Product:

2 Listen again and write the words next to the clues.

~~entrepreneur~~ apply interview successful career set up product boss company

1 A person with great ideas for a job. entrepreneur
2 To show that I'm interested in going on the show. ....
3 To do well. ....
4 They ask a lot of questions in an ....
5 To create a new company. ....
6 To work with other kids and start a ....
7 This is something that you can sell. ....
8 Ronald Stump could be your ....
9 A job for the future. ....

Chapter 9 88

Vocabulary

Lesson objectives: identify and use business vocabulary
Key vocabulary: *apply, boss, career, company, entrepreneur, interview, product, set up, successful*
Materials: Class CD

Warmer: Play "Board Race"

Divide the class into two teams. Give a board pen to one child in each team. Write *Professions* at the top of the board and divide the board into two. Give the children two minutes to write as many names of professions as possible, each word being written by a different team member. Only one child from each team is allowed at the board. The team with the most professions wins.

1 2.24 Listen and complete the form for Sophie.

- Have the children read the advertisement. Ask *Could you apply? Do you think you'd like to do this when you're older?*
- Play the CD. The children listen and complete the form. Elicit answers.

Audioscript

Ben: *Look at this website, Sophie. TV3 is looking for a young entrepreneur—a person with great ideas for jobs.*
Sophie: *Why?*
Ben: *For their new TV show* Young Entrepreneur*. You have to be 16 or older.*
Sophie: *I love that show! I'm 17, and I have a lot of ideas. How do I show that I'm interested in going on the show and that I want to be an entrepreneur?*
Ben: *You probably need to apply.*
Sophie: *OK, I'm going to apply!*
Ben: *Um, just fill in this form and email it to TV3. If you're successful and do well at the application you'll be invited to meet them.*
Sophie: *That's nice. I like meeting new people.*
Ben: *You will be asked to go to an interview.*
Sophie: *Yikes! I bet they ask a lot of questions in an interview. Then what will happen if I succeed?*
Ben: *Um … after a second interview you might get on the show. You will work with some other kids and start something new—set up a new company. You'll have to think of a name for the company you start and you'll have to think of a product—something that you can sell.*
Sophie: *I'll call my company The Cake Company and I'll sell cakes. That's my product. I'm good at baking!*
Ben: *Good idea! The person who has the best business brain wins and gets a job with the most successful business person in the world as your boss. Imagine! Ronald Stump could be your boss!*
Sophie: *Wow! It sounds fantastic.*
Ben: *Uh-huh. You might get a job for the future!*
Sophie: *Yeah! It could be the start of a great career!*

Answers

Name: Sophie *Age:* 17 *Company Name:* The Cake Company *Product:* cakes

2 2.24 Listen again and write the words next to the clues.

- Play the CD again. The children listen and write the word described in each clue, using the words supplied.
- Elicit answers.

Answers

1 entrepreneur **2** apply **3** successful **4** interview **5** set up **6** company **7** product **8** boss **9** career

Optional activity: Associated ideas

Write the key vocabulary (*entrepreneur, apply, interview, successful, career, set up, product, boss, company*) on the board. Elicit words associated with one of the items (e.g, verbs, nouns, company names). Then have the children brainstorm more words for all the items with a friend and write them in their notebooks.

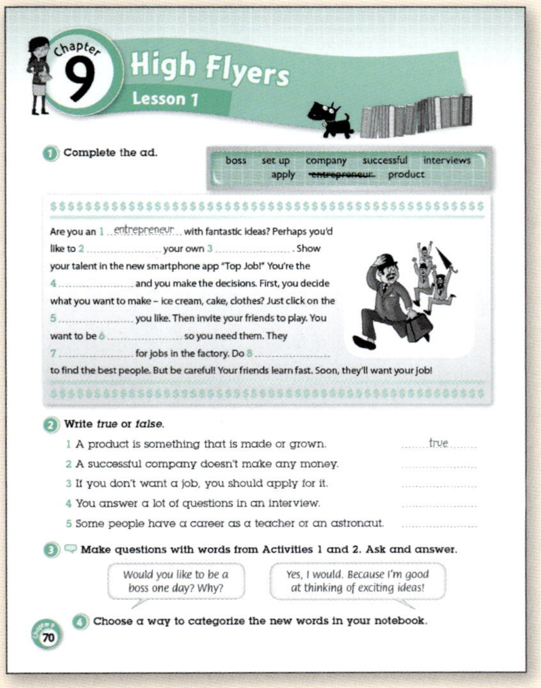

Chapter 9 High Flyers
Lesson 1

1 Complete the ad.

boss set up company successful interviews apply ~~entrepreneur~~ product

Are you an 1 ..entrepreneur.. with fantastic ideas? Perhaps you'd like to 2 .... your own 3 .... Show your talent in the new smartphone app "Top Job!" You're the 4 .... and you make the decisions. First, you decide what you want to make – ice cream, cake, clothes? Just click on the 5 .... you like. Then invite your friends to play. You want to be 6 .... so you need them. They 7 .... for jobs in the factory. Do 8 .... to find the best people. But be careful! Your friends learn fast. Soon, they'll want your job!

2 Write *true* or *false*.

1 A product is something that is made or grown. ......true......
2 A successful company doesn't make any money. ....
3 If you don't want a job, you should apply for it. ....
4 You answer a lot of questions in an interview. ....
5 Some people have a career as a teacher or an astronaut. ....

3 Make questions with words from Activities 1 and 2. Ask and answer.

4 Choose a way to categorize the new words in your notebook.

70

1 Complete the ad.

The children complete the ad using the words supplied. Elicit answers.

Answers

1 entrepreneur **2** set up **3** company **4** boss **5** product **6** successful **7** apply **8** interviews

2 Write *true* or *false*.

The children write true or false for each sentence. Elicit answers.

Answers

1 true **2** false **3** false **4** true **5** true

3 Make questions with words from Activities 1 and 2. Ask and answer.

Elicit a few questions using words from Activities 1 and 2. The children make questions to ask and answer in pairs. Have pairs ask and answer for the class.

4 Choose a way to categorize the new words in your notebook.

Brainstorm appropriate categories, e.g. *verbs/nouns/adjectives, alphabetical order, would like to be or do or have/wouldn't like to be or do or have*. The children choose the best categories for them and list the words in their notebook.

Answers

Children's own answers.

Cooler: Alliterative entrepreneurs

Have the children think of a company name and product for themselves or a friend. The company name will be their name, and the product has to start with the same letter as the name. Give an example for yourself (e.g. *Donna's Dresses, Ben's Beds*). Elicit names and ask *Which company do you think will be the most successful?*

Competency Focus

Think! Critical Thinking

The children use critical thinking skills to understand the new vocabulary by using visual clues and processing the written and spoken forms.

Presentation Kit • Use Vocabulary Tool 9A to pre-teach key vocabulary. Use *Slideshow* to introduce the words and *Distort* to review/test.

- Play "Kim's Game" with the new vocabulary. *Spotlight* the word bank in SB Activity 2. Have the class read the words aloud. Use *Stopwatch* to give the class one minute to memorize the words, then one minute to recall them. Repeat several times.
- TIP Use the arrow in the *Audio* pop-up window to see the audioscript for SB Activity 1.

Lesson 2

1 Read. Why do you think Scott enjoys his job?

I'm Scott and when I was young I liked art. I had always enjoyed drawing and painting, but at school I realized I liked working in 3D as well. So I went to college and studied sculpture. I applied for a job at the movie studio six years ago and I've been working here since then.

The models are made of clay. Then they're painted carefully. They're made of hundreds of parts. Each character has different heads, hands, and mouths, as well as different costumes. On set we move the model a tiny amount, take a picture, then move it again. It takes about four years to make a movie.

The movies have been very successful. It's a great company to work for. Jonathan, who set up the company, is a great boss and a great entrepreneur. He has very creative ideas about the business and he always believes it will work. It's such an interesting career. I'm going to stay here for a long time.

2 Write the questions in the correct tense.

1 Why / take so long to make a movie?
Why does it take so long to make a movie?
2 What / he like to do when he was young?
3 How long / Scott / work at the movie studio?
4 the movies / be / successful?
5 Why / Jonathan / great entrepreneur?
6 How long / Scott / stay at the company?

3 Talk to a friend. Ask and answer the questions in Activity 2.

A: *Why does it take so long to make a movie?*
B: *Because they have to move the model and take a lot of pictures.*

Grammar Central
Using different tenses
Find examples of these tenses in the text.
simple present ... has ...
simple past ...
past perfect ...
present perfect ...
present perfect progressive ...
going to for future ...
present passive ...

Chapter 9 89

Grammar

Lesson objective: talk about someone's job using a range of tenses
Key grammar: different tenses
Secondary language: *clay, a tiny amount, sculpture*
Materials: Grammar Worksheet 9A [TRC printout] (optional)

Warmer: Class mingle

Write on the board *How do you go to school? What had you done before you had breakfast? How long have you known me? How long have you been learning English?* Have the children mingle and ask and answer the questions.

1 Read. Why do you think Scott enjoys his job?

- Have the children read the article. Elicit which person is Scott. Ask *Why do you think Scott enjoys his job?*

Grammar Central

Using different tenses

Ask *Which tense do we use to talk about something … which is always true?* (*simple present*) … *at a specific time in the past?* (*simple past*) … *that happened earlier in the past?* (*past perfect*) … *with no specific time in the past?* (*present perfect*) … *which started in the past and is still happening now?* (*present perfect progressive*) … *which is a plan for the future?* (*going to*) … *which focuses on the object not the subject?* (*present passive*) See also the Grammar Reference sections in the Student Book (p. 103) and Activity Book (p. 104) for further explanation and practice.

Grammar Central Answers: (e.g.) has, liked, had enjoyed, have been, 've been working, 'm going to stay, are made

AB Answers Activity 1: 1 've started **2** are given **3** played **4** has been learning **5** 's **6** had won **7** 'm going to practice

2 Write the questions in the correct tense.

- Draw the children's attention to the completed answer and elicit why it is correct. (*It's something that is always true, so we use the present simple:* do/does + *subject* + *verb*) Remind the children of this word order for all tenses: auxiliary + subject + verb.
- Have the children do the activity individually and then compare with a friend.
- Elicit the questions.

Answers

1 Why does it take so long to make a movie? **2** What did he like to do when he was young? **3** How long has Scott been working at the movie studio? **4** Have the movies been successful? **5** Why is Jonathan a great entrepreneur? **6** How long is Scott going to stay at the company?

3 Talk to a friend. Ask and answer the questions in Activity 2.

- A pair read out the example question and answer.
- The children find the answers to the Activity 2 questions in pairs. Have pairs ask and answer for the class.

Optional activity: Your own company

Have the children imagine their own company. They can use their company names from the Cooler in Lesson 1. They write a short paragraph about working in their company using a number of tenses, then compare with a friend. Have children read their paragraphs to the class.

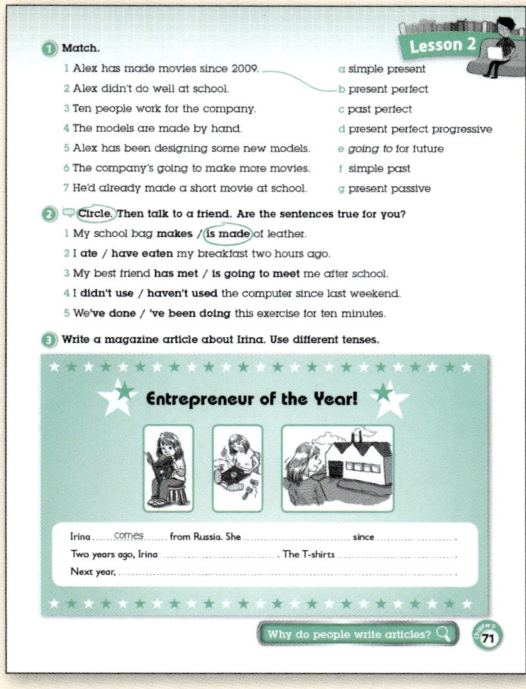

Lesson 2

1 Match.

1 Alex has made movies since 2009. — a simple present
2 Alex didn't do well at school. — b present perfect
3 Ten people work for the company. — c past perfect
4 The models are made by hand. — d present perfect progressive
5 Alex has been designing some new models. — e *going to* for future
6 The company's going to make more movies. — f simple past
7 He'd already made a short movie at school. — g present passive

2 Circle. Then talk to a friend. Are the sentences true for you?

1 My school bag **makes** / **is made** of leather.
2 I **ate** / **have eaten** my breakfast two hours ago.
3 My best friend **has met** / **is going to meet** me after school.
4 I **didn't use** / **haven't used** the computer since last weekend.
5 **We've done** / **'ve been doing** this exercise for ten minutes.

3 Write a magazine article about Irina. Use different tenses.

Entrepreneur of the Year!

Irina ......comes...... from Russia. She .... since ....
Two years ago, Irina .... The T-shirts ....
Next year, ...

Why do people write articles?

71

1 Match.

The children match the sentences to the correct tense. Elicit answers.

Answers

1 b **2** f **3** a **4** g **5** d **6** e **7** c

2 Circle. Then talk to a friend. Are the sentences true for you?

The children complete the sentences by circling the correct option from two each time. Elicit answers. They then discuss in pairs whether the sentences are true for them.

Answers

1 is made **2** ate **3** is going to meet **4** haven't used **5** 've been doing

3 Write a magazine article about Irina. Use different tenses.

The children use the picture prompts to write a magazine article about young entrepreneur Irina. Then, they compare with a friend. Ask *Why do people write articles?* (*They want to give information about a person/a thing/a place.*)

Answers

Children's own answers.

Cooler: Play "Disappearing Words"

Play the game with common verbs in different tenses, e.g. *going to see*, *had been*, *have been learning*, etc. (see Games Bank p. 222).

Competency Focus

Learn

The children integrate previously acquired vocabulary into new grammar and structure, and adapt the language to show an understanding of the topic.

Presentation Kit • To give feedback on AB Activity 2, have children use *Pen* to circle the correct answers. If the class disagrees, use *Eraser* to clear for another child to write. Confirm answers using *Answer Key*.

- TIP Use *Notepad* to note weaknesses in the children's vocabulary, grammar, or pronunciation so you can revisit in later lessons.

Teacher's Resource Center • For extra grammar practice, print out Grammar Worksheet 9A.

Student's Resource Center • The children can use Interactive Grammar 9A at home.

Reading: Story Extract

Lesson objectives: talk about future careers; use the title and pictures to predict story content; read the extract from the modern fairy tale *A Fairy Tale Life* (beginning)
Functional language: *Would you like a career in …? No way! But I'd like a career in …*
Secondary language: *rags to riches*
Materials: Class CD

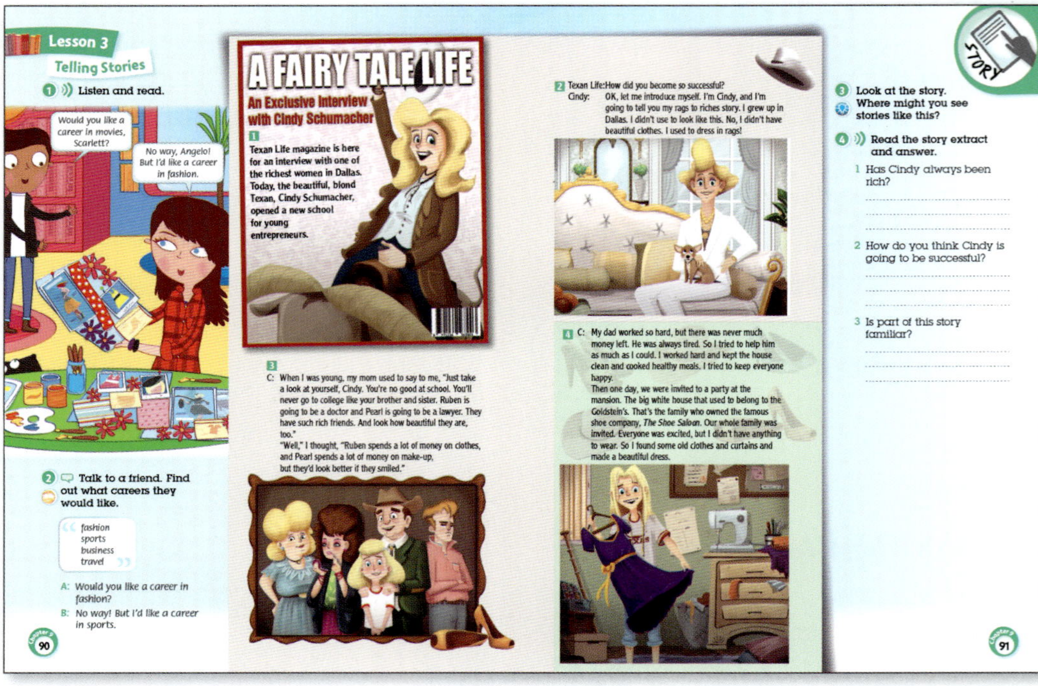

Lesson 3
Telling Stories
1 Listen and read.

2 Talk to a friend. Find out what careers they would like.

fashion
sports
business
travel

A: Would you like a career in fashion?
B: No way! But I'd like a career in sports.

90

A FAIRY TALE LIFE
An Exclusive Interview with Cindy Schumacher

1 Texan Life magazine is here for an interview with one of the richest women in Dallas. Today, the beautiful, blond Texan, Cindy Schumacher, opened a new school for young entrepreneurs.

2 Texan Life: How did you become so successful?
Cindy: OK, let me introduce myself. I'm Cindy, and I'm going to tell you my rags to riches story. I grew up in Dallas. I didn't use to look like this. No, I didn't have beautiful clothes. I used to dress in rags!

3 C: When I was young, my mom used to say to me, "Just take a look at yourself, Cindy. You're no good at school. You'll never go to college like your brother and sister. Ruben is going to be a doctor and Pearl is going to be a lawyer. They have such rich friends. And look how beautiful they are, too."
"Well," I thought, "Ruben spends a lot of money on clothes, and Pearl spends a lot of money on make-up, but they'd look better if they smiled."

4 C: My dad worked so hard, but there was never much money left. He was always tired. So I tried to help him as much as I could. I worked hard and kept the house clean and cooked healthy meals. I tried to keep everyone happy.
Then one day, we were invited to a party at the mansion. The big white house that used to belong to the Goldstein's. That's the family who owned the famous shoe company, *The Shoe Saloon*. Our whole family was invited. Everyone was excited, but I didn't have anything to wear. So I found some old clothes and curtains and made a beautiful dress.

STORY

3 Look at the story. Where might you see stories like this?

4 Read the story extract and answer.

1 Has Cindy always been rich?

2 How do you think Cindy is going to be successful?

3 Is part of this story familiar?

91

Warmer: Famous careers

Write famous people and professions on the board in two columns: *Bill Gates, J. K. Rowling, Barack Obama, Maria Sharapova, Oprah Winfrey, Brad Pitt; TV presenter, politician, author, actor, entrepreneur, sportsperson*. The children match the names and the professions. Elicit which careers they would most and least like to follow.

Functional language

1 2.25 Listen and read.

- Play the CD. The children listen and read along. Ask *Are Angelo and Scarlett talking about the present or the future?* (*future*) *Is Scarlett sure about not working in movies?* (*Yes—she says "No way!"*)
- Play the CD again, pausing for them to repeat.
- Divide the class into pairs to practice the dialogue.

2 Talk to a friend. Find out what careers they would like.

- Choose two children to read the example dialogue. Elicit other examples using the prompts supplied.
- The children practice in pairs. Have pairs perform a dialogue for the class.

Before reading

3 Look at the story. Where might you see stories like this?

- Have the children study the story title and pictures. Ask *Where might you see stories like this?* (*a magazine*)

4 2.26 Read the story extract and answer.

- Play the CD. The children listen and read along. Have them answer question 1. Elicit the answer.

- Play the CD again so they can write their ideas for questions 2 and 3. Encourage them to use reading skills to infer meaning and make predictions.
- Elicit answers, but do not confirm predictions: explain they will have to read the story to find out.

Answers

1 No. (She used to dress in rags.) **2** Children's own answers. / She's going to set up a business. **3** Children's own answers. / It's like the Cinderella fairy tale.

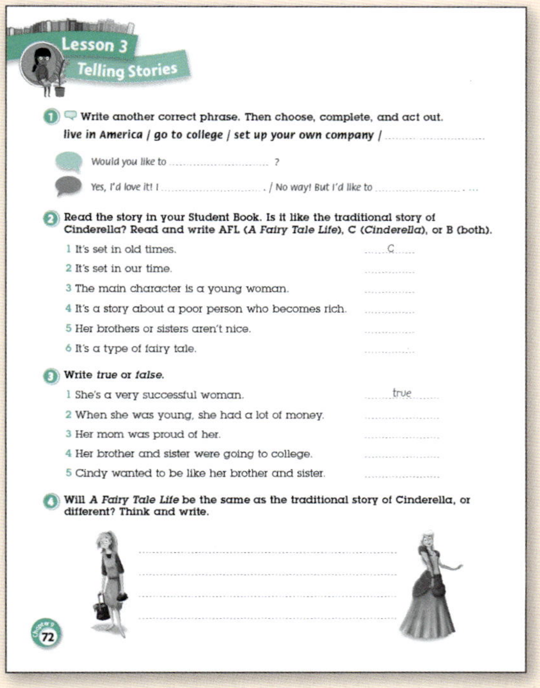

Lesson 3
Telling Stories

1 Write another correct phrase. Then choose, complete, and act out.

live in America / go to college / set up your own company / ....

Would you like to .... ?

Yes, I'd love it! I .... / No way! But I'd like to ....

2 Read the story in your Student Book. Is it like the traditional story of Cinderella? Read and write AFL (*A Fairy Tale Life*), C (*Cinderella*), or B (both).

1 It's set in old times. ......C......
2 It's set in our time. ....
3 The main character is a young woman. ....
4 It's a story about a poor person who becomes rich. ....
5 Her brothers or sisters aren't nice. ....
6 It's a type of fairy tale. ....

3 Write *true* or *false*.

1 She's a very successful woman. ......true......
2 When she was young, she had a lot of money. ....
3 Her mom was proud of her. ....
4 Her brother and sister were going to college. ....
5 Cindy wanted to be like her brother and sister. ....

4 Will *A Fairy Tale Life* be the same as the traditional story of Cinderella, or different? Think and write.

Chapter 9 72

1 Write another correct phrase. Then choose, complete, and act out.

Elicit other phrases that could follow *Would you like to … ?* The children choose a phrase and complete the dialogue. They then act it out in pairs. Encourage the children to use what they know to adapt and extend the dialogue. Have pairs act out their dialogue for the class.

2 Read the story in your Student Book. Is it like the traditional story of Cinderella? Read and write AFL (A Fairy Tale Life), C (Cinderella), or B (both).

The children read the Student Book story extract again, then decide whether each sentence describes *A Fairy Tale Life*, the traditional *Cinderella* story, or both of them, writing AFL, C, or B, as appropriate.

Answers

1 C **2** AFL **3** B **4** B **5** B **6** B

3 Write *true* or *false*.

The children write true or false for each sentence. Elicit answers.

Answers

1 true **2** false **3** false **4** true **5** false

4 Will *A Fairy Tale Life* be the same as the traditional story of Cinderella, or different? Think and write.

Elicit suggestions. The children write their own ideas, then compare with a friend. Elicit ideas.

Answers

Children's own answers.

Cooler: The last word

2.26

Play the story extract, stopping after key words in the text to elicit what the last word was.

Competency Focus

Collaborate and Communicate

The children work together to practice, perform, and adapt the new functional language learned.

Think

The children use critical thinking skills to identify the setting of the story by looking at the text and story artwork.

Presentation Kit • Display the AB page for Activity 4 review. Have a child use *Pen* to write a comparison between *A Fairy Tale Life* and *Cinderella*. Elicit if the class had the same ideas. Use *Eraser* to clear and repeat with children who have different ideas.

- TIP Give children the opportunity to be your assistant! Ask a child to be responsible for choosing the relevant buttons.
- TIP With *Answer Key*, you can show the answers all at once or one by one to customize feedback.

A FAIRY TALE LIFE

1 An Exclusive Interview with Cindy Schumacher

***Texan Life* magazine is here for an interview with one of the richest women in Dallas. Today, the beautiful, blond Texan Cindy Schumacher opened a new school for young entrepreneurs.**

2

Texan Life: How did you become so successful?

Cindy: OK, let me introduce myself. I'm Cindy, and I'm going to tell you my rags to riches story. I grew up in Dallas. I didn't use to look like this. No, I didn't have beautiful clothes. I used to dress in rags!

3

When I was young, my mom used to say to me, "Just take a look at yourself, Cindy. You're no good at school. You'll never go to college like your brother and sister. Ruben is going to be a doctor and Pearl is going to be a lawyer. They have such rich friends. And look how beautiful they are, too."

"Well," I thought, "Ruben spends a lot of money on clothes, and Pearl spends a lot of money on make-up, but they'd look better if they smiled."

4

My dad worked so hard, but there was never much money left. He was always tired. So I tried to help him as much as I could. I worked hard and kept the house clean and cooked healthy meals. I tried to keep everyone happy.

Then one day, we were invited to a party at the mansion. The big white house that used to belong to the Goldsteins. That's the family who owned the famous shoe company, *The Shoe Saloon*. Our whole family was invited. Everyone was excited, but I didn't have anything to wear. So I found some old clothes and curtains and made a beautiful dress.

5

Texan Life: I'm guessing this is a short story. Did you go to the ball and marry the heir to *The Shoe Saloon*?

Cindy: No! I decided to give the dress to my friend. It looked better on her and she loved it. And I loved creating it so much that I stayed home that evening and started working on another dress.

6

Texan Life: So what happened?

Cindy: Well, that evening I had an idea for a business. Soon after, I set up a company selling the clothes I had designed, and was successful very quickly. Some of my friends came to work for me, too. We had a lot of fun.

7

Texan Life: Wow! You're quite an entrepreneur. But you didn't go to the ball. I don't understand how you now own *The Shoe Saloon*?

Cindy: I never liked the way *The Shoe Saloon* was managed. The people who worked there weren't happy and they were badly paid. So, three years later, I bought the company! Now I'm the boss there. The staff is much happier and we buy leather from local farmers to make the best product in town—cowboy boots!

8

Texan Life: Oh! I thought I knew your story, but your career has surprised me.

Cindy: Well, I always say you can't judge a book by its cover. And you can't just wait for a prince to rescue you, can you? But I do think my life has been like a fairy tale.

Lesson objective: read and understand the modern fairy tale *A Fairy Tale Life* in the Reader
Materials: Class CD; Reader; Oral Storytelling Video Worksheet 9 [TRC printout] (optional)

Warmer: Is this Cindy?

Write on the board *rich, poor, lazy, creative, tired, nice, hardworking, helpful, successful, crazy*. Have the children discuss in pairs which adjectives could refer to Cindy from the story extract, giving reasons. Elicit ideas.

Story Summary

Cindy Schumacher, from a poor Texan background, has worked hard and is now a successful entrepreneur. She started by making her own clothes, then set up her own business, and now owns *The Shoe Saloon*.

Theme: the benefits of hard work

2.27 While reading

- Have the children look at the pictures in the Reader. Ask *What kind of business does Cindy have now?* (*a business that makes shoes*)
- Play the CD. The children listen and read along. Ask *Has Cindy been successful?* (*yes*) *How?* (*She set up a company and now owns The Shoe Saloon.*)
- Ask questions to check comprehension, e.g. *Was Cindy's family nice to her?* (*no*) *How talented was Cindy at making clothes?* (*very*) *What material do they use at The Shoe Saloon?* (*leather from local farmers*)
- Have the class read the story aloud with children taking turns playing the interviewer (see **Story Time**).

After reading: Reflect

Ask questions to give the children the opportunity to think about the issues raised by the story, e.g. *Did Cindy deserve her success? What do you think happened to her brother and sister?*

Optional activity: Different roles

Brainstorm the different roles Cindy played (*daughter, sister, friend, entrepreneur, boss*). Have the children discuss in pairs if they think Cindy was good in these roles or not, and why. Then ask *Were the other people in the story good at what they did?* Elicit answers.

Story Time

Interacting with the CD

In a story like this, which has a question/answer format, the children (as a class) can be the interviewer. The CD provides answers. This makes the children feel really involved with the story, as they seem to direct the interaction. Keep the CD low as they read out the questions, turning it up again for each answer.

Reading Strategy

Audio-assisted Reading

With audio-assisted reading, the children read the story aloud as they listen to you read or to the story audio. They can do this individually or as a group. It helps them improve their reading skills, pronunciation, and intonation.

For additional explanation and activities, see the Literacy Handbook on the Teacher's Resource Center.

Cooler: Tell the story

Re-tell Cindy's story around the class, with each child saying one word. Start with *Cindy* …

Presentation Kit • Use *Mask* to conceal the story. Uncover random points and elicit what the children can see. Elicit revised predictions of what will happen.

- Oral Storytelling Video 9 contains a different story on a related theme (*Achilles, the Great Greek Warrior*). Watch and discuss it together at the end of the lesson.

Teacher's Resource Center • Print out Oral Storytelling Video Worksheet 9 to help you get the most out of the video.

Student's Resource Center • The children can watch Oral Storytelling Video 9 at home.

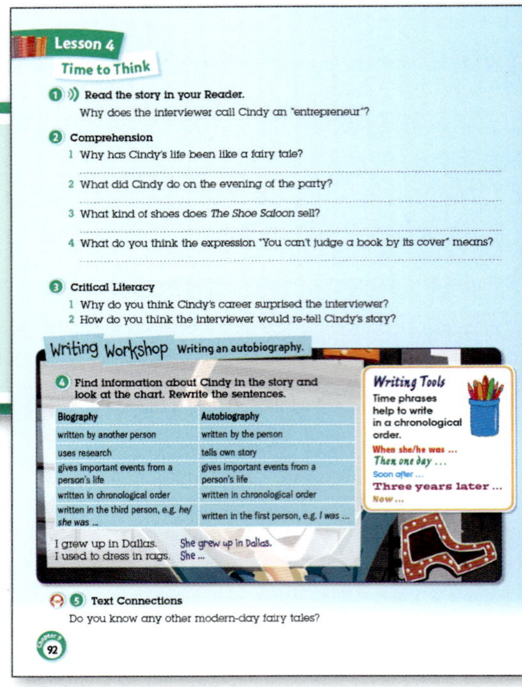
Lesson 4

Time to Think

1 Read the story in your Reader.

Why does the interviewer call Cindy an "entrepreneur"?

2 Comprehension

1 Why has Cindy's life been like a fairy tale?

2 What did Cindy do on the evening of the party?

3 What kind of shoes does *The Shoe Saloon* sell?

4 What do you think the expression "You can't judge a book by its cover" means?

3 Critical Literacy

1 Why do you think Cindy's career surprised the interviewer?

2 How do you think the interviewer would re-tell Cindy's story?

Writing Workshop Writing an autobiography.

4 Find information about Cindy in the story and look at the chart. Rewrite the sentences.

Biography	Autobiography
written by another person	written by the person
uses research	tells own story
gives important events from a person's life	gives important events from a person's life
written in chronological order	written in chronological order
written in the third person, e.g. *he/she was ...*	written in the first person, e.g. *I was ...*

I grew up in Dallas. She grew up in Dallas.

I used to dress in rags. She ...

Writing Tools

Time phrases help to write in a chronological order.

When she/he was ...

Then one day ...

Soon after ...

Three years later ...

Now ...

5 Text Connections

Do you know any other modern-day fairy tales?

Chapter 9 92

Reading Comprehension and Critical Literacy

Lesson objectives: understand and evaluate the story; relate story theme to personal experience; focus on the use of time phrases to make chronological order clear

Materials: Class CD; Reader; Oral Storytelling Video Worksheet 9 [TRC printout] (optional)

Note: Please ensure that your class has read the Reader story before you do this lesson.

Warmer: Change the title

Write on the board *A Modern Cinderella / Rags to Riches / A Texas Girl / How to Be Best / There's Money in Shoes!* The children discuss in pairs which are good alternative titles for the Reader story. Elicit ideas with reasons.

1 2.27 Read the story in your Reader.

- Have the children read the story. (Alternatively, play the CD and have them read along.)
- Elicit whether the children were correct in their predictions in Lesson 3 Activity 4. Ask *Why does the interviewer call Cindy an "entrepreneur?"* (*because she had an idea for a business / she set up a company selling the clothes she had designed*)

2 Comprehension

- The children write answers to the first three questions. Elicit answers.
- Discuss question 4. Elicit ideas with reasons.

Answers

1 Children's own answers. / Because it has a happy ending / it's like the Cinderella fairy tale. **2** She stayed home and started making a dress. / She had an idea for a business. **3** cowboy boots **4** Children's own answers. / You can't tell what someone is really like by how they look.

3 Critical Literacy

- Have the children discuss the answers to the questions with a friend.
- Elicit ideas and have a class discussion. Encourage children to give reasons for their opinions. Ask *What do you think was the interviewer's first impression of Cindy?* Analyzing the interviewer's behavior and attitudes in this way develops critical literacy.

Answers

Children's own answers.

Writing Workshop

Writing an autobiography

4 Find information about Cindy in the story and look at the chart. Rewrite the sentences.

Have a child read the example. Elicit ways to write in chronological order, using phrases from the **Writing Tools** box. The children find information about Cindy in the story. They rewrite sentences about her in their notebook using time phrases to structure their writing, then compare with a friend. Elicit responses.

Answers

Children's own answers.

5 Text Connections

- Ask *Do you know any other modern-day fairy tales?* Elicit ideas and discuss as a class.

Optional activity: Biography or autobiography?

Write on the board the following sentences:
It was the best day of my life.
Julia was nervous on her first day of school.
She was good at math, but she loved English.
An idea came to her for a new business.
Ask *Are these from a biography, autobiography, or both?* Have the children decide in pairs. Elicit answers.

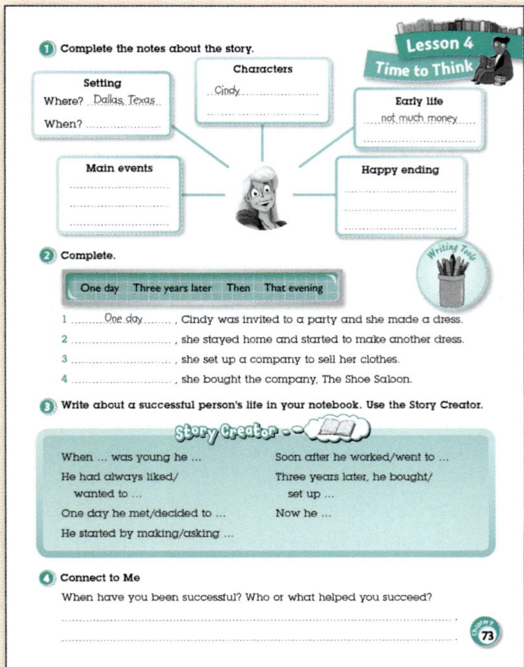

Lesson 4
Time to Think

1 Complete the notes about the story.

Setting
Where? Dallas, Texas
When? ....

Characters
Cindy

Early life
not much money

Main events

Happy ending

2 Complete.

Writing Tools

One day Three years later Then That evening

1 One day, Cindy was invited to a party and she made a dress.
2 ...., she stayed home and started to make another dress.
3 ...., she set up a company to sell her clothes.
4 ...., she bought the company, The Shoe Saloon.

3 Write about a successful person's life in your notebook. Use the Story Creator.

Story Creator

When ... was young he ...
He had always liked/wanted to ...
One day he met/decided to ...
He started by making/asking ...
Soon after he worked/went to ...
Three years later, he bought/set up ...
Now he ...

4 Connect to Me

When have you been successful? Who or what helped you succeed?

Chapter 9 73

1 Complete the notes about the story.

The children write notes about the different features of the story. Elicit responses.

Answers (suggested)

Setting: Where? Dallas, Texas When? modern day/now
Characters: Cindy, mom, dad, brother, sister, friends, the Goldsteins
Early life: They didn't have much money. Try to help dad.
Main events: Party—C started making clothes. Set up a company. Bought The Shoe Saloon.
Happy ending: C boss at The Shoe Saloon. Buy leather from local farmers. Everyone happy.

2 Complete.

The children complete the sentences using the words supplied. Elicit answers.

Answers

1 One day **2** That evening **3** Then **4** Three years later

3 Write about a successful person's life in your notebook. Use the Story Creator.

Use the **Story Creator** prompts to elicit ideas. The children write about a successful person's life in their notebook, then compare with a friend. Have children read out their texts for the class.

4 Connect to Me

Elicit examples of successes the children have had and who or what helped them to be successful, e.g. *I won a race at sports day. My teacher helped me practice.* The children write their own response, then compare with a friend. Elicit responses.

Cooler: Browse the biographies

Have the children leave the biographies they wrote in Activity Book Activity 3 on their desk and walk around the room, looking at their friends' biographies. Ask them to look for good use of time phrases and interesting details. Elicit which biographies are well written.

Competency Focus

Me: Critical Literacy

The children use critical literacy skills to reflect on the story and relate it to their own experiences.

Presentation Kit • Show the Reader story, picture by picture, without *Audio*. Minimize the screen. Use *Stopwatch* to give the children two minutes to recall the main events of the story in pairs. Elicit answers, showing the story pictures to confirm.

- Children use *Highlighter* to identify the time phrases in the Reader story.
- If you haven't already, show Oral Storytelling Video 9 (a different story on a related theme).

Teacher's Resource Center • If you haven't already, print out Oral Storytelling Video Worksheet 9.

Grammar and Reading

Lesson objective: talk about preferences
Key grammar: *prefer … to, would rather … than*
Secondary language: *look up facts, e-reader, My battery is dead.*
Materials: Class CD; Grammar Worksheet 9B [TRC printout] (optional)

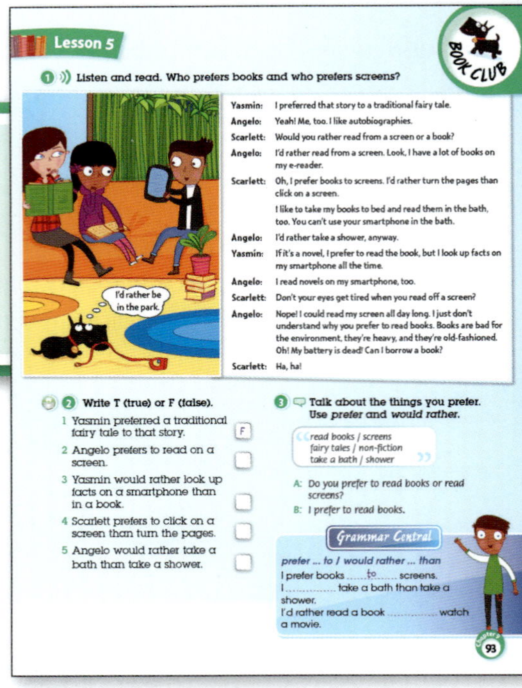
Lesson 5

BOOK CLUB

1 Listen and read. Who prefers books and who prefers screens?

Yasmin: I preferred that story to a traditional fairy tale.
Angelo: Yeah! Me, too. I like autobiographies.
Scarlett: Would you rather read from a screen or a book?
Angelo: I'd rather read from a screen. Look, I have a lot of books on my e-reader.
Scarlett: Oh, I prefer books to screens. I'd rather turn the pages than click on a screen.
I like to take my books to bed and read them in the bath, too. You can't use your smartphone in the bath.
Angelo: I'd rather take a shower, anyway.
Yasmin: If it's a novel, I prefer to read the book, but I look up facts on my smartphone all the time.
Angelo: I read novels on my smartphone, too.
Scarlett: Don't your eyes get tired when you read off a screen?
Angelo: Nope! I could read my screen all day long. I just don't understand why you prefer to read books. Books are bad for the environment, they're heavy, and they're old-fashioned. Oh! My battery is dead! Can I borrow a book?
Scarlett: Ha, ha!

2 Write T (true) or F (false).
1 Yasmin preferred a traditional fairy tale to that story. F
2 Angelo prefers to read on a screen.
3 Yasmin would rather look up facts on a smartphone than in a book.
4 Scarlett prefers to click on a screen than turn the pages.
5 Angelo would rather take a bath than take a shower.

3 Talk about the things you prefer. Use *prefer* and *would rather.*
read books / screens
fairy tales / non-fiction
take a bath / shower
A: *Do you prefer to read books or read screens?*
B: *I prefer to read books.*

Grammar Central
prefer … to / would rather … than
I prefer books ...to... screens.
I .... take a bath than take a shower.
I'd rather read a book .... watch a movie.

Chapter 9 93

Warmer: Categorize the words

Write the following words on the board in random order: *e-reader, novel, comic, autobiography, page, chapter, title, illustration, fairy tale, myth, mystery, play*. Have the children work in pairs to put the words into categories of their own choosing (e.g. *types of book/parts of a book/types of story*). Elicit answers.

1 2.28 Listen and read. Who prefers books and who prefers screens?

- Play the CD. The children listen and read along. Ask *Who prefers books and who prefers screens?* (*Scarlett prefers books. Angelo prefers screens. Yasmin prefers books for novels/fiction and screens for facts/non-fiction.*)
- Play the CD again and stop after key phrases (especially questions with *prefer* or *would rather*). Have the children repeat the phrases.

2 Write T (true) or F (false).

- Read out the first sentence and elicit why it is false. (*She says she preferred that story to a traditional fairy tale.*) The children write T (true) or F (false) for the other sentences. Elicit answers, including the correct version of the false sentences.

Answers

1 F **2** T **3** T **4** F **5** F

Grammar Central

prefer … to / would rather … than

Have the children complete the grammar examples. Elicit answers. Elicit how we say we like one thing more than another. (*prefer … to; would rather … than*) The children write further examples in their notebook. See also the Grammar Reference sections in the Student Book (p. 103) and Activity Book (p. 104) for further explanation and practice.

Grammar Central Answers: to, 'd/would rather, than

3 Talk about the things you prefer. Use *prefer* and *would rather.*

- Choose two children to read the example dialogue.
- Divide the class into pairs to practice the dialogue using the prompts supplied and their own ideas. Have pairs perform for the class.

Optional activity: The next activity

Write *pairs / groups / speaking / writing / sitting / standing* on the board. Ask *How would you like to do the next activity?* (but do not say what the activity is yet). Elicit preferences using *prefer … to* or *would rather … than*. Then have the children discuss their answers in pairs. Ask *Did you have the same ideas?*

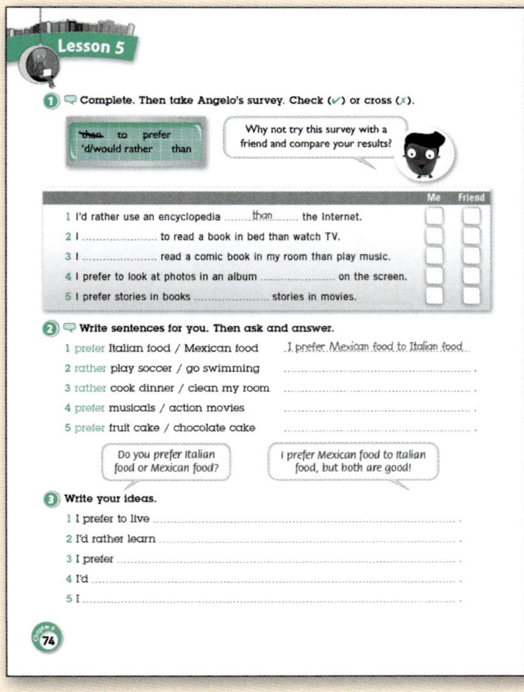

Lesson 5

1 Complete. Then take Angelo's survey. Check (✓) or cross (✗).

~~than~~ to prefer 'd/would rather than

Why not try this survey with a friend and compare your results?

	Me	Friend
1 I'd rather use an encyclopedia ....than.... the Internet.		
2 I .... to read a book in bed than watch TV.		
3 I .... read a comic book in my room than play music.		
4 I prefer to look at photos in an album .... on the screen.		
5 I prefer stories in books .... stories in movies.		

2 Write sentences for you. Then ask and answer.

1 prefer Italian food / Mexican food I prefer Mexican food to Italian food.
2 rather play soccer / go swimming ....
3 rather cook dinner / clean my room ....
4 prefer musicals / action movies ....
5 prefer fruit cake / chocolate cake ....

Do you prefer Italian food or Mexican food?

I prefer Mexican food to Italian food, but both are good!

3 Write your ideas.

1 I prefer to live ....
2 I'd rather learn ....
3 I prefer ....
4 I'd ....
5 I ....

Chapter 9 74

Competency Focus

Learn

The children demonstrate their understanding of the new language by reading the dialogue and completing the activity.

1 Complete. Then take Angelo's survey. Check (✓) or cross (✗).

The children complete the survey using the words supplied. Then they complete the survey in pairs, noting their own and their friend's answers. Elicit responses.

Answers

1 than **2** prefer **3** 'd/would rather **4** than **5** to

2 Write sentences for you. Then ask and answer.

The children write sentences about their own preferences using the prompts supplied. Then they ask and answer on preferences in pairs.

Answers

1 I prefer … to … **2** I'd rather … than … **3** I'd rather … than … **4** I prefer … to … **5** I prefer … to …

3 Write your ideas.

Elicit possible ways to complete the first sentence. The children write their own ideas. They then compare with a friend. Elicit ideas.

Answers

Children's own answers.

Cooler: Play "Change the Text"

Play the game with sentences from the survey in Activity Book Activity 1 (see Games Bank p. 222).

Presentation Kit • Use *Mask* to hide parts of sentences in SB Activity 1 text, e.g. *I prefer ~~books~~ to screens*. Elicit the missing word(s).

• Have groups of five discuss their ideas for AB Activity 3. Children use *Pen* to write responses, each child completing one sentence. Take a vote on which sentence the class agrees with most. Repeat with other groups.

Teacher's Resource Center • For extra grammar practice, print out Grammar Worksheet 9B.

Student's Resource Center • The children can use Interactive Grammar 9B at home.

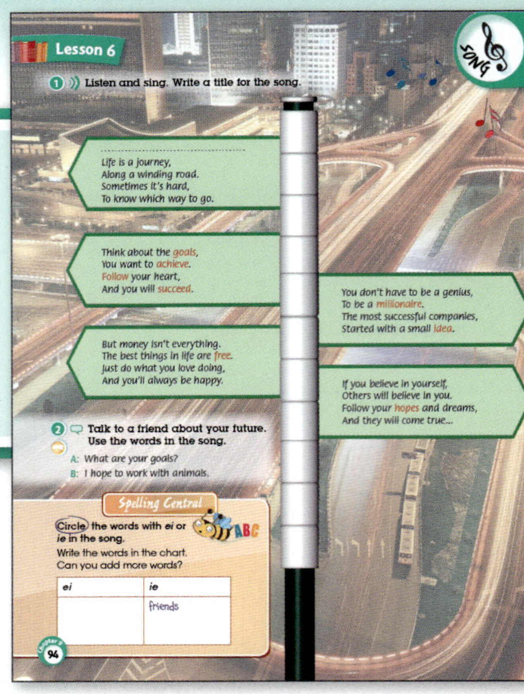

Vocabulary, Song, and Spelling

Lesson objectives: identify and use vocabulary connected to future goals; practice spelling words with *ei* or *ie*

Key vocabulary: *achieve, follow, free, goals, hopes, idea, millionaire, succeed*

Secondary language: *winding road, genius, believe in yourself*

Materials: Class CD; envelopes (optional)

Warmer: Pre-teach vocabulary

Pre-teach the vocabulary by giving definitions or sentences showing the words in context, e.g. *My goal is to remember ten new words a week.* Repeat the definitions/sentences, stopping before the key word to elicit it from the class.

1 2.29 Listen and sing. Write a title for the song.

- Play the CD. The children listen and think about a title. Ask *Is the song about now or the future?* (*the future*)
- Ask them to write a title and compare with a friend. Elicit ideas for titles.
- Play the CD again for the children to sing along.

Answer

Children's own answers.

2 Talk to a friend about your future. Use the words in the song.

- Have two children read out the example.
- Have a child ask you the question. Give your response.
- Divide the class into pairs. They take turns asking and answering the question.
- Ask all the children to tell the class about their future goals.

Spelling Central

Words with *ei* or *ie*

Have the children find words with *ei* and *ie* on the page and complete the chart. They then add other words in each category. (e.g. *eight, their, neighbor, weight, weird*; *field, thief, piece, fierce*) Elicit answers, asking children to write them on the board. Highlight how the letters are pronounced, pointing out the exceptions *weird* and *friends*.

Answers

ei: –

ie: friends, achieve, companies, believe

Optional activity: Write a letter to your future self

Have the children write a short letter to their future selves and encourage them to use vocabulary from the song. They can compare letters with a friend. They then seal it and address it to themselves with the words: *To open only in* ______ (*the year when they will be 25 years old*).

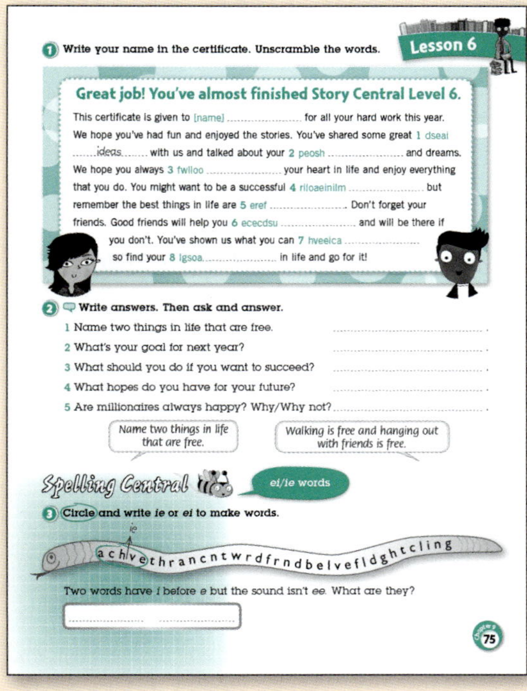

1 Write your name in the certificate. Unscramble the words. Lesson 6

Great job! You've almost finished Story Central Level 6.

This certificate is given to [name] .... for all your hard work this year. We hope you've had fun and enjoyed the stories. You've shared some great 1 dseai ....ideas.... with us and talked about your 2 peosh .... and dreams. We hope you always 3 fwlloo .... your heart in life and enjoy everything that you do. You might want to be a successful 4 rlloaeinilm .... but remember the best things in life are 5 eref .... Don't forget your friends. Good friends will help you 6 ececdsu .... and will be there if you don't. You've shown us what you can 7 hveeica .... so find your 8 igsoa.................. in life and go for it!

2 Write answers. Then ask and answer.

1 Name two things in life that are free. ....
2 What's your goal for next year? ....
3 What should you do if you want to succeed? ....
4 What hopes do you have for your future? ....
5 Are millionaires always happy? Why/Why not? ....

Spelling Central ei/ie words

3 Circle and write ie or ei to make words.

Two words have i before e but the sound isn't ee. What are they?

....

75

1 Write your name in the certificate. Unscramble the words.

The children write their name and complete the certificate by writing the words correctly. Elicit answers.

Answers

1 ideas **2** hopes **3** follow **4** millionaire **5** free **6** succeed **7** achieve **8** goals

2 Write answers. Then ask and answer.

The children write answers for themselves. Then they ask and answer in pairs.

Answers

Children's own answers.

3 Circle and write *ie* or *ei* to make words.

To practice the **Spelling Central** feature, the children identify the different words in the wordsnake, adding *ie* or *ei* as appropriate to complete the word each time. Then, they identify which two of the words have *ie* which is not pronounced *ee*. Elicit answers.

Answers

achieve, their, ancient, weird, friend, believe, field, eight, ceiling

Not pronounced ee: ancient, friend

Cooler: *ie* or *ei*?

Have the children draw a big *IE* on one piece of paper and a big *EI* on another. Call out words from **Spelling Central**. The children hold up the *IE* or *EI* piece of paper as appropriate, depending on the spelling of the word.

Competency Focus

Collaborate and Communicate

The children work together to share their ideas on the topic, incorporating the new vocabulary.

Presentation Kit • Use Vocabulary Tool 9B to pre-teach key vocabulary. Use *Slideshow* to introduce the words and *Picture Dictionary* to review/test.

• For SB Activity 1, choose Music Video 9 and encourage the children to sing along, using the graphic lyrics on screen. Pause *Video* for the children to continue singing. Monitor to check the children are participating and identify any who are struggling.

Student's Resource Center • Remind the children they can access Music Video 9 at home to practice the song.

CLIL: Social sciences—Young entrepreneurs

Lesson objective: find out about successful young businesspeople
Materials: CLIL Graphic Organizer 9 [TRC printout] (optional)

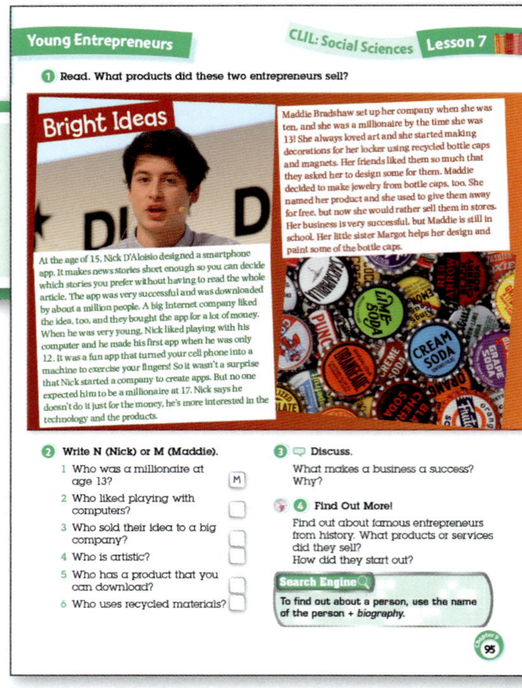

Young Entrepreneurs CLIL: Social Sciences Lesson 7

1 Read. What products did these two entrepreneurs sell?

Bright Ideas

At the age of 15, Nick D'Aloisio designed a smartphone app. It makes news stories short enough so you can decide which stories you prefer without having to read the whole article. The app was very successful and was downloaded by about a million people. A big Internet company liked the idea, too, and they bought the app for a lot of money. When he was very young, Nick liked playing with his computer and he made his first app when he was only 12. It was a fun app that turned your cell phone into a machine to exercise your fingers! So it wasn't a surprise that Nick started a company to create apps. But no one expected him to be a millionaire at 17. Nick says he doesn't do it just for the money, he's more interested in the technology and the products.

Maddie Bradshaw set up her company when she was ten, and she was a millionaire by the time she was 13! She always loved art and she started making decorations for her locker using recycled bottle caps and magnets. Her friends liked them so much that they asked her to design some for them. Maddie decided to make jewelry from bottle caps, too. She named her product and she used to give them away for free, but now she would rather sell them in stores. Her business is very successful, but Maddie is still in school. Her little sister Margot helps her design and paint some of the bottle caps.

2 Write N (Nick) or M (Maddie).

1 Who was a millionaire at age 13? M
2 Who liked playing with computers?
3 Who sold their idea to a big company?
4 Who is artistic?
5 Who has a product that you can download?
6 Who uses recycled materials?

3 Discuss.

What makes a business a success? Why?

4 Find Out More!

Find out about famous entrepreneurs from history. What products or services did they sell?
How did they start out?

Search Engine
To find out about a person, use the name of the person + *biography*.

Chapter 9 95

Warmer: Matching

Write two column headings INVENTIONS and DATES on the board. Write the inventions in the left-hand column in the order shown here and the dates in the right-hand column in random order (shown with the inventions here for reference only): *airplane (1903), YouTube (2005), smartphone (1993), World Wide Web (1990), DVD (1995), games console (1972), TV (1926).* Have the children guess the date for each invention. Connect the correct ones until all inventions and dates are matched.

1 Read. What products did these two entrepreneurs sell?

- Have the children read the text quickly and find the answer to the question.
- Ask *What products did these two entrepreneurs sell? (Nick D'Aloisio sold smartphone apps. Maddie Bradshaw sold decorations and jewelry made from bottle caps.)*

2 Write N (Nick) or M (Maddie).

- The children read the questions and decide who is described in each one, writing N (Nick) or M (Maddie) as appropriate.
- Elicit answers.

Answers

1 M **2** N **3** N **4** M **5** N **6** M

3 Discuss.

- Have a child read out the discussion question.
- Have the children talk about their ideas in small groups, then share ideas as a class.

4 Find Out More!

- The children research famous entrepreneurs from history. The **Search Engine** feature gives support on where to look. The children will need to complete this research before doing the follow-up activity in the Activity Book. (It could be set as homework.)

Optional activity: Design an app

Ask *What kind of apps do you use most?* Elicit responses. Then have the children work in pairs to think of a new app. Give an example yourself, e.g. *I invented an app which you can use to take a picture of the dishes in your kitchen and it will tell you how long it will take to wash them.* Elicit ideas and vote for the best app.

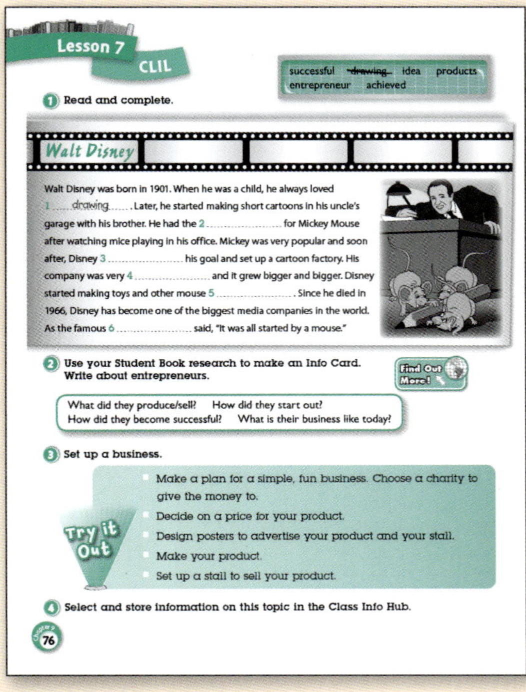
Lesson 7 CLIL

successful ~~drawing~~ idea products entrepreneur achieved

1 Read and complete.

Walt Disney

Walt Disney was born in 1901. When he was a child, he always loved 1 ......drawing...... . Later, he started making short cartoons in his uncle's garage with his brother. He had the 2 .... for Mickey Mouse after watching mice playing in his office. Mickey was very popular and soon after, Disney 3 .... his goal and set up a cartoon factory. His company was very 4 .... and it grew bigger and bigger. Disney started making toys and other mouse 5 .... Since he died in 1966, Disney has become one of the biggest media companies in the world. As the famous 6 .... said, "It was all started by a mouse."

2 Use your Student Book research to make an Info Card. Write about entrepreneurs.

Find Out More!

What did they produce/sell? How did they start out?
How did they become successful? What is their business like today?

3 Set up a business.

Try it Out

- Make a plan for a simple, fun business. Choose a charity to give the money to.
- Decide on a price for your product.
- Design posters to advertise your product and your stall.
- Make your product.
- Set up a stall to sell your product.

4 Select and store information on this topic in the Class Info Hub.

Chapter 9 76

1 Read and complete.

The children read and complete the text using the words supplied. Elicit answers.

Answers

1 drawing **2** idea **3** achieved **4** successful **5** products **6** entrepreneur

2 Use your Student Book research to make an Info Card. Write about entrepreneurs.

Divide the class into groups. Have the children pool the information they learned from their research in the Student Book and the Activity Book. The children write about and illustrate their ideas individually. Have the groups present their Info Cards to the class.

3 Set up a business.

In their groups, the children follow the **Try It Out** instructions to set up a business. This could be done as a class project or as part of a bigger school initiative.

4 Select and store information on this topic in the Class Info Hub.

Have the children vote for the five most interesting Info Cards. Archive these in your Class Hub (see p. 41) in a folder called **Chapter 9 Entrepreneurs**.

Cooler: Play "Sentence Builders"

Play the game with text from the lesson (see Games Bank p. 222).

Competency Focus

Act

The children carry out research to find out about famous entrepreneurs and their products or ideas. This helps them expand their learning and relate it to their world, both inside and outside the classroom.

Presentation Kit • TIP When using the board for "heads-up" teaching, give the children as much opportunity as possible to participate. Make sure you ask plenty of questions to give them the chance to engage with the text.

• TIP You can position the Navigation Pane and Tool Bar on the left or right of the screen. Choose *Swap sides* to change.

Teacher's Resource Center • Print out CLIL Graphic Organizer 9 for the children to use in collating their Find Out More! research.

Writing Project

Lesson objectives: review language from Chapter 9; write an autobiography and present it to the class

Materials: Writing Template 9 [TRC printout] (optional)

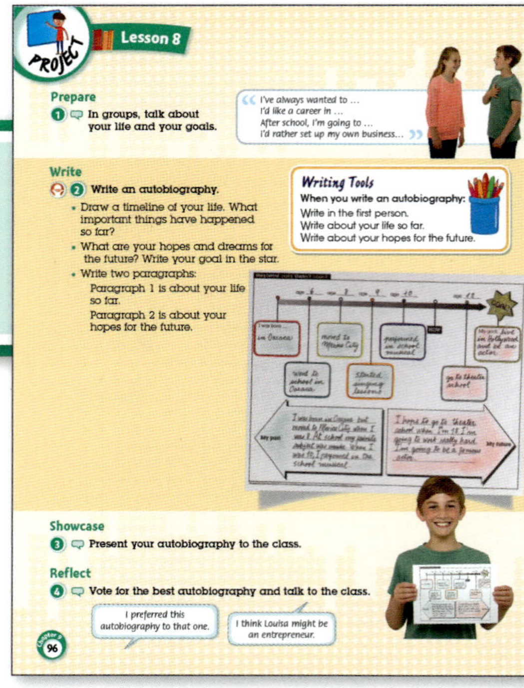

PROJECT Lesson 8

Prepare

1 In groups, talk about your life and your goals.

I've always wanted to …
I'd like a career in …
After school, I'm going to …
I'd rather set up my own business…

Write

2 Write an autobiography.

- Draw a timeline of your life. What important things have happened so far?
- What are your hopes and dreams for the future? Write your goal in the star.
- Write two paragraphs:
  Paragraph 1 is about your life so far.
  Paragraph 2 is about your hopes for the future.

Writing Tools
When you write an autobiography:
Write in the first person.
Write about your life so far.
Write about your hopes for the future.

Showcase

3 Present your autobiography to the class.

Reflect

4 Vote for the best autobiography and talk to the class.

I preferred this autobiography to that one.
I think Louisa might be an entrepreneur.

Chapter 9 96

Warmer: Teacher's timeline

Draw a timeline on the board with dates that are important in your life. Below this, write events in random order, e.g. *learned to drive, started school, became a teacher*, etc. The children discuss in pairs and make guesses about when you did these things. Elicit ideas. Match events to dates when the children guess correctly.

Prepare

1 In groups, talk about your life and your goals.

- Elicit possible ways to finish the example sentence openings.
- Have the children talk to friends in small groups. Remind the children their goals can be things they enjoy doing which they want to do more of.
- Elicit ideas and sentences.

Write

2 Write an autobiography.

- Read the **Writing Tools** box together. Elicit examples of the information to include in an autobiography.
- The children prepare an outline using a timeline. They write about their life so far, then compare with a friend. Give support as necessary.

Showcase

3 Present your autobiography to the class.

- Choose children to read their autobiography to the class. Ask the class to listen and say which are the most similar.

Reflect

4 Vote for the best autobiography and talk to the class.

- Have the children comment on which autobiography was the best and why. Have a class vote to identify their favorite.

Optional activity: Invent an autobiography

Have the children work in pairs to write an autobiography as though they were an imaginary famous person. Have the children leave the autobiographies on their desks and read others' work around the class. Elicit any similarities.

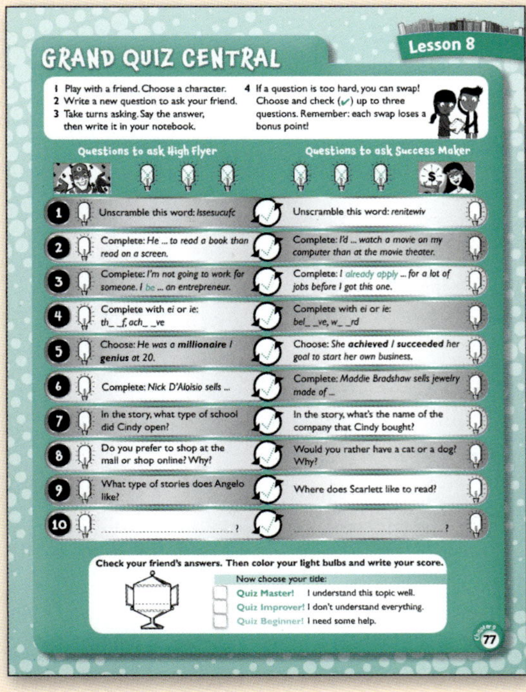
Lesson 8

GRAND QUIZ CENTRAL

1 Play with a friend. Choose a character.
2 Write a new question to ask your friend.
3 Take turns asking. Say the answer, then write it in your notebook.
4 If a question is too hard, you can swap! Choose and check (✓) up to three questions. Remember: each swap loses a bonus point!

	Questions to ask High Flyer	Questions to ask Success Maker
1	Unscramble this word: *lssesucufc*	Unscramble this word: *renitewiv*
2	Complete: *He ... to read a book than read on a screen.*	Complete: *I'd ... watch a movie on my computer than at the movie theater.*
3	Complete: *I'm not going to work for someone. I be ... an entrepreneur.*	Complete: *I already apply ... for a lot of jobs before I got this one.*
4	Complete with *ei* or *ie*: *th_ _f, ach_ _ve*	Complete with *ei* or *ie*: *bel_ _ve, w_ _rd*
5	Choose: *He was a* ***millionaire / genius*** *at 20.*	Choose: *She* ***achieved / succeeded*** *her goal to start her own business.*
6	Complete: *Nick D'Aloisio sells ...*	Complete: *Maddie Bradshaw sells jewelry made of ...*
7	In the story, what type of school did Cindy open?	In the story, what's the name of the company that Cindy bought?
8	Do you prefer to shop at the mall or shop online? Why?	Would you rather have a cat or a dog? Why?
9	What type of stories does Angelo like?	Where does Scarlett like to read?
10	..........................?	..........................?

Check your friend's answers. Then color your light bulbs and write your score.

Now choose your title:
- Quiz Master! I understand this topic well.
- Quiz Improver! I don't understand everything.
- Quiz Beginner! I need some help.

Chapter 9 77

Grand Quiz Central

See p. 43 for details of how to take the quiz.

Answers

1 successful / interview **2** prefers / rather **3** 'm going to be / had already applied **4** thief, achieve / believe, weird **5** millionaire / achieved **6** smartphone apps / bottle caps **7** a school for young entrepreneurs / The Shoe Saloon **8** Children's own answers: I prefer to shop … / I'd rather have a … **9** autobiographies / in bed or in the bath **10** Children's own answers.

Cooler: The teacher's life

Have the children recount your biography around the class, one word each. You can intervene and add words when you want to redirect the sentence. Children can make corrections when the sentence goes wrong.

Competency Focus

Me

The children write their autobiography. This helps them reflect on the important events in their life so far.

Presentation Kit • Have children use *Highlighter* to identify examples of autobiography features in the SB model text: first person narrative, details of life so far, hopes for the future.

- Have children tally the SB Activity 4 vote results and write the scores on *Notepad*.

Student's Resource Center • The class chooses one topic from Chapters 1–9. The children review the vocabulary from that topic at home, using the appropriate Vocabulary Tool, in preparation for a quiz that you can have in your next class.

Language Review

Lesson objective: review language from Chapter 9
Materials: Class CD

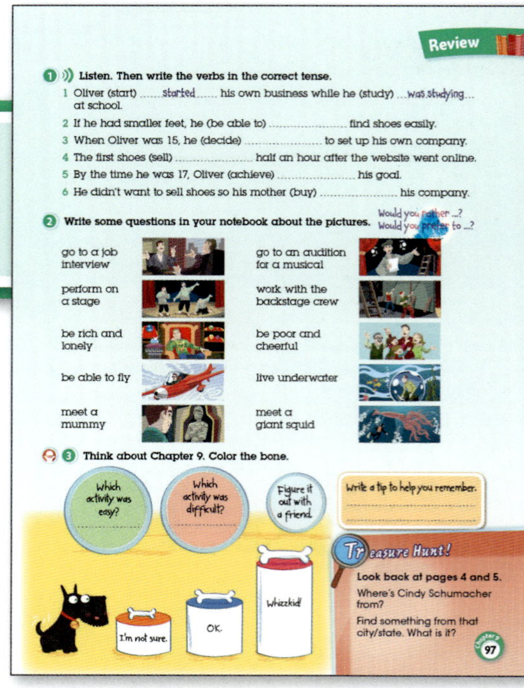
Review

1 Listen. Then write the verbs in the correct tense.

1 Oliver (start) ......started...... his own business while he (study) ...was studying... at school.
2 If he had smaller feet, he (be able to) .... find shoes easily.
3 When Oliver was 15, he (decide) .... to set up his own company.
4 The first shoes (sell) .... half an hour after the website went online.
5 By the time he was 17, Oliver (achieve) .... his goal.
6 He didn't want to sell shoes so his mother (buy) .... his company.

2 Write some questions in your notebook about the pictures. Would you rather ...? Would you prefer to ...?

go to a job interview | go to an audition for a musical
perform on a stage | work with the backstage crew
be rich and lonely | be poor and cheerful
be able to fly | live underwater
meet a mummy | meet a giant squid

3 Think about Chapter 9. Color the bone.

Which activity was easy?
Which activity was difficult?
Figure it out with a friend.
Write a tip to help you remember.
I'm not sure.
OK.
Whizzkid!

Treasure Hunt!
Look back at pages 4 and 5.
Where's Cindy Schumacher from?
Find something from that city/state. What is it?

Chapter 9 97

Warmer: Play "Tic-Tac-Toe"

Play the game with collocations: *young—entrepreneur, a successful—company, creative—ideas, a fairy—tale, soon—after that, I prefer books—to screens, old-—fashioned, follow—your heart, download—an app* (see Games Bank p. 222).

1 2.30 Listen. Then write the verbs in the correct tense.

- Have the children read the sentence prompts. Ask *What do you think we're going to hear about?* Elicit ideas.
- Play the CD twice. The children listen and complete the sentences.
- Elicit answers.

Audioscript

Oliver Bridge started his own business while he was studying at school. As a school boy, he couldn't find shoes to fit his big feet. He looked on the Internet but there weren't any online stores selling large shoes. When he was fifteen, Oliver decided to set up his own company. He called it Bigger Feet, and he contacted shoe makers and arranged to sell their biggest sizes through his online store. His first pair of shoes was sold half an hour after his website went online. Soon, his business was very successful. Oliver had achieved his goal by the time he was 17, but he didn't want to sell shoes as a career so he sold his company to his mother.

Answers

1 started, was studying **2** would be able to **3** decided **4** were sold **5** had achieved **6** bought

2 Write some questions in your notebook about the pictures.

- Have the children look at the pictures. Elicit a question for the first two pictures.
- The children then write questions in their notebook.
- Elicit the questions.

Answers

Children's own answers.

3 Think about Chapter 9. Color the bone.

- Have the children look back at Chapter 9 and color the bone to evaluate their progress (self-evaluation).
- Discuss ideas for adapting model texts, e.g. in speaking activities underline words in examples that you can change, etc. The children choose and write a tip in their Student Book.

Treasure Hunt

Ask *Where is Cindy Schumacher from?* (*Dallas, Texas, in the USA*) Ask the children to look at pp. 4–5 to find something that people in Texas might buy from The Shoe Saloon. (*cowboy boots*)

Chapter 9 Review

1 Reading and Writing.
Read and write the words.

~~a millionaire~~ an idea a product a business a company a boss goals an interview a career an entrepreneur

Example.
A very rich person. ....a millionaire....

1 A job you do for a long time. ....
2 Something that is made and sold. ....
3 This is a person at work who tells other people what to do. ....
4 These are things that you want to achieve. ....
5 This is a meeting where you answer questions about yourself because you want a job.
....

2 Listening.
Listen and color, write, or draw.

94 95

1 Reading and Writing. Read and write the words.

The children write the words defined by the sentences, using the words supplied. Check answers.

Answers

1 a career **2** a product **3** a boss **4** goals **5** an interview

2 2.39 Listening. Listen and color, write, or draw.

Play the CD twice. The children listen and color, write, or draw the objects according to the recording. Check answers.

Answers (Audioscript on p. 224)

1 Boy's t-shirt has GOAL written on it.
2 Girl with long hair: hair colored brown.
3 Smartphone drawn on desk next to notebook.
4 Woman with hat in café: hat colored yellow.
5 Dog's ball: colored red.

Cooler: Visualization

Have the children close their eyes and imagine their dream job. Ask *Where are you? What are you doing? Are you alone? What's happening? How do you feel? Do you help other people? Do you make things? Do other people like what you do? Are you happy?* Then, have the children open their eyes and tell a friend what they imagined in their future life. Elicit responses.

Competency Focus

Me: Self-evaluation

The children reflect on the chapter, express their personal opinions about their own progress, and look for ways to improve. This encourages them to evaluate and make decisions about what they need to revisit and how they can learn better.

Presentation Kit • Use *Answer Key* to give feedback on AB Chapter Review activities. You can show the answers all at once or one by one to customize feedback.

Teacher's Resource Center • Print out Test Chapter 9 and End-of-year Test to use at the end of this lesson. The Test Generator also allows you to create customized tests.

• For the CEYLT (Cambridge YLE) exam preparation activities, there are Speaking prompts available for this chapter.

Back to the Board

Divide the class into pairs. Have one child sit facing away from the board. Write a word/phrase from the lesson on the board. The child facing the board defines the word/phrase for the other child to guess. (They cannot use the actual word(s).) Repeat with other words, with the children taking turns prompting and guessing.

Board Pelmanism

Prepare two sets of cards (big enough to be visible on the board) showing the target vocabulary (word halves or split phrases). A child turns over a pair of cards. If they match, the child wins them and the cards are removed. Play until all the pairs have been matched.

Variation: Children match pairs of the same word, then give a sentence using the word to win the pair.

Change the Text

Write a text (35–40 words) on the board. Explain the idea is to change the text completely by changing one or two words at a time, e.g. *Ravi lives with his mother … Take out "mother" and put in "teddy bear."* Erase *mother* and write *teddy bear* in its place. You have to replace with the same type of word each time. Elicit suggestions until all the possible words are changed but the sentence structure is still the same.

Collocations

Choose eight phrases from a text or the chapter, e.g. *discover the tomb*, *have an audition*, etc. Write the phrases in two columns (one word in each column), mixing up the order in the second column. Children come to the board and draw a line to make a link. Ask for class agreement. Continue until all the phrases are linked.

Disappearing Text

Write sentences or a short text on the board (30–35 words). The children read the text aloud. Erase a word and have the children read the text again, including the missing word. Continue in this way until the children are saying the text with no visual prompt on the board.

Disappearing Words

Write key vocabulary on the board. Give the children one minute to memorize them in pairs, then erase them. The children then have one minute to recall and write as many of the words as possible. Pairs swap answers with another pair to check. Elicit answers.

Variation: Write ten words on the board. Have the children look at them, then close their eyes. Erase one word. Have the children look again and say the missing word. Repeat until there are no more words on the board.

Ready, Set, Draw!

Put the children in teams. Secretly give a child from each team a word to draw on the board. The first team to identify the word correctly wins a point. You could award an extra point if they spell it correctly, too.

Variation: Teams take turns choosing a word for the other team to guess. Set a time limit for the team guessing.

Sentence Builders

Divide the class into teams. Give each team a large sheet of paper (positioned so that the other team cannot see it) and a pen. Read out a sentence/question using key language twice. The first child writes the first word only, then gives the pen to the next child to continue. When finished, each team checks another team's sentence. Each correct word wins a point.

The Chain Game

Have the class stand. Start off a chain, e.g. *I went to the store and I bought apples*. Each child repeats the chain so far and adds an object, e.g. *I went to the store and I bought apples and oranges*. If a child makes a mistake or cannot think of an item, they are out and sit down. The last child standing wins.

Tic-Tac-Toe

Divide the class into two teams (O and X). Draw a Tic-Tac-Toe grid on the board, and number the spaces 1–9. You can include short prompts or just give these orally. Have one team choose a number. Ask a question (e.g. *How old are you?*) or give a challenge (*Name four animals. Spell "dictionary."*, etc.). If the team answers correctly, mark their chosen square O or X. The first team to make a diagonal or straight line wins.

NB W = *Woman*, **M** = *Man*, **G** = *Girl*, **B** = *boy*

2.31 Chapter 1 Audioscript

E **W:** *How was the art competition at school, Charlie?*
B: *It was great. Everyone worked really hard to make some fantastic things. We all used recyclable materials like old clothes. I was really happy with my map of Mexico. The teacher helped me cut some wood and I painted it.*

W: *What did the others do?*
B: *Sophie loves masks so she made a beautiful one. She got her idea from some vacation pictures she took in Italy. She might do more one day and sell them.*
W: *What about Mark? He's very artistic, isn't he?*
B: *Yes. He wanted to show that we're losing places where birds and bees can live so he made a wildlife area. It had a river in the middle of it. I think that was an old blue plastic bag. Then he made a lot of tall trees with small birds in them. We all liked it.*
W: *Did Luis make anything?*
B: *Yes, he usually makes planes. You know, the ones you buy, but in the competition it can't be something from a shop. So he made a beast from a movie he saw. It had big scary teeth.*
W: *And how about Amy?*
B: *Well, Amy loves two things, jewelry and clothes. She decided to use old clothes to make some silk bracelets. They must be good because all the girls in the class want one!*
W: *Did anyone make a building?*
B: *Lily copied a pyramid in Egypt from a book at school —it was amazing! The teacher wants to keep it in the classroom because it's so good.*

2.32 Chapter 2 Audioscript

E **W:** *If you want to come to the new craft club, Ben, it starts at four thirty.*
B: *Great.*

B: *Can I come today?*
W: *I'm afraid we stopped doing it on Tuesdays, Wednesdays, and Fridays because the school has other clubs on those days. But you're welcome on Monday and Thursday.*
B: *Is it expensive?*
W: *No. Because we use a lot of recycled things, it's only two dollars for each class. That's 14 dollars if you do it to the end of the semester.*
B: *I'd like to make models. Can I do that in the club?*
W: *We've already made some models of buildings. We'll do some more next month. This week, we're doing photography. John Bailey is visiting us tomorrow, that's B-A-I-L-E-Y. He's a photographer who's going to tell us how to take good pictures of wildlife.*
B: *That's cool. I'd like to practice taking pictures. I wish I had a camera.*
W: *Why don't you call Max? He has two cameras and he's offered to lend one to anyone in the club.*
B: *Do you have his number?*
W: *Yes, it's seven, eight, six, three, nine, four, seven, seven, four, two.*
B: *Thanks, Mrs. White. I'll call him now.*

2.33 Chapter 3 Audioscript

E **M:** *You're late today, Grace. School finishes at 3 o'clock.*
G: *I know, Dad, but I went to the recycling club after school. I was there until five thirty.*
M: *Oh, I forgot about that. You're normally here at three thirty.*

1 **G:** *We had a really good time at the club. Each week, we make something different from old things. It can be old clothes, plastic, paper ... we use everything.*
M: *That's right. Last week, you painted glass bottles. They were nice.*
G: *Yes, but this week we saved all our old cardboard boxes and we made a boat for children to play in.*
M: *What a great idea!*
2 **M:** *Are you hungry?*
G: *Yes, I am. Something smells nice. Are we having pizza for dinner?*
M: *No. I couldn't find any tomatoes so I've made something else with chicken.*
G: *Oh, my favorite. Can we have fries with it?*
M: *Sorry, I made a nice green salad.*
G: *Oh, that's OK.*
3 **M:** *Do you want to do your homework before dinner?*
G: *Yes. If I can use your computer, it won't take long. I need to do this exercise. We have to write the number of people who live in these countries. We're learning about world population in geography.*
M: *That sounds interesting. Do you want some help?*
G: *Yes, please.*

2.34 Chapter 4 Audioscript

E **M:** *Do you like this picture?*
B: *Yes, look at the superhero. He's coming to save the world!*
M: *Yes, he looks very strong and brave!*
B: *What's he wearing?*
M: *A superhero costume, of course. Can you see his T-shirt?*
B: *Yes, I'll color it.*
M: *Great—make it green.*

1 **M:** *Can you see the boy?*
B: *There are three boys.*
M: *Yes, the one who's riding his skateboard. Can you color his hat blue?*
B: *OK.*
2 **B:** *Can I color something else?*
M: *In a minute. You're going to write something now. One of the other boys is carrying a sports bag. Can you see him?*
B: *Yes.*
M: *Good. Write the word "STAR" on the bag.*
3 **M:** *You can draw something now.*
B: *Great. I'm good at drawing.*
M: *Can you see the lady at the bus stop?*
B: *Yes, she's reading a book.*
M: *That's right. Can you draw a suitcase next to her?*
B: *OK. She might be going on vacation.*
4 **M:** *Good. Now, two girls are waiting for the bus.*
B: *Yes, I can see them. One girl is taking a picture.*
M: *That's right. Can you color her phone?*
B: *Yes. I'll make it red.*
5 **M:** *OK, last one.*
B: *Can I write something else?*
M: *Yes, look at the bus. Above the driver's head, there's a square.*
B: *Oh, yes, that's for the number of the bus.*
M: *You're right. Can you write X70 in the square?*
B: *Yes. I've done it.*

2.35 Chapter 5 Audioscript

E **G:** *Look, Dad, there's a group of people from my school. They're going scuba diving.*
M: *Do you know them?*
G: *Yes, that's Jake.*
M: *The boy wearing sunglasses?*
G: *Yes. He'll need to take his sandals off before he gets into the boat!*

1 **M:** *Who's the girl with the long hair next to Jake?*
G: *Which one?*
M: *She's holding a towel.*
G: *That's Sonia. She lives on our street.*
M: *Oh, I knew I had seen her before.*
G: *They're going to put their diving masks on soon.*

2 **M:** *Who's that boy? He looks very cold.*
G: *That's Daniel. He's the youngest. He loves diving.*
M: *But only when it's sunny!*

3 **G:** *Can you see my friend Alice?*
M: *Is she the girl waving?*
G: *Yes. She's already wearing her mask. Alice has done a lot of scuba diving. She's a champion.*

4 **G:** *Oh, and that boy is Patrick.*
M: *Is he sitting down?*
G: *No, he's getting into the boat. He's carrying his mask.*

5 **M:** *What's that boy doing with his bag?*
G: *He's probably looking for his mask. It's Charlie and he always brings his own.*
M: *He should hurry up. They're getting ready to go.*

2.36 Chapter 6 Audioscript

E **W:** *How was your school musical, James?*
B: *It was fantastic, thanks. Everyone worked really hard on the stage and backstage. We sold food and drinks and made some money for the school. I made fifty bags of popcorn at home and sold them during the break. I didn't even have a bag for myself!*

W: *Did anyone else make anything?*
B: *Well, Daisy was really good. She loves cooking. She was going to make a few big cakes, then she had an idea to make cupcakes. They were all different colors and they sold very quickly.*
W: *What other snacks did you have?*
B: *Well, we wanted to have ice creams, but it was very hot inside the theater. Jim had a better idea. He brought some ice and put it in buckets so he could sell cold drinks.*
W: *Were a lot of people helping?*
B: *Oh, yes. Dan was there, too. At first, he had a problem with his camera but in the end, he took some great pictures for the school magazine. I'll show them to you.*
W: *Who was working backstage?*
B: *Oh, there were a lot of people. Anna did a great job because she's very artistic. She's been taking a course in make-up at college and she painted everyone's faces. The make-up was great.*
W: *Did anyone make a DVD of the musical? I'd love to watch it at home.*
B: *Oh, we all wanted a video and Holly offered to do one but there wasn't enough time. On that night, she was very busy. She had to collect tickets and show people where to sit. Maybe we'll do another musical and next time, we'll make a DVD, too.*

2.37 Chapter 7 Audioscript

E **W:** *What are you doing on Saturday, David?*
M: *I'm going to try the new Theater Club.*
W: *That's a good idea. Where is it?*
M: *It's in a new building next to the old fire station.*

W: *Is everyone invited?*
M: *Yes, of course, but you have to be interested in singing and dancing.*
W: *Oh, are they doing a show?*
M: *Yes, it's called Big Top, that's two words: B-I-G then T-O-P. It's a musical about the circus.*
W: *Fantastic. Does the club last all day?*
M: *No, it lasts for four hours—from ten o'clock until two in the afternoon. After that, they have to prepare for the evening's show.*
W: *Can I join?*
M: *Of course, but you have to call the theater with your name.*
W: *OK. What's the number?*
M: *It's five seven six, two four six, six nine oh two.*
W: *Great, I'll call now ... Oh, no, it's busy.*
M: *You should just go there.*
W: *OK. Where is it again?*
M: *It's on Market Street. If you walk quickly, you'll get there before it closes.*
W: *Thanks.*

2.38 Chapter 8 Audioscript

E **W:** *Hi, Will. Are you OK?*
B: *Hi, Mom. I need to do something online for school but I've forgotten the password. I can't remember if it's Apple three two three or three two four.*
W: *No, we changed it. It's Apple three three four.*
B: *Oh, that's right.*

1 **W:** *Are you going to do your homework?*
B: *Yes, we've been studying the weather at school. We looked at a world map and saw how many problems were caused by bad weather. Do you know the number of disasters has gone up a lot?*
W: *Yes, I know.*
B: *I want to look for photos that were taken after hurricanes and bad storms. Then I can put them in my notebook.*
W: *That's a good idea.*

2 **B:** *I need some more glue for these photos.*
W: *There's some in the kitchen. I'll get it. Do you want the scissors, too?*
B: *No, I've got some, but I'd like some crayons.*
W: *We have a new pack. Here you go.*
B: *Oh, good. Thanks.*

3 **W:** *Oh, is that your phone?*
B: *Yes, I'll get it. It's in the kitchen.*
W: *Yes, I think it's on the table, next to your keys.*
B: *Got it! It was under my books!*

2.39 Chapter 9 Audioscript

E **W:** *Hi, Alice, do you want to color this picture?*
G: *Yes, it's a factory, isn't it? They're making robots.*
W: *Yes, what do you want to color first?*
G: *Can I color a robot?*
W: *Yes, which one?*
G: *I'll color the big one at the end of the table. It's going to be green.*

1 **G:** *What can I color now?*
W: *Now you're going to write something.*
G: *OK.*
W: *Do you see the boys who are making robots?*
G: *Yes, there are two.*
W: *One of them is wearing a T-shirt. Can you write GOAL on it?*
G: *OK, I've done that.*

2 **W:** *Now, can you see the two girls?*
G: *Yes, one girl is painting.*
W: *That's right. The girl next to her has long hair.*
G: *Yes, I can see that.*
W: *Color her hair brown.*

3 **G:** *What should I color now?*
W: *Now, you're going to draw something. Can you see the woman in the chair by the computer?*
G: *Yes, I think that man is in an interview.*
W: *You're right. Can you draw a smartphone?*
G: *Sure. Where?*
W: *Draw it next to the notebook.*
G: *OK.*

4 **W:** *Now, you're going to color again.*
G: *I see.*
W: *Can you see the woman in the café?*
G: *There are two women. Which one?*
W: *The woman who has a plate in her hand.*
G: *Oh, yes.*
W: *Color her hat.*
G: *I'll make it yellow.*

5 **W:** *Last thing, now. There's a dog in a basket. Can you see it?*
G: *Yes, it's in the office. It's sleeping next to the desk.*
W: *That's right. There's a ball next to the basket. Color it red.*
G: *OK. I've finished.*